COSMOPOLITA

War is about individuals maiming and killing e          , ... yet, it seems that
it is also irreducibly collective, as it is fought by groups of people and more
often than not for the sake of communal values such as territorial integrity and
national self-determination. Cécile Fabre articulates and defends an ethical
account of war in which the individual, as a moral and rational agent, is the
fundamental focus for concern and respect—both as a combatant whose acts of
killing need justifying and as a non-combatant whose suffering also needs
justifying. She takes as her starting point a political morality to which the
individual, rather than the nation-state, is central, namely cosmopolitanism.
According to cosmopolitanism, individuals all matter equally, irrespective of
their membership in this or that political community. Traditional war ethics
already accepts this principle, since it holds that unarmed civilians are illegitimate targets even though they belong to the enemy community. However,
although the traditional account of whom we may kill in wars is broadly
faithful to that principle, the traditional account of why we may kill and of
who may kill is not. Cosmopolitan theorists, for their part, do not address the
ethical issues raised by war in any depth. Fabre's *Cosmopolitan War* seeks to fill
this gap, and defends its account of just and unjust wars by addressing the
ethics of different kinds of war: wars of national defence, wars over scarce
resources, civil wars, humanitarian intervention, wars involving private military forces, and asymmetrical wars.

**Cécile Fabre** is Professor of Political Philosophy at the University of Oxford,
and a Fellow of Lincoln College.

# Cosmopolitan War

CÉCILE FABRE

OXFORD
UNIVERSITY PRESS

# OXFORD
## UNIVERSITY PRESS

Great Clarendon Street, Oxford, OX2 6DP,
United Kingdom

Oxford University Press is a department of the University of Oxford.
It furthers the University's objective of excellence in research, scholarship,
and education by publishing worldwide. Oxford is a registered trade mark of
Oxford University Press in the UK and in certain other countries

First Edition published in 2012
First published in paperback 2014

Published in the United States of America by Oxford University Press
198 Madison Avenue, New York, NY 10016, United States of America

British Library Cataloguing in Publication Data
Data available

Library of Congress Cataloging in Publication Data
Data available

ISBN 978–0–19–956716–4 (Hbk.)
ISBN 978–0–19–870857–5 (Pbk.)

To my grandparents
Marcel (*d.*) and Simone Fabre
Philippe and Marie-Louise Thélot

# *Acknowledgements*

I started thinking about some of the material contained in this book in 1989 whilst preparing for the French Baccalauréat. History and philosophy are compulsory subjects in the Baccalauréat, and I was fortunate enough to be taught in both by two outstanding teachers: Anne-Marie Ramon and Barbara de Négroni. Not only did they have unstinting intellectual respect for each other's discipline; they were also committed to showing to us on the one hand how to think about history philosophically, and on the other hand to bring our knowledge of the past to bear on our philosophizing. Thus, we were invited in history classes to bring to bear Rousseau's writings on our under-standing of World War II, the wars of decolonization, and the Cold War; conversely, we were asked in philosophy classes to think about historical examples when grappling with the concept of rights and the notion of the social contract. The fact that the entire country (but for its tiny royalist minority) was celebrating the bicentenary of the French Revolution provided a fertile and propitious background for this two-pronged inquiry about both transnational and civil wars—particularly in my hometown, Versailles, of all places.

To this day, I can remember both the intellectual joy I felt during that year when reflecting on war, and the distress I experienced when reading about its horrors. I thought for a long while that I would never be able to write about war—too complex, too depressing, enough of it in the newspapers and on the 10 o'clock news, and so on. I gave in, though not without enduring ambiva-lence. Fortunately, I have benefitted throughout from the support of the three institutions in which I have worked since I began this project: the London School of Economics, the University of Edinburgh, and the University of Oxford. At all three, I have met historians who have been more than willing to answer my endless questions about a particular conflict or other; scholars of international relations who have tried (not as successfully as they might wish) to impress on me that relations between states are nothing at all like relations between individuals; literary scholars who have pointed me in the direction of a particular piece of literature describing war; and philosophers, of course, who have constantly pushed me to be more rigorous, to write more clearly, to think harder. I am particularly grateful to the Oxford Faculty of Philosophy and to the Fellows and Rector of Lincoln College for granting me a one-term sabbatical leave only a year after my arrival, which enabled me to bring this book to completion, and much more importantly, for welcoming me back to Oxford and giving me an academic home after a ten-year-long absence.

As I argue at some length in this book, however, institutions do not really matter *per se*: individuals ultimately do. Fittingly, I owe a considerable debt of gratitude to those many individuals who have commented, orally and in writing, on parts of the typescript. I am thankful to audiences and participants at the following conferences and seminars where I have presented most of the book's chapters: the Philosophy Research Seminar at the University of St Andrews, the Edinburgh Political Theory Research Seminar, the Stirling Philosophy Seminar, the 2008 Conference for the Society for Applied Philosophy (Manchester), the 2008 Brave New World Conference (Manchester), the 2007 UCL Graduate Conference in Political Philosophy; the 2008 UKVIR Conference; the 2010 UCL Colloquium in Legal, Moral, and Political Philosophy; the 2010 ELAC Conference; the 2010 Oxford Moral Philosophy Seminar; the 2011 Warwick Political Philosophy Workshop. Last but not least, in that vein, the Oxford Social Justice Seminar, the Nuffield Political Theory Workshop, and the Oxford War Group have been rich and demanding sources of comments.

Oral comments are one thing. Written feedback, which takes an enormous amount of time to produce, is another. I should like to thank the following commentators for their penetrating criticisms (with heartfelt apologies to those whom I have unwittingly omitted to record): Krister Bykvist, Idil Boran, Alejandro Chehtman, Liz Cripps, Liz Cripps, Janina Dill, George Grech, Robert Jubb, Seth Lazar, Jeff McMahan, Marco Meyer, Toby Ord, Michael Otsuka, Avia Pasternak, Felix Pinkert, Thomas Pogge, Mike Ravvin, David Rodin, Cheyney Ryan, Craig Scott, Henry Shue, Nicholas Southwood, Zofia Stemplowska, Laura Valentini, Gerard Vong, Ralph Wedgewood, and Leif Wenar. Two anonymous referees for Oxford University Press, and the Press's Philosophy Commissioning Editor, Peter Momtchiloff, provided useful suggestions and staunch support.

Some sections of the book first appeared as articles. A few paragraphs from Chapter 1 appeared in 'Global Distributive Justice: An Egalitarian Perspective', *Canadian Journal of Philosophy (Supplementary)* 31 (2005): 139–64. Parts of Chapter 2 appeared in *Proceedings of the Aristotelian Society* as 'Permissible Rescue Killings', 109, Issue 1 (August 2009), 149–64. Parts of Chapter 4 first appeared as 'Cosmopolitanism, Just War Theory and Legitimate Authority', in *International Affairs* (London), 84, number 5 (September 2008), 963–76, and Chapter 6 first appeared as 'In Defence of Mercenarism', *British Journal of Political Science* 40, Issue 3 (2010), 539–59. I am grateful to the publishers and editors of those journals for giving me permission to reprint those pieces here.

I have some further and deeper intellectual debts to acknowledge. One of my central contentions in this book is that whether soldiers may kill enemy combatants largely depends on the justness or unjustness of the cause for which they fight. This is not a widely accepted view, and yet I cannot remember a time when I did not endorse it. But I would not have been able to articulate my vague pre-theoretic intuitions had it not been for Jeff McMahan's sustained and ground-breaking work. Like so many others in our field, I owe him more than I can ever give back. As nice counterpoints to Jeff's undeniable influence on my own thinking, David Miller and Henry Shue have regularly insisted that I pay more attention to real-world cases and rely less on abstract hypotheticals. I have not been fully successful in this, at least by their standards, but I am nevertheless grateful for their gentle admonishments. And for the best part of the last decade, Tamar Meisels and Jonathan Quong have read and commented on more or less every single paper I have written on the ethics of war and the ethics of killing. They read the book's penultimate draft in its entirety and supplied dozens (literally) of suggestions which I have done my best to accommodate here. To be the recipient of such intellectual generosity is humbling. For that, and for the friendships which developed along the way, I am deeply thankful.

Last, but not least, as the years went by, three of my four grandparents have added layers of a much more personal kind to my research by sharing their experiences and memories of the wars in which they were caught. They did so very reluctantly at first, for fear of reopening badly healed wounds, but increasingly willingly in more recent times. I thus dedicate this book, with love and gratitude, to Marcel Fabre, who died in 1978 but was born in 1902, and thus enjoyed the enormous good brute luck of being too young to be conscripted in the First World War and too old to be sent to fight in the Second; to Simone Fabre, born in 1911, who still remembers the toll of the bell calling the men up to their regiments on 1 August 1914 and bringing too few of them back home on 11 November 1918; to Philippe Thélot, born in 1922, who volunteered to work with the British medical staff at Bergen-Belsen in the spring of 1945 and saw first-hand both the worst and the best of which human beings are capable; and to Marie-Louise Thélot, born in 1922, who had to share her home (literally) with five German soldiers during much of the Second World War and who, when telling me her story, quietly and without fuss urged me never to lose sight of our enemies' humanity.

Lincoln College, Oxford
Remembrance Day, 2011

# *Contents*

# Introduction

On the eve of the battle of Borodino, Prince Andrei Bolkonsky, one of the main characters in *War and Peace* and, in that scene at least, Tolstoy's mouthpiece, describes war as follows:

The aim of war is murder; the methods of war are spying, treachery, and their encourage-ment, the ruin of a country's inhabitants, robbing them or stealing to provision the army, and fraud and falsehood termed military craft....[Soldiers] meet, as we shall meet tomorrow, to murder one another; they kill and maim tens of thousands, and then have thanksgiving services for having killed so many people (they even exaggerate the number) and they announce a victory, supposing that the more people they have killed the greater their achievement...[1]

Compare this with Wilfred Owen's well-known rejection of the romanticism of war in *Dulce and Decorum est:*

> If you could hear, at every jolt, the blood
> Come gargling from the froth-corrupted lungs,
> Obscene as cancer, bitter as the cud
> Of vile, incurable sores on innocent tongues,
> My friend, you would not tell with such high zest
> To children ardent for some desperate glory,
> The old Lie: *Dulce et Decorum est*
> *Pro patria mori.*[2]

For both Tolstoy and Owen, war is about individuals maiming and killing each other, and it is precisely that which elicits the former's cold fury and the latter's bitter anger. And yet, it seems that war is also irreducibly collective: it is fought by groups of people, and more often than not, as Owen himself painfully reminds us, for the sake of communal values such as territorial integrity and national self-determination.

[1] L. Tolstoy. *War and Peace*, ed. H. Gifford (Oxford: Oxford University Press, 1991), 831.
[2] W. Owen, *Dulce et Decorum Est*, ed. O. Knowles (London: Wordsworth, 2002).

In this book I articulate and defend an ethical account of war (by which I shall mean an armed conflict involving[3] large groups of individuals over social and political ends) in which the individual, as a moral and rational agent, is the fundamental focus for concern and respect—both as a combatant whose acts of killing need justifying and as a non-combatant whose suffering also needs justifying. I do so by taking as my starting point a political morality to which the individual, rather than the nation-state, is central: namely, cosmopolitanism. According to cosmopolitanism (across its many variants), individuals each matter, and in some important sense matter equally, irrespective of their membership in this or that political community. Traditional war ethics already accepts this principle, since it holds (across its own many variants) that unarmed civilians are illegitimate targets even though they belong to the enemy community. However, although its account of whom we may kill in wars is broadly faithful to that principle, its account of why we may kill and of who may kill is not. In particular, and interestingly, there is a growing sense amongst some scholars of warfare that classic, statist, accounts of war need revising in the light of (1) forms of warfare as witnessed in former Yugoslavia in the 1990s and in sub-Saharan Africa in the last twenty years, as well as (2) theoretical developments in the law and political philosophy towards less state-centric approaches to the norms which ought to govern violent relationships between individuals themselves, but also between individuals on the one hand and coercive structures on the other hand.[4]

Both the ethics of war and cosmopolitanism are familiar areas of inquiry, and both have known a strong resurgence in the last four decades, so much so that the former is a dominant branch of applied ethics and the latter a dominant branch of political philosophy. Interestingly, however, they have developed along separate tracks. Book-length normative accounts of war either give a general account of the standard principles of the just war or tackle

---

[3] I use 'involving' deliberately vaguely, to denote either political and social (armed) conflicts in which large groups of individuals themselves fight, or conflicts in which some people fight on behalf of large groups. As the *Oxford English Dictionary* has it, war is a 'Hostile contention by means of armed forces, carried on between nations, states, or rulers, or between parties in the same nation or state; the employment of armed forces against a foreign power, or against an opposing party in the state.' I shall dissent from the *OED*'s focus on states in Section 4.3.

[4] I am not suggesting here that we are witnessing a new form of warfare which is drastically different from so-called old wars. In fact, I am rather sceptical of the 'new war thesis', as articulated in, for example, I. Duyvesteyn and J. Angstrom (ed.), *Rethinking the Nature of War* (London: Frank Cass, 2005); M. Kaldor, *New and Old Wars*, 2nd edn. (Cambridge: Polity, 2006); H. Munkler, *The New Wars* (Cambridge: Polity, 2005). For scepticism, see, for example, M. Berdal, 'The "New Wars" Thesis Revisited', in H. Strachan and S. Scheipers (ed.), *The Changing Character of War* (Oxford: Oxford University Press, 2011). My point is merely that, whether old or new, the features mentioned at the outset of this (in-text) paragraph are present in contemporary forms of warfare and that they warrant normative scrutiny.

specific dimensions of war such as the killing of combatants, national self-defence, terrorism, non-combatant-immunity, pre-emptive wars, or humanitarian intervention: to my knowledge, there is no systematic book-length cosmopolitan theory of the just war.[5] Cosmopolitans, for their part, have tended to focus on defending principles of distributive justice as well as normative guidelines for world governance, but have not devoted much attention to articulating norms for the use of military force, or have done so only partially. For example, Moellendorf restricts his cosmopolitan account to *jus ad bellum*. Caney, for his part, frames his inquiry largely as a response to Walzer's seminal *Just and Unjust War*, and does not address issues such as terrorism, asymmetrical warfare, subsistence wars, and *jus post bellum* with the degree of detail which a full cosmopolitan account of warfare would require. Others, such as Ian Atack, press that cosmopolitan justice, concerned as it is with ensuring that all human beings are to be treated with equal concern and respect, should be construed as an ethics of peace, and not an ethics of war. In conceiving of humanitarian intervention and peace-building as cosmopolitan responses to injustice, however, those authors overlook the serious normative difficulties raised by military interventions which necessitate acts of killing.[6]

The claim that all individuals are owed equal concern and respect, which flows from a deeper concern with preserving their dignity as human beings and minimising their suffering, is compatible with both the thesis (which

[5] For general principles for the just war, see, for example, A. J. Coates, *The Ethics of War* (Manchester: Manchester University Press, 1997); B. Orend, *The Morality of War* (Peterborough, Ontario: Broadview Press, 2006); D. P. Lackey, *The Ethics of War and Peace* (Upper Saddle River, NJ: Prentice Hall, 1989); P. Christopher, *The Ethics of War and Peace: An Introduction to Legal and Moral Issues* (Upple Saddle River, NJ: Prentice Hall, 1999). For issue-specific books, see, for example, J. McMahan, *Killing in War* (Oxford: Oxford University Press, 2009); R. E. Goodin, *What's Wrong with Terrorism?* (Cambridge: Polity, 2006); D. Rodin, *War and Self-Defense* (Oxford: Clarendon Press, 2002); U. Steinhoff, *On the Ethics of War and Terrorism* (Oxford: Oxford University Press, 2007); D. Rodin and H. Shue (ed.), *Preemption: Military Action and Moral Justification* (Oxford: Oxford University Press, 2007); D. Rodin and H. Shue (ed.), *Just and Unjust Warriors* (Oxford: Oxford University Press, 2008); I. Primoratz (ed.), *Civilian Immunity in War* (Oxford: Oxford University Press, 2007); T. Nardin and M. Williams (ed.), *Humanitarian Intervention*, vol. XLVII (New York: New York University Press, 2006); J. Pattison, *Humanitarian Intervention and the Responsibility to Protect: Who Should Intervene?* (Oxford: Oxford University Press, 2010); and N. J. Wheeler, *Saving Strangers: Humanitarian Intervention in International Society* (Oxford: Oxford University Press, 2002).

[6] D. Moellendorf, *Cosmopolitan justice* (Boulder, CO: Westview Press, 2002); S. Caney, *Justice Beyond Borders: A Global Political Theory* (Oxford: Oxford University Press, 2005); I. Atack, *The Ethics of Peace and War: from State Security to World Community* (Edinburgh: Edinburgh University Press, 2005). For a thoughtful discussion of war from a cosmopolitan perspective with strong pacifist leanings, see N. Dower, *The Ethics of War and Peace: Cosmopolitan and Other Perspectives* (Cambridge: Polity Press, 2009). For a recent articulation of the view that just-war theory needs revising in the light of cosmopolitan principles of morality, see G. Palmer-Fernandez, 'Cosmpolitan Revisions to Just War Theory', in M. Boylan (ed.), *The Morality and Global Justice Reader* (Boulder, CO: Westview Press, 2011).

I certainly do not reject) that we should strive for peace and, accordingly, endeavour to construct an ethics of peace-building, and the view that we sometimes have the right to resort to war precisely when our or other people's fundamental rights are violated. A cosmopolitan need not, and indeed as I shall argue throughout, should not, be a pacifist—at least on those variants of pacifism which condemn war *per se* as morally unacceptable.[7] In fact, just as war ethicists would do well to draw on the insights of cosmopolitan moral theory, cosmopolitans for their part would do well to start thinking more deeply than they have done so far about war. For cosmopolitan thinking, which is profoundly sceptical of the normative weight of national identity, has mostly focused on two areas of international relations—to wit, distributive justice, and governance structures: its credentials as a plausible normative framework for international relations in general would be severely impaired if it could not provide a plausible account of the just war in particular.

My aim, in other words, is to offer a cosmopolitan theory of the just war. In the first chapter I shall begin by outlining and defending a relatively moderate account of cosmopolitan justice. In subsequent chapters I shall make a number of revisions to some fundamental principles of the morality of war (either with respect to their content, or with respect to their justification, or both.) I shall describe the chapters in greater detail presently. Meanwhile, a general comment on the book's strategy is in order. The ethics of war is standardly divided into three sets of principles: principles which govern the resort to war (*jus ad bellum*), principles which regulate combatants' conduct during war (*jus in bello*), and principles which constrain belligerents' conduct towards one another once the war has ended (*jus post bellum*.) The specific contents of those principles are a matter of some controversy, but the following list is relatively canonical:

*Jus ad bellum*

1. The war must have a just cause.
2. It must be waged by a legitimate authority.

---

[7] For good accounts of pacifism, see, for example, Atack, *The Ethics of Peace and War*, ch. 6; M. Ceadel, *Thinking about Peace and War* (Oxford: Oxford University Press, 1987); Coates, *The Ethics of War*, ch. 3; Dower, *The Ethics of War and Peace*, ch. 5; J. Teichman, *Pacifism and the Just War* (Oxford: Blackwell, 1986). For a trenchant philosophical argument against pacifism, see J. Narveson, 'Pacifism: A Philosophical Analysis', *Ethics* 75 (1965): 259–71. For a thoughtfully pacifist view on the permissibility of self-defensive killing, see C. Ryan, 'Self-Defense, Pacifism, and the Permissibility of Killing', *Ethics* 93 (1983): 508–24. Incidentally, I shall focus on the act of killing throughout the book. But there is much interesting work to be done still on the ethics of using non-lethal weapons. As Michael Gross points out, our views on the relative badness of killing versus, for example, causing blindness in combatants, are neither wholly consistent not stable. I prescind from addressing those issues here. See M. L. Gross, *Moral Dilemmas of Modern War: Torture, Assassination, and Blackmail in an Age of Asymmetric Conflict* (Cambridge: Cambridge University Press, 2010), ch. 4.

3. It must be waged with the right intentions.
4. It must be the option of last resort.
5. It must stand a reasonable chance of success.
6. The good which it brings about must outweigh the harms which it causes.

*Jus in bello*

1. Combatants must only carry out missions which are necessary to the achievement of military objectives.
2. They may kill enemy combatants but must not target non-combatants.
3. The harms which combatants cause to other agents must not be out of proportion relative to the good which they produce.

*Jus post bellum*

1. Victorious belligerents may bring wrongdoers to trial subject to fair criminal procedures.
2. Compensation for the war ought to be paid by the wrongdoing party/parties to its/their victims, subject to proportionality considerations.
3. Victorious belligerents ought to assist in the reconstruction of the vanquished country/countries.
4. Victorious belligerents ought to respect the sovereignty of the vanquished country/countries.

In this book I shall tackle *jus ad bellum* and *jus in bello*—leaving the multi-pronged issue of *jus post bellum* for another time. But I shall not scrutinize all nine principles one after the other and consider how they each should be interpreted from a cosmopolitan perspective. Instead, each of the chapters (once cosmopolitan justice in general is defended in Chapter 1) addresses a particular kind of war: wars of collective self-defence (Chapter 2); subsistence wars (Chapter 3); civil wars (Chapter 4); humanitarian wars (Chapter 5); commodified wars (Chapter 6); asymmetrical wars (Chapter 7).

My reasons for proceeding in this way are twofold. First, the 'cataloguing strategy' is a route well-travelled—albeit not by cosmopolitans—so well-travelled, in fact, that alternative routes which explore similarities and differences between various forms of conflict are regrettably neglected. More importantly, not all of those requirements admit of a specifically cosmopolitan interpretation: in particular, the requirements of last resort, necessity, and reasonable chance of success remain the same whether or not one believes that justice is global rather than national in scope. For they all stem from the thought that war inflicts so much pain and suffering that it must not do so in vain and must cede way to peaceful means for conflict resolution when those are available. One can hold that view and yet at the same time firmly believe that borders and political membership are profoundly relevant, morally speaking, to how we should treat one another. By contrast, the requirements of just cause, legitimate authority, and proportionality, as well as the principle of discrimination between combatants and non-combatants need revising in the light of the relatively minimalist cosmopolitan theory of justice which I (amongst many other philosophers) take as my starting point. The different kinds of war which the book will study from an ethical point of view have thus been chosen partly because they should be of concern to us, here and now, but also because they raise (precisely) the issues of just cause and legitimate authority; they also present specific problems for the ethics of killing combatants and non-combatants, particularly with respect to targetting decisions and to calculations of costs and benefits. To anticipate briefly on the longer summary to follow: we shall see that a greater range of rights violations than is standardly thought gives rise to just causes for war, be it in transnational wars of self-defence against aggression, transnational wars waged in defence of victims of tyrannical regimes, or civil wars. We shall also see that the requirement of legitimate authority, which holds that a war is just only if it is waged by a state, coalition of states, or quasi-state, is not sound. Finally, we shall see that both prongs of the principle of discrimination stand in need of considerable qualification; in so doing, we shall be led to conclude that orthodox views about the relative weight to be given to combatants' and non-combatants' lives ought to be modified.[8] Its first prong, which we may call the principle of combatant liability, stipulates that combatants are legitimate targets precisely because they are armed and pose lethal threats, and this irrespective of the justness of their cause. Its second prong, known as the principle of non-combatant immunity, holds that non-combatants are not legitimate targets, precisely because they do not take part in the hostilities, and this irrespective of the moral status of the cause for which their country fights. I shall argue that only some combatants are liable to being killed—those who (*modulo* some qualifications to be introduced below) fight for an unjust cause—and that some non-combatants are also liable to being killed—those who in fact do take part, in relevant ways to be described later, in an unjust war.

---

[8] I shall discuss the requirement of proportionality mostly in the course of scrutinizing the principle of discrimination. But goods and bads other than lives saved or destroyed must be included in the proportionality calculus, whether in its *ad bellum* or in its *in bello* variants. I shall briefly mention the ways in which my cosmopolitan account of justice affects those goods and bads as I go along. For a recent discussion of proportionality, see T. Hurka, 'Proportionality in the Morality of War', *Philosophy & Public Affairs* 33 (2005): 34–66.

The book unfolds as follows. In Chapter 1 I present and defend a cosmopolitan theory of justice. I first sketch out a rights-based sufficientist theory of justice, whereby individuals[9] have rights to the resources and freedoms which they need in order to lead a minimally decent life. Once the needy have those resources, I argue, the well-off have the autonomy-based right to pursue their goals and life-projects. In addition, the chapter deals with two further issues. First, when elaborating on the principle of autonomy, I claim that freedom of association—especially political association—is an important value which ought to be given due place in a cosmopolitan morality. Those associations, or political communities, are legitimate only if they respect and promote the fundamental human rights of their members as well as of outsiders. Second, the well-off are not under a duty to help the needy at the cost of their own prospects for a minimally decent life.

In a second step I argue that all individuals, wherever they reside, have the aforementioned rights against everyone else, irrespective of residence. Were we to impose on members of a political community the relevant duties, this would not be for the substantive moral reason that one may give priority to one's compatriots when meeting the demands of justice, but for the instrumental reason that such an allocation is the best way for all to discharge their duties to all. Within that framework, cosmopolitan sufficientism is compatible with some degree of patriotic preference for the resident members of one's political community—precisely because a just world is one in which individuals do have the freedom to associate with whomever they wish and, once sufficiency is met, to allocate amongst themselves the benefits which result from their mutual cooperation. In so arguing, I develop an account of group rights which makes sense of individuals' collective interest in self-determination but remains firmly grounded in the interests of those communities' individual members.

Having thus sketched out a cosmopolitan theory of justice, I embark on the task of delineating cosmopolitan principles for a just war. In order to be deserving of the label 'cosmopolitan', such principles must meet the following

---

[9] My cosmopolitan account of the just war is human-centric. Perhaps that is an arbitrary restriction—perhaps we should include non-human animals in our global community. This might in turn have far-reaching implications for our understanding of the just war. In particular, we would need to work out whether 'animalarian intervention' (to protect animals from one another, or from human beings) would be justified; whether to include the bads accruing to non-human animals as a result of the war in our proportionality calculus; indeed, whether it is permissible to conscript animals. My intuitions on those questions are far too rough at this point to be worth setting out here—hence the restricted scope in that respect of the present inquiry. But I am grateful to Jon Quong for raising the issue, and to Sue Donaldson and Will Kymlicka for prompting me to turn my attention to it—eventually.

two conditions. First, they must ascribe pre-eminence to individuals and not conceive of groups as having independent moral status; accordingly, the rights and duties they delineate must be those of individuals, not of groups as such. Second, they must not make individuals' basic entitlements dependent on their membership in a political community—nor, in fact, on their membership in any kind of group, when such membership is irrelevant to the interests which those entitlements protect. As will be apparent at the close of this chapter, my starting point will be a relatively minimalist account of cosmopolitan justice. As will be no less clear by the end of the book, this relatively minimalist account generates rather controversial conclusions concerning the legitimate recourse to military force.

I start, in Chapter 2, by providing an account of wars of collective self-defence against an unwarranted military aggression—the paradigmatic case of a just war, and yet the kind of war, precisely, which might seem to pose insuperable problems for cosmopolitanism, since it pits sovereign political communities against one another. I begin the chapter by delineating a normative account of defensive killings in private, domestic contexts, which I then apply to the case of collective self-defence against a foreign aggressor. In a nutshell, I argue that combatants who fight a just war of self-defence have the right to kill combatants who fight an unjust war of aggression, but that the latter may not, in turn, retaliate in their own defence: *pace* orthodox just-war theory, whether or not combatants have the right to kill enemy combatants (largely) depends on the moral status of the cause for which they fight. The defence of the territorial integrity and political self-determination of one's political community against unwarranted aggression is a just cause, I further claim, because of the importance to individuals of those collective goods. Having thus shown that members of a wrongfully aggressed country have the right to authorize their leaders to wage war on their behalf in defence of their collective rights to territorial integrity and collective self-determination, I then examine some tensions between, on the one hand, the cosmopolitan claim that membership in a given political community is irrelevant to the conferral and infringement of rights, and on the other hand, the collateral killing of enemy non-combatants.

Chapter 3 takes us into relatively uncharted territory. If, as I argue in Chapter 2, the right to wage war is a right to resort to large-scale lethal force in defence of one's rights, is it the case that violations of *subsistence* rights (to the material resources we need to lead a minimally decent life) provide victims with a just cause for war? I argue that they do, partly because severe mass poverty undermines collective interests in collective self-determination, but also on the deeper grounds that threats to one's life, of which starvation is one,

warrant defensive killing. The claim holds not merely when the rights violations take the form of a wrongful action but also (more controversially) when
they take the form of a wrongful omission. Having thus expanded on the
account of just causes for war offered in Chapter 2, I make a first foray into the
issue of legitimate authority, and argue that the right to wage a subsistence war
is held not merely by states whose populations suffer unjustly from severe
poverty and which are not themselves responsible for that predicament, but
also (controversially) by responsible states, as well as by victims themselves.
I end the chapter with an account of the grounds upon which individual
affluent members of affluent communities who are derelict in their duty to the
very poor are legitimate targets in war.

   In those two chapters I examine cases where the rights of members of a
given political community are violated by a foreign regime. In Chapter 4
I turn to instances where those rights are violated by the victims' own
regime—in other words, to civil wars. Civil wars are currently the most
common, and most lethal, form of conflict: they might also be thought to
fall outside the remit of a cosmopolitan inquiry of war, since they are fought
*within* sovereign political communities, and since cosmopolitanism's distinctive contribution bears on such communities' conduct *vis-à-vis* one another.
And yet, I show that civil wars—which incidentally are consistently over-
looked in the philosophical literature—bear scrutinizing at the bar of cosmopolitan justice. In particular, I argue that if a given right-violation constitutes a
just cause for an inter-state war, then it also constitutes a just cause for a civil
war—though (as we shall also see) whether the war is inter- or intra-state can
have a bearing on the degree to which the war meets other requirements for a
just war. I then revisit a thesis which I began defending in Chapter 3, to the
effect that individuals in their private capacity may hold the right to wage war.
Here I argue, more incisively, that it is not a necessary condition for *all* wars to
be just that they be waged by state-actors—which thus opens the door (contra
some important strands within the tradition) for the view that a civil war can
be just on the side of the insurgents. Finally, I close with some comments on
agents' liability to lethal harm in civil wars, with particular focus on civil wars
fought under the shadow of a foreign occupier.

   Whilst Chapters 2 to 4 focus on self-defensive wars (wars, in other words,
which belligerents fight in defence of their own rights), Chapter 5, by contrast,
examines the conditions under which the violations of the rights *of others*
provide some actor(s) A with a just cause for using military force against rights
violator regime B. Humanitarian intervention raises a number of issues which
normative accounts of self-defensive wars do not address. First, and most
obviously, any argument in favour of the right to intervene must set out the

conditions under which regime B forfeits its right to govern over community B and, thereby, its right not to be attacked by A. Second, whereas self-defensive wars raise the issue of the right to kill in (individual and collective) self-defence, humanitarian wars also raise that of the duty to kill in defence of others. My aim, in the chapter, is four-fold: to provide an argument for the right to intervene which draws on the account of defensive killings offered in Chapter 2; to defend the duty to intervene; to offer an account of whose right and whose duty it is; to tackle the serious normative difficulties raised by the fact that, in such a war, intervening forces not only will kill combatants who are not themselves complicitous in the often egregious rights violations which provide interveners with a just cause, but will also kill a number of those very victims on whose behalf the war is waged.

Chapters 2 to 5 provide a cosmopolitan account of different kinds of war, by focusing on the notions of just cause, legitimate authority. and liability to being killed. In Chapter 6 I offer an account of what I call commodified wars—wars, in other words, in which private actors take on important roles alongside or in replacement of regular armed forces. One might wonder why a book-length *cosmopolitan* account of the just war should tackle mercenarism, since there seems to be nothing distinctively cosmopolitan about it. Yet the issue is worth addressing, if only because cosmopolitanism is more hospitable than other moral and political theories to loosening states' normative grip, as it were, on a wide range of practices. Moreover, my aim in this book is not simply to articulate and defend a cosmopolitan account of the just war: it is to bring to bear that account on the kinds of wars which we are currently witnessing—of which commodified warfare is one. I offer a qualified defence of mercenarism which, drawing on the account of defensive killings presented in Chapter 2, appeals to the importance of enabling just defensive killing. If the war is just, I argue, individuals have the right to hire themselves out for military services; political communities have the right to contract with them for those purposes; and private military corporations have the right to act as intermediaries between them. I then dispose of five objections to mercenarism and end with some remarks on mercenaries', as contrasted with uniformed combatants', right to kill in war.

Throughout those five chapters, both prongs of the principle of discrimination are addressed alongside those of just cause and legitimate authority, as each chapter tackles the issues of combatants' and non-combatants' liability to attack. The final chapter, by contrast, is wholly given over to the second part of the principle: namely, the principle of non-combatant immunity, which is the cornerstone of *jus in bello*. It does so in the context of military asymmetry between belligerents. The problem of military asymmetry has acquired new prominence in contemporary Western strategic circles, due in part to the ease with which small groups of individuals can procure weapons which would have been beyond their reach two decades ago, the concomitant rise in asymmetrical wars, and powerful states' greater vulnerability in such wars. Contemporary wars are often asymmetrical both militarily and morally: that is, weaker belligerents (from a military point of view) are now increasingly resorting to means of warfare which are in violation of the rules of *jus in bello* (most notably the deliberate targeting of innocent non-combatants), *and* are exploiting their adversary's unwillingness similarly to violate those rules.

Asymmetrical wars (in both senses) are of particular concern for the cosmopolitan theory of the just war which I defend in this book. For the requirement of legitimate authority as reinterpreted in Chapters 3 and 4 confers the status of lawful combatants and/or belligerents on small groups of individuals, indeed individuals as such—actors, in other words, who are unlikely to be in a position to further their ends by conventional means. In this chapter I assume that the weaker belligerent has a just cause, fights for just ends, and has legitimate authority. With those assumptions in hand, I scrutinise three tactics which weaker belligerents typically employ: the direct targeting of non-combatants; the use of non-combatants as human shields; and the use of deception such as pretending to be a non-combatant in order the better to approach the enemy and kill him. I argue that deliberate targeting is impermissible, that (controversially) the use of human shields is sometimes permissible, and that deceitful tactics are largely unproblematic from a moral point of view.

A further few *caveat*. In claiming to construct a cosmopolitan theory of the just war, I do not mean to imply that non-cosmopolitans cannot endorse the principles I defend here. Nor do I mean to imply that all the justifications I offer in favour of those principles are available only to cosmopolitans. Thus, one clearly need not be a cosmopolitan to hold the view that unwarranted military aggression on a sovereign community's territory is a just cause for war, or that humanitarian intervention is sometimes morally legitimate. However, some conclusions which non-cosmopolitans endorse are *in fact* cosmopolitan—such as, most notably, the view that innocent non-combatants who belong to the enemy are not legitimate targets, since that view supposes that borders are irrelevant to those individuals' entitlements. Moreover, many of the justifications which I shall provide in support of those conclusions markedly differ from those advanced by non-cosmopolitans. In so far as it is important to be clear as to what one's justifications are and whether they are sound, there is merit to the task of defending cosmopolitan justifications for principles the content of which is generally not in dispute. *A fortiori*, it is worth working out which principles ought to be substantively revised in the light of the central tenets of cosmopolitan morality.

Furthermore, my concern throughout is with the moral principles which should guide our resort to and conduct in war, and not with the laws of war as articulated in, for example, the Geneva Conventions. I shall not say anything at all about the extent to which the latter can, or indeed ought to, reflect the former. Thus, in arguing that combatants who fight in an unjust war (*prima facie*) do not have the right to kill enemy combatants, I am not committing myself to the view that the laws of war should reflect that important principle in such a way that unjust combatants ought to stand trial for murder. In so proceeding, I am assuming (without defending that assumption here) that one can speak of moral principles for war independently of their applicability—in just the same way as (I note elsewhere) one can coherently speak of the demands of distributive justice independently of the degree to which those demands can be cashed out, as such, into public policy. I concede that a full normative account of war should not merely delineate first-best principles for war, but also (morally directed) second-best principles which can be enshrined in the law. Mine is therefore incomplete. Unearthing first-best principles is important in its own right, however, if only because one cannot know what the law should prescribe and proscribe unless one brings into view the moral ideals to which it should aspire.[10]

In embarking on that task, I often appeal to pre-theoretic intuitions which I unearth either by constructing hypothetical scenarios or by referring to historical examples of military conflicts (more on which presently), and which will be examined in the light of other intuitions and more considered judgements. The mode of reasoning at play in this book is thus best

---

[10] See C. Fabre, 'Guns, Food, and Liability to Attack', *Ethics* 120 (2009): 36–63, esp. 39. The view of the relationship between first-best and second-best principle (of war, or of distributive justice) which I endorse is broadly similar to G. A. Cohen's as it applies to distributive justice. (See G. A. Cohen, *Rescuing Justice and Equality* (Cambridge, MA: Harvard University Press, 2008).) But it differs from J. McMahan's as it applies to war. On McMahan's view, the morality of war is not in any way conventional: its norms are true independently of what we may think of them. By contrast, the laws of war are conventional means for limiting the commissions of unjust acts in war. However, effectiveness (on that front) is not the only consideration that matters when deciding whether legally to prohibit or permit a given act. As David Rodin points out, we would deem unjust a law permitting the (grievously wrong) ritualistic killing of one innocent person as a means to avert a much greater number of rights violations, however effective such killing would be. Standards of 'moral directedness', as it were, for the laws of war are more closely connected to deep moral norms of war than McMahan seems to allow. See J. McMahan, 'The Morality of War and the Law of War', in D. Rodin and H. Shue (ed.), *Just and Unjust Warriors* (Oxford: Oxford University Press, 2008), and D. Rodin, 'Morality and Law in War', in H. Strachan and S. Scheipers (ed.), *The Changing Character of War* (Oxford: Oxford University Press, 2011). For further extensive criticism of McMahan's position, see, for example, A. Roberts, 'The Principle of Equal Application of the Laws of War', in D. Rodin and H. Shue (ed.), *Just and Unjust Warriors* (Oxford: Oxford University Press, 2008), H. Shue, 'Do We Need a "Morality of War"?', in D. Rodin and H. Shue (ed.), *Just and Unjust Warriors* (Oxford: Oxford University Press, 2008); S. Lazar, 'The Morality and Law of War', in A. Marmor (ed.), *Routledge Companion to the Philosophy of Law* (London: Routledge, forthcoming).

understood as a combination of casuistry and (to use Rawls' apt phrase) reflective equilibrium, which has become a rather standard way to proceed in applied ethics and political philosophy. Admittedly, its reliance on moral intuitions and hypotheticals makes it unappealing to many. Intuitions, it is sometimes said, are too unstable to have any moral authority, too reflective of the prevailing moral ethos and thus too conservative to lead to progressive philosophy. Hypotheticals, it is also said, are too abstract and too detached from reality to be of much use; indeed, by grossly distorting what really is happening in the real world, they can have the pernicious effect of justifying practices which ought never to be condoned.[11]

There is something to be said for those claims. However, if used sparingly and judiciously, hypotheticals do help us isolate morally relevant features of particular cases and thereby uncover our intuitions. This is not to imply that intuitions are the only sources of moral knowledge: far from it; rather, they are one such source—the raw data, if you will—of our moral thinking. Moreover, as we shall see at various points in this book, some of the intuitions which underpin my considered account of the morality of war are rather radical and immune from the charge of undue conservatism.

There is one respect, however, where my overall approach is unashamedly standard. I endorse neither absolutist deontology, whereby (broadly put) one can never under any circumstances infringe the rights of an innocent party, nor consequentialism, whereby (broadly put) the goodness or badness of consequences is the only morally relevant factor for assessing the rightness or wrongness of our actions. I agree with deontologists, of whom I am, that *pace* consequentialists, some acts are intrinsically right or, as the case may be, intrinsically wrong, irrespective of their consequences. In particular, I agree that the ways in which a certain state of affairs is brought about, and the intentions of the agents which do bring it about, matter a great deal to the rightness or wrongness. However, I also take on board the quasi-consequentialist point that consequences sometimes do matter a great deal. The resulting theory might seem an *ad hoc*, unhappy hybrid of deontological and consequentialist intuitions. I do not deny this. But '*ad hoc*ness'

---

[11] For the view thus described of moral intuitions, see, for example, P. Singer, 'Sidgwick and Reflective Equilibrium', *The Monist* 58 (1974): 490–517. The paradigmatic example of a pernicious hypothetical is the ticking-bomb scenario, which is routinely invoked in support of torture. For a pithy criticism of over-reliance on hypotheticals in general and of the ticking-bomb scenario in particular, see, for example, D. Luban, 'Unthinking the Ticking Bomb', in C. R. Beitz and R. E. Goodin (ed.), *Global Basic Rights* (Oxford: Oxford University Press, 2009); H. Shue, 'Torture', *Philosophy & Public Affairs* 7 (1978): 124–43. The approach I outline in this paragraph is described and defended at greater length, and with characteristic clarity, by Jeff McMahan, in J. McMahan, 'Moral Intuitions', in H. LaFollette (ed.), *The Blackwell Guide to Ethical Theory* (Oxford: Blackwell Publishing, 2000).

seems to me to be a price worth paying to avoid incurring the much higher cost of the jarring implausibility inherent in the views that consequences *never* matter or that they are the *only* thing that matters.

In endorsing this hybrid view, I take for granted the following two familiar doctrines: to wit, the doctrine of acts and omissions on the one hand, and the doctrine of double effect on the other hand. Both doctrines have been characterized in many different ways. Here I assume, in agreement with the doctrine of acts and omissions, that wrongfully harming someone is morally worse than wrongfully allowing harm to happen to them, at least *ceteris paribus*. I also assume, in agreement with the doctrine of double effect, that deliberately harming an innocent person as a means to bring about a good end is morally worse than harming her foreseeably but intentionally as a side-effect of one's attempt to bring about a good end—again, *ceteris paribus*. Notwithstanding the criticisms which they have elicited in recent years, those two doctrines, in this and others of their formulations, remain central to much of our moral and legal traditions, so much so that the normative costs attendant on abandoning them strike me as too high to warrant incurring. More precisely, both doctrines rely on a particular understanding of normative agency, whereby morally responsible agents stand in a particular relationship to one another on the one hand and to the causal processes in which they operate on the other hand. The doctrine of acts and omissions, in its relatively standard justifications, confers greater moral weight on the acts whereby agents bring about certain states of affairs than on the fact of their not acting, precisely because of the special value to be attached to the exercise of responsible agency. The doctrine of double effect, for its part, standardly locates the moral 'worseness' of the deliberate infliction of harm as a means to bring about some good in a failure on the part of agents properly to respect other such agents by using them solely as means to their or other parties' ends. Both points will prove important at various junctures in this book.[12]

---

[12] For classic expositions and defences of the doctrine of double effect, see P. Foot, 'The Problem of Abortion and the Doctrine of the Double Effect', in P. Foot, *Virtues and Vices* (Oxford: 1978); W. S. Quinn, 'Actions, Intentions, and Consequences: The Doctrine of Double Effect', *Philosophy & Public Affairs* 18 (1989): 334–51; for a book-length account of its various characterizations and its role in normative and applied ethics, see T. A. Cavanaugh, *Double-Effect Reasoning: Doing Good and Avoiding Evil* (Oxford: Oxford University Press, 2006). For a recent defence, see A. Hills, 'Defending Double Effect', *Philosophical Studies: An International Journal for Philosophy in the Analytic Tradition* 116 (2003): 133–52. For an indirect defence, which emphasizes the costs for the criminal law (where intentions are central to the determination of wrongdoing) of abandoning the view that intentions are relevant to permissibility, see D. Husak, 'The Costs to Criminal Theory of Supposing that Intentions are Irrelevant to Permissibility', *Criminal Law and Philosophy* 3 (2009): 51–70. For criticisms of the doctrine, see, for example, S. Kagan, *The Limits of Morality* (Oxford: Oxford University Press, 1989); A. McIntyre, 'Doing Away with Double Effect', *Ethics* 111 (2001):

Finally, a word on my use of historical cases. Michael Walzer's seminal *Just and Unjust Wars: A Moral Argument with Historical Illustrations* revived the field of just-war ethics in the 1970s. It did so as much due to its thoughtful and normatively driven study of history as through the conduit of intricately analytical arguments. Yet much of contemporary war ethics is extraordinarily analytical and pays rather scant attention to the historical cases which often and implicitly drive its conclusions. This is not a philosophical failure: one can make a perfectly coherent argument about, for example, the permissibility of a war of humanitarian intervention without saying anything at all about any of the interventions which did actually take place (such as India's intervention in what was then East Pakistan in 1971), or those which did not but should have taken place (such as the UN's and its members' conspicuous failure to halt the Rwandan genocide in 1994.) In this book, however, I adopt a resolutely Walzerian approach to writing on war as far as historical examples are concerned. My extensive use of such examples is not just self-indulgence on my part (I started out as an historian and still sometimes hanker after history as an academic discipline); nor is it solely a mean to relieve the inevitable tedium, if not of reading, at least of writing, a long philosophical argument. Rather, it is informed by the thought that war is unfortunately ubiquitous and that it would be odd to think about it from a normative point of view without alluding at all to its historical manifestations. That said, I am not an historian and thus do not claim to speak with any degree of historiographical authority on the wars which I mention here. All I can do is put forward relatively accepted accounts thereof, based on secondary sources which, in their relevant sub-fields and as far as I can tell (or, indeed, have been told), are widely regarded as seminal or at least important.

Without further ado, then, let us begin.

219–55; T. M. Scanlon, *Moral Dimensions: Permissibility, Meaning, Blame* (Cambridge, MA: Harvard University Press, 2008), ch. 1. For classic expositions and defences of the doctrine of acts and omissions (or, as it is sometimes called, doing and allowing, or killing and letting die), see Foot, ibid.; J. McMahan, 'Killing, Letting Die, and Withdrawing Aid', *Ethics* 103 (1993): 250–79; W. S. Quinn, 'Actions, Intentions, and Consequences: The Doctrine of Doing and Allowing', *The Philosophical Review* 98 (1989): 287–312; S. Scheffler, 'Doing and Allowing', *Ethics* 114 (2004): 215–39; J. J. Thomson, 'Killing, Letting Die and the Trolley Problem', in *Rights, Restitution, and Risk: Essays in Moral Theory* (Cambridge, MA: 1986) For criticisms, see Kagan, *The Limits of Morality*; P. Unger, *Living High and Letting Die* (Oxford: Oxford University Press, 1996); K. Draper, 'Rights and the Doctrine of Doing and Allowing', *Philosophy & Public Affairs* 33 (2005): 253–80.

# 1

# Cosmopolitanism

## 1.1 INTRODUCTION

Cosmopolitanism is the view that human beings are the fundamental and primary *loci* for moral concern and respect and have equal moral worth. It is individualist, egalitarian, and universal, and insists that political borders are arbitrary from a moral point of view, and more precisely ought not to have a bearing on individuals' prospects for a flourishing life. Thus, it takes a stand not so much on the *content* of principles of justice, but rather, on their *scope*. In this chapter I sketch a rights-based theory of cosmopolitan justice according to which individuals should be guaranteed, as a matter of right, equal opportunities for a minimally decent life—and this irrespective of political borders—and where, once all have such a life, those who have more resources at their disposal are not under further duties towards the worse off—again, irrespective of borders.

The chapter proceeds as follows. In Section 1.2 I outline what I take justice to require *within* borders. In Section 1.3 I defend the view that political borders are irrelevant to individuals' just entitlements. In Section 1.4 I give an account of the right to political self-determination and of the notion of state legitimacy which is compatible with the central tenets of cosmopolitan justice as articulated in the previous two sections.

Before I start I will make a few remarks. First, some points of terminology: by 'the state', I shall mean (a) the set of institutions and the individuals who occupy roles within those institutions, (b) which together govern over a given territory and people, (c) which decide whom to admit on to that territory; (d) whose rules and decisions are *de facto* binding over both that territory and people, and (e) which coercively enforce those rules and decisions. By 'political community' I shall mean a group of individuals linked by a set of shared political values and ideals who inhabit a given territory. By 'country' I shall mean the state, the community over which it has jurisdiction, and that territory itself. By 'regime' I shall mean a subset of those institutions—more precisely, those which are tasked with enacting and enforcing the laws which apply to all residents, such as nationally elected representatives, the government, the judiciary, the police, and the armed forces.

Second, a plea for both understanding and patience. All the issues I shall address here (equality, justice, rights, cosmopolitanism, state legitimacy, political self-determination) are the focus of enormous bodies of literature. Space will not permit me to engage fully with them. Instead, I shall aim to proceed directly to the most persuasive arguments in support of the cosmopolitan principles which I favour, and will tackle only those objections to cosmopolitanism which are particularly relevant to its merits as a theory of war. Even so, the chapter is nevertheless quite long. Setting the stage does take time, however, particularly when every single one of its constitutive planks is needed to frame and support the ensuing narrative.

## 1.2 JUSTICE: A SUFFICIENTIST ACCOUNT

A complete theory of distributive justice sets out the *scope* of its constitutive principles, their *site*, their *content*, and their *strength*. By the content of justice I mean that which justice prescribes should be given or done to others. By the strength of justice I have in mind the degree to which it is important, morally speaking, that the requirements of justice should be respected. By the site of justice I have in mind the question of where justice applies—more precisely, whether it applies to political institutions with coercive powers (what some call, following Rawls, the basic structure), or whether it also applies to individuals' choices within the interstices of the law.[1] Finally, by the scope of justice I mean those to whom the requirements of justice apply. In this section I attend to the content, strength, and site of justice, leaving the question of its scope to Section 1.3. More precisely, I claim, with respect to its content, that justice requires that individuals be treated with equal concern and respect, which in turn requires that they have equal opportunities for a minimally decent life. With respect to its strength, I claim that the freedoms and resources which individuals must enjoy if they are to have opportunities for a minimally decent life must be secured to them as a matter of rights. With respect to its site, I aver that the requirements of justice do not merely apply to the basic structure: they also apply to individuals' choices within it—those

---

[1] See J. Rawls, *A Theory of Justice* (Cambridge, MA: Harvard University Press, 1971). For an illuminating critical discussion of Rawls' account of the basic structure in particular, and of the site of justice in general, see G. A. Cohen, 'Where the Action Is: On the Site of Distributive Justice', *Philosophy & Public Affairs* 26 (1997): 3–30; *Rescuing Justice and Equality*. The term 'site' derives from Cohen.

choices, that is, which for a number of reasons ought not to be subject to the scrutiny of the law but which can nevertheless impair third parties' opportunities for a minimally decent life.

### 1.2.1 On the content of justice

Let me start with the uncontroversial claim that individuals have a fundamental interest in being able to frame, revise, and pursue a conception of the good life—for which they need standard civil and political freedoms as well as some material resources. The question which is at the heart of competing theories of distributive justice is that of how much of such resources they should be guaranteed. The claim that a world in which individuals lack opportunities for a minimally decent life is unjust is more demanding than conceptions of distributive justice which require that individuals' *basic* material needs be met by way of resources transfers. The difficulty with basic needs views, however, is that their rationale for mandating resource transfers—that individuals whose basic needs are not met do not live a life worthy of a human being—demands more than they are prepared to concede. On basic needs views, a world in which individuals have enough to subsist but not enough for their life to be described in any way as decent is not an unjust state of affairs. Yet it is hard to see how someone whose life is not in any way decent leads a life worthy of a human being.

At this juncture, some—so-called radical egalitarians—will undoubtedly press that justice requires much more than providing individuals with (material) opportunities for a minimally decent life: rather, it requires that no one be worse off than others through no fault of his own. Radical egalitarians disagree amongst themselves on the best way to understand 'worse off'. But they do agree that unchosen inequalities call for remedial action and that a world in which some have opportunities for a minimally decent life, *whereas others*, in that world, have opportunities for a maximally flourishing life is an unfair world if those inequalities are not traceable to agents' choices; so is a world in which some individuals lack opportunities for a minimally decent life through no fault of their own *whilst others* enjoy such opportunities.[2]

Radical egalitarianism is standardly condemned for being too demanding on the better off (since the latter, it is alleged, would have to transfer all of their

[2] For classic defences and different conceptions of radical egalitarianism, see R. Arneson, 'Equality and Equal Opportunity for Welfare', *Philosophical Studies* 56 (1989); G. A. Cohen, 'On the Currency of Egalitarian Justice', *Ethics* 99 (1989): 916–44; R. Dworkin, 'What is Equality? Part One: Equality of Welfare', *Philosophy & Public Affairs* 10 (1981): 185–246; 'What is Equality? Part Two: Equality of Resources', *Philosophy & Public Affairs* 10 (1981): 283–345.

surplus resources to the worse off until equality obtains); for conferring too much weight on individuals' responsibility for how their life goes and in so doing for allowing those who make bad choices to fall below subsistence levels; for committing itself to the view that a world in which all individuals have nothing is preferable to a world in which some have a little and others have more; for being insensitive to the importance of giving priority to the very worst off; and most importantly for riding roughshod over the intuition that what matters, from the point of view of justice, is not whether individuals have more or less than others but, rather, whether they have *enough*.[3]

Space does not permit me to engage in that debate. Instead, I should like to take as my starting point a relatively minimalist theory of justice, on which theorists unsatisfied with the basic needs approach will agree broadly: namely, the view that a world in which individuals lack, yet could enjoy, equal opportunities for a minimally decent life through no fault of their own is an unjust world. More specifically, a minimally decent life, I posit, is one in which individuals enjoy a set of basic capabilities. I refer to the capabilities approach (as outlined by Sen and Nussbaum) for two related reasons: its increasing prominence in development economics, and its fit, as it were, with the Universal Declaration of Human Rights. Of course, there is wide debate on what the capabilities are and how to measure them. I shall restrict myself to the following list, which I hope is as uncontroversial as possible: life, body, and health; bodily integrity; basic health and average longevity; emotional and intellectual flourishing (creativity and imagination, ability to engage in meaningful relationships with others); control over material resources as well control over one's social and political environment (the exercise of both of which is constrained by an obligation not to impair other people's capabilities.[4])

---

[3] Those criticisms can be found, in various forms, in (*inter alia*), E. Anderson, 'What Is the Point of Equality?', *Ethics* 100 (1990): 287–337; Y. Benbaji, 'The Doctrine of Sufficiency: A Defence', *Utilitas* 17 (2005): 310–32; R. Crisp, 'Equality, Priority, and Compassion', *Ethics* 113 (2003): 745–63; H. Frankfurt, 'Equality as a Moral Ideal', *Ethics* 98 (1987): 21–43; R. Huseby, 'Sufficiency: Restated and Defended', *Journal of Political Philosophy* 18 (2010): 178–97. For influential defences of egalitarianism against those criticisms, see R. J. Arneson, 'Luck Egalitarianism and Prioritarianism', *Ethics* 110 (2000): 339–49; P. Casal, 'Why Sufficiency Is Not Enough', *Ethics* 117 (2007): 296–326; L. Temkin, 'Egalitarianism Defended', *Ethics* 113 (2003): 764–82. For influential discussions of the debate between radical egalitarianism and its critics, see, for example, A. Mason, *Levelling the Playing Field: The Idea of Equal Opportunity and its Place in Egalitarian Thought* (Oxford: Oxford University Press, 2006); D. Parfit, 'Equality and Priority', *Ratio* 10 (1997): 202–21; L. Temkin, *Inequality* (Oxford: Oxford University Press, 1993).

[4] See M. C. Nussbaum, 'The Supreme Court 2006 Term. Foreword: Constitutions and Capabilities: "Perceptions" against lofty formalism', *Harvard Law Review* 121 (2006): 5–97, for a recent statement of the capabilities approach by one of its foremost proponents. The *locus classicus* is M. C. Nussbaum, *Women and Human Development: The Capabilities Approach* (Cambridge: Cambridge University Press, 2000). See also A. K. Sen, *Development as Freedom* (New York: Oxford University Press, 1999); A. K. Sen, 'Elements of a Theory of Human Rights', *Philosophy*

The view that justice requires that those who have more than enough help those who have less than enough is often termed 'sufficientist', or 'sufficientarian'. Sufficientists disagree about a number of things. In particular, they disagree about the precise location of the sufficiency threshold and about the role to be played in their theory, if any at all, by the value of equality. On the latter point, some sufficientists seem to believe that equality in the distribution of goods and resources does not matter at all. Others believe that equality matters only past the sufficiency threshold. Others still hold that equality only has instrumental value, in the sense that a society in which there are considerable material inequalities is one in which many individuals are far less likely to have enough. Notwithstanding those disagreements, sufficientists claim that individuals should have *equal* chances of having enough, and thus ground their principles of justice in the principle of fundamental equality whereby individuals have equal moral worth and should treat one another with equal concern and respect. Though radical egalitarians will insist that sufficientists are not egalitarian enough, there nevertheless is a sense in which they too belong to the broad church of egalitarianism.

That said, the principle of fundamental equality warrants further explanation. In mandating individuals to treat one another with respect, it holds that individuals must be granted the freedoms which they need in order to lead a minimally decent life—such as freedom of movement, freedom of association, freedom of expression, freedom to control what happens to their body, and so on. But the requirement of respect does not merely dictate duties of non-interference with individuals' freedom(s). It also informs the kind of considerations which we may invoke for granting, or denying, those resources and freedoms. In particular, to treat individuals with respect is to give them those freedoms and resources out of recognition of their equal worth. Thus, a hitherto white segregationist who agrees to the abolition of segregation on the grounds that he will be better off for it as a businessman does not treat blacks with respect. Likewise, a wealthy entrepreneur who agrees to coercive resource transfers to the needy as a means to thwart the progress of socialism ('if we give them a bit they will not ask for too much') is not treating the needy with respect.

In a similar vein, to treat individuals with respect is to not deny them those freedoms and resources on morally arbitrary grounds. The charge of moral arbitrariness is at the heart of many defences of egalitarian theories of

*& Public Affairs* 32 (2004): 315–56. Note that the foregoing account is entirely compatible with the claim that a world in which some have, and others lack, such opportunities is bad (what Parfit calls *telic egalitarianism*), as distinct from unjust (or *deontic egalitarianism*), in virtue of being ridden with inequalities. See Parfit, 'Equality and Priority'.

distributive justice (sufficientist or otherwise), and plays an important role (as we shall see in Section 1.3) in arguments to the effect that justice is global in scope. It also needs disambiguating. On one prominent account, the charge of arbitrariness holds that individuals should not be made worse off, or (in a sufficientist light) should not have less than enough, as a result of factors for which individuals are not responsible.[5] On another account, however, to deny someone a good or a freedom arbitrarily is to invoke in support of that denial traits or features which, whether or not their bearers have chosen them, are irrelevant to the matter at hand. Thus, it is one thing to say that Andrew has a claim to food as he is not responsible for the fact that he is needy; it is another to hold that it is his need for food, and not the fact that he chose to dye his hair blond, which grounds his claim. It is a matter for considerable debate, amongst sufficientist theories of justice, whether or not agents should be denied those resources if they are responsible for their predicament. I shall not take a stand on that issue either. What does seem beyond dispute is the thought that *if* individuals are not responsible, *then* they have a claim at the bar of justice, and I shall thus take that thought as fixed throughout the book. What is also beyond dispute is the claim that individuals should not be denied freedoms and resources on the basis of features, whether chosen or not, which are irrelevant to the matter at hand. Finally, the commitment to showing concern for the needy implies that, under conditions of epistemic uncertainty as to whether or not agents are responsible for their predicament, it is better to err on the side of giving them more than that to which they may perhaps have a claim, by deeming them not to be responsible, than to err on the side of withholding that to which they do in fact have a claim, by deeming them responsible.[6]

Finally, although justice requires that the well off help the needy secure opportunities for a minimally decent life as defined above, it does not require that they do more than enough. In fact, a just world is one in which individuals are permitted to confer greater weight on their own goals, projects, and attachments, in two cases: once the needy have such opportunities, and when securing such opportunities for them would require of the better off to sacrifice their own opportunities for a minimally decent life. The prerogative

---

[5] Rawls, *A Theory of Justice*, 72–3.

[6] To anticipate my ensuing discussion of the right to kill, this point is compatible with the claim that *if* their right to a good or freedom warrants defending by using lethal force, and *if* we are not sure as to whether or not they have that right, then we should proceed on the assumption that they do not have it, and we should thus refrain from exercising lethal force on their behalf. Incidentally, that claim strikes me as plausible: as per the doctrine of acts and omissions, it is better to err on the side of wrongfully failing to help someone in need and in so doing preserve the life of someone who is liable to being killed, than to err on the side of helping someone who lacks a claim to assistance by wrongfully killing someone who is not liable. I am grateful to Tamar Meisels for pressing me on this.

has two facets. First, it permits material inequalities above the sufficiency threshold such that some individuals are in a better position than others to pursue their conception of the good life, both individually and as part of the associations which they have formed with others.[7] Second, the prerogative permits them not to do so much for others as to impair their own opportunities for a minimally decent life. Note, however, that although agents are not under a duty to assist others at that particular cost, they are (I submit) under a (*prima facie*) duty not to harm others in order to secure their own opportunities, at least when those others are not in any way causally related to the fact that they themselves are in such predicament. In other words, they are not under a (*prima facie*) duty to divest themselves of the resources they need for a minimally decent life in order to save others from death by hunger; but they are under a (*prima facie*) duty not to kill innocent bystanders in order to procure for themselves life-saving food. As we shall see, agents sometimes are justified in infringing bystanders' rights not to be grievously harmed in the course of defending theirs or other people's fundamental rights—not only unintentionally (when the harm they inflict is a foreseen but intended side-effect of their defensive move) but also intentionally (in which case the justificatory bar is higher than when the harm is inflicted unintentionally.) Nevertheless, there generally is a greater constraint on harming than on not assisting, for which different reasons have been offered. Samuel Scheffler's Kantian proposal strikes me as particularly convincing. It holds that moral and rational agents should conceive of themselves as bound to norms of individual responsibility for the states of affairs which they cause as well as for those which they allow to happen. Holding oneself to norms of responsibility consists in calibrating one's conduct on those norms; in so doing, one exercises 'fully-fledged agency'. As Scheffler puts it, 'to view oneself as subject to such norms is already to attach a special importance to, and to see oneself as having special responsibility for, what one does', as distinct from what one merely allows to happen.[8]

As should be clear, the mere fact that one is not as responsible for harms which one allows to happen as for harms which one causes does not entail that one has no responsibility at all for the ongoing harms which one fails to block.

---

[7] Even as radical an egalitarian as G. A. Cohen did concede the prerogative to critics who claimed that radical egalitarianism was too demanding. The (enormous) difficulty, for egalitarians, lies in working out when the prerogative 'kicks in'. See Cohen, *Rescuing Justice and Equality*, esp. ch. 5. As a reader for OUP pointed out to me, my account implies that an agent is under a duty to save the life of a child not merely at the cost of a ruined suit (in Peter Singer's original example), but also at the cost of three of his own fingers. I think that this is actually correct—however demanding it is.

[8] Scheffler, 'Doing and Allowing', 222.

If it did, it would not make sense to say that justice requires that the well off help the badly off. Rather, that fact helps us to distinguish, within cases where my opportunities for a minimally decent life are impaired, those where we may confer greater weight on our ends than on those of others from those where we may not do so.[9]

## 1.2.2 On the strength of justice

So much, then, for the content of the principles of justice. With respect to their strength, I take justice to pertain to what we owe to each other as a matter of rights. This is not by any means uncontroversial, for justice, after all, has variously been taken to refer to giving individuals their due, treating them fairly, fulfilling enforceable duties to them, and so on.[10] Still, the view that justice is about rights does capture the intuition that we owe certain things to one another in a way that leaves us with no discretion as to whether we must or simply may so act. Often, however, our rights are under threat at the hands of others. Justice, then, is also about what we may and indeed have the right to do in defence of our rights. That question in turn divides into three questions: (a) what we may and have the right to do to those who wrongfully threaten our rights; (b) what we may and have the right to do to those who do threaten our rights but have a justification for so acting; and (c) what we may and have the right to do to those who are causally innocent of those threats, where harming them, whether or not intentionally, would enable us to protect our rights.

Much of the book is given over to tackling those three questions in the context of war. At this juncture, suffice it to elucidate what is meant by the claim 'some agent has a right'. I shall assume throughout that to say that someone has a right is to say that an interest of hers is important enough to impose on third parties duties not to interfere with her pursuit of that or some related interest, as well as duties to promote that interest. I shall further postulate that an interest in a good G or freedom F acquires that importance

---

[9] I shall return to the case of killing over food—in other words, subsistence wars—at great length in Chapter 3, and to the issue of the deliberate killing of the innocent to secure one's survival in general in Chapter 7 (where I shall argue that the prohibition against deliberately killing the innocent may be relaxed when such killing is a necessary means to avert a greater evil.) Note that the view I am defending here is compatible with the thesis that one's duties not to harm are not *always* more stringent than one's duties to help (numbers of lives saved or destroyed might make a difference, for example.) For a recent and thoughtful discussion of the 'greater stringency view' (one which focuses on harms—such as pollution—caused by multitudes of agents), see J. Lichtenberg, 'Negative Duties, Positive Duties, and the 'New Harms'', *Ethics* 120 (2010): 557–78.

[10] For a very good overview of the different ways in which the word 'justice' is used, see P. Vallentyne, 'Justice in General: An Introduction', in P. Vallentyne (ed.), *Equality and Justice: Justice in General* (London: Routledge, 2003).

when the agent would not enjoy a minimally decent life if she did not have G or F. By implication, the content of rights-correlative obligations is determinate (securing G or F); so are their recipients (those who need G or F to have a minimally decent life); and so are the bearers of the corresponding obligations.[11]

The foregoing remarks require elaborating along four dimensions. First, to say that X has a right to something, or in respect of something, is not simply to say that X is better off for having that thing. It is to say, more strongly, that third parties *prima facie* lack discretion as to whether or not X should enjoy that thing—or, to put it differently, that the burden of proof is on them to show why they may desist from respecting or promoting the interest protected by the right, and that the burden, moreover, is very onerous indeed. (As we shall see later, notably in Section 2.2, there sometimes are justifications for infringing rights.) The difficulty, of course, is to articulate when that thing is something which X *ought* to have. The sufficientist account of justice I deployed in Section 1.2.1. sought to do precisely that.

Second, and relatedly, by the claim that X has an interest in G or F, I shall mean that it is in the interest of X to get G or enjoy F, where 'in the interest of' is not to be construed in either purely subjective or purely objective terms. More precisely, I shall mean that G either contributes to X's pursuit of some goal or project of his and there is no other goal that X would rather have if he thought rationally about alternatives; or that G contributes to X's acquiring that other goal.[12] This conception of interests advantageously blocks two implausible views: namely, the view that interests are mere wants (in which case it would be in the interest of the drug addict to get the shot of heroin he desperately wants), as well as the view that interests are not in any way related to agents' preferences (in which case it would be in the interest of the religious worshipper on a fast to get the food he desperately does *not* want.) With that point in hand, the claim 'G, or F, is *important enough* to be protected by a right' must be interpreted as follows: it is important *to X*, in the light of his

[11] The contemporary *locus classicus* for the interest theory of rights is J. Raz, *The Morality of Freedom* (Oxford: Clarendon Press, 1986), chs. 7–8. Brilliant discussions and defences of the theory can be found in M. H. Kramer, 'Rights Without Trimmings', in M. H. Kramer, N. E. Simmonds, and H. Steiner, *A Debate Over Rights* (Oxford: Oxford University Press, 1998); 'Getting Rights Right', in M. H. Kramer (ed.), *Rights, Wrongs, and Responsibilities* (Basingstoke: Palgrave, 2001). For trenchant criticisms, see N. E. Simmonds, 'Rights at the Cutting Edge', in *A Debate Over Rights*; H. Steiner, 'Working Rights', in *A Debate Over Rights*. The view that justice consists in allocating rights has a long pedigree in moral philosophy. For a relatively recent and forceful statement, see G. Vlastos, 'Justice and Equality', in J. Waldron (ed.), *Theories of Rights* (Oxford: Oxford University Press, 1984), 60.

[12] I make a similar point, almost verbatim, in C. Fabre, *Whose Body is it Anyway? Justice and the Integrity of the Person* (Oxford: Oxford University Press, 2006), 18.

goals and projects so construed, that he should get G or enjoy F; the fact that it has that importance to X plays an important part in determining whether it is important enough, all things considered, to impose the relevant duties upon third parties. Appealing to the agent-relative standpoint of interest-bearers is important in so far as it properly accounts for the fact that agents are uniquely (and appropriately so) situated in relation to their own goals and projects. In that vein, it is important not merely that—as matter of substantive justice—agents should effectively enjoy and exercise the rights (specified below) to the protection and promotion of their fundamental interests; it is also impor-tant—as matter of procedural justice—that the right person or body should decide *whether* or not they should have those goods and freedoms as a matter of fact.[13] For although the claim that X has a right to G implies that duty-bearers *prima facie* have no discretion in the matter, X himself, however, should have such discretion, at least if he has the capacity for rational and moral agency. To illustrate, it matters not merely that the hungry should be fed; it also matters who decides whether the hungry do actually get the food: namely, the hungry themselves, who might have an overriding interest in not being made to accept the food—for example, because they are fasting, or more likely, because they have chosen to go on a hunger strike as a means to further some political goal.

Third, as W. N. Hohfeld famously noted, when we use the word 'right to *p*', we often conflate quite different points: a claim in respect of *p*, which does indeed correlate with a duty on third parties to act or not to act in certain ways; a liberty, whereby one is not under a duty with respect to *p*; a power, whereby one is able to change the set of one's claims, liberties (and indeed powers themselves) *vis-à-vis p*, and an immunity, whereby one is protected against others' attempt to change one's relationship to *p* without one's consent. Throughout this book I shall have opportunities to distinguish between those different jural relations. It is particularly important to do so, for as we shall see at various junctures, the statement that an agent is at liberty to kill another in self- or other- defence (that is to say, may do so) is not the same as the statement that she has the claim to do so; likewise, the view that the right to govern is in fact a power to do so is not the same as the view that it is a claim to do so. Unless otherwise stated, I use the word 'right' to denote a claim, correlating with duties not to interfere (when rights protect interests in freedoms), or to help (when they protect interests in material resources.)[14]

---

[13] For the distinction between substantive and procedural justice as drawn here, see R. Dworkin, *Law's Empire* (London: Fontana Press, 1986), 177.

[14] W. N. Hohfeld, *Fundamental Conceptions as Applied in Judicial Reasoning* (New Haven, CT: Yale University Press, 1919).

Fourth, a statement to the effect that 'X has a right (with respect to) *p* against Y' presupposes an account of the grounds upon which X has that right and Y is the bearer of the correlative duty (or, as the case may be, liability when X's power is at issue.) With respect to the justification for rights, the latter standardly divide into so-called general and special rights: general rights are rights which agents have in virtue of being human, whereas special rights are rights which they have in virtue of something that they do or of a relationship in which they stand to another party. With respect to the assignment of duties, rights can be held *in rem*—that is, against the world at large—or *in personam*—that is, against specific individuals and institutions. Although the distinction between general and special rights is often assumed to overlap exactly with the distinction between rights *in rem* and rights *in personam*, they do in fact come apart. Thus, an agent might have a general right in virtue of being human (such as a right to food) against a specific party (such as her parents, or her state); she might also have a special right (for example, if we are to believe Locke, to the product of her labour) against the world at large (in other words, a right that no one else should interfere with her rightful use of her property.)[15]

With those clarifications in hand, we are now in a position to set out the rights which individuals must have in a just society: civil and political rights such as rights not to be killed, not to be raped, tortured, or mutilated, and rights to associate with whomever they want, to vote and to run for office; welfare rights not to have their basic health wilfully impaired by others, to be given necessities of life (some income, shelter, clothing, basic healthcare), and not to be interfered with when attempting to secure those resources. Broadly speaking, those rights, which are general rights, divide into negative rights that others not act in such a way as to bring us below the sufficient threshold or to constrain our legitimate exercise of our personal prerogative, and positive rights that they provide us the required resources if we fall below that threshold.[16]

---

[15] For the distinction between general and special rights, see H. L. A. Hart, 'Are There Any Natural Rights?', *The Philosophical Review* 64 (1955): 175–91. For a very clear discussion of the connections between the distinctions general versus special rights and rights *in rem* versus rights *in personam*, see J. Waldron, *The Right to Private Property* (Oxford: Oxford University Press, 1988), pp. 106–9. In fact, the distinction rights *in rem*/rights *in personam* is too rough, since many rights are likely to impose some duties on specific individuals as well as other duties against the world at large. (For example, my son has a right against me, his mother, that I protect him from harm, as well as a right against all other individuals that they protect him if I am not there to help.)

[16] For a classic statement of the distinction between negative and positive rights, see C. Fried, *Right and Wrong* (Cambridge, MA: Harvard University Press, 1978), 110.

### 1.2.3 On the site of justice

It remains to determine, in this section, where the site of justice is—that is, whether justice applies only to political institutions with coercive powers, whether it also applies to individuals' choices as made within the interstices of the law, or whether it applies not merely to coercive institutions but also (and only) to major, but non-coercive, social and economic institutions such as the family, economic corporations, or the market. Now, if justice is to apply anywhere at all, it ought at least to apply to coercive institutions. At a minimum, then, justice requires the establishment of political institutions which enable citizens to exercise some degree of control over their social and political environment (typically, broadly democratic institutions), as well as laws which enable them to have the resources needed for a minimally decent life (typically, coercively directed resource transfers.) By implication it requires of citizens and public officials that they set up, maintain, and support those institutions and policies over time.

Difficulties arise, however, as soon as one moves away from institutions and considers the following cases. Suppose, first, that there is no decent publicly funded medical provision for those who (through no fault of their own) cannot purchase medical insurance. Are the better off under an obligation of justice to help the needy through charitable giving, even though they are not under a legal duty to do so? Or suppose that the law prohibits employers from discriminating against prospective employees on grounds of race, disability, gender, and sexual orientation, and that it grants all adults of sound mind the power unilaterally to divorce their spouse. However, young girls who belong to a particular religious minority are systematically bullied and put down by their parents and community peers if they show aspirations to have a career outside the home; they are also pressurized, in subtle, non-physically coercive but pervasive ways into marrying at a very young age and into not seeking a divorce, however abusive their marriage might be. Assume for the sake of argument that such treatments impair their opportunities for a minimally decent life, and that their parents and peers are thus guilty of wrongdoing. Assume too that there are very good reasons not to legally enforce those young girls' right not to be so treated—such as, for example, the fact that, as they are not being physically or sexually abused, to unearth evidence of their mistreatment would be an enormously costly invasion of the value of privacy in intimate relationships. Are we to say that as the law must remain silent, those young girls are not victims of an injustice at the hands of their kin? Or suppose, finally, that those who lack opportunities for a minimally decent life will not reach the sufficiency threshold unless talented individuals enter socially useful professions such as doctoring or teaching, that the latter can make that choice without unacceptably compromising their personal prerogative to confer greater weight on their own projects, but that there are good, normative as well as practical reasons not to compel them to do so. Are we to say that the better off, by entering their preferred professions irrespective of the consequences of their choice on the badly off, are acting unjustly?

Some would deny that the well off, the young girls' kin, or the talented are acting unjustly, precisely because justice, they would claim, is a property of institutions, not of individual conduct. Others, by contrast, would argue that they are acting unjustly.[17] I for one am susceptible to the intuitive pull of the thought that the silence of the law on a particular issue is no bar to the determination of an agents' conduct as unjust (as when parents, for example, systematically and grossly discriminate in favour of one of their children on grounds of gender when handing out treats, pocket money, and presents.) In fact, that thought is not as controversial as it may seem. Those who have resisted it have tended to focus on its implications for duties of beneficence. By way of example, and to anticipate my argument for the cosmopolitan scope of justice in Section 1.3, let us suppose that protectionist tariffs as currently imposed by rich countries on foodstuff from Third World countries are very harmful to the latter's producers. We may find it relatively unproblematic to claim that, as a matter of justice, French farmers who benefit from such tariffs and who also enjoy considerable welfare benefits from their state are acting unjustly if they support the policy, and thus are under a duty of justice to support its abolition. But many will find it utterly implausible to hold them under a duty unilaterally to raise the price of their products in order to give their Kenyan counterparts a fighting chance on Western markets.

I suspect that the reason why holding French farmers under such duty seems implausible has partly to do with the fact that positive duties of that kind can only be discharged collectively through appropriate institutions. To hold individuals under such duties in their daily lives is to make short shrift of the fact that they simply cannot know how best to conduct themselves—by how much, for example, they should each individually raise the price of their foodstuff—as a result of which they will either do nothing at all or do more than they are expected to do. I do not want to settle that particular question here, if only because my aim is to sketch out a relatively *un*controversial account of justice. I shall posit that justice does not require of individuals in their purely private capacity that they should try to remedy their society's institutional failure to implement the sufficiency principle. However, it does

---

[17] The foremost proponent of that demanding view, which he discusses in the context of career choices, is G. A. Cohen. See his *Rescuing Justice and Equality*, ch. 5.

require of them that they not breach the requirement of respect in their daily lives: for example, that they not discriminate against others on the basis of race, gender, and disability, whether or not the law commands them not to do so. It also mandates them to provide assistance to those who are clearly and identifiably in need of it when they chance upon them, if they are in a position to do so (the typical drowning-baby case). In that respect, justice is not a property of institutions only: it also informs some individual choices within the societal and legal framework provided by those institutions. Moreover, in so far as it does apply to those institutions, it applies not merely to the state's legal and formal apparatus but also to other major organisations such as economic corporations, firms and, to some extent, the market in general— in other words, to the basic structure as Rawls understood it.[18] In so doing, it regulates some of the agents' choices with respect to those institutions. Thus, it does not require of agents that they refuse to enter a profession and its organizing structures on the grounds that it is not socially useful. However, it clearly requires of them that they refuse to join an organisation which is unjust through and through—the Mafia, for example—or that they refuse to take part in an unjust endeavour within partly just firms or organizations, again whether or not those endeavours are banned by the law.

That last point might be thought unduly demanding of agents, since it charges them with unjust conduct for participating in collective endeavours to which their individual contributions are only marginally significant. The objection proves too much, however, for if it does apply to employees' participation in unjust practices, it must also apply to citizens' use for their (individual) right to vote—which would thus implausibly clear German citizens who voted for the Nazi Party in December 1932 of any wrongdoing. That said, it draws our attention to the difficult issues raised by individuals' responsibility for harmful collective actions—issues to which we will attend recurrently, particularly when discussing soldiers' individual participation in, and responsibility for, unjust wars. I shall hold that individuals can be said to act jointly towards a particular goal and to be individually responsible for its occurrence when they intentionally contribute to an enterprise of which this goal is a part; further, this is so even though they need not intend to bring about that goal itself, provided that they can be reasonably expected to know

---

[18] As Susan M. Okin has shown with respect to the family, and Cohen with respect to the market, broadening the site of justice to non-coercive institutions supposes that those of individuals' choices which do not fall within the purview of the law are subject to critical evaluation *at the bar of justice*, contrary to what Rawls seems to suppose—with devastating consequences (at least according to Cohen) for his justification of material inequalities. See Cohen, *Rescuing Justice and Equality*, esp. chs. 1–3, and S. M. Okin, *Justice, Gender and the Family* (New York: Basic Books, 1989), ch. 5.

that other individuals not only also do so but have at least overlapping understandings of what that larger enterprise consists in.[19] Imagine a veterinary biologist who works in the farming industry. Amongst other things useful to good and just ends, his factory manufactures a growth hormone for livestock which, he can be reasonably expected to know, causes illness in meat consumers who suffer from Crohn's disease. Suppose further that he synthesizes a product which on the one hand makes it possible for livestock to digest this hormone, and on the other hand serves some other, good, end. Even though he cannot be described as *intending* to do his part in the production of the growth hormone, he can be described as intending to do his part in the company's collective venture which is best described as 'manufacturing and selling products'. In so far as he has good reasons to believe that one part of this collective venture consists in producing a growth hormone which is harmful to humans, as his acts are part of a collective venture, and as that collective venture constitutes a serious violation of its victims' rights not to be grievously harmed (or so I plausibly assume), the engineer can be deemed to commit an injustice.

   To recapitulate, individuals are not under a positive duty of justice to provide assistance to others in their daily life *qua* private actors, within the interstices of the law (except in cases where immediate assistance is required, here and now, failing which the person will die—as in the drowning-baby case.) Nor are they under a negative duty of justice, in their daily life, not to take part in unstructured practices the effects of which are severely harmful to others. However, *qua* citizens and public officials, individuals are under a duty of justice to (respectively) support and implement just institutions, laws, and policies; they are also under negative duties not to support and bring about unjust policies, not to take part in structured and organized practices the effects of which are severely harmful to others, and not to violate the requirement of respect in their daily lives—for example, by discriminating against others on the basis of arbitrary factors. Whether or not those duties, which, you recall, correlate into rights, extend across borders (in other words, are rights *in rem*) remains to be seen; and to this issue I now turn.

---

    [19] See C. Kutz, *Complicity: Ethics and Law for a Collective Age* (Cambridge and New York: Cambridge University Press, 2000) p. 103, and ch. 3 in general. The example that follows in the text is drawn from pp. 158–9 of that book. See also C. List and P. Pettit, *Group Agency: The Possibility, Design, and Status of Corporate Agents* (Oxford: Oxford University Press, 2011), pp. 33ff. Note that (*pace* List and Pettit) I am not taking a stand on whether there is such a thing as *group* agency. The view of collective responsibility which I sketch here is compatible with the view that there is as it is with the claim that there is not.

## 1.3 ON THE SCOPE OF JUSTICE: THE MORAL ARBITRARINESS OF BORDERS

### 1.3.1 Cosmopolitan justice: a sketch

I noted at the outset that a complete theory of justice must attend not merely to its content, strength, and site, but also to its scope, by which I meant the question of which individuals are both the beneficiaries and agents of its principles. In this section I shall argue that at the bar of justice, (1) all individuals, irrespective of political borders, have the aforementioned civil, political, and welfare rights, that (2) all individuals are under the relevant correlative duties to rights-bearers, irrespective of political borders, and (3) that there is no principled reason (other than flowing from the imperative to bring about global justice or from a general permission to privilege one's interest in leading a minimally decent life) for duty-bearers to confer priority on compatriots or fellow residents when faced with conflicts between rights.

It is in that three-pronged sense, thus, that my account of justice is cosmopolitan: an account which would affirm (1) but deny (2)—on the grounds, for example, that the requirements of *justice* apply only to, or are stronger in, domestic settings—would not be cosmopolitan. Nor would a theory which would affirm both (1) and (2), and yet deny (3) on the grounds, for example, that when faced with scarce resources, we may choose to give food to a compatriot *qua* compatriot simply on grounds of common membership. Nor, finally, can we deem cosmopolitan a moral theory which affirms that political borders are irrelevant yet at the same time denies fundamental rights and freedoms to some individuals on the basis of, for example, skin colour, gender, or religious beliefs.

In this sub-section I attend to claims (1) and (2), leaving the issue of legitimate scope for patriotic partiality until Section 1.3.2. Before I begin, however, it is worth distinguishing between different kinds of cosmopolitanism. A *cultural cosmopolitan*, to draw on Waldron's influential account, is someone whose cultural identity is composed of any possible set or subset of the world's cultural resources—for example, someone whose culinary tastes may be firmly South Asian, whose musical preferences lean towards Baroque music, and whose religious beliefs are a composite of Early Christian and Buddhist views. A *moral cosmopolitan*, by contrast, may well see her identity as being inescapably defined by the culture in which she grew up; however, she takes the view that the fate of distant strangers (by whom I mean, throughout this book, those with whom she shares neither residence nor nationality) matters to her as much as the fate of her compatriots morally speaking. Finally, a *political or institutional cosmopolitan* typically takes the view that supra-national institutions are best placed to bring about cosmopolitan normative principles. As should be clear, one can be a moral cosmopolitan and at the same time reject cultural cosmopolitanism (on the grounds that how one conceives of one's cultural identity has nothing to do with the content of one's moral beliefs) and political cosmopolitanism (on the grounds that territorially bounded states are the best mechanisms for delivering cosmopolitan justice.) One can also be a cultural cosmopolitan without endorsing either moral or political cosmopolitanism. One can also—perhaps surprisingly—be a political cosmopolitan and yet reject the moral demands of cosmopolitanism—as when one argues that supra-national institutions are best equipped to deliver justice in a globalized world, but that one's primary moral obligations are to fellow community members, other things equal.[20]

My focus, in this book, is on moral cosmopolitanism in general and rights-based cosmopolitanism—or what I shall call cosmopolitan justice—in particular. This, of course, is not the only cosmopolitan account that there is: just as there are many different kinds of moral theories, there are many different kinds of moral cosmopolitanism, from utilitarian cosmopolitanism, to duties-based cosmopolitanism, cosmopolitanism as an ethics of care, and rights-based cosmopolitanism. Moreover, just as one can be a rights-based prioritarian, or a sufficientist, or a radical egalitarian when it comes to justice within borders, one can be a rights-based prioritarian, or sufficientist, or radical egalitarian when it comes to justice beyond borders. Yet I offered a sufficientist account of justice in Section 1.2; given that, as per my argument in this section, borders are morally irrelevant to justice, I thus endorse a sufficientist account of cosmopolitan justice.[21]

---

[20] For an influential account of cultural cosmopolitanism, see J. Waldron, 'What is Cosmopolitan?', *Journal of Political Philosophy* 8 (2000): 227–43. For an influential defence of moral cosmopolitanism, see M. C. Nussbaum, 'Patriotism and Cosmopolitanism', in J. Cohen (ed.), *For Love of Country: Debating the Limits of Patriotism. Martha C. Nussbaum with Respondents* (Boston: Beacon Press, 1996). For useful surveys of different kinds of moral cosmopolitanism, see, for example, K.-C. Tan, *Justice Without Borders: Cosmopolitanism, Nationalism and Patriotism* (Cambridge: Cambridge University Press, 2004), ch. 3; Caney, *Justice Beyond Borders*, pp. 1–7; S. Scheffler, 'Conceptions of Cosmopolitanism', *Utilitas* 11 (1999): 255–76. For an interesting distinction between telic and deontic cosmopolitanism (though he does not refer to them as such), see D. Miller, *National Responsibility and Global Justice* (Oxford: Oxford University Press, 2007), 28. For a particularly crisp statement of the distinction between political (or institutional) cosmopolitanism and moral cosmopolitanism, see C. D. Jones, *Global Justice: Defending Cosmopolitanism* (New York: Oxford University Press, 1999), 228–9. My account of the requirements of cosmopolitan justice is similar to Gillian Brock's, though (unlike me) she arrives at it by way of a broadly Rawlsian deliberative procedure. See G. Brock, *Global Justice: A Cosmopolitan Account* (Oxford: Oxford University Press, 2009), esp. ch. 3.

[21] The seminal work in utilitarian cosmopolitanism is P. Singer, 'Famine, Affluence, and Morality', *Philosophy & Public Affairs* 1 (1972): 229–43. For an equally classic account of duties-based cosmopolitanism, see O. O'Neill, 'Bounds of Justice', in O. O'Neill, *Bounds of Justice*

All individuals, I submit, have rights to the freedoms and resources which they need in order to lead a minimally decent life, wherever they reside. The rationale for broadening the scope of justice to the whole of humanity is the simple thought (sometimes expressed as a requirement of impartial treatment) that if possession of a particular characteristic $x$ provides a justification for treating one individual who has $x$ in certain ways, then one must treat all bearers of $x$ in those same ways unless one can point to morally relevant differences between members of the set such as to justify differential treatment. By implication, then, *if* it is the fact that some freedoms and resources are needed to live a life worthy of a human being that provides a justification for securing those goods and freedoms to any given human being as a matter of right, then that fact also provides a justification for securing them to all other human beings—unless there are differences between humans such as to provide a legitimate basis for differential treatment. Given that this fact is the rationale for the conferral of those rights on individuals within a given society, it is also a rationale for conferring those rights to all individuals, irrespective of borders.

I shall not dwell on those points, familiar as they are to anyone with passing acquaintance with the field. Rather, let me turn to the second prong of cosmopolitan justice, whereby all individuals are under the relevant correlative duties to rights-bearers, irrespective of political borders. Universalism of rights does not entail universalism of the correlative duties: the claim that all individuals wherever they are have the aforementioned rights is compatible with both the view that those rights are held against fellow community members only, and the view that they are held against distant strangers as well. It is the latter which is at the heart of the debate between cosmopolitans and their critics. The most common reason which cosmopolitans invoke in support of the universalism of duties is the claim that political borders are arbitrary from a moral point of view. In Section 1.2.1 I distinguished between two interpretations of the claim 'whether or not an agent possesses a given characteristic $x$ is arbitrary from a moral point of view and thus should not affect that agent's entitlements.' On one interpretation, an agent should

(Cambridge: Cambridge University Press, 2000). Cosmopolitanism as an ethics of care is articulated in F. Robinson, 'After Liberalism in World Politics? Towards an International Political Theory of Care', *Ethics and Social Welfare* 4 (2010): 130–44, and S. C. Miller, 'Cosmopolitan Care', *Ethics and Social Welfare* 4 (2010): 145–57. For rights-based cosmopolitanism, see, *inter alia*, Caney, *Justice Beyond Borders*; Jones, *Global Justice*; Moellendorf, *Cosmopolitan Justice*; T. Pogge, *World Poverty and Human Rights* (Cambridge: Polity Press, 2000); Tan, *Justice Without Borders*. In addition to the works I have cited so far and shall cite throughout, a very useful two-volume collection of seminal essays on cosmopolitanism and its critics is T. Pogge and K. Horton (ed.), *Global Ethics. Seminal Essays: Global Responsibilities*, vol. II (St Paul, MN: Paragon House, 2008); T. Pogge and D. Moellendorf (ed.), *Global Justice. Seminal Essays: Global Responsibilities*, vol. I (St Paul, MN: Paragon House, 2008).

not lack opportunities for a minimally decent life on the basis of $x$ because she is not responsible for possessing $x$. On another interpretation, an agent should not lack such opportunities on the basis of $x$ because, whether or not he has chosen $x$, the possession of $x$ (such as hair colour) is entirely irrelevant to the agent's interest in the freedoms and resources needed to secure those opportunities. It is worth noting that the charge of moral arbitrariness is usually invoked to reject both the claim that only some people have a given right and the claim that only some people are under a duty to respect that right. In what follows I deploy the charge, in both its interpretations, in support of the view that the scope of duties of justice extends across borders.

Consider the 'irrelevance interpretation' of the charge of arbitrariness. Egalitarian and liberal theories of domestic justice claim that the assignment of duties to respect those freedoms and to transfer resources does not depend on one's geographical location within a given community. They claim, thus, that those who live in Worcestershire do not have stronger obligations of justice towards one another than they do towards those who live in Oxfordshire, that those who live in Massachusetts do not have stronger obligations of justice to Bostonians than to inhabitants of San Francisco, and that those who live in southern Kenya do not have stronger obligations of justice to one another than to fellow Kenyans who live in the north. The strongest argument in support of that view is that whether I live in Oxfordshire or in Worcestershire, in Massachusetts or in California, in the north or in the south of Kenya, my interest in secure freedoms and my need for the resources I need to live a minimally decent life are the same. By that token, the assignment of duties of justice does not depend on one's geographical location on the planet.[22]

I find that argument utterly persuasive—though it has recently been challenged by a number of authors. However, before addressing that challenge it is worth examining a second argument in favour of cosmopolitan justice, which invokes the 'no responsibility' interpretation of arbitrariness.[23] According to that argument, the fact that some individuals lack opportunities for a minimally decent life whereas other agents have them is traceable to individuals' location with respect to natural resources or to their nationality. In so far as we are not responsible for being badly located with respect to natural resources or for being of a certain nationality, those differences in individuals' opportunities are unjust, which in turn places rich members of rich countries

[22] For powerful arguments to that effect, see Caney, *Justice Beyond Borders*, chs. 3–4, and S. Black, 'Individualism at an Impasse', *Canadian Journal of Philosophy* 21 (1991): 347–77.

[23] Here I follow section 2 of my article on global egalitarianism—which I adapt to sufficientist theories of justice. See C. Fabre, 'Global Distributive Justice: An Egalitarian Perspective', *Canadian Journal of Philosophy (Supplementary)* 31 (2005): 139–64.

under an obligation of justice to distribute part of their wealth to poor members of poor countries.[24]

If it is indeed the case that individuals ought not to lack prospects for a minimally decent life for reasons outside their control, then the argument is sound. But its causal account of global inequality is problematic. For a start, neither geographical location with respect to natural resources nor nationality captures precisely what is at stake in debates over the distribution of resources at global level, whereas residence in a given country does. Geographical location does not work, because two countries could be equally well endowed with natural resources, and yet have vastly divergent standards of living. If one takes geographical location to be the explanation for unequal opportunities for a minimally decent life, it follows, counter-intuitively, that individuals who enjoy close proximity to natural resources but are very poor through being unable to exploit them should contribute to international transfers of resources, whereas individuals which are poorly endowed with natural resources but good at producing wealth are exonerated from such an obligation. Nationality will not do either, for one may have greater opportunities for a minimally decent life, simply by living in a given country, than someone else who happens to live in another country, whether or not one is a national of that country. In fact, residence, and neither proximity to natural resources nor nationality, is the most salient of the considerations which should lead us to conceive of distributive justice globally, and not domestically: for it is in virtue of residing somewhere that we have or lack access to the infrastructure, networks of exchange, and groups of productive people which we need in order to convert natural resources into wealth.

It remains to be seen whether residence is arbitrary in the sense of 'unchosen'. Clearly, we do not decide where we first reside, any more than we decide whether to come into existence. However, many of us do subsequently choose to emigrate—often to flee persecution or escape debilitating poverty, sometimes to have a maximally flourishing life. Conversely, it is also true that many of us choose not to emigrate, even though we could raise our opportunities for a minimally decent life if we did. Moreover, even if it is true that we do not choose whether to stay or go, it may be that we do not share responsibility for the fact that our residence harms our prospects for a minimally decent life to the point

---

[24] See, for example, C. R. Beitz, *Political Theory and International Relations* (Princeton: Princeton University Press, 1980), and B. Barry, 'Humanity and Justice in Global Perspective', in B. Barry, *Liberty and Justice: Essays in Political Theory*, vol. 1 (Oxford: 1991). See also T. Pogge, *Realizing Rawls* (Ithaca: Cornell University Press, 1989), 247. Beitz and Pogge regard geographical location and nationality (respectively) as arbitrary causes for global inequalities, but I take it that they would also regard them as arbitrary causes for individuals' economic location, as it were, on either side of the subsistence threshold.

where we fall below the subsistence threshold. For in many cases, we are not entirely responsible for our government's policy failures. We may not even have a say in the way policies are decided and conducted; even if we do, and vote against justice, we may do so out of utterly unavoidable ignorance; and if we vote for the policies required by justice, we may be in the minority. In such cases, cosmopolitan justice requires that residents of poor countries who do not have prospects for a minimally decent life have a *prima facie* claim to extra shares of resources against individuals who already enjoy such opportunities, whether or not the latter are fellow residents (again, subject to institutional considerations relative to the implementation of justice.)

A full theory of cosmopolitan justice would need to set out the conditions under which we can be said really *not* to be responsible for our government's efforts, or lack thereof, to bring about sufficiency amongst ourselves. This is a rather difficult issue, with which I cannot hope to deal fully here. It is plausible to assume, however, that at least at present, far many more individuals are not responsible for their lack of prospects for a minimally decent life than are responsible, especially in countries which lack any kind of welfare provision. Accordingly, we are more likely to bring about justice by helping all, irrespective of considerations of responsibility, than by helping none. Justice thus requires that we should set aside the no-responsibility proviso.

In summary, and drawing together the argument made here and the theory of justice I sketched in Section 1.2, we are now in a position to affirm the following: citizens and public officials are under a duty of justice to (respectively) support and implement just institutions, laws, and policies, and not to support or implement unjust ones, for the sake of distant strangers; they are also in their daily life under negative duties not to take part in structured and organized practices the effects of which are similarly harmful to those individuals. However, they are not under a positive duty of justice (as a duty of assistance) to act accordingly, in their daily life, in the interstices of the law—by, for example, giving money to Oxfam as remedy to their community's failure to operate resource transfers towards the very deprived abroad. Nor are they under a negative duty of justice, in their daily life, not to take part in unstructured practices the effects of which are severely harmful to distant strangers. In so far as the rights into which those duties correlate are held by all, irrespective of race, gender, sexual orientation, disability, and residence, and are justified by appeal to the conditions necessary for life worthy of human beings, I shall call them, unsurprisingly, *human* rights.[25]

---

[25] My account of human rights is thus more expansive than Griffin's recent and influential theory, which explicitly rejects appeals to human flourishing as part of a justification for those rights. Human

## 1.3.2 Cosmopolitan justice and patriotic partiality

Cosmopolitanism has many critics. Some non-cosmopolitans admit that we do owe some duties of justice to distant strangers, such as negative duties not to harm them deliberately (for example, by waging a war of aggression), as well as positive duties to help them meet their very basic needs; but they claim that those positive duties are not duties of justice, but rather, duties of humanity, and that we do not owe distant strangers more than that.[26] Others, by contrast, agree that positive duties are duties of justice and thus correlate with rights, but affirm that justice's requirements are more stringent within borders than across them.[27] At the heart of those objections is the view that cosmopolitanism is insufficiently sensitive to the very special ties which bind together members of national communities. To belong to a national community (the objection goes) is not merely to be part of a relationship of co-citizenship: it is also to be provided with a rich cultural and moral context within which we grow, develop, and form a conception of who we are and where we stand in the world. To do justice to that special relationship (the objection continues), one must allow individuals to show partiality towards their compatriots when deciding how to allocate scarce resources; in fact, on an even stronger reading of the objection, the fact that we stand in a special relationship to compatriots generates not merely a permission

rights, on his view, protect personhood. My account is also more expansive than another recent and influential theory, that deployed by Beitz, which argues that states and other institutions (as opposed to individuals acting in their private capacity) are the bearers of the correlative duties. See J. Griffin, *On Human Rights* (Oxford: Oxford University Press, 2008), esp. ch.1; C. Beitz, *The Idea of Human Rights* (Oxford: Oxford University Press, 2009), 5.

[26] See, for example, Barry, 'Humanity and Justice in Global Perspective'. I also take this to be Rawls' view. See J. Rawls, *The Law of Peoples* (Cambridge, MA: Harvard University Press, 1999). For trenchant criticisms of Rawls, see A. Abizadeh, 'Cooperation, Pervasive Impact, and Coercion: On the Scope (not Site) of Distributive Justice', *Philosophy & Public Affairs* 35 (2007): 318–58; C. R. Beitz, 'Rawls's Law of Peoples', *Ethics* 110 (2000): 669–96; A. E. Buchanan, 'Rawls's Law of Peoples: Rules for a Vanished Westphalian World', *Ethics* 110 (2000): 697–722.

[27] See, for example, M. Blake, 'Distributive Justice, State Coercion, and Autonomy', *Philosophy & Public Affairs* 30 (2001): 257–96; A. Mason, 'Special Obligations to Compatriots', *Ethics* 107 (1997): 427–47; Miller, *National Responsibility and Global Justice*, esp. chs. 2 and 7; T. Nagel, 'The Problem of Global Justice', *Philosophy & Public Affairs* 33 (2005): 113–47; A. Sangiovanni, 'Global Justice, Reciprocity and the State', *Philosophy & Public Affairs* 35 (2007): 3–39; C. H. Wellman, 'Relational Facts in Liberal Political Theory: Is There Magic in the Pronoun "My"?', *Ethics* 110 (2000): 537–62. An important point of clarification: Miller distinguishes between weak and strong cosmopolitanism, whereby a weak cosmopolitan shows equal concern to all, and a strong cosmopolitan gives equal substantive treatment to all, irrespective of borders. According to Miller, weak cosmopolitanism yields a justice requirement to help the very poor by providing them with basic levels of resources, whereas strong cosmopolitanism issues in differential requirements of justice within and across borders. Likewise, Sangiovanni, whose views are very similar to Miller's, also describes himself as a cosmopolitan in that weak sense. I shall reserve the label '(moral) cosmopolitan' for theories which hold that prior to institutional considerations as to the best way of implementing justice, individuals' just entitlements do not depend on borders.

to treat them more favourably than we treat distant strangers, but also an obligation to do so.[28]

It is not difficult to see the intuitive appeal of the objection, drawing as it does on the familiar thought that we may not treat all other human beings in a way that is deaf to the nuances and features of our relationship to them. *Pace* Godwin, if I cannot save both my father and Archbishop Fenelon from a raging fire, I may, indeed must, choose the former.[29] For it is in the nature of this relationship that its participants should have greater concern and regard for one another than for strangers. By analogy, it is in the nature of one's relationship with one's compatriots that one should give them priority over distant strangers. Or so some might be taken to aver.

And yet, by insisting that individuals' basic rights not be made to depend on political and/or national membership, I have in effect rejected the patriotic objection to cosmopolitan justice. Without wanting to retrace a well-trodden route, note that what seems to do the work, in most responses to Godwin, is the thought that we have a shared, personal, intimate history with our family members or other close associates such as friends, and it is that which generates special permissions or even obligations. But our relationship to compatriots *qua* compatriots is very different—so different, in fact, that it is hard to see how it could generate such special permissions and duties. Imagine that you are standing in front of a burning building in which two individuals are trapped, that you cannot save both, and that you do not know either of them. Imagine further that you are confident of being able to save one of them. Hearing them scream for help, you realize that one is a compatriot, the other a foreigner. According to the objection under study, at the very least you may—indeed, some would say, must—save your compatriot, simply in virtue of the fact that he is, precisely, a compatriot. But that claim strikes me as utterly indefensible—as indefensible, in fact, as the claim that one may save someone of one's skin colour to the detriment of someone of another skin colour. True, you do need to make a choice, since you cannot save both. But other things equal (that is, assuming that it would not be easier to save one than the other, that they are the same age, and so on), the only fair, just procedure is to use a lottery, since it would give each of them an equal chance of being saved.

---

[28] The view sketched here on the normative importance of nationality has been developed by, for example, D. Miller, *On Nationality* (Oxford and New York: Clarendon Press, 1995); Y. Tamir, *Liberal Nationalism* (Princeton, NJ: Princeton University Press, 1992).

[29] W. Godwin, *An Enquiry Concerning Political Justice.* (London: 1793), II–2.

## 1.4 SELF-DETERMINATION, GROUP RIGHTS, AND STATE LEGITIMACY

None of this is to deny, crucially, that the theory of cosmopolitan justice I have articulated in this chapter makes space for the view that we have some rights and duties *vis-à-vis* fellow citizens which we do not have towards distant strangers. For a start, special relationships between fellow citizens have instrumental value in so far as they might be the best vehicle through which to ensure that all individuals have the resources they need to lead a minimally decent life—just as a parent is usually better placed than anyone else to ensure that her child is fed on a regular basis.[30] There are at least two reasons why that might be the case. First, transfer costs are likely to be higher the greater the distance, as it were, between recipients and donors of resources. Second, although all individuals, wherever they reside, have rights to the material resources needed for a minimally decent life, the content of rights to the relevant resources will vary so as to take account of local climactic, geographical, and social conditions. It makes sense, therefore, to entrust the task of making that assessment to local states, as opposed to their distant donors.

In addition, those special relationships have value in so far as they are the vehicle through which a specific cultural identity (broadly understood) can flourish: it certainly matters a little to me, as a French citizen brought up in France, that the French state rather than, for example, the UNESCO should maintain my country's architectural heritage. Cosmopolitan sufficientism can and does accommodate this claim. For according to the personal prerogative, once all individuals have the goods and freedoms which are constitutive of a minimally decent life, the well off have rights as permitted by justice to pursue their goals and life-projects—again, irrespective of borders—which include the right to allocate amongst themselves the benefits from the cooperative ventures and associations to which they belong and, in so doing, to confer on one another specific rights and duties *vis-à-vis* one another (for example, with respect to promoting and maintaining a distinct cultural identity over time) that distant strangers lack *vis-à-vis* them. Whilst some of those associations are

---

[30] For strong arguments to the effect that special duties between a state and its citizens can (often) be seen as instantiations of general duties, see R. E. Goodin, 'What Is So Special about Our Fellow Countrymen?', *Ethics* 98 (1988): 663–86, and H. Shue, 'Mediating Duties', *Ethics* 98 (1988): 687–704. A standard contemporary discussion of the social relativity of needs is D. Wiggins, 'Claims of Need', in *Needs, Values, Truth: Essays in the Philosophy of Value* (Oxford: Oxford University Press, 1987). For the stronger view that cosmopolitan values are best promoted by recognizing the importance of politically sovereign and discrete associations, see L. Ypi, 'Statist cosmopolitanism', *Journal of Political Philosophy* 16 (2008): 48–71.

formed at the sub-state level, others consist in territorially bounded states or unions of states. The right to political self-determination, in other words, is not antithetical to cosmopolitan justice so long as it is constrained by obligations of justice to distant strangers.[31]

Sceptics will press that those obligations are so stringent as to render the right to political self-determination nugatory. They will argue that individuals' putative right to have some degree of control over their social and political environment—a capability which, I myself suggested in Section 1.2.1, is part of a minimally decent life—is so heavily constrained by the imperative of giving others what they are owed as a matter of justice that one wonders, really, whether it has any worth at all. To summarize an argument I have made elsewhere, however, cosmopolitan justice does leave scope for some degree of political self-determination.[32] Not only does it not rule out the constitution of political associations (as we have just seen): moreover, the resource transfers which it requires are compatible with political self-determination on a number of counts. First, if the value of political self-determination is paramount, then one may need to constrain the rights of wealthy communities over their own future for the sake of ensuring that those communities which are not in a position properly to determine their own future exercise those very same rights. Cosmopolitan sufficientism, far from rendering political self-determination nugatory in general, may instead be a means towards a redistribution of the natural resources which it requires. Second, whilst it is true that cosmopolitan sufficientism requires wealthy communities to transfer resources to distant strangers who lack prospects for a minimally decent life—for example, by way of a global tax—it leaves it up to them to decide how to levy the tax on their well off members and redistribute it amongst the needy. Third, cosmopolitan sufficientism is not oblivious to the fact that inequalities in opportunities for a minimally decent life may arise between individuals, wherever they reside, which are not due to residence, such as disabilities, race, familial background, gender, lack of remunerative talents, and so on. It makes sense to entrust the government of each country with the task to redress them. Here again, different policies might achieve the same end whilst

[31] For strong arguments to that effect, see, for example, S. Scheffler, *Boundaries and Allegiances: Problems of Justice and Responsibility in Liberal Thought* (Oxford: Oxford University Press, 2002); Tan, *Justice without Borders*; K. Nielsen, 'Cosmopolitan Nationalism', *Monist* 82 (1999): 446–68. Much more would need to be said about the grounds upon which special relationships in general (which include one's relationships to one's relatives, one's colleagues, and so on) can generate duties. I restrict my inquiry to the relationship of co-citizenship, and do not mean to imply that my sketchy account of the value of that relationship, and the rights and duties which it can generate, also applies to other special relationships. For a good review of different accounts of associative duties, see S. Lazar, *War and Associative Duties*, Oxford D.Phil thesis, 2009.

[32] See Fabre, 'Global Distributive Justice: An Egalitarian Perspective'.

being, perhaps, more acceptable in some countries than in others. Note that my point is not the familiar one that it is appropriate for citizens of a given country to confer special advantages and burdens on one another as the best way to implement cosmopolitan sufficientism. Rather, I am suggesting that they are entitled to invoke the relationship in which they stand together, and in particular the political, social, and cultural norms and values which are constitutive of it, when ensuring that no inequalities arise between them as a result of arbitrary factors. And the reason why they are so entitled is not that it would better promote cosmopolitan sufficientism (although it may do so): it is that such relationship does (or at least can) have, for its parties, value which is not reducible to its effectiveness as a means to satisfying the demands of justice.

One might think that one feature of the theory of justice which I defended in Section 1.2 supports patriotic partiality even when it adversely affects distant strangers' opportunities for a minimally decent life. For as we saw there, a just society is one in which agents are not under a duty to benefit others at the cost of their own opportunities for such a life. Does the no-undue-sacrifice principle apply to political communities, in such a way that political community A could object to transferring resources to needy political community B—in an exercise of its right to self-determination—on the grounds that doing so would threaten its survival as a community? Yes, and no. No, because at the bar of cosmopolitan justice a community does not have a moral status independent from that of its individual members; accordingly, community A cannot object to transferring resources to the needier members of community B on the grounds that doing so would threaten its own survival. Rather (and this is the 'yes' part), its members would have to show that transferring those resources to B's needy members would jeopardize their own opportunities, as individuals, for a minimally decent life. The rationale for resisting a duty to transfer would thus be based not on priority for compatriots *qua* compatriots, but on the claim that inability to transfer to one's compatriots rather than distant strangers would destroy one's own opportunities for a minimally decent life.

The latter point presupposes that group rights—of which the right to self-determination is a paradigmatic example—are grounded in individual interests. It might sound odd to some to argue, as I do here, that an individualistic morality can make space for group rights. Yet some of the interests which individuals typically have are interests in communal goods and resources—goods, in other words, which have worth to each of those individuals only in so far as they have worth to other similarly situated individuals.[33] Consider the value for

[33] My account of group rights broadly follows Jeremy Waldron's and Peter Jones'. See J. Waldron, 'Can Communal Goods be Human Rights?', in , J. Waldron *Liberal Rights* (Cambridge:

some individuals of the political self-determination of their community. Self-determination is a communal good in the sense that it can be enjoyed only if a sufficiently high number of community members value it: if I am the only one to participate in those elections, my participation is valueless to me, since it cannot result in anything which we would regard as an expression of popular sovereignty. Moreover, although the self-determination of my country is important to me (for example, because it enables me to shape the social and political environment in which I live), it is only *qua* member of that country that I can value it. Political self-determination thus understood is an example of a good which is jointly valuable and whose worth can only be understood as the worth it has to individuals *qua* members of the group. But it remains the case that the justification for granting that right to individuals *qua* group members is precisely the fact that it serves to promote a particular dimension of their flourishing *as individuals*. There is nothing odd, thus, in the thought that there can be group rights within a cosmopolitan theory of justice.

Moreover, in the light of the foregoing discussion, the rights which individuals have against their fellow citizens are both special (in that individuals have them in virtue of standing in a special relationship to their compatriots) and *in personam* (in that they are held against those individuals specifically.) Those rights divide into two kinds. On the one hand, some of those special rights are direct instantiations of the general rights which partake of justice. Thus John has a right, as a human being, to form a political community with other individuals and to shape that community's future; but it is in virtue of his special relationship with fellow Britons that he has a right to shape the future of the specific political community known as the United Kingdom. Likewise, John has a right to the material resources necessary to live a minimally decent life, but it is in virtue of his special relationship to fellow Britons that he has a right against the British state that the latter give him whatever amount is necessary in Britain so to live. On the other hand, other special rights are only indirect instantiations of general rights. Thus, once all human beings in the world have opportunities for a minimally decent life, Britons have the right to share amongst themselves the benefits of their social and economic cooperation. Whilst they have that right in virtue of being

Cambridge University Press, 1993); P. Jones, 'Group Rights and Group Oppression', *Journal of Political Philosophy* 7 (1999): 353–77. For other influential discussions of group rights, see, for example, Raz, *The Morality of Freedom*, p. 208; M. McDonald, 'Should Communities Have Rights? Reflections on Liberal Individualism', *Canadian Journal of Jurisprudence* 4 (1991): 217–37; D. Reaume, 'Individuals, Groups, and Rights to Public Goods', *University of Toronto Law Journal* 38 (1988): 1–27. For a conception of group rights which is similar to mine and is explicitly brought to bear on the value of self-determination, see A. Altman and C. H. Wellman, *A Liberal Theory of International Justice* (Oxford: Oxford University Press, 2009), ch. 2.

human, the very specific rights which flow from their exercise of their associative prerogative and which they have against one another are not requirements of justice. Were the British people to decide, by an Act of Parliament, that every adult should receive an additional £5,000 a year out of the public purse, John would have a right so to benefit against fellow Britons, as well as a right against outsiders that they not make it impossible for his fellow Britons to fulfil their commitment to him. But were his compatriots suddenly to decide, again via another Act of Parliament, to rescind their earlier decision (and against his wishes), they would not be violating a general right of his to that extra amount, since he does not have such a right in the first instance.

Our cosmopolitan picture of the value of collective self-determination and of the special relationship to which fellow members of a political community stand *vis-à-vis* one another is incomplete: it is one thing to say that individuals have the rights to form and shape a politically sovereign community; it is another to claim that they have the jointly held rights to govern over a given territory. For whilst it might seem obvious that a community cannot be properly self-determining and sovereign unless it exercises exclusive jurisdiction (constrained by the demands of cosmopolitan justice) over *a* territory, it is not at all obvious why it might have a claim to do so over *this* rather than *that* territory. Territorial rights, in other words, still stand in need of justification once a group's right to collective self-determination has been established.

At first glance it might seem as if cosmopolitan justice does not have the resources to justify territorial rights, since it holds that borders, which are territorial if anything is, are irrelevant to agents' fundamental entitlements. However, recall that justice mandates that all individuals have equal opportunities for a minimally decent life, and rights to the required freedoms, goods, and resources. Remember, moreover, that the demands of both sufficientism and the personal prerogative might be best served by individuals' exercise of a jointly held right to self-determination. Such a collective right cannot be securely exercised, nor can individual rights be securely enjoyed, if their holders are constantly vulnerable to being forcibly expelled from where they live and thus to being torn asunder from the interconnected networks of relationships—familial, professional, social—which form the fabric of their lives. The *prima facie* case is for letting them stay where they are, not forcing them out. If, then, it is necessary for individual members of a group to have such opportunities that they should live on, and together exercise jurisdiction over, a given territory rather than another, or that they should not be removed from that territory if they have longed lived within its borders, then they have the right to do so—provided (crucially) that the territory in question has not come to acquire that importance for them as a result of a wrongdoing which they themselves committed. Thus, let us assume for the sake of argument (but plausibly, I think) that white settlers wrongfully took territory away from Native Americans in the nineteenth century in such a way that, and as a result of which, the latter's prospects for a minimally decent life were severely diminished. Even if forcibly removing the settlers from those territories had caused them to live a less than minimally decent life, it would have been permitted, precisely because of their own, initial wrongdoing. Contrastingly, descendants of those settlers ought not to be made to leave if their forcible removal would cause them to lead a less than minimally decent life, and even though they currently occupy a land which their ancestors wrongfully took. This, of course, is compatible with the further claim that they may well owe compensation to victims' descendants—particularly if the latter's prospects for a minimally decent life are still below par as a result of the initial act of wrongful annexation. Cosmopolitan justice thus can make space for territorial rights—though admittedly rather restricted space, since it accepts neither first-occupancy justifications for territorial claims nor the view that the existence of a strong cultural, identity-based connection between a people and a land is a sufficient condition for granting rights to the former over the latter.[34]

Let us accept, then, that individuals, as such and *qua* members of political communities, have rights to the freedoms and resources necessary for a minimally decent life; correlatively, let us accept that, as individuals and members of political communities, they are under duties to act in such a way as to secure those freedoms and resources for one another, irrespective of residence. Let us also grant that they have the right to associate with one another and thus to constitute self-determining political community as well as the right to exercise jurisdiction over a given territory. Let us finally endorse the view that they have the right to display partiality towards fellow members with respect to the distribution of resources once outsiders have prospects for a minimally decent life. As we saw in Section 1.3.2, special relationships between fellow residents of a political community have value in so far as they are the best setting within which to ensure that individuals' universal rights to the conditions for a minimally decent life are respected and

[34] For the view that cosmopolitanism cannot justify territorial rights, see A. Kolers, *Land, Conflict, and Justice: A Political Theory of Territory* (Cambridge: Cambridge University Press, 2009). More widely, as first-cuts in the voluminous literature on territorial rights, see, for example, T. Meisels, *Territorial Rights* (Dordrecht: Springer, 2005); H. Steiner, 'Territorial Justice', in S. Caney, D. George, and P. Jones (ed.), *National Rights, International Obligations* (Boulder, CO: Westview Press, 1996); C. Gans, *The Limits of Nationalism* (Oxford: Oxford University Press, 2003), ch. 5. The view of territorial rights which I sketch out here is broadly similar to that defended by A. Stilz in a pair of recent articles. See A. Stilz, 'Why do states have territorial rights?', *International Theory* 1 (2009): 185–213; A. Stilz, 'Nations, States, and Territory', *Ethics* 121 (2011): 572–601.

promoted; they can also have value in so far as they matter *per se* for individual flourishing above and beyond the sufficiency threshold. To the extent, then, that states are the institutional vehicle, as it were, through which citizens discharge their duties to one another, they have value as well.

To say that the state has value, however, is not the same as to say that it is legitimate, and it is to that latter question that we finally turn. The state, you will recall, is (a) the set of institutions (b) which, via their agents, together govern over a given territory and people, (c) which decide whom to admit onto that territory, (d) whose rules and decisions are claimed by its actors to be *de facto* authoritative over both that territory and people, and (e) which enforce those rules and decisions. A state is legitimate, it is standardly said, in so far as it has the moral *right* to govern. Strictly speaking, of course, the state does not have rights; its officials do, in that capacity. Moreover, we must distinguish between two rather different understandings of the right to govern. On the one hand, it is a moral claim to govern which correlates with a duty on the part of those subject to obey its laws. On the other hand, it is also thought of as a morally justified power to change members' and outsiders' bundles of claims, duties, privileges, and powers, which correlates with those individuals' liability to have their bundles so modified. Space does not permit me fully to defend what I take to be a plausible account of either the right to govern in its Hohfeldian components or of the conditions under which the state is legitimate. Instead, I shall simply posit the following. In the light of the foregoing account of political self-determination, whereby individuals have the right to constitute themselves in political communities and, once so constituted, to shape their collective future, state officials' right to govern is a fiduciary right which they exercise on behalf of citizens. It is best understood, first and foremost, as a (fiduciary) power to change citizens' and outsiders' bundles of claims, duties, privileges, and powers via the enactment and enforcement of the law. However, to conceive of that right solely as a power would be a mistake. For 'naked powers'—powers without the protection afforded by duties of non-interference with their exercise—are worthless: for all that he may have the power to hand down a prison sentence on a convicted criminal, a judge will not be able to exercise it unless he is actually able to present himself at the Crown Court. To prevent his going to the Court or, more radically still, to try to remove him from office without due process, is to wrong him—not merely in the general sense that one ought not to physically restrain people without just cause or treat them without due process, but in the special sense that he, *as a judge*, has an interest in being able effectively to discharge the task for which he has been granted powers. Likewise, a head of government not merely has the power to implement the law; she also has a claim, *qua* head of government, against both state members and outsiders (such as foreign governments and individuals) that they not prevent her from exercising her power (and thereby discharging her obligations) by, for example, assassinating her. To say that state officials' have the right to govern, then, is not just to say that they have the power to enact and enforce laws; it is also to say that they have a claim against those to whom the law applies that they not interfere with them when they go about the business of government. Finally, it is also to say more generally that they have the (fiduciary) right to demand compliance on the part of those who are subject to their directives.[35]

The right to govern, thus, is a morally justified and protected fiduciary power. But that conceptual point about the nature of the right does not touch on the question of the conditions under which state officials have it—in other words, under which the state is legitimate. Nor does it provide an answer to the question of the reason why agents must regard the state's directive as binding. In the light of the account of rights which I have deployed so far, I shall posit, throughout this book, that a state is legitimate—that is, that its officials have the moral right to govern over a given territory and the people within it—if and only if its institutions and officials, through the laws which they vote and enforce and the executive decisions which they make on the basis of those laws, respect and promote the fundamental rights of both the state's members and outsiders. Moreover, it is precisely because those directives provide agents with better conditions for the protection of their moral

---

[35] In these paragraphs and those that follow, I thus endorse a (broadly) Lockean account of state legitimacy. See J. Locke, *'Two Treatises of Government'*, in ed. P. Laslett (Cambridge: Cambridge University Press, 1960). For a classic account of the state's right to govern as a normative power, see J. Raz, *The Authority of Law: Essays on Law and Morality* (Oxford: Clarendon Press, 1979); 'Authority and Justification', *Philosophy & Public Affairs* 14 (1985): 3–29. For a recent discussion of the differences between the right-duty approach and the power-liability approach, see A. I. Applbaum, 'Legitimacy without the Duty to Obey', *Philosophy & Public Affairs* 38 (2010): 215–39. See also D. Copp, 'The Idea of a Legitimate State', *Philosophy & Public Affairs* 28 (1999): 3–45. The main difference (as I see it) between Copp's and my account is that he conceives of duties of obedience and non-interference as owed to the state itself. So does Allen Buchanan, whose account of the conditions under which a state is legitimate (respect for human rights) is similar to mine. See A. E. Buchanan, *Justice, Legitimacy, and Self-Determination: Moral Foundations for International Law* (Oxford: Oxford University Press, 2003), esp. ch. 5. The claim that the legitimacy of a state need not imply that there is a duty to obey the law is also defended in, for example, L. Green, *The Authority of the State* (Oxford: Oxford University Press, 1988); see also W. A. Edmundson, 'Legitimate Authority without Political Obligation', *Law and Philosophy* 17 (1998): 43–60. Edmundson's argument rests on a distinction between the duty to obey the law (which we do not have) and the duty not to interfere with the administration of the law (which we do have.) It is not clear to me that the distinction can bear the weight of the argument: the latter duty really seems to me to be tantamount to the former.

rights and the fulfilment of their moral duties than they would have absent the state that agents have a reason for regarding those directives as binding.

So conceived, this conception of state legitimacy, when coupled with the (conceptual) account of the state's right to govern which I articulated above, has three features which are worth bringing out here. First, whether the state is legitimate does not solely depend on the degree to which it protects the rights of its members: its treatment of outsiders, by which I mean not merely foreign residents but also outsiders who are not subject to its jurisdiction, is equally relevant to the determination of its legitimacy. For example, if my regime embarks on a wholly unjust course of systematic colonial expansion, I have good reasons to deem it illegitimate and deny that it has the right to rule over me (though I might have very good reasons to abide by its directives—for example, the impact that disobedience would have on myself or my family.)

Second, a state might be illegitimate for failing to respect and promote the fundamental rights of its members and outsiders, but nevertheless issue specific directives in some areas with which citizens have good reasons to comply. However illegitimate the Nazi and Soviet regimes were, German and Soviet citizens had good reasons to obey their traffic laws, in so far as those laws enabled German and Soviet drivers better to fulfil their duty to drive responsibly.[36]

Third, state's officials can have the power to act wrongly, within limits. The thought that there can be such a thing as the power to do wrong should not elicit greater scepticism than the view that there can be such a thing as the claim to do wrong. Nevertheless, some kinds of wrongdoings are so egregious that state officials lack the morally justified power to commit them. More strongly still, state officials who commit such wrongdoings in a systematic way and over a significant period of time, or who negligently or wilfully fail to stop the commission of those wrongdoings by private actors, forfeit their protected (and not only their naked) power to govern. More precisely, they are no longer (morally) competent to change individuals' bundles of rights, duties, privileges, and powers; nor, moreover, do they have a claim against those individuals not to be impeded in their exercise of now-invalid power or not to be removed from office. However—and this is absolutely crucial—the claim that in a given case state officials have forfeited their right to govern is entirely compatible with the two-pronged view that the state's members are under a duty to one another to obey those laws which enable them better to fulfil their moral duties, and that outsiders are under a duty to those members not to interfere in the affairs of their community. On the first count, it could very well be that although state officials

---

[36] I owe this example to Tamar Meisels.

would not themselves be wronged if impeded in the exercise of their powers, general disobedience to the law would create a state of affairs in which individuals' fundamental rights are less likely to be respected and promoted. On the second count, and as we shall see in Chapter 5 when discussing humanitarian intervention, it could very well be that further conditions must be met (in addition to the state officials' forfeiture of their right to govern) in order for an intervention to be permissible.

Before I conclude, one loose end needs tying. Taken together, my accounts of territorial rights and state legitimacy imply that state officials have the right to govern over a given territory only if their directives protect and promote members' and outsiders' human rights. Now, suppose that citizens and residents of political community B would do better at the bar of justice if they were governed by officials from state A than by their own state's which, though not grossly illegitimate, nevertheless does not quite succeed at providing everyone within its borders with the resources necessary for a minimally decent life. It might seem as if officials from B do not in fact have a claim to govern political community B. May A invade B? Or suppose that A's leaders and army rightfully mount a military invasion of political community B on the grounds that the latter's regime is guilty of gross human rights violations both at home and abroad, and that A's regime would be able to govern over B—respecting and promoting its members' basic human rights—very effectively. May A annex political community B instead of giving its members full sovereignty rights over their territory? Intuitively at least, it seems that in both cases A would act *ultra vires*. Fortunately, the foregoing accounts need not imply that aggression and annexation in cases such as these are permissible. For as we saw in Section 1.2.2, it is a necessary condition for an individual permissibly to be given that to which she has a right that she should (in some sense) consent to it. By parity of reasoning, it is a necessary condition for a community of individuals who are already bound together by a shared history of cooperation to be given the freedoms and resources to which they have both individual and jointly held rights that they consent to it. It is also sufficient, for them to be denied those rights and resources, that they consent to such denial. If, then, A has good reasons to believe that B would not consent either to aggression or annexion, and if, moreover, B would not endorse grossly illegitimate institutions of their own (such as would carry out genocidal policies towards a sub-set of B), then state A lacks the right to govern over their territory.[37] We shall revisit this issue in Chapters 2 and 5.

---

[37] For a discussion of the problem of annexion along those broadly similar lines, see Stilz, 'Nations, States, and Territory', 590ff.

## 1.5 CONCLUSION

In this chapter I have sketched out a rights-based theory of cosmopolitan justice in virtue of which individuals have rights to the freedoms and resources which they need in order to enjoy a minimally decent life. According to the personal prerogative, individuals are not under a duty to sacrifice their own prospects for a minimally decent life for the sake of helping others; and once those who lack the requisite resources are catered for, the well off have the right to pursue their goals and life-projects. In a second step I argued that borders are irrelevant to the conferral of those entitlements. In other words, all individuals, wherever they reside, have the aforementioned positive and negative rights against everyone else, irrespective of residence. Thus, were we to impose on members of a political community the relevant positive and negative duties, this would not be for the substantive moral reason that agents are in general morally permitted or obliged to give priority to their compatriots, but for the instrumental reason that such an allocation is the best way for all to discharge their duties to all. Under such an allocative model, individuals are under positive duties (in the sense articulated in Section 1.3) to help distant strangers if the latter are unable to provide for themselves; they are also under negative duties not to prevent one another from discharging their (instrumentally justified) duties to the needy. Within that framework, cosmopolitan sufficientism is compatible with some degree of patriotic partiality for the resident members of one's political community—precisely because a just world is one in which individuals have the personal prerogative to associate with whomever they wish, and, once sufficiency is met, to allocate amongst themselves the benefits which result from their mutual cooperation. In so arguing, I developed an account of group rights which makes sense of political communities' collective interest in self-determination (to which continuing occupancy of a territory is crucial) whilst being grounded in the interests of those communities' individual members.

Having thus delineated what I take to be a plausible, relatively minimalist theory of cosmopolitan justice, I now embark on the task of delineating a cosmopolitan theory of the just war. In order to be deserving of the label 'cosmopolitan', such a theory must meet the following two conditions. First, its central tenets must ascribe pre-eminence to individuals and not conceive of groups as having independent moral status; accordingly, the rights and duties they delineate must be those of individuals, not of groups *qua* groups. Second, it can allow individuals, *qua* group members, to confer greater weight on fellow members' interests as against the interests of outsiders only as an exercise of the personal prerogative (here in the form of patriotic partiality) suitably constrained by the demands of cosmopolitan sufficientism. With those two requirements in hand, I begin with wars of collective self-defence against unwarranted military aggression which pit sovereign political communities against one another.

# 2

# Collective self-defence

## 2.1 INTRODUCTION

On 24 June 1812 Napoleon ordered his forces to cross the Niemen river into what was then Russian territory. On 4 August 1914 the German Army invaded Belgium and quickly made its way to France which, though not neutral, nevertheless had not declared war upon either Germany or her allies. On 22 September 1980 the Iraqi government ordered its army to carry out an air and land invasion into Iran's territory. On 2 August 1990 it gave a similar order, this time against Kuwait. The resulting wars were of the paradigmatic kind: namely, wars of collective self-defence by a state against a military aggression carried out by another state. Yet states, I argued in Chapter 1, are legitimate only if and to the extent that their institutions and officials, through the laws which they vote and enforce and the executive decisions which they make on the basis of those laws, do not violate the fundamental rights of both the state's members and outsiders. Moreover, the rights, powers, immunities, and liberties of state officials flow from and supervene on the rights, powers, immunities, and liberties of citizens. It follows that a state, *qua* state, does not have the right to defend itself, in the sense that it does not, *qua* state, have rights in the first instance; it also follows that individuals *qua* members of a sovereign political community do not have the unconditional collective right to defend the latter's territorial integrity and institutional structures. Rather, they have it only if the military aggression to which they are subject is unwarranted.

The view that unwarranted aggression provides its victims with a just cause for war has always been central to the tradition. Indeed, the so-called fathers of codified international law (Vitoria, Grotius, and Vattel) are notorious for their highly moralized interpretation of the *jus gentium*. Yet international law from the eighteenth century to the early decades of the twentieth century conferred on states the unlimited rights both to protect their sovereignty and to resort to war as an instrument of foreign policy: neither the invasion of Russia by Napoleon nor the invasion of France and Belgium by Germany were deemed unlawful at the time. Clearly, however, a world in which states and their leaders are entitled to go to war at will is not one in which state sovereignty can flourish. Nor is it one which is particularly conducive to human flourishing. It took two world wars and the concomitant death of dozens of millions of people for the international community to revise the law. Key legal sources, in that regard, are the Charter of the United Nations (1945) and the Rome Statute instituting the International Criminal Court (1998). The Charter prohibits UN members from using or threatening to use armed force against the territorial integrity or collective self-determination of another state (Article 2(4)), but confers on them the right to defend themselves against a military attack (Article 51). The Rome Statute, for its part, explicitly lists aggression as one of four crimes over which the ICC claims jurisdiction (Article 5 (1, d).) What counts as aggression is by no means uncontroversial in the law—as evidenced by the facts that the UN and the ICC did not provide their own definition of it until, respectively, 1974 (by way of General Assembly resolution 3314) and 2010 (by way of a resolution passed by the ICC Assembly of state parties.) By and large, international law defines aggression as the use of force by a state against another state, which includes, *inter alia*, land invasion, air bombardment, and blockades. *Unlawful* aggression consists in the use of such force other than as (a) a response to provocation which itself imminently threatens territorial integrity and collective self-determination, (b) in self-defence or other defence, or (c) as a result of UN authorization.[1]

The international law of war has thus rediscovered its roots in the just-war tradition. And in that tradition, Russia, Belgium, France, Iran, and Kuwait, faced as they were with a large-scale armed attack onto their territorial integrity and political sovereignty, had a just cause for using military force to repel their aggressor. Recently, however, some contemporary cosmopolitan theorists have argued that in the face of changes in the nature of warfare, statist accounts of war as an instance of national self-defence ought to be abandoned. On their views, wars should instead be regarded as a police operation undertaken by international peacekeeping forces with a view to enforcing the fundamental human rights of individuals. I reject the enforcement model of war elsewhere, on the grounds that it cannot, on its own, fully account for the fact that the right to wage and fight a war includes, *inter alia*, a right to kill and maim other persons in defence of one's and compatriots' rights. The enforcement model, I argue there, does not provide a justification for that particular

---

[1] On the international law of aggression, see Y. Dinstein, *War, Aggression and Self-Defence*, 3rd edn. (Cambridge: Cambridge University Press, 2001). For a philosophical treatment of that particular body of law, see L. May, *Aggression and Crimes Against Peace* (Cambridge: Cambridge University Press, 2008).

right.[2] Moreover, the intuition that a territorially bounded and sovereign community has the right to defend itself by force against an unwarranted aggression is too deeply rooted in common-sense morality to warrant abandoning without attempting to defend it against its critics. In this chapter my primary aim is thus to offer a normative account of those wars to which the right to kill is central and which is compatible with the tenets of cosmopolitan justice as set out in Chapter 1. The task is not as straightforward as it may seem. For if membership in such a community is largely irrelevant to individuals' basic entitlements, it is not clear, as first sight, how the protection of territorial integrity and collective self-determination can warrant *killing* human beings, particularly (as will more often than not happen in such a war) civilians who are not themselves directly responsible for the wrongful aggression carried out by their military forces.

The chapter proceeds as follows. In Section 2.2 I sketch a normative account of defensive killings in private, domestic contexts. I bring that account to bear on the case of collective self-defence in Section 2.3. Having thus shown that members of a wrongfully aggressed country have the right to authorize their leaders to wage war on their behalf in defence of their rights to territorial integrity and collective self-determination, I examine, in Section 2.4, some tensions between, on the one hand, the cosmopolitan claim that membership in a given political community is irrelevant to the conferral and infringement of rights, and on the other hand, the view that the collateral killing of enemy non-combatants is (at least sometimes) permitted.

Let me make one further comment before I begin. In Chapter 1 I argued that inequalities in prospects for a minimally decent life are traceable to residence in, rather than nationality or citizenship of, a given sovereign political community. Clearly, long-term residents in a country who do not have citizenship rights often have a vested interest in that country's not being wrongfully invaded. However, the rights which an aggression primarily harms, to wit, interests in controlling both access to the country's territory (which includes its airspace and territorial waters) and its institutions, are held by citizens, and it is on that special relationship such as obtains between fellow citizens or compatriots on which I shall focus in this chapter.

---

[2] For avowedly cosmopolitan defences of the model, see Atack, *The Ethics of Peace and War*; D. Held, 'Violence, Law and Justice in a Global Age', no. (2001), http://www.theglobalsite.ac.uk/ press/112held.htm; M. Kaldor, *Global Ccivil Ssociety: An Answer to War* (Cambridge: Polity Press, 2003), esp. ch. 5. I reject the model in C. Fabre, 'Cosmopolitanism and Wars of Self-Defence', unpublished typescript.

## 2.2 DEFENSIVE RIGHTS

As I noted in Section 1.2.2, a theory of justice must provide an account of what agents may and have the right to do in defence of their rights. The right to wage a war of collective self-defence, I shall argue below, consists in a right to maim or kill enemy combatants in defence of one's individual and jointly held rights. But here a difficulty arises, pertaining to what some have called the dual morality of war.[3] War, typically, is waged by groups against other groups in the name of communal and often national values; however, those who do the actual fighting and die from it are not groups as such but individuals acting together. The alleged dual morality of war—as waged by groups *ad bellum* and fought by individuals *in bello*—is thought to pose a particular problem for standard justifications of the right to wage and kill in war. Those justifications divide into so-called analogical and reductive strategies. The analogical strategy claims that just as an individual has a right to defend herself from a lethal threat by killing her attacker, states have a right to defend their territorial integrity and sovereignty from other aggressive states. The eighteenth-century European jurists Vattel and Wolff, who sought to apply to states the natural laws which regulate individuals' conduct towards one another, were foremost proponents of the analogical strategy—which underpins much of the international laws of war.[4]

The problem with the analogical strategy is twofold. First, it fails to account for the fact that war is about killing and maiming, and that those acts are committed by individuals. Second, it should be clear from the accounts of cosmopolitan justice and group rights which I deployed in Chapter 1 that a cosmopolitan theory of the just war cannot subscribe to it, since it confers on groups, and in particular states, rights which are not reducible to the rights of their individual members. From a cosmopolitan point of view, the right to wage war must be explainable in terms of, or by reference to, some rights of individuals. The reductive strategy seems more promising in that respect, for it regards individual rights as central to the right to wage war. That said, it has a collectivist and an individualistic variants. In its collectivist variant it confers

---

[3] See Atack, *The Ethics of Peace and War*; N. Zohar, 'Collective War and Individualistic Ethics: Against the Conscription of "Self-Defense"', *Political Theory* 21 (1993): 606–22.

[4] E. d. Vattel, *Le droit des gens, ou, Principes de la loi naturelle appliqués á la conduite et aux affaires des nations et des souverains* (London: 1758); C. Wolff, *Jus gentium methodo scientifica pertractatum* (Oxford: Clarendon Press, 1934). For an analysis of the international law pertaining to aggression, see Dinstein, *War, Aggression and Self-Defence*; and for a recent defence of the analogical strategy, see G. P. Fletcher and J. D. Ohlin, *Defending Humanity* (Oxford: Oxford University Press, 2008).

on the state the right to wage war in defence of the fundamental rights of its citizens.[5] As we saw in Chapter 1, however, the rights of state officials are reducible to rights held by individuals, either *qua* individuals or *qua* group members. Accordingly, state officials' right to defend the rights of fellow citizens cannot be justified other than by justifying a citizen's very same right.[6] The right to wage war, therefore, is a right as held by individuals to kill in defence of their rights—as per the individualistic variant of the strategy.

In what follows, I sketch out the account of defensive rights which underpins my account of the right to wage war in general and a war of collective self-defence in particular. By defensive rights I mean both the right to kill in self-defence and the right to kill in defence of others. The qualification is crucial, because in a war of collective self-defence, combatants do not kill merely in defence of their lives; they also kill in defence of their comrades' lives, as well as in defence of the lives and other fundamental rights of non-combatants back on the home front. Accordingly, when thinking about killing in wars of collective self-defence, we should not focus solely on one-to-one cases where a lone victim V is subject to a lethal attack at the hands of a lone attacker A. We should also bear in mind cases where a number of victims are subject to a lethal attack at the hands of a number of attackers, and where those victims, when killing those attackers, not merely each defend their own lives but also defend the lives of fellow victims.

That said, justifications for the right to kill in defence of others flow from arguments in favour of the right to kill in self-defence, so we should start with the latter. Consider the following *scenarii*, involving a victim (V) and her

[5] For the individualistic variant, see J. McMahan, 'Innocence, Self-Defense and Killing in War', *Journal of Political Philosophy* 2 (1994): 193–221; 'Self-Defense and the Problem of the Innocent Attacker', *Ethics* 104 (1994): 252–90; 'The Ethics of Killing in War', *Ethics* 114 (2004): 693–733; 'Just Cause for War', *Ethics & International Affairs* 19 (2005): 1–21; 'War as Self-Defense', *Ethics & International Affairs* 18 (2004): 75–80. For a recent book-length restatement and refinement of the views he expressed in those articles, see *Killing in War*. Both Nagel and Luban also insist that war pits *individuals* against one another (T. Nagel, 'War and Massacre', *Philosophy & Public Affairs* 1 (1972): 123–44; and D. Luban, 'Just War and Human Rights', *Philosophy & Public Affairs* 9 (1980): 160–81.) Walzer himself seems to hold that view, alongside the analogical view, so that his overall account of the justification for the right to wage war is ambiguous. See M. Walzer, *Just and Unjust Wars: A Moral Argument with Historical Illustrations*, 4th edn. (New York: Basic Books, 2006), 51. For the collectivist variant, see H. Grotius, *The Rights of War and Peace*. ed. R. Tuck. (Indianapolis, IN: Liberty Fund, 2005); F. R. Tesón, *Humanitarian Intervention: An Inquiry into Law and Morality*, 2nd edn. (Irvington-on-Hudson, NY: Transnational, 1997); F. de Vitoria, *On the Law of War*, in F. de Vitoria, *Political Writings*, ed. A. Pagden and J. Lawrance (Cambridge: Cambridge University Press, 1991), and N. Zohar, 'Collective War and Individualistic Ethics: Against the Conscription of "Self-Defense"', *Political Theory* 21 (1993): 606–22.

[6] From now on, therefore, when I refer to the reductive strategy I shall mean the strategy in its individualistic form (unless stated otherwise).

attacker (A), both of which are drawn from Judith Thomson's seminal article on self-defence:[7]

*Villainous truck driver.* V is walking in the park minding her own business. A is a villainous truck-driver who drives at speed towards V with the manifest intention of killing her— though she has not provoked him in any way.
*Psychotic gunman.* V is walking in the park minding her own business. A is in the grip of a psychotic breakdown and is convinced that he must kill V—though she has not provoked him in any way.

Those two cases differ from yet another Thomson case—that of the innocent passive threat (T):

*Falling man.* V is having a picnic on a beach. T, who is a very fat man, is pushed off the cliff above V by some villain. T will crush V to death unless the latter pulverises him in mid-air, but will survive if he lands on V.

Whereas the villainous truck-driver is morally responsible for his action, T is not, any more than is the psychotic gunman. But whereas the latter deliberately (though not culpably) imposes a harm onto V, the threat to which V is subject in *Falling man* is not the product of T's exercise of his agency: it comes about purely as a result of the location and velocity of his body, over which, in this instance, he has absolutely no control. Finally, the truck driver and the psychotic gunman have this in common that they both act in such a way as to subject V to a threat of lethal harm, for which they lack a positive and objective moral justification.

One of the most important questions in the ethics of self-defence is whether one may kill innocent attackers and passive threats in self-defence or other defence. According to Thomson, A (in both cases) and T violate V's right not to be killed and thus forfeit their own right not to be killed, which is why V may kill them in self-defence. Many have persuasively argued that it is not appropriate to say of the psychotic gunman, who is not in any way morally responsible for his actions, that he *violates* A's rights—any more than it is appropriate to say of a murderously hungry tiger which jumps at my throat for the kill that he violates my right not to be eaten alive. It seems even less appropriate to charge T with a rights violation.[8] Nonetheless, I agree with

---

[7] J. J. Thomson, 'Self-Defense', *Philosophy & Public Affairs* 20 (1991): 283–310. The literature of defensive killings is enormous, and the most important contributions are referenced in the next few footnotes.

[8] McMahan, 'Self-Defense and the Problem of the Innocent Attacker', *Ethics* 104 (1994): 252–90; M. Otsuka, 'Killing the Innocent in Self-Defense', *Philosophy & Public Affairs* 23 (1994): 74–94; J. Quong, 'Killing in Self-Defence', *Ethics* 119 (2009): 507–37. In that article, McMahan argues that whilst we have good reasons to reject the view that killing innocent attackers is impermissible, it is nevertheless very difficult to construct a plausible argument in support of the

Thomson's conclusion (though not with her argument for it) that V may kill all three in self-defence. For to claim, *a contrario*, that the victim of a wrongful threat may not kill her morally innocent attacker or passive threat is to say, by implication, that she is under a duty to allow herself to be killed even though (*ex hypothesi*) she has done nothing to warrant the attack. However, as we saw in Chapter 1, agents generally have a personal prerogative to confer greater weight on their own projects and goals than on other agents' similar projects, which in turn sets limits to the sacrifices which they can be expected to make for the sake of others. I submit that whilst the prerogative does not permit agents to kill a bystander in their own defence (for the bystander himself bears no causal responsibility for their predicament and thus cannot be used as a means only to their ends), it does permit them to kill their attacker if the latter, whatever might be said about their lack of moral responsibility for the situation of forced choice between lives, nevertheless subjects them to a wrongful lethal threat. In other words, agents may not be expected to sacrifice their life for the sake of not bringing about the death of another person when they have done nothing to warrant the threat which he poses to them.[9]

A standard objection to the personal prerogative justification for self-defence is that if it permits the killing of attackers—particularly innocent attackers—then it also licences the deliberate killing of innocent bystanders as a means to one's preservation. For if a victim is permitted to kill her attacker on the grounds that she may give greater weight to the preservation of her own life than to his, then (it is argued) she may kill an innocent bystander

converse claim that such killing is permissible. Otsuka explicitly rejects that claim in one-to-one context. Quong accepts it, on grounds similar to those I adduce below (pertaining to victims' personal prerogative.) Incidentally, the claim that killing innocent attackers in self-defence is permissible is compatible with the claim that one ought to exercise greater restraint when thwarting them than would be warranted if one were faced with a culpable attacker—at least given equal chances for survival (precisely because they are not responsible for forcing the choice between lives.) See McMahan, 'Self-Defense and the Problem of the Innocent Attacker', 264–5.

9 In Grotius's words, our permission to kill stems 'from the Care of our own Preservation, which *Nature* recommends to every one, and not from the Injustice or Crime of the *Aggressor*.' For Grotius, moreover, the wrongfulness of the act, as opposed to moral fault in the aggressor, does make a difference to the permissibility of self-defensive killing: as Grotius holds, an unjust attacker may not defend himself from his victim unless he has desisted and offered her restitution even though she still threatens his life. (Grotius, *The Rights of War and Peace*, Book II, Ch. 1, para. 3, and Book II, Ch. 1, para. 18.) See also Quong, 'Killing in Self-Defence', and F. M. Kamm, 'Grouping and the Imposition of Loss', *Utilitas* 10 (1998): 292–319, at 310–16. In this piece, Kamm rejects Peter Unger's claim that we must treat ourselves exactly as we may treat others—in other words, that there is no such thing as a personal prerogative. (See Unger, *Living High and Letting Die*.) Note that I use the phrase 'wrongful threat' to denote a threat which its target has not done anything to warrant, such that compensation is owed to her (should she survive the attack). I do not mean to suggest that an innocent attacker can be appropriately described *as acting wrongly* in such cases. In fact, the case of justified attackers show that one can pose a wrongful threat and be justified in so doing.

intentionally, on those very same grounds. Either one accepts, wholly implausibly, that the intentional killing of bystanders is permissible in one-to-one cases, in which case one can endorse partiality as a justification for self-defence albeit at considerable moral costs; or one holds on to the much more plausible prohibition on the killing of bystanders, in which case one has to look elsewhere for an account of V's right to kill her attacker. In so far as we assume at the outset that one may not deliberately kill innocent bystanders in self-defence, the objection, if sound, strikes at the heart of the partiality justification.[10]

The objection invites some qualifications to the partiality-based account, though do not fatally undermine it. Having an interest in $p$, though necessary, is not a sufficient condition for an agent to have a liberty or a right in respect of $p$. Accordingly, the partiality justification is not committed to regarding the fact that one's interest in survival is under threat as a sufficient condition for being permitted, let alone having the right, to kill in self-defence. In fact, it can allow that there are limits to the extent to which one may give priority to one's interests, such as (in that instance) whether the target of one's self-defensive move causes one to be under threat. Innocent bystanders, by definition, are not, whereas attackers are. Partiality is also compatible with the entirely plausible claim that a culpable attacker, such as our villainous truck-driver, is not permitted to kill his victim in his *own* defence. Thus, the partiality argument for self-defence can and should stipulate that one is permitted intentionally to kill in self-defence (on grounds of partiality) only if one is directly threatened by the target of one's self-defensive actions.

Opponents of the partiality view will remain unconvinced. They will maintain that partiality cannot on its own discriminate between cases where V has the right to kill and cases such as that of the bystander (B), where V must desist. What justifies V's permission to kill, therefore, is not partiality, but whatever consideration we invoke to distinguish A from B. Such considerations typically take the following form: by culpably attacking V, A has forfeited his right not to be killed, and V is permitted to defend herself by killing him precisely because he no longer has a right to be killed. The bystander has not attacked V and therefore has not forfeited his right not to be killed by her. Consequently, V is not permitted (and lacks the right) to kill him. We thus have a criterion for distinguishing A from B—a criterion which partiality is unable to provide.

---

[10] See, for example, McMahan, 'Self-Defense and the Problem of the Innocent Attacker', at 270ff. The rejoinder that follows appears in C. Fabre, 'Permissible Rescue Killings', *Proceedings of the Aristotelian Society* 109 (2009): 149–64.

Now, I agree that partiality cannot, *on its own*, explain why V may kill A and not B—put differently, that the judgement that V is directly threatened by A and not B is not one that is made on grounds of partiality. However, that claim does not entail that partiality has no role to play in justifying self-defensive (and, as we shall see, other-defensive) killings. In fact, unlike agent-neutral justifications for self-defensive killings, partiality makes sense of the intuition that V has a special reason for killing her attacker which others lack: he is threatening *her life*, and no one else's, and accordingly she has a vested interest, which others (on the whole) lack, in thwarting his attack. That factual point about V's special location, as it were, in relation to her own survival, does not merely capture the fact that V's has special prudential reasons to kill A: it has some normative implications as well. In particular, her special stake in thwarting A's attack may sometimes give her latitude which she would lack if she only had impartial, agent-neutral reasons for stopping him. Thus, she would have greater latitude *vis-à-vis* innocent bystanders who might be killed as a result of the defensive steps which she would take; she would also have greater latitude for deciding that A really does subject her to a lethal threat.

I shall return to this issue below when discussing rescue killings. Meanwhile, the claim that V may kill A or T in self-defence does not entail that she has the right to do so. For V to have that right means that the target of her self-defensive move is under a duty not to defend himself. Now, given that the falling man exercises no agency whatsoever, it would be unfair to withhold from him the permission to defend his own life from V. In this case, although V may kill him, she lacks the right to do so. By contrast, if the villainous truck driver is unsuccessful in his attempt on V's life at $t_1$, and if she starts shooting at $t_2$, he clearly may not defend his life from her at $t_3$. The reason why that is so is not merely that he triggers a forced choice between their lives: it is also that he does so without (objective) justification whatsoever, which in turn supports the view that V not merely is permitted but also has the right to kill him. More controversially, I also believe that a morally non-responsible attacker such as the psychotic gunman loses his right not to be killed—and thus that V has the right to kill him—precisely because he too acts without (objective) justification. For to claim that V in those cases lacks that right is to claim that third parties are not under a duty to her either not to interfere with her self-defensive steps by helping her attacker, or to help her by thwarting him. This strikes me as extraordinarily implausible. It would mean, for example, that the police would be permitted (*vis-à-vis* her) either to prevent a severely abused woman from defending herself from her psychotic husband, or to refuse to intervene as he is about to kill her even if she would die as a result.

I should add that whether victims have the right to kill morally innocent attackers is a matter of controversy. Fortunately, not much in this book hinges on the soundness of that claim, since the overwhelming majority of war cases do not involve psychotic attackers—with the admittedly problematic case of child soldiers, some (but not all) of whom cannot in any way be regarded as morally responsible agents. The key point, rather, is that if an agent lacks an objective justification for attacking V, the latter has the right to use lethal force in self-defence.[11] Sometimes, however, agents are justified in subjecting others to a threat of lethal harm which they have not warranted—in other words, to what I shall call a wrongful threat. Whereas the (morally responsible) attacker who acts without justification is standardly said to *violate* V's rights, the attacker who does have such a justification is said to (justifiably) *infringe* it. Consider the following case, drawn (with slight modification) from McMahan's recent book on the ethics of killing in war:[12]

*Ambulance driver.* An ambulance driver drives at speed to the hospital, though not recklessly so by ambulance-driving standards, with a grievously injured patient who will die unless he receives medical help within twenty minutes. On the way, some freakish event causes the driver to lose control of the ambulance, which veers towards a pedestrian.

---

[11] One further point on innocent attackers. Some attackers are what Catholic theologians call 'invincibly ignorant', in that they cannot possibly know, or be expected to know, that they are inflicting harm on someone else (consider, for example, the case of someone who dreams that he is about to drown, who gesticulates in an attempt—he thinks—to claw his way back to the surface of the water by holding on to a branch, but who in fact is strangling his wife.) On my account, in so far as an invincibly ignorant attacker lacks an objective justification for attacking V, the latter has the right to kill him. This too is a very controversial claim, though the overwhelming majority of war cases do not involve invincibly ignorant combatants. More generally, on the view I articulate here, whether or not A has an *objective* justification for attacking V is decisive for determining whether V has the right to kill A. Whether A has a subjective justification (or an excuse) is another matter. For a detailed scrutiny of the complex relationship between excuses and justifications in the context of war, see McMahan, *Killing in War*, ch. 3. For an account of permissible self-defence which assigns a central role to subjective justifications, see H. Frowe, 'A Practical Account of Self-Defence', *Law and Philosophy* 29 (2010): 245–72. For normative accounts of the killing of child soldiers, see, for example, McMahan, *Killing in War*, pp. 198–202, and M. Vaha, 'Child Soldiers and Killing in Self-Defence: Challenging the "Moral View" on Killing in War', *Journal of Military Ethics* 10 (2011): 36–52. For an empirical account, see P. W. Singer, *Children at War* (New York: Pantheon Books, 2005).
[12] See McMahan, *Killing in War*, p. 165, for the case of the ambulance-driver. McMahan agrees that the ambulance-driver has a subjective justification for acting as he does, but denies that he is objectively justified in subjecting the pedestrian to a risk of being killed. On his account, then, the pedestrian has the right to kill the driver—the latter, in other words, is under a duty not to save his own life. I submit, on the contrary, that the ambulance-driver has an objective justification for so acting. For penetrating criticisms of McMahan's position on this and, more generally, of his account of the right to kill, see S. Lazar, 'Responsibility, Risk, and Killing in Self-Defense', *Ethics* 119 (2009): 699–728. More generally, my account of defensive rights implies that it is sometimes permissible to kill innocent obstructors, *pace* (for example) Zohar, 'Collective War and Individualistic Ethics'; N. Zohar, 'Innocence and Complex Threats: Upholding the War Ethics and the Condemnation of Terrorism', *Ethics* 114 (2004): 734–51. Note, finally, that on my view, culpability is not relevant to liability (on which point McMahan clearly disagrees).

Suppose that the only way the pedestrian can survive is by killing the driver. True the driver poses a wrongful threat of harm to the pedestrian. But in so far as he is justified, indeed is under a duty, to drive at speed, to claim that he violates the pedestrian's right not to be killed and thus that he may not defend himself from the latter's self-defensive move seems grossly unfair indeed. In this case, both are permitted to defend themselves but neither has the right (at least against the other) to do so.

To recapitulate, V is permitted to kill A in self-defence in so far as she is permitted more generally to attach greater importance to her life than to A's, provided that the latter is causally responsible (or, as I shall sometimes say, bears contributory responsibility) for the fact that she is subjected to a wrongful threat of lethal harm. Describing morally innocent attackers as causally *responsible* for their victim's predicament might seem tendentious in so far as the use of the term 'responsibility', evoking as it does the notion of *moral* responsibility, loads the philosophical dice, as it were, in favour of killing them. I myself do not hear or read 'causal responsibility' in that way. Still, to avoid any and all possible ambiguity: by causal responsibility, I mean *just that*—that the agent acts in such a way that another party is subject to a lethal harm, no less, and no more. And it is that fact about him which turns him into a legitimate target, whilst it is another fact, about his victim, which provides her with a special justification for killing him. To put the point differently, prior to his attack, A, like any other similar agent, as a right *in rem* not to be killed—a right, in other words, which he holds against everyone else. By attacking V, A loses his right that no one kills him. However, it does not follow from the claim that A has lost his right that no one kill him, that he is a legitimate target for any individual against whom he had that right. That claim only suggests that it is no longer the case that *everyone* is under a duty not to kill him. Whether or not *any* of all those against whom he previously had that right is now at liberty to kill him is precisely what needs to be shown. Partiality, as I have argued, offers a convincing reason as to why V may kill A: if A has lost his right not to be killed against anyone, then surely he has lost it *against his victim*. V, thus, is permitted to kill A in self-defence. Moreover, she has the right to do so if A acts without justification. In those cases where V has the right to kill A, I shall say that A is liable to being killed by her. Note, moreover, that it is not a necessary condition for V permissibly or rightfully to kill A in self-defence that the latter actually *pose* the threat himself. If he contributes significantly to it, for example by instigating it, authorizing it, ordering someone else to carry it out, or supplying the means by which it is carried out, and if V can save her life by killing him, then she may, and sometimes has the right, to do so.

So much, then, for self-defence. Let us now turn to the defence of others. A standard objection to victim-centred accounts of the right to kill in self-defence is that they do not justify the right to kill in defence of others. For although it is easy to see why a victim may give priority to her life over her attacker's, it is not so easy to see why a rescuer may choose V's life over A's on victim-centred grounds, particularly if R is not V's friend or relative. I disagree. Suppose that a potential rescuer, R, is on the scene. In the conflict which opposes V and A, and on the assumption that A no longer has a right not to be killed, R's options are the following:

(1) Do nothing and remain neutral between A and V.
(2) Intervene on A's side and help him kill V.
(3) Intervene on V's side and help her kill A.

Clearly R may not opt for (2): for if V's interest in remaining alive is important enough to hold A under a duty not to save his own life by killing her in self-defence, surely it is important enough to hold third parties under a duty not to prevent her from picking the gun. Likewise, it would be wrong of them to thwart V by helping A obtain the additional weapon he would need in order to overcome V's self-defensive action—let alone by killing her (indeed, in most jurisdictions, they would be charged with the criminal offence of aiding and abetting in the commission of a crime.[13]) Not only may R *not* side with A and against V: more strongly still, R has a right to come to V's rescue and kill A, precisely because V has defensive rights at the bar of the prerogative. According to the interest theory of rights, you recall (as per Section 1.2.2), to say that an agent has a right is to say that an interest of his is important enough to hold some other person(s) under some duty. As applied to permissions, to say that an agent is permitted to $\phi$ is to say that an interest of his is important enough to deem it (morally) permissible for him to $\phi$. Not only does the interest theory account for rights and liberties; it also accounts for powers—the ability to change not merely one's own but also others' moral or legal relationships by granting them rights and liberties. In the case at hand, V's fundamental interest in surviving A's attack is not merely protected by a right to kill A: it is also protected by a *prima facie* power to transfer that right to R. For if V's interest in survival is important enough (as it surely is) to be protected by a permission and a right so to act, then surely it is important enough on principle to be protected by a *prima facie* power to transfer that right to third

---

[13] This is so even if R is related to A, and even if A is not morally responsible for his action. I do not believe, therfore, that a mother is justified in siding with her psychotic son against the latter's victims (though she may be excused for so doing.)

parties. To claim otherwise is to impose an arbitrary restriction on V's ability to promote this fundamental interest of hers. By analogy, to say, on the one hand, that V has a right to procure food for herself and thus that others are under a duty to let her do so, and on the other hand that she lacks the power to get others to procure food on her behalf, is to fail to protect her interest in getting food.

None of this is to deny that R might *also* have agent-neutral reasons for killing A—as reside in the importance of blocking wrongful attacks in general. Moreover, the claim that R might have agent-neutral reasons for killing A does not imply that agent-relative justifications for defensive killings are redundant to those reasons. In making space for agents' personal prerogative, one allows them to confer greater weight on their own goals than on the goals of others, but one also recognizes that they have a standpoint *vis-à-vis* those goals that others lack. The point is important in two respects. First, by that token, V may desist from killing A, because she may confer lesser weight on her life than on his—which means that, in some cases at least, it is up to her and to no one else to decide who will survive the attack. Put differently, and to bring to bear on this issue the distinction between procedural and substantive justice which was drawn at the close of Section 1.2.2, it is up to her to decide whether or not to exercise her right not to be killed. This will prove relevant in subsequent accounts of humanitarian wars and civil wars. Humanitarian wars are fought on behalf and for the sake of individuals who often do not take part in belligerents' decision-making procedures; civil wars are often fought by actors who have not been given an explicit mandate by their compatriots. In both cases, the issue of consent is crucial.

Second, V's special stake in A's demise may sometimes give her latitude which R lacks *vis-à-vis* innocent bystanders who might be killed as a result of the defensive steps which either she, or R, will take. This is why I claimed two paragraphs ago that V's interest in her own survival, if important enough to be protected by a permission or a right, is on principle important enough to be protected by a *prima facie* (and not all things considered) power. Suppose that V, in the course of firing at the villainous truck-driver, is at risk of unintentionally though foreseeably killing a pedestrian who happens to pass by. She may well have a justified personal prerogative so to act; but even if that is so, this is not enough to show that R himself may do so on her behalf. To be sure, he may well have agent-neutral reasons to prevent the truck-driver from killing V. But those reasons, stemming as they do from interests of his (and of everyone else's) in not living in a world in which wrongful attackers are allowed a free rein, are not as powerful as agent-relative reasons (here, V's) which stem from one's interest in survival. Accordingly, before concluding that R may kill innocent bystanders (who have not lost their right not to be killed) on V's behalf, we must thus establish that his (agent-neutral) interest (which is lesser than an interest in survival) in blocking the villainous truck-driver is strong enough to justify causing him to die. In this particular case it is not clear that R may so act—though he may (I submit) shoot at A if in so doing he will merely inflict a slight injury to B's arm. In other cases, agent-neutral reasons would justify R's act, as where (for example) the only way to rescue 500 hostages from two attackers is by storming the theatre in which they are held and, in so doing, foreseeably but unintentionally kill a bystander who cannot be evacuated in time. To put the point in a language familiar to just war theory, rescuers who do not have a special relationship to the victim must confer greater weight than the latter on the interests of innocent bystanders when assessing whether their defensive move is a proportionate response to the wrongdoing which they would thereby block. The point will prove important for assessing the permissibility of inflicting collateral damage in wars of humanitarian intervention (Section 5.5.2) and scrutinizing the ethics of contracting private soldiers into helping us fight our own wars of defence (Section 6.4).

Let us now turn to cases where A is a justified attacker (JA), and where V and A thus are permitted, though lack the right, to kill each other in self-defence. In the face of a conflict of permissions between JA and V—between, for example, the pedestrian and the ambulance driver—and in the light of the view that killing is generally worse than letting die, it might be tempting to think that R not only may but in fact must remain neutral. But suppose that the number of letting-dies which would take place were R remain neutral far exceed the number of killings which R would have to commit in order to prevent those deaths—to such a degree, in fact, that R is permitted to intervene.[14] That both JA and V have an equal permission to kill, as grounded in their interest in survival, does not imply that they both have the power to transfer their permission to R. For there is an asymmetry between them, which resides in JA's having a positive moral justification for starting a chain of

[14] For the view that R must remain neutral, as applied to conflicts between innocent passive threats and victims, where (it is said) the former are permitted to kill the latter in self-defence and *vice versa*, see N. Davis, 'Abortion and Self-Defense', *Philosophy & Public Affairs* 13 (1984): 175–297. To anticipate Chapter 5, unless we are really prepared to condemn more or less all humanitarian interventions as wrong, we must accept that letting many die is sometimes worse than killing a few. For if third parties intervene, they almost always inevitably kill innocent victims (though unintentionally so). If they do not intervene, they will let (some of) those victims die at the hands of their regime. To say that intervening is permissible is tantamount to claiming that, in those cases at least, killing is permissible though the alternative is 'merely letting die'. More strongly still, to say that intervening is mandatory is tantamount to claiming that letting die, in those cases, is *worse* than killing.

events leading to a forced choice between their lives. Consider the following case, which takes us closer to lethal conflicts in war:

*Bank robbery.* A bank customer C is under a lethal threat from a gangster who is carrying out a bank robbery and has already killed some other customers. C is armed, and pulls out his gun to defend himself and the remaining customers. However, unless another customer, R, also armed, shoots at C, the latter will inevitably (though unintentionally) kill someone else, V, in the process of killing the gunman. Suppose that V would not die anyway at the hands of the gangster.

There is an asymmetry between C and V in this case, for although both are at risk of dying, C also has a positive moral justification for subjecting V to a lethal threat, in that he is stopping a gangster from robbing a bank and more importantly from killing more people. One might think that V is under a duty to let C kill her, precisely because C has a justification for acting as he does. However, to hold that V is under a duty to make that sacrifice would fly in the face of the personal prerogative. It seems, thus, that V has not lost her right not to be killed and thus may defend herself from C on grounds of partiality. On the assumption that R may step in, he ought to side with C rather than V, for if he kills C he allows the continuation of a seriously wrongful process in which the fundamental rights (not to be killed or seriously injured) of a number of individuals are violated. Agent-neutral considerations in this case outweigh V's interest in conferring on R the permission to kill C. Put differently, it is (sometimes) permissible deliberately to kill morally and causally innocent agents whose lives are under threat at the hands of justified attackers if they turn themselves into (justified) attackers and, in so doing, threaten to undermine the successful completion of the justified attackers' rightful course of action.

I shall return to these difficult issues in Section 2.4 when examining the issues of collateral damage and patriotic partiality in wars of collective self-defence. In the next section I apply the foregoing account of defensive rights to the right (deliberately) to kill enemy combatants in such wars.

## 2.3 WARS OF COLLECTIVE SELF-DEFENCE

### 2.3.1 The right to wage a war of collective self-defence: a first cut

We saw in Section 1.4 that political self-determination is a communal good which has worth to individuals in so far as it helps fulfil the demands of sufficientist cosmopolitanism and offers citizens the opportunity to exercise their legitimate personal prerogative to associate with one another. Given that it cannot be exercised other than over a bounded territory, large-scale attacks on that territory itself undermine it and thereby the rights which it serves. When they are backed by lethal force, as they typically are, those attacks sometimes give rise to a just cause for war—and more specifically provide the victims of aggression with a justification for killing their aggressors in self-defence. Let us suppose that the government of country A orders its army to invade country V in a bid for territorial expansion, with strict instructions to its combatants to kill anyone from V's community who attempts to resist the invasion. Let us also take it as fixed throughout that A's invasion of V is wrongful. V's government sends its own army to repel the invasion by force. According to the reductive strategy, V's right to wage that particular war against A is best understood as a right, held by V's citizens, to resort to force in defence of their homeland—a right which they have the Hohfeldian power to transfer to their army and its individual members. Combatants$_V$ thus have a right to use force, on behalf of their own citizens, against combatants$_A$. In the course of defending their individual and jointly held rights, combatants$_V$ are subject to lethal attacks from combatants$_A$. So are non-combatants$_V$, in fact, if combatants$_A$ do not restrict their military operations to the battlefield but also seek to destroy V's infrastructure and, in so doing, inflict lethal collateral damage on them. The right of combatants$_V$ to wage war, thus, is not simply a right to defend their compatriots' and their (jointly held) rights to, for example, territorial integrity and political sovereignty: it is a right to defend their and others' life from lethal threats which combatants$_A$ pose to them in the course of prosecuting their war. Moreover, in some cases, violations of those rights by way of a military aggression lead to further violations of the rights not to be killed or maimed of V's members, not merely in the sense that the latter's refusal to surrender causes combatants$_A$ to attack them, but in the sense that A's regime, were it to win the war, might carry out genocidal policies against V's population, engage in the systematic torture of opponents, and so on. Similarly, were A to win, its war of aggression might lead to systematic and severe poverty within V's borders as a result of A's grossly incompetent mismanagement of V's resources; it might also lead to the establishment of a dictatorship. In other words, violations of the rights to territorial integrity and political sovereignty warrant resistance by lethal force not just because they are themselves backed by lethal force, but also in so far as a defeat would result in violations of the requirements of justice within V.[15] By analogy, we have the right to use lethal force against an intruder who

---

[15] In another paper I scrutinise cases of so-called bloodless invasions, where A violates V's sovereignty rights without killing anyone within V. I argue that even in (some of) those cases,

threatens to kill us unless we let him stay in our house, as well as against an intruder who, were we to lay down our arms as he crosses the threshold, would still kill us, maim us, cause us to live a less than minimally decent life, and so on. It is in that sense that the right to wage war is simply the right to use lethal force against those whose deadly threat is one which they pose (as combatants), or contribute to posing (as those combatants' leaders) in furtherance of, or as a prelude to, the violation of our fundamental rights.

At this juncture, the following objection might be raised. Imagine that on 1 July 1914 two Frenchmen, André and Bernard, are taking a stroll in the French countryside and are unjustifiably attacked by a German individual, Carl. On my account of defensive rights, André and Bernard each have the right to kill Carl in self-defence as well as the Hohfeldian power to transfer that right to potential rescuers and thus to each other: put differently, André has the right to kill Carl in defence of Bernard, and *vice versa*. As should be clear, the reason why that is so has nothing to do with the fact that André and Bernard are compatriots and everything to do with the fact that Carl is unjustifiably subjecting them to a wrongful threat of lethal harm. And indeed, to claim, *a contrario*, that André and Bernard have the right to kill Carl in defence of each other *just because* they are compatriots (whilst Carl is a German) would violate the central tenets of cosmopolitan justice: as we saw in Sections 1.2.1 and 1.3.1, the principle of fundamental equality forbids agents deliberately to harm one another on the basis of morally arbitrary factors, of which political membership *per se* is one. So far, so good. But now, fast-forward to 6 September 1914: France and Germany are at war, and André and Bernard are conscripted into the French army and fight alongside each other at the Battle of the Marne.[16] By happenstance, Carl, who survived their defensive move two months earlier by fleeing, is fighting them as part of the German army. In this case, it does seem as if André has the right to kill Carl in defence of Bernard and *vice versa* precisely because André and Bernard are compatriots whose rights (both individual and jointly held) are under threat at the hands of Carl and other German soldiers. And if that is the case, then (the objection might continue) my account of André's and Bernard's right to kill Carl in defence of each other on 1 July 1914 does not support their right to kill him in defence of each other on 6 September 1914.

combatants$_V$ have the right to use force in defence of those rights. See Fabre, 'Cosmopolitanism and Wars of Self-Defence', unpublished typescript.

[16] The Battle of the Marne, which lasted only a few days and saw dozens of thousands of casualties on all sides, was the first major battle of the First World War. It more or less stopped the German advance into French territory, and marked the start of trench warfare. See H. Strachan, *The First World War: To Arms*, vol. 1 (Oxford: Oxford University Press, 2001), 242–62.

The difficulty is more apparent than real. For suppose that on 1 July 1914 Carl throws an incendiary bomb on a house which André and Bernard jointly own and currently occupy—with a view to forcing them to relinquish their rights to him. André and Bernard have the right to kill him in defence of their own lives, in defence of each other's life, *and* in defence of their jointly held right of ownership over the house. In this example the fact that they are compatriots is irrelevant, because the right at issue is not one which they have in virtue of that particular relationship. By contrast, the jointly held rights which are under threat in a war of collective self-defence are rights which compatriots together have with respect to the territorial integrity and political sovereignty of the national or political community to which they belong. Notwithstanding this difference between this case and the scenario involving joint rights over a house, the point just made holds. When violating those rights by using lethal force, Carl (and his fellow German soldiers) provide André and Bernard with a justification for killing him in defence of their own life as well as in defence of each other's life; he also provides them with a justification for killing him in defence of their rights to territorial integrity and collective self-determination—which rights they happen to hold jointly as members of the same political community.

Two points of clarification are required before we proceed further. First, it is worth stressing, once more, that I am not endorsing the claim that individuals may kill in defence of their compatriots *qua* compatriots. Second, my point is not that we may give priority to those with whom we have a special relationship in general only if that special relationship generates jointly held rights, and if, therefore, one's own interest is at stake. (For if that were so, then we would not be permitted either to give priority to our children over other children, or to do for our children certain things which we would be permitted to do for ourselves—which in some cases at least is absurd.) My focus here is on the relationship of co-citizenship. When that relationship is under threat it is because the jointly held rights which are constitutive of it are also under threat, and it is that, in turn, which sometimes confers on actors in that relationship the right to exercise lethal force in its defence.

Note that the argument presupposes that agents may kill wrongdoers in defence of jointly held rights, which are of lesser importance than the right not to be killed and whose violations themselves need not lead to the loss of that particular right. On some views this undermines the reductive strategy, for in private cases (they will press) one may kill only if one is subject to a lethal threat.[17] However, in some jurisdictions the law does permit individuals to kill in

---

[17] Rodin, *War and Self-Defense*, 128 and 132–8; R. J. Norman, *Ethics, Killing, and War* (Cambridge: Cambridge University Press, 1995), 128–31.

defence of lesser rights than the right to life—such as, for example, the rights not to be raped, kidnapped, and enslaved. I believe that the law has got it right. Killing someone without justification is an egregious wrongdoing because it treats the victim as less than a person. In killing V (non-accidentally) the attacker shows, in effect, that *she* counts for nothing, that she is not in any way worthy of his concern and respect, and thus that she can appropriately be treated as a means only to his ends, and not as an end in herself. So do rapists, kidnappers, and slave-owners: for rape, kidnapping, and enslavement also treat their victims as less than persons. If V may kill her lethal attacker on the grounds (in part) that she cannot be held under a moral duty to let him treat her as nothing better than an object, then she may kill him when he treats her in dehumanizing ways which come close to inflicting on her the loss of her life.

More controversially, contrary to what the law stipulates in most jurisdiction, killing is not a disproportionate response to the threatened loss of one's property—at least in those cases where threats to one's property rights are backed by force or severely jeopardise one's prospects for a minimally decent life. Suppose that your house is wrongfully invaded by a group of individuals who intend to stay there permanently and who use coercive force against you if you dissent with whatever decision they make with respect to your house. Or suppose that you are (non-lethally) coerced by an attacker into signing over all your possessions, with no possibility for you to get compensation or help from anyone *ex post*. And suppose, finally, that in all those cases you have a choice between fully complying with wrongdoers' demands or killing them. I cannot think of any plausible justification for the view that you lack the right to kill your aggressors. To reiterate, there are limits to the sacrifices which we may be expected to incur for the sake of others. In particular, we are not under a duty to lead a less than minimally decent life for their sake. Whilst this does not permit us deliberately to kill innocent bystanders for the sake of living such a life, it does permit us (subject to considerations of proportionality, chance of success, and so on) deliberately to kill those who wrongfully placed us in a position where we have to choose between agreeing to live such a life, or being coerced into living it if we refuse to accede to their (wrongful) demands.[18]

Clearly, this is what a war of aggression is like. When country A's army invades country V, and when A's government insists that V comply with its

---

[18] The argument which I deployed one paragraph ago regarding killing as a means to block rape (roughly) follows F. Leverick, *Killing in Self-Defence* (Oxford: Oxford University Press, 2006), ch. 8. For interesting parallels between the right to use force in defence of one's home and the right to wage a war of collective self-defence, see Hurka, 'Proportionality in the Morality of War', at 55–66.

demands as a condition for withdrawing, A is typically subjecting V to a multi-pronged attack which is very similar to that described in the previous paragraph: it is, typically, an attack on the rights of V's members to determine their own future and decide who will live on, and dispose of, their territory. Moreover, it is an attack that is more often than not accompanied by threats to some of the most fundamental rights of V's individual members, such as the right not to be killed, raped, beaten up, maimed, and so on.

Here is another way to put the point. A just cause for war is standardly seen as a wrongdoing of such magnitude as to warrant a retaliatory lethal attack by its victims, understood collectively as a group of individuals, on the wrongdoer, also understood in those terms. Yet we ought to distinguish between a narrow just cause and a wide just cause. A narrow just cause is a justification for killing wrongdoers, whilst a wide just cause is a justification for using non-lethal force even though one plausibly foresees that wrongdoers will counter this defensive move by lethal means—the use of which is not warranted and provides victims with a narrow just cause for killing. When we speak of a just cause for war, therefore, we might speak either of a narrow just cause or of a wide just cause. Now, not all rights are so important that their violation on its own provides their holders with a narrow just cause for subjecting wrongdoers to a lethal attack. Suppose that A's forces bloodlessly invade a tiny empty island over which V claims sovereignty, but which is located many thousands miles away from V's mainland. The invasion alone does not provide V with a narrow just cause for sending its soldiers to kill combatants$_A$. This is because the violation of this particular right of V's does not in this case undermine the prospects of V's members for a minimally decent life. However, A's act of aggression does provide V with a wide just cause for using non-lethal force against combatants$_A$. If combatants$_A$ *then* pose a lethal threat to combatants$_V$, the latter have a narrow just cause for killing or seriously maiming them. By contrast, A's large-scale traditionally military invasion of V's mainland *would*, on its own, constitute a narrow just cause for combatants$_V$ to kill combatants$_A$, to the extent that those combatants could take it as read from that particular act that the invaders will kill them unless they surrender, or that they have very strong reasons to believe that A's regime, if unopposed and thus victorious, would commit further violations of their fundamental human rights.

An important question at this juncture is that of the grounds upon which—if any at all—illegitimate states can have the right to wage a war of collective self-defence. As we saw in Section 1.4, a state is legitimate—that is, its officials collectively have a moral right to govern—provided, and to the extent that, it respects the fundamental rights of both citizens and outsiders; moreover, the right to govern is a fiduciary right which the state's agents hold as trustees acting on behalf of citizens, who are under an obligation to obey those agents' directives only if their fundamental rights are thereby better protected by those directives than if they disobeyed. By that token, the right to wage war as held by the state's agents is one which they have as trustees acting on behalf of those individuals. If the latter do better in the face of severe rights violations, such as territorial aggression by another state, by obeying the agents' directives during the war than they would do without it, those agents collectively have the right to wage war on their behalf, even though the fact that they are themselves guilty of severe rights violations provides citizens with a justification for overthrowing them once the war is over. The example of the USSR during the Second World War illustrates the point. That the Soviet regime was illegitimate is absolutely beyond question. But it does not allow us to conclude that Germany did not violate the rights to sovereignty, territorial integrity, and life, of Soviet citizens, and that Stalin and his henchmen therefore did not have the right (acting on behalf of those citizens) to take the steps necessary to repel the invasion. The latter clearly did have that right, but, to repeat, only as the agents of Soviet citizens, who had morally-directed pragmatic reasons to defer to their orders. Had Soviet citizens decided to overthrow Stalin and his regime in the aftermath of the war, they would not have wronged them in any way at all.[19]

## 2.3.2 The moral status of combatants

Taken together, my account of defensive rights and the account of the right to wage and kill in wars of collective self-defence which it underpins imply that whether combatants may—indeed, have the right to—kill enemy combatants (in large part) depends on the moral status of their war *ad bellum* in general and whether it has a just cause in particular. In private killings, V has the right to kill A in self-defence on the grounds that the latter is subjecting her to a wrongful threat, but (as we saw) A clearly may not retaliate in his *own* defence. If A's lethal threat is unjustified at time $t_1$, such that V may take defensive steps against him at $t_2$, then surely he may not continue to threaten V at $t_3$, even if the latter, at that point, is threatening his life. To claim otherwise

---

[19] For the view that only legitimate regimes have the right to wage war, see Orend, *The Morality of War*, 35ff. For the view that illegitimate (on cosmopolitan grounds) regimes nevertheless may have a just cause for war, see Caney, *Justice Beyond Borders*, 203–4. Caney argues that to deny illegitimate regimes the right to go to war—on the grounds that, illegitimate as they are, they cannot have a just cause—is to overlook the fact that for them not to wage war would create greater injustice. Though he does not explicitly distinguish (at this juncture of his discussion) between the rights of political regimes and the (individual and collective) rights of the latters' members, I essentially agree with him.

would be to say, wildly implausibly, that an armed bank-robber may kill the cashier who, furnished with good reasons to believe that the robber would start shooting, pulls out his gun and mounts a self-defensive and other-defensive attack. By parity of reasoning, if an act of aggression as carried out by A's army against the territorial integrity and sovereignty of community V is morally wrong, then its constitutive elements are morally wrong as well, and combatants$_A$ are therefore committing a wrongdoing. If it is morally wrong for A's army to cross over the border into V's territory, it is morally wrong for combatants$_A$ to do precisely that. Crucially, if it is morally wrong for combatants$_A$ to threaten, at $t_1$, the lives of those of combatants$_V$ who stand in their way, then it is wrong for those individual combatants to kill combatants$_V$ in self-defence at $t_3$. On that view, German soldiers who killed Belgian soldiers in pursuit of their army's wrongful invasion in the summer of 1914 were not permitted so to act, even when they were attempting to defend their own lives from the Belgians' own self-defensive steps.

This view, variants of which have been revived recently by, *inter alia*, Tony Coady, David Rodin, and Jeff McMahan, is not altogether new: thus, writing in the sixteenth century, Francisco de Vitoria avers that combatants fighting on the objectively unjust side are acting impermissibly.[20] But to many, this is unacceptable. As Walzer puts it, once the war has started, combatants lose their right not to be killed by the enemy simply in virtue of posing a lethal threat to them, and thus are legitimate targets (subjects to considerations of proportionality and necessity), irrespective of the justness, or lack thereof, of the side for which they are fighting. The point is not merely a point of law—for the laws of war do treat combatants on a par—but also a claim of morality. The modern just-war tradition and the body of laws which it underpins do not draw any distinction between German and Belgian combatants in 1914.[21]

---

[20] C. A. J. Coady, *Morality and Political Violence* (Cambridge: Cambridge University Press, 2008); Vitoria, *On the Law of War*; McMahan, *Killing in War*; Rodin, *War and Self-Defense*.

[21] Walzer, *Just and Unjust Wars*, ch. 9. For spirited and recent defences of the orthodox account and the moral symmetry thesis, see Y. Benbaji, 'The Responsibility of Soldiers and the Ethics of Killing in War', *Philosophical Quarterly* 57 (2007): 558–72; 'A Defence of the Traditional War Convention', *Ethics* 118 (2008): 464–95; L. May, *War Crimes and Just War* (Cambridge: Cambridge University Press, 2007); P. Emerton and T. Handfield, 'Order and Affray: Defensive Privileges in Warfare', *Philosophy & Public Affairs* 37 (2009). See also Rodin and Shue (ed.), *Just and Unjust Warriors*, for a very good set of essays on the dispute. For criticisms of McMahan's position specifically, see Lazar, 'Responsibility, Risk, and Killing in Self-Defense'; 'The Responsibility Dilemma for *Killing in War*: A Review Essay', *Philosophy & Public Affairs* 38 (2010): 180–213. It is worth stressing here, once more, that there is one crucially important difference between McMahan's account and my own account. Whereas he locates the basis for liability in moral responsibility for a wrongful threat (for which there is no justification), and thus holds that one does not have the right to kill morally innocent attackers, I locate it in contributory responsibility alone.

The dispute between proponents of that older view (which under their penmanship is known as the 'neo-classical account') and proponents of the orthodox account of war killings as articulated by Walzer is at the frontier of contemporary war ethics, and exploring its participants' various moves and counter-moves in depth is beyond the scope of this chapter. Instead, I shall briefly tackle three objections which are standardly levelled against the neo-classical account: the duress objection, the epistemic objection, and the lack-of-control objection. Strictly speaking, those objections target an interpretation of that account which I do not endorse—to wit, that one may, indeed has the right, to kill an attacker only if the latter is *morally responsible* for a wrongful lethal harm. However, it is worth discussing them here, just in case moral responsibility *is* necessary for liability—contrary to what I argued in Section 2.2.

Briefly put, the objections claim, respectively, that combatants act under duress, that they cannot be expected to know whether they are fighting for a just cause, and that they lack control over their country's foreign policy; they then insist that as a result, combatants are not to be held morally responsible for the killings which they commit during that war, and conclude that they have therefore not lost their right not to be killed, which implies that they may kill enemy combatants in self-defence even if their cause is unjust.

I do not think that either duress, or epistemic difficulties, or lack of control, furnish combatants who take part in an unjust aggression on another country's territory and sovereignty with the kind of excuses which would enable them permissibly to kill enemy combatants in self-defence.[22] Consider duress. That it is felt by many combatants is beyond question—though far less so in those countries which no longer resort to conscription. It is worth noting, however, that private actors who kill in the course of, for example, drug-related gang warfare, are also subjected to considerable duress. Yet one would not say that a gang hit-man may kill his victim, should he fail at first try and should she be armed, in his own defence: duress, in those cases, is not fully exculpatory, and so it is hard to see how, exactly, war differs (with respect to duress) from private killings.

The epistemic objection for its part need not claim that soldiers are acting under duress. Rather, it asserts that they act under conditions of severe epistemic uncertainty. For in most cases, the objection presses, determining

---

[22] For powerful rebuttals of the duress and epistemic objections, see McMahan, *Killing in War*, ch. 3. For further decisive criticisms of the epistemic objection, see D. Rodin, 'The Moral Inequality of Soldiers: Why *jus in bello* Asymmetry is Half Right', in D. Rodin and H. Shue (ed.), *Just and Unjust Warriors* (Oxford: Oxford University Press, 2008).

whether the war is just *ad bellum* is so complex as to be beyond the cognitive reach of ordinary soldiers. Consequently, even if soldiers are objectively in the wrong when killing in the prosecution of an unjust war, they have very strong subjective justifications for so doing—such as to warrant regarding them as morally on a par with their enemy on the battlefield. By contrast, private actors can be expected to know whether or not they are killing rightfully.[23]

However, the objection assumes—somewhat disrespectfully and without much empirical basis—that combatants are incapable of determining whether the war is just. Relatedly, a decision to join the army and thereby go to war can be, and in many cases is, made in the light of information about the facts of the case. Finally, proponents of the objection are more than willing to hold soldiers morally responsible for the acts of killing which they commit in violation of *jus in bello*, such as the deliberate killing of non-combatants, even though the conditions under which they have to fight ('the fog of war') might make it extremely difficult for them to judge whether or not the orders they are given are just. If epistemic uncertainty in the fog of war does not constitute a justification for a wrongful killing, it is not clear why it would constitute a justification for taking part in an unjust war when the decision so to act can be made in the safety of the barracks.[24] I do not mean to deny that there are good reasons in practice for treating combatants *as if* they were morally on a par, which would mean, in particular, not prosecuting for murder those who fight an unjust war. Such reasons include, for example, the fact that combatants who fear prosecution may be less likely to obey *just* orders, or more likely to fight without restraint if they sense that they will, in any event, be punished. But that is not the same as to say that combatants *are* morally on a par, and in so far as my concern, in this book, is with the moral

---

[23] See, for example, Shue, 'Do We Need a "Morality of War"?', 99ff; see also C. A. J. Coady, 'The Status of Combatants', in D. Rodin and H. Shue (ed.), *Just and Unjust Warriors* (Oxford: Oxford University Press, 2008), 164ff. A full treatment (either in defence or in rebuttal) of the epistemic objection would require distinguishing soldiers' putative ignorance of the empirical facts at hand (for example, did Saddam Hussein's regime have nuclear weapons, and did it conceal them from UN inspectors?), and their putative ignorance of the moral facts at hand (for example, assuming that Saddam Hussein did have and conceal such weapons, did this constitute a justification for invading Iraq?). It would also have to trace the connection, or identify the lack thereof, between ignorance (and knowledge) of either kind and moral responsibility for the ensuing war.

[24] A point pithily made, for example, by L. McPherson, 'Innocence and Responsibility in War', *Canadian Journal of Philosophy* 34 (2004): 485–506. There is a sense in which soldiers might be deemed closer to the facts as pertain to targeting decisions made once the war has started, than they are with respect to the *ad bellum* decision to resort to war in the first instance. Perhaps. But there is also a sense in which the circumstances under which they find themselves are much more conducive to dispassionate reflexion on whatever facts they have *ad bellum* than *in bello*. And that, surely, is highly relevant—to a degree that the epistemic objection overlooks. I am grateful to Jon Quong for pressing me on this.

permissions and moral rights which agents *do* have in war rather than morally directed laws of war, the epistemic objection leaves the moral responsibility-variant account of the right to kill untouched.

Finally, the lack-of-control objection insists that most combatants have no influence on the overall course of action taken by their army or, for that matter, their regime; as a result, to withhold from them the permission to defend their lives on the grounds that they are participants in their army's collective wrongdoing is to subsume them under their collective identity. The objection is worth scrutinizing, because in so far as it is a central premise of cosmopolitanism that agents are not reducible to their membership in a group, the objection, if correct, is seriously damaging to any cosmopolitan theory of the just war. Again, however, gang members too often have little control over the decisions made by gang leaders. If lack of control in such cases is not thought to provide gang members with a subjective justification for killing wrongfully, then it is not clear why it should furnish combatants with a subjective justification for taking part, and killing, in an unjust war. In any event, although it is true that rank-and-file soldiers have close to little influence on their political leaders' decision wrongfully to invade a neighbour-ing country, acting as such they do have control (for the most) over their own decision to stay in the army, to board the aircraft which will take them to the border on the eve of the invasion, to drive their tanks over the border, and, most importantly, to fire at enemy soldiers who refuse to let them pass through. They cannot invoke lack of control as an excuse, let alone a justificatory excuse, for committing those lesser wrongdoings, and particularly for backing those wrongdoings with the threat of (lethal) force. Moreover, drawing on the account of individual responsibility for collective wrongdoings which was set out in Section 1.2.3, to the extent that they have a choice as to whether or not to participate in this particular wrongful collective venture (their army's aggression against V), and to the extent that they intend to do that which they know is part of that collective venture, they can be held responsible for the wrongdoing which consists, not just in setting foot into V's territory without V's consent, but, in doing so collectively, in invading V. The claim that soldiers are not morally on a par, thus described and defended, is entirely of a piece with the individualistic principles of cosmopolitan justice.

To recapitulate, I have argued that even if, *pace* my argument in Section 2.2, attackers are liable to being killed only if they are morally responsible for the wrongful threat which they pose to their victims, whether or not soldiers have the right to kill enemy soldiers largely depends on the moral status of their war. That said, the foregoing discussion raises the further and important issue of the liabilities of agents other than combatants$_A$—such as A's non-combatting officials who play a significant role in the decision to wage the war of aggression and in its subsequent prosecution, or A's citizens who elected those officials in the first place. It might seem tempting to suppose that only combatants are legitimate targets, on the grounds that they alone *pose* a threat to combatants$_V$. On that view, however, A's leaders, and perhaps some of its citizens, are not liable—which, in some cases at least, seems counter-intuitive. To give but one example, it is not plausible on the one hand to claim that generals who give unjust orders to their soldiers are liable to being killed whilst those generals' civilian prime minister or head of state, who took the decision to wage the war in the first instance, is not liable. It thus seems more plausible to say that causal responsibility for a wrongful threat posed by unjustifiable action is the basis for liability. The difficulty here is that more often than not, individual wrongdoers' contributions to the collective harm which they inflict on V's members are very marginal and not significant enough on their own to warrant the judgement that they have lost their right not to be killed. To give but one example, we might be reluctant to claim that citizens who elect a warmongering leader are legitimate targets, on the grounds that the act of casting a vote, when taken on its own, cannot possibly justify killing the voter.

The reason why casting a vote is not a basis for liability in this particular case is that the voter makes an exceedingly small contribution to the resultant war. Causal significance often greatly matters: the secretaries who were sharpening the pencils used by the German General Staff during World War II were not liable; the generals themselves clearly were, and not merely in virtue of being soldiers. However, one should not infer that making a significant contribution to a wrongful threat of lethal harm is a necessary condition for liability. For there are cases where an agent is liable to being killed even when his contribution to such a harm is very small. Suppose that 20,000 individuals are sending 10V of electricity into the body of an innocent victim, as a result of which she dies. Or suppose that a mob of thousands of people are each throwing a small stone at a woman on the grounds that she committed adultery, as a result of which she too dies. Imagine that a rescuer could save the victim's life, in both cases, by killing one, and simply one, wrongdoer (for example, because the others would flee, fearing for their lives.) I believe that each and every one of those torturers or stone-casters has lost their right not to be killed in this case—in other words, is liable to being killed—even though their contribution to V's fate, each taken on their own, is very small. An important difference between those two cases on the one hand and the aforementioned voting example on the other hand is that torturers and stone-casters would be liable to less-than-lethal force if they acted alone, since they would be inflicting a wrongful (though lesser) harm onto their victim; voters, by contrast, would not be liable for a single voter cannot on its own inflict a wrongful harm to third parties (at least in cases where outcomes are not settled by margins of one vote only). I believe that this difference matters to the determination of agents' liability to being killed when their individual contributions to collective wrongdoings are marginal. If an agent's contribution is such that he has lost his right not to have force used against him, then he is liable to being killed for his participation (subject to other conditions such as necessity.) On the other hand, if his individual contribution is such that one would violate his right by resorting to force as a means to block the harm to which the individual contributes, then that agent is not liable to being killed for his participation in a collective (wrongful) lethal harm.[25] That said, the fact that agents who are not liable to being killed in the sense just defined but nevertheless unjustifiably contribute to the imposition of a wrongdoing provides their victims, or agents acting on her behalf, with a justification for deliberately imposing a lesser harm (than the loss of their life) on them collectively. It may also provide victims and their rescuers with a justification for acting in such a way as to kill them unintentionally, though foreseeably. In many cases, of course, we will not be in a position to ascertain whether civilians who belong to the enemy do in fact contribute to the latter's wrongdoing—notably in those cases where the wrongdoing occurs as a result of collective actions or omissions involving thousands of individual agents. Under conditions of epistemic uncertainty of that kind, we ought to err on the side of caution and proceed on the assumption that those agents are innocent. The rationale for adopting this precautionary principle lies in the familiar two-pronged thought that the deliberate imposition of harm, rather than immunity from it, stands in need of justification, and that agents generally ought to be regarded as (causally) innocent of wrongdoing until proven (causally)

---

[25] I used to think that an agent's contribution to a grievous wrongdoing had to meet a certain threshold of causal significance in order for the agent to be deemed liable to being killed. I develop that point in Fabre, 'Guns, Food, and Liability to Attack', part V. As is clear here, I now think that I was wrong, and that causal significance is not a necessary condition for liability (though it often matters). I owe this change of mind to Jon Quong, to whom I grateful for saving me from that mistake. The torturers example is loosely drawn from Parfit's well-known discussion of collective responsibility in D. Parfit, *Reasons and Persons* (Oxford: Clarendon, 1984), 70. The example of the stone-casting is Quong's. The criterion for distinguishing marginal contributions which render one liable from those which do not is mine. The criterion of causal significance has a troublesome implication, which was brought to my attention by both Quong and Krister Bykvist: to wit, that individuals acting together can avoid being liable to lethal force by distributing responsibilities in such a way that the act of every single one of them has a negligible probability of harming third parties (as negligible as the probability of one's vote being a casting vote, for example.) In the cases at hand, however, where at least some policy decisions have to be made by small groups of people, it is not clear to me that there would be no agent whose contribution would warrant attacking him.

responsible for it. I shall revisit those questions in Section 3.4 in the course of my normative account of subsistence wars.[26] Meanwhile, let me present the conclusion reached so far in the following way. As we saw in the Introduction, the principle of discrimination is central to both the morality and the laws of war. In its orthodox mainstream interpretations, it holds that combatants are legitimate targets, irrespective of their cause, just because they pose a threat to one another; by contrast, non-combatants are not legitimate targets, precisely because they do not take part in hostilities. On my account, by contrast, not all combatants are legitimate targets, whereas some non-combatants are.

An important qualification is in order. Although my account of the right to kill in a war of collective self-defence implies that the *ad bellum* justness, or lack thereof, of the war is a decisive consideration for evaluating combatants' *in bello* rights and liabilities *vis-à-vis* one another, it does not entail that combatants who take part in an unjust war may never kill enemy combatants.[27] Thus, even if combatants$_V$ are at liberty to kill combatants$_A$, they are not permitted to use whatever means they wish. For example, they may not use weapons which are designed not merely to kill but to kill atrociously painfully. If they do, combatants$_A$ are permitted to retaliate against combatants$_V$' self-defensive steps. Moreover, to the extent that combatants who are unjust (for lacking a just cause) at time $t_1$ may come to acquire a just cause for continuing with the war at time $t_2$, they may and should, *in those phases*, be regarded as just combatants.

Nor does the account entail that combatants who take part in a just war always have the right to kill combatants from the *ad bellum* unjust side. Suppose that country A wrongfully invades V. V, I assume, has a just cause for waging a war of self-defence against A but goes into war for additional unjust reasons—such as the seizure of A's diamond mines, over which it has no legitimate claim. Some of combatants$_V$ will be deployed to repel the invasion and in so doing will act justly, whilst others will be sent deep into A's territory to take control of the mines and in so doing will act unjustly.[28] By

---

[26] The precautionary principle I set out here dovetails with the view (which was defended in Section 1.2.1) that pending information to the contrary, a needy individual is not responsible for his predicament, and *prima facie* has a claim to our assistance. Note that my discussion in this paragraph partly follows McMahan's account of the complex relationship between just cause and proportionality in McMahan, *Killing in War*, 21–32. I say 'partly' because McMahan rejects appeals to thresholds in general (ibid.,), and because he believes that moral (as opposed to merely causal) responsibility for a wrongful threat (by way of unjustified action) is the basis for liability.

[27] *Pace* Tesón, 'Self-Defense in International Law and Rights of Persons'. I phrase the point by reference to combatants for ease of exposition, but it applies to participants in war in general.

[28] See McMahan, 'The Morality of War and the Law of War', 31, the argument of which I follow closely in the remainder of this paragraph. McMahan's own example—that of an oil field—appears in another context. I use the case of a diamond mine to forestall the objection that, as A's army relies on regular supplies of oil to fight its unjust war, V might be wholly justified in seizing its fields.

implication, those of combatants$_A$ who oppose V's self-defensive steps act unjustly; but those who kill V's soldiers in protection of the diamond field act justly. Or suppose that although A went to war against V at $t_1$ without a just cause, it subsequently acquired a just cause for continuing with the war at $t_5$. Correspondingly, combatants$_A$ who, at $t_1$, posed a wrongful threat to their enemy, are acting permissibly at $t_5$. And so on. A full account of combatants' moral status *vis-à-vis* one another—which it is not my aim to provide here— would offer more fine-grained principles for discerning, on the basis of the justness of the war *ad bellum*, when combatants are liable to being killed and are permitted to kill, and when they are not. I shall return to this difficult issue in Section 7.5, where I shall examine the moral status of *ad bellum* just combatants who use unjust tactics on the grounds that they cannot win their war in any other way. In the remainder of this chapter, however, I assume that combatants$_A$ are violating the rights of V's members, be they combatants$_V$ or citizens$_V$.

To recapitulate, combatants$_V$ have the right to kill combatants$_A$ in one another's defence and in defence of their compatriots in so far as combatants$_A$ violate their jointly held rights to territorial integrity and political sovereignty via the use of lethal force. The point might seem entirely straightforward once one rejects the thesis that combatants are *not* on a par once the war has started. But one of its very controversial implications is worth drawing out. *Ex hypothesi*, combatants$_A$ are unjust attackers. Suppose that they are sent on a mission to kill some combatants$_V$. Whilst it might be tempting to describe war killings in collective terms—'platoon A killed soldiers of platoon V'—they are, in fact, carried out by individuals against other individuals. In the lethal conflict which pits those two sets of individual enemy combatants, individual combatants$_A$ will often kill, not so much, or not merely, in their own defence, but also in defence of their comrades. However, in so far an individual combatant$_A$ lacks the right to kill an individual combatant$_V$ in his own defence, he lacks the power to authorize his comrades to kill the latter—and thus his comrades may not kill combatant$_V$ in his defence. More strongly still, if combatants$_A$ who are not themselves directly threatened by combatants$_V$ decide to intervene in the set of lethal interaction which pits their comrades with combatants$_V$, then they must intervene *on the side of combatants$_V$* (or, indeed, of non-combatants$_V$ who are unjustifiably threatened by their comrades). In other words, they must kill fellow members of A rather than members of V. Moreover, *if* there is such a thing as a duty to kill unjustified attackers in defence of their victims (and I shall argue in Section 5.3 that there is), then combatants$_A$ not only are permitted, but are under a duty, to kill other combatants$_A$ in defence of combatants$_V$, non-combatants$_V$, or any other innocent third party who might be embroiled in that conflict.

That conclusion will seem unacceptable to many: for how could it be that combatants$_A$ may, let alone must, turn against their own side? And yet I believe that there is no place for patriotic partiality under those circumstances. The point is entirely uncontroversial in private cases. Suppose that, as André and Bernard are taking a stroll in the countryside, Bernard (this time) unjustifiably attacks Carl, who attempts to defend himself. One does not need to be a cosmopolitan to affirm that the fact that André and Bernard are both French whereas Carl is German does not provide André with a justification for killing Carl in defence of Bernard: one just may not come to the help of an unjust attacker by killing his victim. The same applies to the case of war. As we saw in Section 1.3, individuals can act in such way as to deliberately confer greater weight on the interests of fellow members in two cases: once the demands of sufficiency have been met, and if not giving greater weight to patriotic partiality (than to the demands of non-community-members) would threaten the very survival of the community as a politically sovereign body. But although cosmopolitan justice does allow individuals to confer greater weight on their political community's projects and goals in such cases, it forbids them to do so in furtherance of grievous wrongdoings such as unjustifiable and wrongful killings. Accordingly, for combatants$_A$ to kill combatants$_V$ in defence of other combatants$_A$ simply on the grounds of common membership in A would constitute such participation, and is therefore wrongful.

I suspect that at this juncture some would be tempted to insist that war sharply differs from the private case I have just described, in that *soldiers* who belong to the same army—an institution whose task it is to defend communal interest, and which trains its members to perform that task by creating and fostering very strong ties of loyalty between them—are permitted, or at the very least have the right, to defend one another at the expense of the enemy, even if the war is unjust *ad bellum*. More strongly still, some might object, at the very least they must not side with the enemy.

On that view, what does the work is a combination of patriotic partiality and the contractual and associational duties and rights which soldiers are putatively said to have towards one another. Again, however, it is not clear at all whether killing enemy combatants, who *ex hypothesi* are just combatants, falls within the remit of legitimate patriotic-*cum*-role-based partiality. Partiality so construed would not, I think, forbid combatants$_A$ from killing *fellow* combatants$_A$ if the latter are unjustifiably subjecting innocent noncombatants to a wrongful lethal attack. Take the case of the My Lai massacre. On 16 March 1968, American Warrant Office Hugh Thompson—a helicopter pilot during the Vietnam War—flew over My Lai and noticed injured and dead bodies of Vietnamese civilians. Upon realizing that the latter were being randomly killed by American soldiers (led by Lt Calley), he landed his helicopter between victims and attackers, and as he and his crew started lifting some of the injured villagers to safety, (allegedly) instructed his men to fire at the Americans if the latter kept shooting at the Vietnamese.[29] At the bar of cosmopolitan justice there is no doubt that Thompson acted justifiably—that the fact that he shared US citizenship with Calley and his men could not possibly constitute a consideration in favour of letting them commit such a grievously wrongful killing, let alone in favour of helping them in that task by taking part in the killing themselves. Why, then, should shared citizenship (combined with shared membership in the army) be a consideration in favour of helping one's fellow soldiers kill morally justified enemy combatants?

Because, some will undoubtedly argue, combatants are armed, whereas the Vietnamese villagers were not: it is one thing to kill (or threaten to kill) combatants of one's own army when the latter are wrongfully killing the unarmed; it is another to do so when they are themselves under threat. But clearly this putative reply will not do. For even though $combatants_A$ might have a greater excuse for killing $combatants_V$ than for killing unarmed non-combatants, *ex hypothesi*, $combatants_A$ are no more permitted, indeed no more have the right, (deliberately) to kill $combatants_V$ in self-defence than they are permitted, let alone have the right, (deliberately) to kill innocent civilians at first strike. And so if patriotic partiality cannot forbid $combatants_A$ to kill their comrades in defence of those civilians, it cannot forbid them to kill them in defence of $combatants_V$. If cosmopolitan justice permits, indeed mandates, $combatants_A$ to kill fellow $combatants_A$ in defence of unarmed innocent civilians, then it also permits, indeed mandates, them to do so in defence of armed justified $combatants_V$. Pending further considerations to the contrary, in other words, *prima facie* they are under a duty to defect to the *ad bellum* just side, however controversial the point might be.

---

[29] I say 'allegedly' because accounts differ as to whether Thompson really issued that threat. See D. L. Anderson (ed.), *Facing My Lai* (Lawrence, KS: University Press of Kansas, 1998), 27ff, for Thompson's own recounting of the massacre at a 1994 conference organised by Tulane University—at which he does not, in fact, unambiguously either deny or admit having used those words. See also M. Bilton and K. Sim, *Four Hours in My Lai* (Harmondsworth: Penguin Books, 1992), esp. 136–40. There is a difference, of course, between one's fellow soldiers attacking unarmed civilians and their attacking just combatants: namely, that at least as things stand, soldiers can reasonably be expected to know that the former is grievously wrong (as well as the most serious offence under the laws of war), whereas they usually will not know that they may not kill enemy combatants in prosecution of an unjust cause (given the training they receive and the enduring appeal of the orthodox account). But lack of knowledge at best provides them with an excuse, and not a justification, for so acting—as does duress, in fact. My concern here is with the latter, not the former. I am grateful to Jonathan Quong for pressing me on this point.

## 2.4 PATRIOTIC PARTIALITY AND
## COLLATERAL DAMAGE

Let us take stock. I noted at the outset that a normative account of wars of collective self-defence must speak to war's constitutive acts of killing. The right to wage and fight in such a war, in other words, is *inter alia* a right to kill. The reductive strategy, which regards the right to kill in wars as a particular example of defensive rights in general, sought to provide such an account against the background of a cosmopolitan theory of justice which on the one hand proscribes agents from inflicting harm upon others solely on the basis of political membership, and on the other hand permits them to kill aggressors in defence of their and their compatriots' jointly held rights to territorial integrity and collective-self-determination. Combatants do not merely kill other combatants, however: they also (usually) kill non-combatants, whose plight is central, as a matter of fact, to both the law and the morality of war. In Section 2.3.2 I noted that participants in an unjust war of aggression contribute to the wrongdoings inflicted on the aggressed parties to different degrees and in different ways, and that only those agents whose contribution would render them liable to the use of force *simpliciter* are liable to being killed. Others, whose contribution does not meet that condition, might lose their right not to be subject to lesser forms of harm or, indeed, might be liable to having their interest in survival somewhat discounted when the aggressed party's military decide which tactical objectives to pursue and thus which civilians will be killed foreseeably though not unintentionally. As we also saw earlier, however, an agent may sometimes have a justification for subjecting *innocent* third parties to a wrongful threat of lethal harm. Often, the agent foresees the harm but does not intend to cause it. In such cases, I argued, even if the agent may kill those individuals, they in turn may kill him in self-defence—precisely because they have not acted in such a way as to warrant the threat which he poses to them. Consider, paradigmatically, tactical bombers$_V$ who target A's munitions factories in the knowledge (though not with the intention) that the bombs will kill scores of non-combatants$_A$ who live in the vicinity. It is a familiar claim, in just war theory, that the justness of their cause furnishes tactical bombers$_V$ with a justification for posing a wrongful threat to non-combatants$_A$. Less familiar, but nevertheless plausible, is the view that although they may kill those non-combatants, the latter in turn may retaliate in their own defence—precisely because they have not acted in such a way as to warrant the threat which tactical bombers$_V$ pose to them.

But now some difficulty arises. For cosmopolitan justice, political member-ship is not, *per se*, an appropriate basis for the conferral or denial of funda-mental human rights. By that token, it is not an appropriate basis for the justified infringement of such rights. In the case at hand, however, comba-tants$_V$ bomb A's munitions factories and foreseeably though unintentionally kill some non-combatants$_A$ in order to weaken A's military effort as a means better to defend their and their compatriots' individual and jointly held rights. Whether one can justify this course of action on cosmopolitan grounds remains to be seen. For it is one thing to confer greater priority on one's interests and on the interests of one's compatriots than on the interests of combatants$_A$ who, *ex hypothesi*, act wrongfully; it is quite another to kill non-combatants$_A$, albeit unintentionally, in self-defence and in defence of the rights of one's compatriots, given that those non-combatants have not lost their own right not to be killed *and* that their membership in A *per se* and combatants$_V$' membership in V *per se* should have no bearing on the latter's justification for so acting. To be clear: the difficulty is not that of justifying collateral damage itself, for on agent-neutral grounds there might well be powerful justifications for permitting combatants who fight in defence, not so much of *their* individual and jointly held rights, but rather as a means to enforce norms against aggression, unintentionally (though foreseeably) to kill innocent bystanders. The difficulty is that of justifying collateral damage from the standpoint of the account of defensive rights which I offered in Sections 2.2 and 2.3.2, to which partiality—here, collectively understood—is central.

Those points raise the following three questions: (1) On what grounds, if any, may combatants$_V$ give priority to their own compatriots by uninten-tionally but foreseeably killing innocent non-combatants$_A$? (2) If non-combatants$_A$ in turn may kill combatants$_V$ in defence of their own lives, do they have the (Hohfeldian) power to transfer their permission to combatants$_A$? (3) If so, does this not undermine the point made in Section 2.3.2 that combatants$_A$, who prosecute an *ad bellum* unjust war, may not kill comba-tants$_V$, who wage an *ad bellum* just war?

Before addressing those questions I need to take one important issue out of the way. My focus in this section is on collateral damage, by which I mean in this instance killing by, for example, dropping bombs on munitions factories which are located in densely populated areas. There are other kinds of harm which combatants and their leaders typically inflict, or contribute to inflicting, on non-combatants, such a shortern life-expectancy, hunger, and general poverty. If it is permissible to inflict lethal collateral damage, then *a fortiori* and other things roughly equal it is permissible to inflict collateral harm that is lesser than (immediate) death. In both kinds of cases, however, it will be appropriate to say that combatants$_V$ justifiably infringe non-combatants' right not to be harmed. As I noted in Section 1.2.1, agents are under a *prima facie* duty not to harm innocent bystanders in the course of defending their or other people's fundamental rights, though are sometimes justified in not fulfilling their duty. But as I also averred then, agents are not under a *prima facie* duty to divest themselves of the resources they need for a minimally decent life, thereby sacrificing their own prospects, in order to save the needy. By deciding to wage, and thus finance, a war of collective self-defence against A, citizens$_V$ might become unable to continue to help needy individuals in other communities without jeopardizing their own prospects for a minimally decent life. There is thus a sense in which their decision to go to war will result in severe harm (which they foresee but do not necessarily intend) for those individuals. In this case however, citizens$_V$ cannot be described as infringing a right of those individuals, since there is no such right in the first instance under those circumstances. To put the point differently, they need not take those harms into account when assessing whether their decision to go to war is a proportionate response to A's wrongdoing.

In other cases, they must take those harms into account. Suppose that V's leaders and citizens face the following choice: they can either wage their war of defence with sophisticated weapons thanks to which only 15,000 non-combatants$_A$ will die in the bombings but 300,000 needy individuals from neutral community N will be left without life-saving resources; or they can wage a cheaper war, in which case 30,000 non-combatants$_A$ will die but only 150,000 needy individuals$_N$ will starve to death (since V will be able to divert extra resources towards them.) V would win their war under both courses of action— that is to say, they would regain the resources and freedoms which are necessary for a minimally decent life. With that stipulation in place, and given that (as we saw in Section 1.3) citizens$_V$ are under a duty of justice to help those in need under those circumstances, it is appropriate to describe them as justifiably infringing the rights of non-combatants$_A$ not to be killed and the rights of individuals$_N$ to receive assistance. If the numbers are roughly equal, then V ought to wage the more expensive war, on the grounds that it is morally worse to kill the innocent than to let them die. But when numbers are not roughly equal, and when V themselves would not be worse off under one course of action than the other, then it is not so clear that V ought to weigh the lives they destroy more heavily than they weigh the lives they allow to be lost. This is one respect in which the cosmopolitan theory of justice I defended in Chapter 1 has important implications for the *ad bellum* principle of proportionality.

In the remainder of this section, however, I focus on combatants$_V$' act of foreseeably though unintentionally killing non-combatants in the course of defending theirs and their compatriots' rights. Let us begin with the first of our three questions: namely, whether the act is permissible. Two paragraphs ago I outlined a scenario where combatants$_V$ must decide whether to bomb a munitions factory in the knowledge that, in so doing, they will kill some non-combatants$_A$. I shall argue presently that patriotic partiality does have a role to play in such cases. Beforehand, however, let us examine a very different scenario, where it does not have place. Suppose that, other things being equal, combatants$_V$ must choose between bombing a munitions factory which is controlled by A but is located on V's territory (factory$_V$), as a result of which they will kill some non-combatants$_V$, and bombing a munitions factory which is controlled by A and is located on A's territory (factory$_A$), as a result of which they will kill some non-combatants$_A$. May they opt for the latter on the grounds that they are generally permitted to give priority to their compatriots over the lives of non-combatants$_A$, however innocent the latter are of the wrongdoing committed by their leaders and combatants$_A$ against V's members? In private, domestic cases, patriotic partiality clearly has no place. Suppose that André, in the course of defending his life, has a choice between killing Carl and foreseeably killing Bernard, and killing Carl and foreseeably killing Werner, a German bystander who is wholly innocent of Carl's wrong-doing. According to cosmopolitan justice he may not confer greater weight on Bernard's life than on Werner's simply on the basis that the former is, whilst the latter is not, a compatriot.[30] Can we infer, then, that combatants$_V$ may not opt to bomb the factory located on A on grounds of patriotic partiality?

We can infer that they may not: whatever justification they may invoke in support of this strategy cannot appeal to patriotic partiality, at least not if one's account of war is to remain resolutely cosmopolitan. That said, there are reasons in support of this particular act of bombing which a cosmopolitan can endorse.[31] By waging war against V, one might hold, A's regime wrongfully impose harm on non-combatants$_V$ which they do not impose on their own compatriots, and combatants$_V$ may thus redistribute harm away from the latter to the former. Put differently, it would be doubly unfair for non-combatants$_V$ to suffer harm at the hands of combatants$_V$ given that they already suffer harm—and unjustly at that—at the hands of combatants$_A$. If non-combatants$_V$ are exposed to a given risk of harm prior to their regime's

---

[30] One need not be a cosmopolitan to endorse that view: David Miller, for example, explicitly claims that in Thomson-type trolley cases one may not redirect the runaway trolley away from five workers stuck on the line towards a foreigner in preference to turning it towards compatriots. See D. Miller, 'Reasonable Partiality towards Compatriots', *Ethical Theory and Moral Practice* 8 (2005): 63–81, 74–5.

[31] I owe the essence of the argument that follows to Jonathan Quong.

defensive steps, and if combatants$_V$ have a choice between lowering this risk by bombing factory$_A$, thereby increasing the risk of harm to non-combatants$_A$, and increasing the risk to their compatriots by bombing factory$_V$, then they may do the former (at least if the total number of non-combatants harmed under both options remains the same.) But note that the harm-distribution argument has nothing to do with patriotic partiality. Suppose that A locates its factories in an area which is not inhabited by A's members, but which is near its borders with neighbouring neutral country N. At the bar of just harm-distribution, V would not have a lesser reason to target those factories, thus unintentionally killing non-combatants$_N$, than it would have to target factories located in the heart of A's urban network. In a similar vein, suppose that some of the factories controlled by A though located on V's territory are surrounded by refugees camps. Those camps are populated by non-V members whose predicament is caused by A's decision to wage a wrongful war against V. Given that those individuals are subject to wrongful harm at the hands of A, other things equal V has no lesser reason to redistribute harm away from them and onto non-combatants$_A$ than it has to redistribute harm away from non-combatants$_V$. To repeat, patriotic partiality plays no role, it seems, in justifying the infliction of collateral damage by combatants$_V$ on non-combatants$_A$.

However, it is central to yet another, fairly standard argument to the effect that combatants$_V$ may so act, to wit, that V's military and civilian officials have a special responsibility to protect their compatriots which provides them with a justification for instructing combatants$_V$ so to act.[32] Once again, this simply cannot be right, for two related reasons. First, the standard argument thus implies that stateless individuals, be they combatants or non-combatants, do not enjoy the protection awarded to state members. On cosmopolitan grounds this is unacceptable: if membership in a given political community rather than another such community is not a legitimate basis for conferring or justifiably infringing basic rights, neither is political membership rather than no membership at all.

Second, as we saw in Section 1.4, the rights, permissions, and duties of state officials supervene on the rights, permissions, and duties of citizens, such that

---

[32] See, for example, Hurka, 'Proportionality in the Morality of War', 60–1; F. M. Kamm, 'Failures of Just War Theory: Terror, Harm, and Justice', *Ethics* 114 (2004): 650–92, 674. Hurka invokes the special responsibility argument not merely in support of a nation's preference for the lives of its civilians as opposed to the lives of enemy civilians, but also in support of its preferences for its own soldiers as opposed to the lives of enemy civilians. For apt criticisms of Hurka's and Kamm's arguments, see D. Lefkowitz, 'Partiality and Weighing Harm to Non-Combatants', *Journal of Moral Philosophy* 6 (2009): 298–316.

they have the right to govern only if and to the extent that they do not violate the fundamental rights of both the state's members and outsiders. Moreover, it is precisely because those officials' directives provide agents with better conditions for the protection of their moral rights and enable them better to comply with their moral duties than they would have absent the state, that those directives are binding. We thus cannot infer from the claim that V's officials have special responsibilities to their compatriots the thought that they may authorize combatants$_V$ unintentionally to kill non-combatants$_A$ in preference to unintentionally killing non-combatants$_V$: we must first discern whether V's members themselves are permitted so to act.

In waging or authorizing a war of collective self-defence against A, V's members act in defence of their individually held rights not to die, be tortured, raped, or maimed at the hands of combatants$_A$, as well as in defence of their jointly held rights to political self-determination and territorial integrity. One might think that the former rights do not permit them to give priority to one another over non-combatants$_A$ (as per the domestic case), whilst the latter rights do, on the grounds that the loss of non-combatants$_V$' lives threatens those rights themselves: as we saw in Section 1.4, self-determination is a communal good, in the sense that it can be enjoyed only if a sufficiently high number of community members value it—which in turn requires that a sufficiently high number of community members actually survive. In the case at hand, however, we assume that combatants$_V$' choice, whether to (unintentionally) kill their compatriots or non-combatants$_A$, would not impair their chances of success overall. With that assumption in hand, the fact that the protection of jointly held rights is at issue, far from providing combatants$_V$ with a justification for targeting factory$_A$, would in fact dictate in favour of factory$_V$: for account must also be taken of the fact that non-combatants$_V$ are *ex ante* beneficiaries of V's war, whereas non-combatants$_A$ are not. The point is not unique to war. Suppose once again that Carl attacks André and Bernard on July 1914, and in so doing violates not merely their right not to be killed but also their jointly held rights over their house. Suppose further that André is in a position to kill Carl, and can do so either by shooting from such an angle as to unintentionally subject Werner to a given risk of death or by shooting from such an angle as to subject Bernard to such a risk. Suppose, finally, that Bernard stands a higher chance of surviving the attack and thus enjoying the aforementioned rights if André takes action than if he desists. Given that Bernard stands to benefit from André's defensive move and that Werner not only does not stand to benefit from it but in addition is innocent of Carl's wrongdoing, André must opt for subjecting Bernard to the risk. Likewise, I submit, with the choice faced by combatants$_V$ in the case at hand—though with two important qualifications. First, the argument from benefitting does not support the bombing of factory$_V$ if the bombing is more likely than not to kill the non-combatants$_V$ in the vicinity *and* if it is more likely than not that *those* non-combatants would not have died had V surrendered to A. Second, non-combatants$_A$ themselves sometimes stand to benefit from V's victory. (It seems clearly plausible that Germans who survived the war and found themselves in what was then to become West Germany did far better in the long term out of the Allies' victory in World War II than they would have done had the Nazis not been defeated.) This may well provide combatants$_V$ with a justification for imposing collateral damage on them, though one which would not in any way appeal to patriotic partiality.[33]

So far, we have examined a case where combatants$_V$ must decide between unintentionally killing non-combatants$_A$ and unintentionally killing non-combatants$_V$. There, I claimed, patriotic partiality has no place. But suppose now, in the standard case of tactical bombing, that they must decide whether to bomb a munitions factory which is located on A's territory, as a result of which some non-combatants$_A$ will die. In this case, there is no alternative in the form of unintentionally killing non-combatants$_V$. V's leaders and combatants thus face the following dilemma: either they protect their fellow compatriots from the harms attendant on losing the war by making strategic choices which will result in the (unintended) deaths of innocent non-combatants$_A$, or they desist from making such choices at all, in which case those non-combatants$_A$ will survive but their own compatriots will suffer those harms at the hands of A's leaders and combatants. Bluntly put, they can either kill non-combatants$_A$ or let their compatriots die. Now, as we saw in the Introduction, *other things equal*, there is a stronger presumption against killing than there is against letting die. In the case at hand, the innocent individuals whose lives are at stake differ in that some have a special relationship with V's leaders and combatants (of co-membership in a sovereign political community), whereas others do not. The question, then, is whether this relationship makes things not equal, such that we have a case where letting one's compatriots die is morally worse than killing non-combatants$_A$—indeed (more strongly put still) is impermissible whilst killing non-combatants$_A$ is permissible.

---

[33] I thus agree with McMahan that one must take into account benefits accruing from the war when considering whether one may subject non-combatants at risk of dying. Unlike McMahan, however, I believe that one must take into account not merely *ex ante* but also *ex post* benefits. See J. McMahan, 'The Just Distribution of Harm Between Combatants and Noncombatants', *Philosophy & Public Affairs* 38 (2010): 342–79, esp. 365. I shall say more about harm-shifting towards those who stand to benefit from a war in Section 5.5.2, where I address the issue of collateral damage in wars of humanitarian intervention.

In private, domestic cases, that special relationship does not tip the balance in favour of killing foreigners *qua* foreigners and against letting one's compatriots *qua* compatriots die—any more than it tips the balance in favour of killing a foreigner and against killing a compatriot. Suppose that André realises that the only way he can save Bernard's life from Carl's attack is by shooting at him from such an angle as to also kill Werner—foreseeably though unintentionally. Now, it is not clear at all (at least to me) that André may so act. But *if* he may so act, it cannot be in virtue of the fact that he and Bernard share the same nationality, whereas Werner is, in that respect at least, an outsider. To repeat, Werner's life should have exactly the same weight in André's eyes as would the life of a French bystander. The challenge, for the cosmopolitan, is to find support for the claim that combatants$_V$ are permitted unintentionally to kill non-combatants$_A$ in the course of missions the end of which is to ensure that their compatriots do not continue to suffer the grievous rights violations which gave V its just cause.

It might be tempting at this juncture to accept that cosmopolitan justice cannot accede to the imposition of collateral lethal damage by V's agents onto non-combatants$_A$ as an alternative to letting their compatriots die. But the costs of such a move would be enormous indeed, since we would have to rule out as unjust any war of collective self-defence which involves the imposition of those harms—in other words, in an age where belligerents have long-range air power and are faced with enemies who are more than willing deliberately to locate their military installations in densely populated areas, more or less any such war. Unless it can find a way to justify the unequal weighing of non-combatants' lives on both sides of the divide without giving undue importance to political membership, cosmopolitan justice seems indeed committed to condemning as unjust all wars of collective self-defence in the modern age. If that is so, there is a strong case for rejecting it as a plausible moral theory, such is the intuitive pull of the thought that sovereign political communities do have the (*prima facie*) right to defend themselves against an unwarranted aggression.

It seems to me that a plausible justification for unequal weighing lies in agents' personal prerogative to confer greater weight on their *own* rights than on the rights of strangers. Let us return to an earlier case, whereby Carl throws an incendiary bomb on a house which André and Bernard jointly own and currently occupy—with a view to forcing them to relinquish their rights over it to him. Assume further (as I did in Section 2.3.1) that the loss of their house would severely compromise André's and Bernard's prospects for a minimally decent life. By killing Carl, André protects his own right not to be killed as well as Bernard's, and their jointly held right of ownership over the house.

Suppose now that the only way in which André can do so is by killing Carl and at the same time cause the death, foreseeably but unintentionally, of bystander Werner. André's permission so to act, *if* he does indeed have it in that particular case, is grounded in the importance to him of securing not only his individual right not to be killed but also his right, which he holds jointly with Bernard, over the house. By parity of reasoning, combatants$_V$, when bombing A's munitions factories and thereby unintentionally killing non-combatants$_A$, defend their own lives as well as the lives of their compatriots, *and* their jointly held rights to territorial integrity and political sovereignty— rights which warrant protecting by force precisely because (as we saw above) they are constitutive of a minimally decent life. Combatants$_V$ do, and indeed may, assign greater weight to their compatriots' fundamental interests than on the lives of non-combatants$_A$ in such cases, in virtue *not* of common membership in V alone, but rather as a necessary means to defend the fundamental rights which they too hold jointly with those other agents.

This defence of patriotic partiality presupposes that V's members, *qua* combatants and/or citizens, are not under a duty to surrender to A, even though their refusal to surrender causes innocent non-combatants$_A$ to die. One might wonder whether V ought not, in fact, to surrender (both in the private and in the war cases), in the light of those particular costs. For suppose that they could surrender immediately and, as a result, 'only' lose control over their territory and institutions: in so doing, they would survive A's admittedly unlawful aggression and would avoid killing innocent persons. *If* the choice, thus, is between, on the one hand, losing rights lesser than the right not to be killed and avoiding innocent deaths, and, on the other hand, successfully defending those rights by causing such deaths, it might seem that they should opt for the former course of action, not the latter. Given what we know of the conduct of unwarrantedly bellicose regimes, I have serious doubts as to how likely it is that a peaceful and immediate surrender would spare the lives of V's members. But let us suppose for the sake of argument that this indeed is the choice with which V's members are faced. To say that they ought to surrender is tantamount to claiming that individuals are under a duty to submit to a regime which, after all, is willing *ex hypothesi* to invade them by force unwarrantedly, and which will in all likelihood unwarrantedly impose its unjust rule by force. It is in effect tantamount to claiming that V's members are under a duty to submit themselves to an oppressive dictatorship, though the latter would seriously impair their prospects for a minimally decent life, for the sake of ensuring that innocent persons should not die, and however unintentional their death. It may well be that V's citizens must surrender if they cannot win their war other than by (unintentionally) killing ten million non-combatants$_A$. But to say that they must do so even if they would kill only a few thousand in the course of defending themselves is far too demanding indeed.

I have assumed so far that A's leaders and combatants violate rights to the freedoms and resources necessary to V's prospects for a minimally decent life. But suppose that they violate rights which protect interests above and beyond the decency threshold. In such cases, to hold V's leaders and combatants under a duty to surrender does not strike me as too demanding. I argued in Section 2.3.1 that the protection of V's right to one of its small empty island provides combatants$_V$ with a justification for killing combatants$_A$ only if the latter subject them to a threat of grievous harm. Suppose that the island is far from V's territory, but very close to A's, and that A's soldiers would employ lethal force if met with resistance. Suppose further that V's officials come to the conclusion that defensive force short of war will not work, and that they can persuade A's forces to leave the island only by bombing their supply lines at their source—in so doing foreseeably though unintentionally killing a number of non-combatants$_A$. Suppose finally that A's regime will not use a successful invasion of the island as a platform from which to mount a large-scale invasion of V's mainland. It is hard to see, in that case, how the loss *per se* of their rights over this small island, which would not cause V's members to have a less than minimally decent life, could justify killing innocent individuals. More controversially still, the point holds even if A invades a portion of V's inhabited mainland under the same circumstances—even if, in other words, A's invasion, if unchecked, would lead to redrawing V's borders without at the same time jeopardizing the prospects for a minimally decent life of V's members. In a nutshell, for the infliction of lethal collateral damage to be permissible, it must occur via defensive steps which are necessary to defending rights the violation of which would undermine rights-holders' prospects for a minimally decent life. If that condition is not met, and if the war cannot be fought and won other than by inflicting such damage, then surrender is mandatory.[34]

Before concluding, it is worth highlighting some of the features of my argument in favour of unequal weighing. First, it is not an argument in favour of conferring lesser weight on non-combatants$_A$ *qua* non-combatants$_A$. Rather, it only supports the view that combatants$_V$ are permitted to give

---

[34] This is another way of making the familiar point that war must be a proportionate response to the wrongdoing inflicted. But note that in the proportionality calculus, only harms to the innocent are included: combatants who carry out the wrongdoing of aggression have lost their claim to have the loss of their lives included in the calculus.

priority to their own compatriots *if* that is the only way to win a war in which their own rights, *qua* citizens, are at stake. Crucially, the justification for the permission also applies when the non-combatants who die as a result of combatants$_V$' actions belong to a neutral community. Suppose that André has a choice between collaterally killing Werner and collaterally killing John— a British subject who happens to pass by. At the bar of cosmopolitan justice, he certainly may not opt to kill Werner rather than John on the grounds that the former shares Carl's nationality. By parity of reasoning, combatants$_V$ may not invoke non-combatants$_A$' shared nationality with wrongdoing combatants$_A$ as a justification for bombing the factories near which the latter live, as opposed to factories which are located next to the border which A shares with neutral community N and the destruction of which would cause the death of non-combatants$_N$.[35] Second, it is not an argument in favour of conferring greater weight on the lives and interests of combatants$_V$ *qua* combatants over the lives of non-combatants$_A$ as such: rather, it is an argument in favour of conferring greater weight on one's lives and interests as well on the lives of one's compatriots precisely to the extent that one's individual *and jointly held* fundamental rights are under attack.

At first sight, the conclusion reached in the standard case of tactical bombing seems inconsistent with the conclusion reached in the case where combatants$_V$ had to choose between the unintentional killing of non-combatants$_V$ and the unintentional killing of non-combatants$_A$. For in the latter case, I argued, patriotic partiality has no role to play. How can it be, then, that combatants$_V$ are not allowed to kill non-combatants$_A$ as a means not to let their compatriots *qua* compatriots die in the first scenario, but are allowed so to act in the second scenario? This is because in the first case, combatants$_V$ themselves are in a position to inflict harm on either one of those two groups as a by-product of the steps which they take in defence of their jointly held rights, and must thus decide how to distribute that harm. In the second case, by contrast, their choice is not a choice between killing some versus killing others; rather, it is a choice between killing some as a result of which others to whom they stand in a special relationship and with whom they hold some fundamental rights will survive, or not killing some as a result of which those others will die and the jointly held fundamental rights will be

---

[35] Kamm also seems to think that members of a political community may confer greater weight on saving themselves as a group, at the cost of the lives of non-combatants who belong to the enemy. On the issue of neutral non-combatants, however, I disagree with her, for she believes that V ought to confer greater weight on the lives of non-combatants$_N$ than on the lives of non-combatants$_A$, on the grounds that the latter belong to the community with which V is at war. See Kamm, 'Failures of Just War Theory: Terror, Harm, and Justice', 674–5.

threatened by combatants$_A$. It is not incoherent to invoke patriotic partiality in support of doing the latter but to deny its appeal for the former, at least on the assumption that, by shifting harm onto non-combatants$_V$, combatants$_V$ do stand a reasonable chance of restoring the rights which they are seeking to defend. Suppose that factory$_V$ and factory$_A$ both manufacture nuclear weapons ten times as powerful as those dropped on Hiroshima and Nagasaki; suppose further that A will subject V to a nuclear attack in the near future unless they either surrender or bomb one of those factories. In opting for bombing either, however, combatants$_V$ would trigger a crippling, large-scale nuclear disaster in the relevant community. Assuming *for the sake of argument* that a community may defend itself in such a way when faced with that particular threat, patriotic partiality would permit them to bomb factory$_A$ rather than factory$_V$.

Furthermore, it might also seem that the argument from benefit, which blocks patriotic partiality in the non-standard case, and the argument from the personal prerogative, which makes room for it in the standard case, pull in radically different directions in yet another, crucially important scenario. Suppose that if tactical bombers$_V$ bomb factories$_A$ at very high altitude, they will incur a 2 per cent risk of being gunned down by A's anti-aerial defence systems and unintentionally kill 500 non-combatants$_A$ in the vicinity. If they fly lower they will be able to identify their targets much more precisely, and thus will kill far fewer non-combatants$_A$, but will run a 10 per cent risk of being gunned down. At the bar of the personal prerogative, given that *their* lives are at stake, it would seem that they may opt for the former strategy. At the bar of the benefitting argument, given that they would benefit from V's victory, it would seem that they ought to redirect the risks attendant on the operation onto them and away from non-combatants$_A$. Remember, however, that harm-redirection is not permitted by the benefit argument if there is a higher than 50 per cent probability that those victims would not have died had V surrendered. Suppose, then, that bombers$_V$ stand a higher chance of surviving if the war is fought *and* fought by them under either course of action, than if they did not participate in it (either because V surrenders, or because they are not called up to fight.) Given that they would kill fewer non-combatants$_V$ by flying low, this is what they should do. But if they stand a lower chance of surviving the war by flying low than they would have if the war were not fought at all or, though fought, not by them, then the personal prerogative permits them to fly high (subject to the numbers of non-combatants killed.)

Finally, it is worth pointing out that my account of the conditions under which V's members are (sometimes) justified in giving priority to one another's fundamental rights over non-combatants$_A$' rights does not support the view that they are under a duty to one another, *qua* compatriots, so to act. For on my account, unequal weighting is justified in virtue of V's citizens' personal prerogative to further their interests in the communal goods of territorial integrity and collective self-determination. Self-interest can at best support a permission but not a duty to one another, so to act. Clearly, *if* V's citizens resort to war as a means of collective self-defence (standardly via their regime), then those of their compatriots who are best equipped to do the fighting (in other words, combatants) must carry out those missions. Theirs, however, is a contractual duty which is constrained by what they as citizens are permitted to do. But it is not a duty which they have, *qua* citizens and together with fellow citizens, to one another *qua* compatriots, to act in such a way as to unintentionally kill innocent non-combatants who belong to the enemy or to neutral parties. Crucially, this point is compatible with the view (which I shall defend at greater length in Section 7.3) that conscription for the sake of national defence is legitimate, provided that it is understood and justified not as a mechanism to enforce citizens' duty to their compatriots to help protect the latter's rights, but rather as a mechanism to enforce citizens' duty not to free-ride on their compatriots' willingness to fight for rights which they all deem in their individual interest to preserve.[36]

To recapitulate, I have argued that combatants$_V$ have a justification (as provided by their just cause) for inflicting collateral damage on innocent non-combatants$_A$. But as we saw in Section 2.2, in so far as the latter have not (*ex hypothesi*) lost their right not to be killed, they would be permitted to kill their justified attackers in their own defence should they have the wherewithal to do so. The question, at this juncture, is whether they have the (Hohfeldian) power to transfer their permission to third parties—most obviously to combatants$_A$. To claim that they do is tantamount to granting the latter the permission to kill combatants$_V$. In Section 2.3.2, however, I argued that combatants$_A$ may not kill combatants$_V$ in their own defence. May they do so in defence of their compatriots? I do not think so. For the latter in transferring their permission to combatants$_A$ would in effect enable those combatants to continue to participate in the grievous wrongdoing of aggression *vis-à-vis* V. Admittedly, in defending themselves by killing combatants$_V$ they too would enable their regime to continue so to act. But whilst they are

---

[36] For if it were understood and justified in that way, conscription would be tantamount to institutionalizing a duty which citizens$_V$ in fact do not have: namely, a duty to their compatriots to protect the latter's rights at the cost of distant and innocent strangers' interest in survival. For the view that the relationship of co-citizenship generates associative duties in war which trump general duties not to harm outsiders, see Lazar, *War and Associative Duties*.

not under a duty to allow themselves to die for the sake of stopping that wrongdoing (of which, crucially, they are innocent), their interest in survival is not strong enough to be protected by a power to allow those very agents who carry out a wrongful war of aggression against V and its members to target justified combatants$_V$—any more than bystander V, caught in the crossfire between a bank robber and a policeman, has the power to permit the former to kill the latter in her own defence. Agent-neutral considerations (in this case, bringing an end to A's wrongful war of aggression against V) outweigh non-combatants$_A$' agent-relative justification for conferring on combatants$_A$ the permission to kill combatants$_V$. Far from killing combatants$_V$, combatants$_A$ ought instead to surrender to them, as a means both to stop their regime's wrongful aggression and to forestall justified attacks by combatants$_V$ on their compatriots.

## 2.5 CONCLUSION

When thinking about wars of collective self-defence, we tend to say, loosely, that 'state A wrongfully attacks V and state V justifiably defends itself against A.' But this will not do, for two reasons. First, so stated, the statement does not do justice to the complex set of actions and actors which characterize an act of military aggression and the concomitant act of collective self-defence. Instead, we ought to mean the following: A's individual agents together violate the rights of V's individual agents, on several levels and in different ways. A's political and military leaders order A's individual combatants (sometimes with the authorization of A's citizens) to act in violation of those rights—for example, by crossing the border into V's territory. Combatants$_A$ in turn acquiesce in those orders, and not only act in the indicated ways but in addition use lethal force against V's attempts to block their attack. V, in that last clause, must be understood in several ways: as V's political and military leaders who, (sometimes) on the authorization (implicit or explicit) of V's individual citizens, order individual combatants$_V$ to use lethal force to block combatants$_A$' attack; as those citizens themselves (when appropriate), and as the combatants tasked with repelling the attack. The resultant war between A and V consists in a series of acts of killing on both sides—some justified, others not. To the extent that the initial wrongdoings committed by A's individual leaders and combatants (acting together) consist in violating the rights of V's members, the right as held by V's individual combatants to kill combatants$_A$ is a right to use lethal force in defence of those rights. To the extent that those wrongdoings are backed by lethal force, the right to go to war is a right that soldiers have, not simply to defend their fundamental basic rights, as individuals or citizens, but also to defend their compatriots' similar rights (in which case they do so by way of the latter's exercise of a justified Hohfeldian power).

Second, the claim that a given rights violation is a just cause for war is too rough. That claim in fact comprises two distinct (though related) sub-claims: the claim that a given right is important enough on principle to warrant defending by force against those who violate it even if one inflicts lethal collateral damage on innocent non-combatants, and the claim that there are identifiable agents who do violate that right in such a way that they are liable to having force used against them. I have argued in this chapter that individual rights not to be killed or grievously maimed, as well as jointly held rights to political self-determination and territorial integrity, are important enough in that sense. In addition, we need to distinguish between a narrow just cause and a wide just cause. The former is a wrongdoing which provides its victims with a justification for launching a lethal attack against wrongdoers; the latter is a wrongdoing which provides its victims with a justification for making a non-lethal forceful defensive move against wrongdoers in the knowledge (or at least on the reasonable assumption) that the latter will retaliate with unwarranted lethal force and thus provide victims with a narrow just cause for (this time) waging war. Paradigmatic cases of collective self-defence against military aggression obscure the distinction, since they typically are responses to a wrongdoing which, carried out as it is through the use of lethal force, gives rise to a narrow just cause. Yet the distinction is absolutely essential, because unless we can identify, in any given case, wrongdoers who are liable to being killed, or wrongdoers who are liable to being subject to non-lethal force (as the first step towards a full-scale war), we will not be able to claim that the war is justified. Subsistence wars, as we shall now see, represent a case in point.

# 3

# Subsistence wars

## 3.1 INTRODUCTION

In Chapter 1 I argued that all individuals, wherever they reside, have fundamental rights to the material resources without which they could not hope to
live a minimally decent life. Those rights—which I have called subsistence
rights and which are held against fellow community members *and* foreigners—include the following: negative rights not to be interfered with when
attempting to secure those resources as well as not to be subject to avoidable ill
health and physical harms (henceforth, human rights not to be *subject* to
severe deprivation—or RSD), and positive rights to be provided with the
assistance they need to lift themselves out of their predicament (human rights
to *receive* help—or RRH.) In Chapter 2 I argued that the right to wage war is a
right held by individuals to use lethal force in defence of their fundamental
collective and individual rights—particularly, though not only, when their
aggressors threaten their lives in the course of a large-scale attack on the
territorial integrity and political sovereignty of their country. Those values,
we saw, are important enough to warrant defending by force (whether lethal
or not, depending on the form which the violation of the relevant rights
takes). My aim in this chapter is to assess whether, and if so, under what
conditions, the very deprived have the right to wage war against the foreign
affluent if the latter violate subsistence rights.

Just war theory tends to neglect subsistence wars.[1] This might be because
they are thought unlikely to occur: the populations of countries which are in a

---

[1] But see David Luban's article 'War and Human Rights', in which he devotes a couple of
paragraphs to the issue. Luban asks us to imagine the case of a landlocked community A which suffers
from devastating drought, and of its coastal neighbour B which prevents A from accessing water.
Luban's view—which I share, and for which I shall provide a full defence in Section 3.2.2—is that
A has a case for invading B so as to forge a route to the coast. For the view that victims of violations of
positive rights to assistance may kill wrongdoers, see S. Miller, 'Civilian Immunity, Forcing the
Choice, and Collective Responsibility', in I. Primoratz (ed.), *Civilian Immunity in War* (Oxford:
Oxford University Press, 2007), 116ff; 'Osama Bin Laden, Terrorism and Collective Responsibility',
in C. A. J. Coady and M. O'Keefe (ed.), *Terrorism and Justice: Moral Argument in a Threatened World*

position to take part in a large-scale conflict do not (on the whole) suffer from *severe* deprivation, and those who do suffer from it are unlikely ever to be able to go to war against the affluent. Accordingly, whilst an inquiry into subsistence wars is theoretically interesting, it has little practical relevance—or so one might object. However, there always have been conflicts over access to natural resources, in which what is at stake is, more often than not, the livelihood of those who either lack such resources or have them but (to reiterate) do not benefit from them, as set against the vastly more comfortable lifestyle of those who resist attempts to bring about a just distribution. In fact, such wars are also more likely to happen in the near future, particularly over water and oil. Consider the case of water. Without water, we die—of thirst, disease, and hunger; without access to water above and beyond the satisfaction of our daily bodily needs, we are no longer able to enjoy what many regard as a minimally decent life. Water is also in ever scarce supply, as a result both of growing demand and reduced availability, the latter in part brought about by global climate change. We do not know yet how to desalinize sea water cheaply and efficiently; nor do we know how to recycle human waste. We thus have to rely on fresh water to be found in rivers, basins, and aquifers. Unfortunately, however, those sources of water usually service several countries, of whom we simply cannot be sure that they will manage to allocate water shares fairly. Shared water systems have not, on the whole, made for regional peace. The Middle East and south-west Asia—whose water systems include, for the former, the rivers Jordan, Tigris, Euphrates, and Nile, and for the latter, the Indus—have long been beset by territorial disputes, some of which have openly concerned water. Alongside the Nile, for example, there have been military conflagrations between Egypt and the Sudan in border disputes to which water access was crucial. Explosive population growth in the Nile basin is likely to exacerbate the potential for conflicts. In a similar vein, access to the river Jordan has been a major factor in Middle-East conflicts. Finally, some geopolitical strategists have expressed worries about the potential for escalation of the conflict between India and Pakistan over Kashmir, as the river Indus and some of its tributaries run through it, and as aquifers in both countries are being gradually depleted. Unfortunately, we may have to assess sooner rather than later the legitimacy of the recourse to military force by comparatively water-rich communities that do not want to share access to

(Melbourne: Melbourne University Press, 2002), 55. For an expansionist account of justifications for lethal violence which includes violations of subsistence rights, see also T. Honderich, *After the Terror* (Edinburgh: Edinburgh University Press, 2002); *Terrorism for Humanity: Inquiries in Political Philosophy* (London: Pluto Press, 2003).

water with their comparatively water-poor neighbours, or by coastal communities whose governments refuse to relax patenting rights over desalinization technologies for the benefit of communities which do not have access to those technologies.[2]

Water is not the only vital natural resource over which conflicts are or might be occurring: so is oil, which is said by many to have been an important, not to say crucial, factor in both Gulf Wars. Without oil, and absent equivalent alternatives, world economies will perish. Those who have oil use it as a source of wealth which they (sometimes) convert into benefits and much needed infrastructure for their population; those who lack it need it to function—for transportation, industries, and so on. Likewise, *mutatis mutandis*, with natural gas. But oil reserves are not infinite; moreover, they are also located in conflict-prone areas such as the Middle East, or in areas which are the subject of longstanding territorial disputes. When located in land-locked areas, such as the Caspian Sea, they have to be transported through conflict zones, which leads to the increased militarization of oil politics. From the so-called Carter Doctrine, which regards the protection (by force if necessary) of American access to oil as a key part of US foreign policy, to China's growing involvement with oil-rich African countries such as the Sudan, or Russia's determination not to lose control over Chechnya and Dagestan (through which the Azerbadjian–Novorossyisk pipeline passes), oil, now more than ever, has become a national security concern for major and not so major powers, and a trigger point for transnational military conflicts. Conflicts have arisen and are likely to arise over its transport routes, the extent to which its owners make it available to the rest of the world at reasonable prices, and whether countries which share a reserve extract more than is thought legitimate by the others. Thus, disputes over equitable sharing of oil are thought by some to have been one of the reasons for Iraq's invasion of Kuwait in the summer of 1990; and it is not implausible to surmise that the US and Japan would use force to ensure the safe passage of oil through, respectively, the Strait of Hormuz or the South China Sea.[3]

---

[2] For accounts of water conflicts, see M. Klare, *Resource Wars: The New Landscape of Global Conflict* (New York: Henry Holt and Co., 2002), chs. 6 and 7; P. H. Gleick, 'Water and Conflict: Fresh Water Resources and International Security', *International Security* 18 (1993): 79–112; and J. R. Starr, 'Water Wars', *Foreign Policy* (1991): 17–36. For the Middle East case in particular, see, for example, H. Amery, 'Water Wars in the Middle East: A Looming Threat', *The Geographical Journal* 168 (2002): 313–23.

[3] For an analysis of conflicts over oil, see M. Klare, *Blood and Oil* (London: Penguin, 2005), esp. 58ff for an account of the first Gulf War as an oil war; see also his *Resource Wars*. See also, for example, L. Fawcett, 'Rivalry over Territory and Resources and the Balance of Peace and War: the 20th century', in G. a. N. Lundestad, O. (ed.), *War and Peace in the 21st Century and Beyond* (New Jersey: World Scientific, 2002); J. Selby, 'Oil and Water: The Contrasting Anatomies of

To be sure, access to, and control over, vital resources have always been causes for conflicts. There have always been water wars; and control of oil fields in the Persian Gulf has featured heavily in the geostrategic calculations of Britain and the US since the start of the twentieth century. However, there are grounds for believing that resource wars, which are often wars over what is needed for sheer human subsistence, are likely to occur more frequently than has perhaps been thought to be the case. For a start, we are witnessing an exponential population growth, which leads to ever rising demands for natural resources far in excess of what most countries are able to provide out of their own stock. That, in turn, is likely to exacerbate conflicts over disputed territories and exclusive economic zones at sea, and to encourage powerful countries to militarize their energy policy by taking part or, indeed, provoking regional conflicts with a view to securing access to oil. Furthermore, and relatedly, environmental damage contributes to water drought, which in turn adversely affects many countries' agricultural outputs, thereby leading to food shortages which affluent countries, preoccupied as they are to preserve their own standards of living, might not be willing to remedy via resource transfers. In addition, countries which are competing for increasingly scarce resources have tended to militarize their energy policy—for example, through arms transfers to, and military support for, exporting regimes whose grip on power over volatile areas is likely to become increasingly shaky.[4] Finally, and relatedly, the disillusionment felt by the impoverished at the inability or unwillingness of the powerful to remedy the aforementioned effects of resource scarcity (whilst lining up their own bank accounts with the proceeds of, for example, oil sales) is likely (together with the ready availability of small weapons) to provide militant groups with enough manpower to pursue their ends through violent means.[5]

Subsistence wars, therefore, are a salient and ongoing concern, and it is particularly urgent to examine some of the ethical issues which they raise. I argue, controversially, that cosmopolitan justice sometimes permits the very

---

Resource Conflicts', *Government and Opposition* 40 (2005): 200–24. But for a sceptical take on the connection between resource scarcity and war, see, for example, R. Dannreuther, *International Security: The Contemporary Agenda* (Cambridge: Polity Press, 2007). Oil (and for that matter, water) is not merely a resource over which violent conflicts are fought; access to it is also a means of warfare against those countries—most importantly, the USA—which are highly dependent on oil imports.

[4] For the militarization of energy policy, see, for example, M. Klare, *Rising Powers, Shrinking Planet* (Oxford: Oneworld Publications, 2008), esp. ch. 8, and *Resources Wars*.

[5] For a study of some connections between environmental degradation and armed conflict, see, for example, T. F. Homer-Dixon, 'On the Threshold: Environmental Changes as Causes of Acute Conflict', *International Security* 16 (1991): 76–116; 'Environmental Scarcities and Violent Conflict: Evidence from Cases', *International Security* 19 (1994): 5–40.

deprived to wage war against those who treat them unjustly. Subsistence rights, I claim in Section 3.2, are important enough to warrant defending by force provided that wrongdoers who meet the conditions for liability to attack can be identified. Moreover, as I show in Section 3.3, the very deprived themselves, and not merely their state, have the right to wage such a war. Finally, in Section 3.4 I argue that some individuals amongst the affluent are liable to attack for violating the subsistence rights of the very deprived. Note that I content myself with attempting to provide a normative framework for transnational conflicts between the affluent and the very deprived—leaving the case of civil wars to Chapter 4.

Before I begin, consider three comments. First, for the sake of stylistic convenience, I shall refer to those who are derelict in their duties of justice to distant strangers as 'the affluent'. I do not mean to suggest that affluent countries alone fail to act justly towards the world's very deprived. In fact, many of the countries in which severe poverty prevails are resource-rich but ruled by regimes which are either unable or unwilling to use the proceeds of resource exploitation towards alleviating poverty within their borders—a point which will prove important in Section 3.3 when tackling the issue of who may wage subsistence wars.[6] Still, given the vast disparity of wealth between a small number of countries with highly developed economies and a large number of others beset by severe poverty, the disproportionately vast resource consumption of the former relative to the latter, and the tendencies of those highly developed economies to prop up corrupt regimes for the sake of continued access to prized resources, it is not wholly unreasonable or implausible, I surmise, to use this particular label. By 'the very deprived' I shall mean, unless otherwise stated, those individuals in non-affluent countries who are subject to severe deprivation, as well as those states themselves: as we shall see in Section 3.3, it will sometimes be necessary to distinguish the latter from the former.

Second, I shall take for granted the claims, defended in Chapter 2, that the values of territorial integrity and political sovereignty are worth defending by force if need be, on cosmopolitan grounds. I shall also take for granted that

[6] This phenomenon, which is often called the 'resource curse', has been extensively studied. For a very good philosophical analysis (one which stresses the degree to which affluent countries are responsible for the curse), see L. Wenar, 'Property Rights and the Resource Curse', *Philosophy & Public Affairs* 26 (2008): 2–32. On a related note, the argument I deploy in this chapter to defend the right of the very poor to wage subsistence wars against the affluent can, with appropriate modifications, support a right on the part of the affluent to use lethal force against officials of very poor communities if the latter carry out policies which would suddenly and dramatically cause very severe poverty in affluent countries, and if those policies are unjust (subject, of course, to the resort to war meeting the standard requirements of last resort, proportionality, and so on). I am grateful to Tim Williamson for drawing my attention to this point.

combatants who defend those values in furtherance of their personal prerogative both as individuals and citizens may unintentionally (though foreseeably)
kill non-combatants who belong to the wrongdoing party—subject to the
conditions set out in Section 2.4. My aim in this chapter is in part to bring the
conclusions reached in Chapter 2 to bear on violations of subsistence rights.

Finally, the extent to which the policies conducted by the affluent contribute to causing severe deprivation in Third World countries is a fiercely
debated issue. It is a central contention of this book that policies and decisions
made by some communities can have such an enormously detrimental impact
on others as to constitute wrongdoings. With respect to policies currently
conducted by the affluent, let me venture the following, not implausible,
suggestions. Absent protectionist measures designed by the affluent to protect
their own markets from Third World countries' exports, producers in the
latter might have better life prospects. Absent patenting restrictions on vital
medical treatments, particularly for AIDS (which, let us not forget, has a
crippling effects on the society and economy of many sub-Saharan countries),
individuals in Third World countries might also have better prospects. Had
affluent countries paid greater attention to the necessity of combining rapid
and widespread privatization (a precondition for loans to developing
countries) with infrastructural investments, the very deprived might have
stood a better chance against withstanding the devastating impact of the
former. Were many Third World countries not burdened by cripplingly
heavy debt repayments for bad loans pushed on them by the affluent for
geostrategic reasons, their members might have better access to health care and
education. Were affluent countries not supporting dictators who plunder their
own country's natural wealth and divert aid payments to nefarious military
programmes, or worse, their personal bank accounts, those dictators' compatriots might also stand a better chance of living a minimally decent existence.
And so on. With these not implausible points in hand, let us ponder whether
severe deprivation is a just cause for going to war.[7]

---

[7] The policy literature on Third World deprivation is on the voluminous side. As a first cut, see,
for example, J. Sachs, *The End of Poverty* (London: Penguin, 2005); J. Stiglitz, *Globalization and its
Discontents* (New York: W. W. Norton and Company, 2006); W. Easterly, *The White Man's Burden:
Why the West's Efforts to Aid the Rest have done So Much Ill and So Little good* (Oxford: Oxford
University Press, 2006). For scepticism on the connection between trade barriers and the persistence
of severe deprivation in developing countries, see, for example, A. Panagariya, 'Agricultural
Liberalisation and the Least Developed Countries: Six Fallacies', in D. Greenaway (ed.), *The
World Economy: Global Trade Policy* (Oxford: Blackwell, 2005). For scepticism about the extent to
which patents deprive the very deprived of access to drugs, see, for example, A. Attaran, 'How do
Patents and Economic Policies Affect Access to Essential Medicines in Developing Countries?',
*Health Affairs* 23 (2004): 155–66. For a powerful argument to the effect that the IMF, the World
Bank, and their backers failed in Africa partly because of an unduly narrow and ideological

## 3.2  SEVERE DEPRIVATION AS A JUST
## CAUSE FOR GOING TO WAR

In this section I argue that violations of subsistence rights by the affluent towards the very poor sometimes provide the latter with a narrow just cause for going to war against the former—in the sense that those rights protect values which are worth defending by lethal force. Before examining violations of negative duties not to cause severe poverty (in Section 3.2.2) and violations of positive duties to remedy it (in Section 3.2.3), I consider the claim, which is sometimes made in traditional just war theory, that the recovery of wrongfully taken property is a just cause for war (Section 3.2.1). Note that when I say that violations of subsistence are a just cause of war, I mean simply that—that they are a just cause. They do not provide an all-things-considered justification for waging such a war, any more than the claim that violations of territorial rights does.

### 3.2.1  Subsistence wars and the recovery
### of wrongfully taken property

In some important strands of the tradition, severe poverty can be a *prima facie* just cause for war, at least when severe poverty is the result of the wrongful taking of property. It is in Grotius's magisterial *Rights of War and Peace* that we find the clearest exposition of that view.[8] According to Grotius, in the state of nature, things belong to no one in particular, and anything, except for the sea and the air, can be legitimately appropriated, first by commonly agreed division, then by first occupancy and legitimate transfers. Thus, barren and uncultivated land must be given to those who ask for it, even if they are strangers to the community which lives on that land—a point which lends

commitment to marketisation and liberalisation, see, for example, N. Woods, *The Globalizers: The IMF, the World Bank, and Their Borrowers* (Ithaca: Cornell University Press, 2006), esp. ch. 6. My point on debt repayment here is drawn from her discussion of Zaire, ibid., pp. 153 and 195. For a withering critique of the affluent's policies *vis-à-vis* Third World countries, see Pogge, *World Poverty and Human Rights*. For a powerful but ultimately unconvincing argument to the effect that the global order does not harm the very poor, see M. Risse, 'How Does the Global Order Harm the Poor?', *Philosophy & Public Affairs* 33 (2005): 349–76.

[8] Grotius, *The Rights of War and Peace* Book II, ch.II. For an interesting discussion of Grotius' theory of property, see J. Salter, 'Hugo Grotius: Property and Consent', *Political Theory* 29 (2001): 537–55. Grotius's account is internally inconsistent, as Barbeyrac noted in his marginal comments on the book. For Grotius also avers that if a needy agent takes resources from their current possessor, he owes restitution to the latter (II-II-IX). But if that is so, then the current possessor does have a right to those resources, which the needy agent is justified in infringing. That is not compatible with the claim that necessity reverts resources to the common stock.

support to colonial enterprises in, for example, the Americas. Crucially, the institution of private property is a creation of the human will, and is a means to provide human beings with the conditions for commodious living, on the understanding that they all have an equal interest in it. That is why, in cases of absolute necessity, one may take what belongs to someone else, not as permitted by charity, but as implied by the institution of private property itself: for a system of private property without such restrictions on legitimate ownership would not have been consented to, by rational men, as instrumental to commodious living. In case of dire necessity, therefore, 'one might enter again upon the Rights of the primitive Community' (Book II, II–VI.4)— whereby men appropriate from common stock. On Grotius's account, someone who, in the face of someone else's dire needs, holds on to the resources he had previously acquired is acting wrongfully, since he no longer has a right to them. In so far, therefore, as he wrongfully fails to revert property into the common stock, he has lost his right not to be attacked, and the very needy have a just cause for going to war against him. Note that his failure is not a failure not to give to the needy that to which they have a right. Rather, it is a failure not to interfere with their rightful appropriation of the resources they need to live commodiously. In that sense, the affluent are derelict, not in their positive duty to provide assistance to the very poor, but rather, in their negative duty not to prevent them from accessing what they need and what they may rightfully appropriate: if the affluent were to revert those resources to the common stock, and if the very poor proved unable to acquire them, their poverty would not be the result of the former's wrongdoing, and they would not, therefore, have a just cause for war.

Interestingly, Grotius's account of the connection between poverty and just cause was taken up in the eighteenth century by two of the most influential jurists in European legal history, Christian Wolff and Emerich de Vattel, whose treatises (*Jus Gentium Methodo Scientifica Pertractatum* (1749) for the former, and *Le Droit Des Gens* (1757) for the latter) form one of the bases of modern international law. Both argue, with Grotius, that the recovery of wrongfully taken property is a just cause for war, and both characterize the wrongdoing of the affluent nation, not as a refusal to revert resources to the common stock for subsequent appropriation by the very deprived nation, but as a refusal to sell the latter what it needs.[9]

---

[9] See Wolff, *Jus gentium methodo scientifica pertractatum* (Oxford: Clarendon Press, 1934); Vattel, *Le droit des gens, ou, Principes de la loi naturelle appliqués à la conduite et aux affaires des nations et des souverains* (Washington, DC: Carnegie Institute, 1916).

Cosmopolitans could not accept Wolff's and Vattel's claim that *nations* owe a duty to other *nations* not to appropriate resources to such an extent as to leave the latter destitute: for cosmopolitans, such property rights as there are must be held by individuals either taken singly (when they are said privately to own, for example, their house), or *qua* community members (when they are said collectively to own, for example, the oil fields which happen to be located under their community's territory.) Nor need they endorse the historical justification for private property which Grotius and others invoke in support of the view that the recovery of wrongfully taken property is a just cause for war. They do, however, accept the thought, implicit in Grotius's account, that political boundaries are irrelevant to basic entitlements; they can also comfortably agree that a community is guilty of grievous collective wrongdoing (as described in Section 1.2.3) if it holds on to natural resources which it should in fact revert to the common stock in order to enable others to appropriate them. In so far as the right to wage war is a right to use lethal force in defence of fundamental rights, they are thus open, on principle, to the view that such wrongdoing provides its victims with a (*prima facie*) just cause for war.

### 3.2.2 Severe deprivation and self-defence

That said, not all violations of subsistence rights take the form of wrongfully taking property or refusing to revert property to the common stock: severe deprivation also arises as a result of policies which contribute to causing it (in violation of the right not to be subject to severe deprivation), and policies which consist in a refusal to help its sufferers (in violation of the right to receive assistance). At first sight it seems that the view that such policies provide their victims with a just cause for war constitutes a radical departure from orthodox just war theory. This is because in the tradition, other than punishment for wrongdoing, the recovery of wrongfully taken property, and the defence of others, a community may go to war only if (a) its jointly held rights to political self-determination and territorial integrity (b) are subject to an armed attack. Subsistence wars between poor and affluent countries seemingly fail the test for such a war, since they are not a response to armed attacks, and since deprivation affects individuals as such, and not communities (or so one might insist). I shall argue here that subsistence wars meet criterion (a) in so far as they are a response to violations, by the affluent, of the right of the very deprived not to be subject to severe deprivation (RSD). Moreover, even if they did not, the very deprived still would have a just cause for waging a self-defensive war against the affluent. I shall also concede that subsistence wars as a response to violations of RSD (sometimes) fail criterion (b), but that this does not deprive the very deprived of a just cause for waging them. Note, before I begin, that by 'just cause' I shall mean (as per Section 2.3.1) either a narrow just cause for waging war or a wide just cause for using force in the foreknowledge (or at least on the plausible assumption) that war will ensue.

Let us start with (a). As we saw in Chapter 2, the violation of jointly held rights to territorial integrity and political self-determination can coherently be regarded as a just cause for resorting to war, on the grounds that those rights, which are held by individuals *qua* members of a political community, are instrumentally valuable to those individuals' prospects for a minimally decent life. Still, on that reading of the requirement, it seems that just war theory cannot accommodate subsistence wars, since the violation of individuals' right not to be subjected to severe deprivation does not (or so one might think) constitute an instance of aggression against their *jointly held rights*, as a people, to political self-determination and territorial integrity.

Upon further scrutiny, however, subsistence wars can be understood as a means to redress the wrong of aggression on the political self-determination of a political community, both externally (in that the community in question is subjected to the domination of another such community) and internally (in that its individual members no longer have meaningful control over their community's destiny.) RSD, you will recall, imposes on the affluent a duty not to cause distant strangers to suffer severe deprivation. To the extent that violations of that duty consist in seizing or damaging natural resources to which the target community has a (independently defended) valid claim, they are tantamount to attacking the territorial integrity of that community, and, thereby, its capacity for political self-determination.[10]

Moreover, to the extent that they also consist in depriving the members of that community of access to vital resources or in setting up global institutions the rules of which contribute to reducing them to severe deprivation, they are tantamount to attacking the capacity for political self-determination of that community, in at least three ways. First, those of its citizens who are living in severe deprivation are less likely to exercise their political rights of

---

[10] What if, as Mike Ravvin has pointed out to me, the government of a poor country enters into agreements with A, such as to contribute to causing severe deprivation amongst its people? To what extent, in that case, can we say that severe deprivation vitiates its sovereignty? One cannot reach a firm conclusion on such a case without filling in the details. Is the government democratically elected and representative of the very deprived? Does it enter this agreement because it is the least bad of a number of bad options, or as a way for its leaders to line up their bank accounts with corruption money? And so on. There are cases where such a government could not be regarded as legitimate—and where such a political community could not be regarded as sovereign. It would lack internal sovereignty, both in so far as its government takes decisions without the consent of its members, and in so far as the persistence of severe deprivation within its borders (a consequence, *ex hypothesi*, of those decisions) makes it extremely unlikely that it will become able to direct its own future.

citizenship—most notably voting—if and when called upon to do so. It is doubtful, therefore, that the outcomes of those political processes are genuinely democratic and constitute the expression of political self-determination. Second, a community which has to devote most of its resources to helping its members meet their basic needs is unlikely to be able to engage in whatever collective projects it would have wanted to pursue otherwise. As a result, its capacity for political self-determination is likely to be severely impaired. Third, in so far as national security is a precondition for effective self-determination and as severe deprivation undermines national security, severe deprivation undermines self-determination. Accordingly, framing the issues raised by failures to respect RSD in terms of national security might seem odd. However, it has become commonplace in the literature on security that the latter ought not to be couched solely in narrow military terms (whereby a threat to national security is, paradigmatically and most importantly, a military aggression on the target state's territory.) Rather, the literature goes, security is threatened by severe inequalities, environmental degradation, mass migrations of refugees caused by famine, and so on.[11] Seen in that light, *if* the policies conducted by the affluent can be seen as a threat to the security, more widely defined, of poor countries, they can in turn be seen as a threat to their ability to shape their own future. Within the just war paradigm, these policies would provide the very deprived with a just cause for going to war.

That said, although violations of RSD can undermine a political community's territorial integrity and political sovereignty, it would be a mistake to insist that they are a just cause for going to war only in those cases. For the justification for the duty to avoid causing severe deprivation is not merely— indeed, not even mainly—that individuals who are severely poor cannot properly exercise their political rights and collectively shape their future as a people. Rather, it is that we generally ought not to impose severe harm on others.[12] To insist, then, that the violation of RSD is a *just cause* for waging war only when RSD is understood as a right the realization of which is instrumental to the value of political sovereignty is to miss the point.

Furthermore, narrowing the range of *just causes* for waging war down to violations of jointly held rights, to the exclusion of violations of individual

[11] See, for example, B. Buzan, *People, States and Fear: An Agenda for International Security Studies in the Post-Cold War Era*, 2nd edn. (Hemel Hempstead: Wheatsheaf, 1991); A. Hurrell, *On Global Order: Power, Values, and the Constitution of International Society* (Oxford: Oxford University Press, 2007); J. T. Matthews, "Redefining Security", *Foreign Affairs* 68 (1989): 162–77; R. H. Ullman, 'Redefining Security', *International Security* 8 (1983): 129–53.
[12] For a longer argument to that effect, see C. Fabre, *Social Rights under the Constitution: Government and the Decent Life* (Oxford: Oxford Clarendon Press, 2000), chs. 1 and 4.

basic rights, is at best arbitrary and at worst absurd. For it has the following two-pronged implication: that, in 1982, the United Kingdom had a just cause for waging war against Argentina on the grounds that the latter, by invading the Falklands archipelago—6,000 miles from the UK, and with a population of less than 3,000 people—had violated its sovereignty rights over it; *but, by contrast*, that sub-Saharan African countries lack a just cause for waging a war against rich nations even if the latter's policies are contributing to causing starvation on the continent. As we saw in Section 2.3.1, the violation of jointly held rights to territorial integrity and political sovereignty constitutes a just cause for resorting to war on the grounds that those rights are instrumentally valuable to individuals' prospects for a minimally decent life. If so, RSD violations *per se,* irrespective of the fact that they constitute a violation of the jointly held rights to political sovereignty and territorial integrity, provide the very deprived with a just cause. If the impact of a rights violation on such prospects is what renders it a just cause for waging war, then whether the rights are collective or individual is irrelevant. To the extent that the violations of that duty are current, ongoing, and clearly causally related to the untimely deaths and debilitating diseases suffered by the very deprived, measures which the very deprived would take against wrongdoers to stop the threat can appropriately be regarded as a self-defensive step.

Or can they? As I noted at the outset of this section, a just war of self-defence is typically a war waged as a response to an unjust armed attack (criterion (b) above.) Subsistence wars do not meet that criterion—at least in those cases when they are not a response to the seizure by military force of a country's natural resources by another country, but rather, a response to policies which contribute to causing severe deprivation. Such policies may include, for example, the imposition of protectionist tariffs which, in effect, close rich nations' markets to imports from poorer communities; patenting restrictions on access to poverty-reducing technology and health care; the extension of borrowing privileges to corrupt regimes, and the concomitant imposition of crippling debt repayments on those regimes' successors. They may also include the export of industrial hazards by the former to the latter, with devastating effects on the health of some of their most vulnerable members. If being subject to an armed attack is a necessary condition for a war to count as self-defensive, then subsistence wars waged in response to RSD violations are not self-defensive. Moreover, if one takes the view that war is just only if it is waged in self-defence or other defence against a threat, as punishment, or for the sake of recovering wrongfully taken property, then it follows that subsistence wars cannot be just.

A crucial question, therefore, is whether a self-defensive war must be a response to an armed, kinetic, attack. Paradigmatically, a war of self-defence is a war waged against infantry divisions which have crossed our borders, jet-fighters which have invaded our air-space, or vessels which have entered our territorial waters. It seems to me, however, that the paradigm relies on an overly narrow notion of self-defence. Suppose that our enemy hacks into our computers and destroys our air defence system. That is not an *armed* attack—but it is, nonetheless, an attack. To claim that a war of self-defence must, by definition, be waged against the former kind of threat would rule out the possibility of regarding our retaliatory move as defensive (and therefore just), which is absurd.

A defensive war, therefore, can be a response to a non-military, non-kinetic attack. Some subsistence wars clearly fit that definitional bill. Suppose that a nuclear power, A, decides to conduct tests a few hundred miles off the coast of non-nuclear and considerably less powerful country V. Suppose further that it can be reasonably expected to know that there is a correlation between the conduct of such tests and a rising incidence of cancer amongst populations living within a certain radius of the test zone. Its intention (as far as we can judge) is to strengthen its nuclear capability—not to increase cancer rates in the area.[13] Suppose, finally, that V does not have the wherewithal to offer cancer treatments to its members, that A has consistently refused to compensate V for the harm thus caused, but that V can somehow stop the testing by, for example, destroying the test facilities. It seems clear that, definitionally speaking, V would be defending itself against A were it to bomb the facilities. (Whether it may do so is another question: here I focus on what kind of subsistence wars plausibly *count* as self-defensive.)

This particular example might seem too close to a standard instance of military aggression—for example, by way of using chemical agents in V's airspace—to support subsistence wars in those cases where the wrongdoing takes the form of policies such as protectionist tariffs, patent restrictions, and so on. Even then, however, responses by force to those non-military and non-kinetic threats can appropriately be regarded as self-defensive wars (whether the force exercised takes the form of a war, or whether it falls short of war yet is anticipated to trigger a war.) To illustrate, compare the following two scenarios. (1) Country A's troops mount regular incursions two miles into country

[13] There is some evidence that French nuclear testing in the South Pacific may have had similar effects on parts of the (French) South Polynesian population. At the time of writing, France is no longer conducting such tests. See http://www.independent.co.uk/news/wouldeurope/frances-nuclear-tests-in-pacific-gave-islanders-cancer-410474.html (accessed 6 June 2012).

B's territory and in its air-space, causing only limited casualties amongst B's soldiers. (2) Country C's standard of living is considerably higher than its neighbour D's. Suppose further that C imposes highly protectionist tariffs on D's products, as a result of which D's farmers are then unable to sell their crops and are on the brink of starvation, which in turn has severely destabilizing effects on D's economy and society. Suppose that B goes to war against A, and that D goes to war against C. If a war, in order to count as self-defensive (which in turn would permit us, if other conditions obtain, to deem it just), must be a response to a military kinetic threat, then it follows that B is, but D is not, waging a self-defensive war. Yet it seems linguistically arbitrary to hold that B *defends* itself whereas D does not, given that both take steps so as to protect the fundamental rights of their members. To be clear: my point is not a normative claim to the effect that any harmful policy as conducted by the affluent towards the very poor is wrongful, let alone provides the latter with a just cause for war. Rather, my point is a conceptual remark to the effect that on a broader and more plausible understanding of self-defence, a self-defensive war blocks a threat to vital individual and collective interests; that threat may take the form of a kinetic attack, but it may also take the form of seriously harmful economic (or, for that matter, environmental) policies.

### 3.2.3 War and the right to assistance

So far, I have focused on war as a response to the affluent's violations of their duty not to *subject* distant strangers to severe deprivation. As I noted in Chapter 1, however, cosmopolitan justice also imposes on the affluent (positive) duties to provide help for the very deprived should they be unable to access the resources necessary for a minimally decent life. Many would resist the thought that breaches of their right to receive help give the very deprived a just cause for waging a war against the affluent, as follows:

(1) In failing to help others we do not cause harm to happen to them in the first instance, but rather allow harm to happen to them;

(2) allowing lethal harm to happen to them is not tantamount to posing a lethal threat to them;

(3) moreover, only posing, or contributing to posing, a lethal threat, can warrant the loss and destruction attendant on war; therefore

(4) subsistence wars as responses to breach of the duty to help cannot be just.

Premises (1) and (2) of this putative objection invoke the well-known doctrine of acts and omissions whereby, other things equal, doing harm is morally worse than allowing harm to happen. (DDA is agnostic on the issue of liability, as raised by premise (3).) As noted in the Introduction, I endorse the doctrine. However, the use to which it might be put here is questionable. For a start, although it is true (*ex hypothesi*) that the affluent did not cause the harm suffered by the very poor, the fact remains that they are now in a position to act in such a way as to ensure that the harm is no longer an *ongoing* harm—and that fact, I submit, is morally relevant, even if allowing harm to happen is not the same as posing it. Whether the affluent choose to make their surplus resources available to the very deprived or decide to hold on to them does make a difference to the latter—the difference between a minimally decent life and one which is not so, indeed, between life and death. In that sense, in failing to help the very deprived, the affluent are in some important way responsible for their plight, and thus are responsible for the fact that they are subject to an ongoing and, in the worst cases, lethal, harm to them. One cannot make sense of rights *to provide assistance*, and their correlative duties without conceding that point. (This, note, does not elide the distinction between acts and omissions: the view I defend here is compatible with the claim that there is a morally salient difference between (other things equal) actively ensuring that the harm remains ongoing (such as by thwarting the provision of assistance) and abstaining from stopping it by directing one's energy elsewhere).

Is it to say that the omission—which, remember, is of a kind as to be plausibly described as a form of contributory responsibility for the ongoing predicament of the very poor—provides the latter with a just cause for war in either the narrow or wide sense? I believe so. It would be arbitrary on the one hand to claim that contributory responsibility for a wrongful lethal threat constitutes a just cause for war, and on the other hand to insist that merely (though wrongfully) contributing to making the threat an ongoing one does not. Likewise, by parity of reasoning, for ongoing rights violations which provide their victims with a wide just cause. In both cases the threat is severely harmful and is significantly connected to the affluent's actions. It is that, rather than whether or not they have initiated the threat, which is relevant to the question of whether or not the very deprived have a just cause for going to war.

I concede that many will find it impossible to accept the thought that a failure to aid constitutes a contribution to severe poverty. However, they would not be thereby licensed to reject the view that violations of positive rights to assistance constitute a just cause for war. For even if it is true that a failure to help does not constitute a contribution to a harm, and even if it is true that, other things equal, harming someone is morally worse than failing to help, it remains the case that (as per Sections 1.2 and 1.3) the failure does constitute a grievous rights violation. Moreover, the claim that harming is worse than failing to help, other things equal, is compatible with the thought

that when they are not equal (for example, in different-number cases), failing
to help is as bad as, or indeed worse than, harming. It is thus open to the
doctrine of acts and omissions to hold that, for example, deliberately letting
thirty million people die is morally worse than unwarrantedly launching a
military invasion on a country of five million people. With that point in hand,
it is hard to see why the invasion should constitute a just cause if it threatens
the prospects of that country's five million citizens for a decent life, whilst the
systematic violation of the subsistence rights of thirty million individuals
should not. To put the point in general terms, the view that only violations
of negative rights can be a just cause to war whilst violations of positive rights
by definition can *never* have that status seems an *ad hoc* restriction on the
range of wrongdoings which warrant recourse to lethal force.

## 3.3 SUBSISTENCE WAR AND LEGITIMATE AUTHORITY

To recapitulate, I have argued that the very deprived have a just cause for going
to war against the affluent if the latter are in breach of their negative and
positive duties of justice towards them. However, the just cause requirement is
only one of several conditions which a war must meet in order to be just. As we
saw in the Introduction to this book, orthodox just war theory holds that the
war must be fought by a legitimate authority, standardly defined as a sovereign,
independent state with legal and political jurisdiction over a bounded territory,
a coalition of such states, or (in more recent revisions) national liberation
movements. On that view, only states or quasi-states have the right to wage
war. Accordingly, the claim that the very deprived (P) have the right to wage
war against the affluent (A) raises two questions: (1) under what conditions, if
any, can a state, P, in which a large section of the population is very deprived,
hold that right?; and (2) under what conditions, if any, can the very deprived
themselves have that right, independently of what their government may do?

Let me make two terminological points before proceeding further. First, in
this section and unless otherwise explicitly stated, by A and P I mean
(depending on the context) states or regimes A and P, as distinct from their
peoples (there are grounds for distinguishing a state from its regime, but the
distinction is not relevant here). Second, when I say that P can hold the right
to wage war against the affluent I mean that P has the authority to do so, not
that it *has* the right to wage that war, all things considered. Thus, if in waging
such a war P would violate the requirement of proportionality, then we would
conclude that P does not have the all-things-considered right to go to war
against A, even though it has the authority to do so.

The first question—that of state P's right to wage war against affluent state A—is not unique to subsistence wars. It arises in other kinds of wars of collective self-defence—such as defence from a conventional military aggression. Whilst the tradition insists that only the state—or more archaically put, the Prince—has the authority to declare war against the invader, many of its strands concede that should the state be unwilling or unable so to act, the people may resist the aggressor via a so-called *levée en masse*. That said, subsistence wars raise some specific issues of authority. For consider this. As we saw in Section 1.3.1, RSD and RRH impose the following duties: a negative duty, on A's officials and citizens, not to take part in structured practices, or design, implement or support policies, which contribute to causing severe deprivation within P; a positive duty, on A's officials and citizens, to transfer resources to P's very deprived, by way of coercive taxation; a negative duty, on P's officials and (affluent) citizens, not to act in such a way as to contribute to causing severe deprivation within P's borders; a positive duty, on P's officials and (affluent) citizens, to transfer resources to P's very deprived, by way of coercive taxation. Accordingly, in order to assess whether or not P (understood here as a sovereign community of citizens acting through their officials) can hold the (collective) right to wage war against A, we must distinguish cases where P's duty-bearers are not derelict in their duties to their very deprived compatriots from cases where they are. Suppose, for example, that P's duty-bearers do not forcibly withhold from the latter access to basic necessities: on the contrary, they have set up a welfare system which somewhat alleviates deprivation within its population. However, the policies conducted by A's regime (acting on behalf of A's citizens) are such that, notwithstanding P's fulfilment of their own duties, there still is persistent and severe deprivation within P's borders. P's duty-bearers, moreover, simply cannot do more than they currently do without jeopardising the future of their community as a minimally functioning and sovereign political community. In this case, A's defaulting makes it impossible for P to eradicate severe deprivation within its borders. In so far as, *ex hypothesi*, P's duty-bearers are not guilty of the relevant moral wrongdoing towards its very deprived, it seems clear that its citizens, acting collectively through their regime, can hold the right to wage war against A. It is worth noting, incidentally, that this claim, if true, does not imply that P can hold that right only if it is a morally legitimate state—a state, that is, which respects all the fundamental human rights of its members as well as foreigners, and in which decisions are made through democratic procedures. As I noted at the close of Sections 2.3.1, the fact that an illegitimate state—defined as institutions and their actors without the moral right to govern—lacks the right to protect itself against being overthrown in peacetime does not disqualify it from having the fiduciary right to defend the fundamental rights of its individual members against foreign unjust threats. The point is all the stronger when applied to those cases where it is not itself guilty of the kind of injustice committed by its attackers, and even though it thereby ensures its viability as an illegitimate state.

Contrast this with another scenario, where A supports global institutions the policies of which harm the very poor in P, and where, moreover, P's own policies are such as to have that effect as well. In this case the question is whether the fact that P's duty-bearers default on their obligations to its very poor members disqualifies P's regime from holding the (fiduciary) right to wage war against A. One might think that someone who is also guilty of threatening an attacker's victim—in other words, someone who is also an attacker—could not possibly have the right to exercise lethal force in defence of that victim. If that is correct, P lacks the right to inflict widespread damage and destruction on the lives and limbs of members of A—and this precisely because it is itself guilty of the same wrongdoing. Yet I do not think that this is correct. Of course, it is true that P lacks that right in some cases. Suppose that a policy reversal by P would be enough to secure P's very poor prospects for a minimally decent life. Given that there would be an alternative other than war, P ought not to attack A. Or suppose that P is so corrupt (as evidenced by its dereliction of duty towards its citizens) that it will not reform itself once the war is over, and that the war would therefore not in fact stand a chance of success. In those cases, however, the reason why P lacks the right to wage war against A is not that its wrongdoing deprives its officials of the authority to do so: rather, it is because that war would not fulfil the requirements that war be necessary to achieve one's aims and stand a reasonable chance of doing so.

Now imagine, by contrast, that P's very poor will not enjoy such prospects unless A desists. In those cases, the fact that P is guilty of that wrongdoing does not suffice to withhold from it the right to wage war against A on behalf of its very poor. For A does not have a right, at least *prima facie*, that P not resort to war, since *ex hypothesi* its wrongdoing is a just cause for it. Suppose that V is attacked by two villainous truck-drivers, $D_1$ and $D_2$, that $D_2$ changes his mind halfway through, and that V cannot defend herself without assistance. It would be odd to affirm that $D_2$ would wrong $D_1$ by turning against him. In fact, as we saw in Section 2.3.2, unjust combatants who belong to the same army and are linked to one another by the special ties of co-citizenship do not owe it to one another to carry on wrongfully killing the enemy: more strongly still, they may turn against one another in defence of the latter. *A fortiori*, then, P, which has a special (if largely instrumental) duty of care to its own members, may turn against co-wrongdoer A and seek redress for their joint wrongdoing by going to war against the latter. Admittedly one might worry that illegitimate states could then invoke A's dereliction of duty towards their own very deprived members as a pretext for waging a subsistence war which, if successful, would shore them up; and one might further insist that subsistence wars cannot be just if they enable illegitimate states to survive. It might also be that the harms attendant on the illegitimate state remaining in place are such as to count heavily, in the proportionality calculation, against the all-things-considered permissibility of P's going to war against A. Be that as it may, my concern here is with the narrower question of P's *authority* in respect of that particular war. To reiterate, the fact of P's prior wrongdoing does not suffice to undermine P's authority to wage a subsistence war on behalf of its members.

Moreover, the foregoing point is wholly compatible with the thesis that P's very deprived themselves have the right to go to war against A. The point is at variance with orthodox just war theory, which holds that a war is just only if it is fought by states, coalitions of states, or national liberation movements. However, it is a central tenet of cosmopolitan justice not merely that individuals have a human right not to be subjected to severe deprivation, but also that they have a number of other human rights—for example, human rights to fundamental freedoms. If those claims are correct, individuals also have the right—the meta-right, as it were—to protect those very rights themselves. For it would be incoherent, on the one hand, to claim that individuals' fundamental interests in life-saving resources and basic freedoms are important enough to be protected by rights, and on the other hand, to deny that individuals' interest in the protection of those rights is important enough to be protected by a right to defend those rights themselves. This is not to say, of course, that individuals have the right to take matters into their own hands whenever the protection of their human rights is at issue. In fact, to the extent that they would be better off by transferring the meta-right to protect their human rights to an organization like the state, it is in their interest that they should do so: to reiterate a point made in Section 1.4, a state is legitimate only if it respects the human rights of its members and does a better job at protecting those rights than individuals themselves would. But should it fail to do so, the meta-right to protect fundamental human rights reverts back to individuals. Now, war is one of many steps which individuals may be tempted to take in defence of their fundamental human rights. On my account of state legitimacy, individuals have the right so to act. For on that account, the state's right to wage war is one which it has precisely in so far as it does a better job than individuals at protecting the latter's fundamental human rights through the use of lethal force. If it is derelict in its duty to protect its members, the right reverts to the very deprived. For a war to be just, then, it is not necessary that it should be fought by a legitimate authority such as a state. It may be fought by those for whose sake states are normally given the right to wage war, at least in those cases where states are disallowed from exercising it. Moreover, it may be fought by those individuals acting singly, or by their acting together without the attributes of state sovereignty.

I shall revisit individuals' right to go to war outside state structures at much greater length in Chapter 4 when tackling the issue of civil wars. For now, suffice it to say that in principle, the very poor are legitimate holders of the right to defend their subsistence rights against the affluent's dereliction of duty. Still, one might think that when *both* P and A are derelict in their duties towards P's very deprived, the latter should wage war against their own government before they target A, on the grounds that their own government, as such, has primary responsibility for the persistence of severe deprivation within P's borders. Yet suppose that P's members would be much more successful by waging war against A than by going after their state (for example, they would be able to get A to stop supporting their deprivation-causing government, as a result of which the latter would go under.) Under those circumstances, A's regime, rather than P's government, should be their first target, even if their contribution to the plight of P's very poor is of lesser magnitude than the contribution of P's regime (and provided, of course, that their contribution, though of lesser magnitude, is nevertheless of a kind, when taken on its own, as to warrant an attack).

So far, so good, but here is a complication. Suppose that P decides to go to war against A on the grounds that A is derelict in its duty to P's very deprived, and that the latter therefore cannot but live in severe deprivation. Assume, for the sake of argument, that it has a just cause and can be regarded as having the authority so to act. In so far as a successful war requires the deployment of considerable material and human resources, it is likely that P also lacks the wherewithal to win that war since, *ex hypothesi*, it lacks the wherewithal to pick up the costs attendant on A's dereliction. To be sure, waging a war against the affluent might perhaps be less costly than fulfilling the duty to avoid causing severe deprivation. A poor country might be able to build enough bombs to strike at the heart of affluent institutions, or it might be able to finance a guerrilla war which would impose considerable losses to the affluent and at a lesser financial cost than doing A's share would require.[14] It is likely, though, that many such acts would violate some other requirements of the just war, such as the *in bello* requirement of proportionality: generally put, even if a subsistence

---

[14] I owe this suggestion to G. A. Cohen.

war does respect the *jus ad bellum* requirement of a reasonable chance of success, in many cases it will do so only at the cost of being unjust all things considered.

If that is correct, the more impoverished you are by the affluent, the greater your case against them and the less likely, *by that token*, you are to have the wherewithal to go to war. If anything, the difficulty is more acute when a war is waged by individual victims than by individuals acting as agents of the state with the latter's resources. Put starkly, what hope do the scores of desperately poor individuals throughout the world—many of them children and women with burdensome family responsibilities—have to arm themselves and act in defence of their rights? None whatsoever. The question, then, is whether other individuals or groups who have the ability to fight on their behalf can do so and (assuming that they can—a point to which I shall return in Section 4.3) whether they have the means to fight justly. In so far as those fighters would in all likelihood lack the means to fight a conventional war, they would have to resort to non-conventional means such as terrorism. If it turns out that terrorism (however one defines it) is morally wrong, and if it is nevertheless the only way to prosecute a subsistence war in such a case, then such a war is unjust.

To make matters worse, the difficulty seemingly becomes even more insuperable once one brings into view what it means for a subsistence war to *succeed*. In 'standard' cases of self-defence against unjust aggression—an invasion, for example—the aggressed country has won the war once it has rolled its enemy's armies back across its borders and weakened it to such an extent as to forestall future similar threats. Winning the war is signalled, typically, by the enemy's surrender. Subsistence wars differ from the standard case. In failing to fulfil their duty to the very deprived not to subject them to severe deprivation, the affluent pose an ongoing lethal threat to them—and one which, I have argued, is serious enough to provide them with a just cause for waging war. The very deprived, in waging that war, will stop the threat altogether and obtain what they want, in either one of two cases: either their military victory over affluent states is so comprehensive as to destroy them, or (less unlikely) they manage to persuade affluent states to accept a negotiated peace, the terms of which would include the cessation of harmful economic policies. In the latter case, the success of such a war should be defined as the extent to which winning the war places the very deprived in a position to persuade the affluent to reverse their harmful economic policy. (The affluent's surrender to the very deprived might mean that the latter have won the war in a narrow military sense, but it might not be enough to rectify the injustice which provided them with a just cause for starting the war in the first place.) The very deprived, in fact, might need to persuade the affluent to surrender under conditions such that the latter would no longer be able to cause severe deprivation—a goal which the very deprived simply would not be able to achieve. Accordingly, if conducting that war as dictated by the requirement that it stand a reasonable chance of success proves so costly on the very deprived that they simply are not in a position to persuade the affluent to reverse harmful economic policies once the war is over, then the war would be unjust.

In the light of the foregoing considerations, one might think that a subsistence war could never be just—perhaps almost by definition. But that would be too quick. For although such wars might usually succeed only at the cost of a non-negotiable principle of a just conflict, such as the principle of non-combatant immunity, the door remains open, on principle, for deeming just a subsistence war fought in accordance with that principle. Likewise, although the very poor usually might not be in a position to persuade the affluent to reverse their policies, the door remains open, on principle, for deeming just a war which would succeed on that count.

## 3.4 KILLING IN SUBSISTENCE WARS

### 3.4.1 Killing wrongdoers

In Section 3.2 I argued that subsistence rights are worth defending by force. That claim does not, on its own, provide us with much guidance for determining *who*, within affluent communities, are liable to being killed by the very poor. Yet unless we can identify wrongdoers whose contributions to the predicament of the very poor are such as to warrant deliberately attacking them, we cannot conclude that subsistence wars are justified. This is a particularly difficult issue in the case at hand, since those violations do not take the form of an armed attack. To the extent that subsistence wars are not responses to a wrongful armed attack on one's territory, but rather, to a wrongful denial of access to subsistence resources, any argument to the effect that they can be just must identify who, amongst the affluent's populations, is liable to attack. The principle of civilian immunity as standardly invoked is of no help here, since according to the principle, civilians are immune from attack precisely to the extent that they do not take part in the armed conflict. The difficulty, for subsistence wars, is not the familiar thought that civilians often participate in the war—for example, by working in weapons factories, or as private contractors for the army.[15] Rather, the difficulty is that the rights

---

[15] I explore the liabilities of factory workers at some length in Fabre, 'Guns, Food, and Liability to Attack', and will tackle the liabilities of private contractors in Chapter 6. The literature on civilians' immunities and liabilities is enormous. See, for example, Coady, *Morality and Political Violence*;

violations which provide the very poor with a just cause for war are carried out
by civilians. Is this to say, then, that the former have the right to kill the latter
in the course of a subsistence war?

As I argued in Chapter 1, citizens and public officials are under a duty of
justice to (respectively) support and implement just institutions, laws, and
policies, as well as duties not to take part in structured and organized practices
the effects of which are severely harmful to others. The question, then, is
whether those rights violations are such as to provide the very deprived with a
justification for killing those individuals as a matter of right. To begin with,
note that some subsistence wars which are not properly regarded as a response
to a wrongful military attack nevertheless have features which render an
account of civilians' liabilities less problematic than might appear at first
sight. Suppose that a number of nuclear factories from country A are failing
to respect basic health-and-safety measures, that A's government fails to take
action (those factories are located in the desert, employ a largely foreign and
menial workforce, and so on), with the effect that inhabitants in neighbouring
country V are exposed to highly dangerous levels of radiation. Suppose further
that V regularly protests against A—to no avail, and this despite mounting
evidence of a higher incidence of cancer, birth defects, and so on, amongst V's
residents. V, having given A a warning, rightfully (I assume) bombs some of
the latter's industrial (non-nuclear) installations in the middle of the night—
in a case of bloodless attack. A's anti-missile battery operators fire at V's jet-
fighters, thereby subjecting them to a lethal threat. Their threat is wrongful in
so far as *ex hypothesi* V's combatants are acting justly and thus have not lost
their right not to be killed. In this particular case, although some of A's
civilians are guilty of wrongdoing (of working in those installations, failing
to pressurize their government into enforcing health and safety measures, and
so on), V's combatants clearly lack the right to target them but nevertheless
have the right to target the battery operators, in defence of their own lives as
well as of their compatriots' interest in not suffering the severely detrimental
effects of prolonged exposure to high levels of radiation.

Suppose, however, that the very poor cannot further their ends (persuading
the affluent to put a stop to the nefarious activities of their industries) unless
they target civilian wrongdoers. Do they have the right to do so? I surmise that
the following argument to the effect that they lack such right will seem

Kamm, 'Failures of Just War Theory: Terror, Harm, and Justice'; C. McKeogh, *Innocent Civilians: The Morality of Killing in War* (Basingstoke: Palgrave, 2002); Nagel, 'War and Massacre'; Norman, *Ethics, Killing, and War*; G. E. M. Anscombe, 'War and Murder', in *Collected Papers: Ethics, Religion and Politics* (Oxford: Blackwell 1981).

convincing to many: the victim of a grievous wrongdoing has the right to kill the wrongdoer only if the latter *intended* to harm her. If so, the deliberate contaminating of water sources and/or poisoning crops would admittedly constitute acts of aggression on the very deprived and provide them with a *prima facie* justification for directly attacking wrongdoers, irrespective of the latter's status (civilian or military). However, my opponent might maintain, such acts are extremely rare: rather, deprivation is mainly due to individuals' support for national and global institutions the rules of which contribute to causing severe deprivation. Those actors do not intend to cause deprivation abroad: they do not protect their markets from Third World products with the intention that millions of people should die, every year, of avoidable, deprivation-related causes; nor do they impose highly restrictive patenting rights on medical drugs with the intention of depriving the very poor, in Third World countries, of access to those drugs. Rather, their intention is to protect their farmers' and companies' interests. Whilst morally condemnable, their actions are not such as to justify granting the very poor the right to kill them.

Note that this particular objection need not deny that (in this case) the affluent are causally responsible for severe deprivation abroad. Nor need it deny that the affluent are guilty of moral wrongdoing. Its central claim is that indifference to the plight of the very deprived does not warrant the loss by the affluent of their right not to be killed deliberately. However, on the account of defensive rights which I articulated in Section 2.2, agents' intentions are not relevant to victims' right to kill. The following example might help drive the point home. V's laboratory assistant is about to open a jar of mosquitoes, even though he knows that some of them will almost certainly sting V and that V is lethally allergic to their venom. The laboratory assistant does not intend to kill V. He may simply be indifferent to her predicament. All he intends to do is conduct an experiment with those mosquitoes. V lacks the time to warn him and can save her life only by shooting him. If the objection under study here is correct, V's assistant is not liable to being killed, which is to say that V lacks the right to kill him, since he does not intend to cause V's death. On my account, however, V does have that right, simply because he is unjustifiably posing an ongoing and wrongful lethal threat to her life and limbs.[16]

Consider now a military analogy, in the form of the earlier example of nuclear testing. Community A, you recall, conducts tests a few hundred miles off the coast of some other, non-nuclear, and considerably less powerful country, V, in the knowledge that it thereby exposes V's population to a

---

[16] I borrow and adapt this example from Ryan, 'Self-Defense, Pacifism, and the Permissibility of Killing', 518–9.

greater risk of cancer. Assume further that V cannot offer cancer treatment to its members and is not receiving any compensation from A. A's intention is to strengthen its nuclear capability; the engineers who conduct the test and other sundry affiliated personnel may well share that intention; they may also be motivated by professional ambitions, pride in a job well done, and so on. None of those agents, let us assume, *intend* to increase cancer rates in the area. If V's decision to destroy the facilities respects the requirements of proportionality and necessity, it does not seem implausible, in the face of the suffering caused by A and its agents and of their utter disregard for the lives of V's members, to claim that those agents are liable to direct lethal attack: that they do not intend to destroy those lives is irrelevant. And if that is correct, then, by implication, the fact that civilian wrongdoers do not intend to cause severe and life-threatening deprivation in foreign countries does not make them immune from such an attack. To be clear, my point (at this juncture) is not that the very deprived have the right to kill civilian wrongdoers in a subsistence war. My point, rather, is that one cannot object to the conferral of that right on the grounds that they do not intend to subject the very deprived to grievous, life- and limb- threatening hardship.

That said, the claim that the very deprived do have that right when the affluent are derelict in their positive obligations to provide them with assistance, or in their negative duties not to impose unfair trading conditions, is likely to be met with yet another objection, as follows. Those two kinds of wrongdoing, some might argue, cannot confer on their victims the right to kill the wrongdoer, even if the latter's failure to act would result in the former's death. This is because (the objection might continue) *killing* someone who fails to act justly is not the most efficient way (to say the least) of getting them to comply. Compare this with the act of killing a wrongdoer who subjects us to a lethal harm (as distinct from failing to prevent such harm.) In that case, we avert the harm and thereby redress the rights violation. But in killing someone who fails to help us and whose failure contributes to putting our life at risk, or who harms us and ought to conduct himself in a different way towards us, we do not thereby secure the state of affairs which we want. In so far as killing the wrongdoer would not secure redress (or, to put it differently, would not satisfy the requirement of reasonable chance of success), we lack the right so to act.

The objection supposes that someone has the right to kill a wrongdoer only if the act of killing thwarts the threat posed by the wrongdoer himself. Suppose that P is starving to death but is in possession of a gun. Two individuals, $A_1$ and $A_2$, are both in a position to help him by giving him some of their surplus food, but refuse to do so. Let us assume that their refusal, in that instance, is a violation of P's right to subsistence. P cannot get to the food himself (because, say, he is too weak to crawl), but has good reasons to believe that if he threatens $A_1$ unless they help him and makes good on his threat in the face of their refusal, $A_2$ will give in. To say that P lacks the right to kill $A_1$ on the grounds that he will not in so doing get him to stop wronging him is to say that one lacks the right to kill wrongdoers by omission even as a means to get other wrongdoers to do what justice requires of them. But note, for a start, that opportunistic killing (as a means to persuade wrongdoers to desist) is sometimes permissible. Consider the following variant of the torture example presented in Section 2.3.2. Suppose that someone, V, has been kidnapped by an evil scientist bent on experimenting with various forms of torture by electrocution. The scientist's 1,000 henchmen each repeatedly send a 10-volt charge into V's body, with a view to establishing how long it would take V to die. Confident in their ability to subdue V, the henchmen did not search her properly and failed to take her lethal laser-watch from her. Somehow, V manages to free herself. She can kill only one of the torturers (her watch is fast running out of battery power), and she also knows (let us assume) that if she manages to kill the scientist's son (who is one of the torturers), the torture will stop. By killing the son she is eliminating the 10-volt threat he poses to her, but she is not, in virtue of eliminating this 10-volt threat, thereby eliminating the slowly lethal total harm which the other 999 torturers inflict on her. Rather, she kills the son as a means to get the torturers to stop. As I argued in Section 2.3.2, the son's participation in a collective wrongdoing of that kind, together with the nature of his contribution (sending a jolt of electricity into the body of an innocent person), warrants granting her the (*prima facie*) right so to act. And if that is correct, then by implication she is permitted, indeed has the right, to kill him opportunistically. In order to show, then, that the very deprived lack the right to kill affluent individuals whose wrongdoing takes the form of an omission, one would have to show either that opportunistic killing is never permissible, or that it is permissible but that *this* particular wrongdoing does not qualify as a basis for the right to kill.[17]

I shall consider one possible line of argument to that effect presently—one which, in fact, will apply to the affluent's wrongdoing by action. Beforehand, however, it is worth noting that even if one could show that wrongful omissions cannot form the basis of a right to kill wrongdoers, it still would

---

[17] The distinction between eliminative and opportunistic killing, which draws from W. S. Quinn's seminal distinction between eliminative and opportunistic agency, has enjoyed renewed interest in the recent literature. See Quinn, 'Actions, Intentions, and Consequences: The Doctrine of Double Effect'; McMahan, *Killing in War*, 170–3; Quong, 'Killing in Self-Defence'.

not follow that the very deprived *never* have the right to kill affluent wrong-doers. For a start, some of those wrongdoings take the form of active support for unjust institutions—or of a violation of a negative duty not to harm—rather than failure to establish just ones—or of a violation of a positive duty to help. Moreover, to reiterate an earlier and crucial point, even if a dereliction of a positive duty cannot itself justify granting its victim(s) the right to kill the wrongdoer(s), it may well justify granting them the right to use non-lethal force even though they have good reasons to believe that their targets will respond in such a way (by using lethal force) as to then, at that point, justify killing them. Thus, even if P lacks the right, at time $t_1$, to kill either one of $A_1$ or $A_2$ as a means to get them to comply with their duty of justice, he may well have the right to, for instance, non-lethally maim $A_1$ to get him to comply at $t_1$, in the foreknowledge that $A_1$ or, indeed, $A_2$ will then try to kill him at $t_2$, at which point he will in turn have the right (I posit) to kill his aggressor in self-defence at $t_3$. This is so, of course, provided that P stands a reasonable chance of success of securing his just end (getting food) when triggering a lethal confrontation at $t_1$. By implication, the very deprived may well have the right to inflict non-lethal harm on affluent wrongdoers in the foreknowledge that they will be met by a lethal (*ex hypothesi*) unjust defensive move on the part of the soldiers tasked with protecting the latter. Subject to chances of success, such a move would in turn provide the very deprived with a justification, as a matter of right, for killing those soldiers, as well as civilians who actively contribute to what has now become a full-scale (and more conventional) war.

The foregoing considerations are subject to an absolutely crucial *caveat*. Although (as we have just seen), one need not intend to cause wrongful lethal harm to someone in order to be liable to attack, one must contribute to that wrongful harm in particular ways. Killings which are committed in the course of a traditional war of defence are permissible as a matter of right in so far as they target wrongful invaders. Subsistence wars are different, however. The thought is not that the affluent's policies do not cause severe deprivation, or that their effects pale into insignificance when compared with the consequences for the very deprived of their own government's policies, uncontrollable environmental factors, and so on. Rather, the worries are the following. First, one cannot know of most individual members of affluent communities whether they are in fact derelict in their duties of justice towards the distant poor. As I argued in Section 2.3.2, epistemic uncertainty with respect to that particular issue yields the requirement that one should treat those agents as if they were not derelict—and thus desist from targeting them.

Second, even if we could reach such a judgement, it is likely that those agents' *individual* acts or omissions are not of a kind which would justify the recourse to force *simpliciter* if considered on their own. To claim otherwise is to say, rather implausibly, that the following agents (who, I assume here, are derelict in their duties of justice towards deprived distant strangers) are liable to being killed deliberately: citizens of a highly polluting nation who elect an administration whose priority is, *inter alia*, to reduce taxes on oil used for ground transportation; citizens of a rich nation who fail systematically to elect political parties for whom debt reduction is a priority; citizens who support protectionist tariffs; individuals who work in companies only some activities of which are nefarious to distant strangers; citizens who fail to re-elect a government whose priority is to raise taxes with a view to helping the very deprived abroad, and so on. Even if those citizens are to some degree collectively responsible for the harms suffered by the very deprived, to hold them liable to being killed deliberately for having so acted or, *a fortiori*, for having failed to act as required by justice, is to inflict on them a harm which seems disproportionate in relation both to what they actually do (or failed to do) and to their responsibility for it—and this whether they are attacked eliminatively or opportunistically. This having been said, on the account of the right to wage, and kill in, war which I defended in Chapter 2, one cannot rule out, on principle, the possibility that civilians whose individual contributions or omissions have a significant connection with the harms suffered by distant strangers are legitimate targets. To go back to the example of A's nuclear testing, engineers who design those tests do seem to pass the contribution test. So do public officials in affluent or polluting countries who carry out wrongful policies.

Note, furthermore, that my examples so far have pitted affluent political communities against poor political communities. But duties to the very deprived are often discharged through transnational institutions such as the World Bank or the International Monetary Fund. My defence of subsistence wars thus seems to imply that those institutions and (some of) their members are liable to being killed if their policies result in the persistence of severe deprivation in some countries. Some might be tempted to reject that implication on the grounds that officials in either institutions are highly constrained by the resources available to them and the political imperatives of the institutions' most powerful member states. Even if they share causal responsibility for the plight of the very deprived, my opponent might say, they are not morally culpable for it and therefore ought not to be attacked.

However, we saw in Section 2.2 that the victim of a lethal threat has the right to kill her attacker even if the latter is not fully morally responsible for his act as is the case when, appositely, he acts under duress. Accordingly, the claim that those officials lack proper latitude when framing their organizations' policies towards the very deprived does not support the claim that the latter do not have the right to kill them. In any event, it is not altogether clear that international financial institutions can escape blame for the consequences of their policies on the populations of Third World countries. For while they unquestionably operate under the aforementioned constraints, various studies suggest that they have more room for manoeuvre than the objection implies. Thus they are routinely and not unjustifiably criticised for recruiting their staff mostly from North American economics departments which place great emphasis on neo-classical economics and rather little on development economics. They are also routinely—and again, not unjustifiably—accused of making the same recommendations for a whole region, without paying sufficient attention either to the effects of such widespread policies on individual actors in the area or to local differences between countries.[18] To claim, as the objection suggests, that they have no choice but so to act seems to let them off the hook somewhat lightly.

Finally, the fact that an international or, for that matter, intergovernmental, organization operates under externally imposed political and financial constraints does not suffice to exempt it from moral evaluation for the policies which it carries out. Consider, very tentatively, the case of NATO. Although meant as a tool for the collective security of all its members, disagreements over burden-sharing, force commitments, and security objectives have been rife since its inception in 1949. Those disagreements have been partly shaped by member states' domestic political and financial imperatives, and have constrained the choices made by the organization's military commanders on the ground. If the objection under scrutiny is correct, those commanders cannot be held in any way responsible for those choices—even if the latter foreseeably result in breaches of the laws of war. Surely, though, while constraints of that kind may operate as mitigating circumstances, they cannot be wholly exculpatory, on pain of rendering the very notion of individual and collective responsibility nugatory.[19] If the fact that NATO officials act under those constraints does not render them immune from direct attack in war, it

---

[18] Woods, *The Globalizers*, ch. 2.

[19] On the role of NATO and the burden-sharing controversies, see, for example, J. Duffield, 'The North Atlantic Treaty Organization: Alliance Theory', in N. Woods (ed.), *Explaining International Relations since 1945* (Oxford: Oxford University Press, 1996). For a fascinating history of NATO, see L. Kaplan, *NATO Divided, NATO United* (Westport, CN: Praeger, 2004), and in particular pp. 124ff, where Kaplan argues that the choices made by NATO's military forces during the 1999 air campaign in Kosovo, and particularly the Organization's Supreme Allied Commander for Europe, General W. Clark, were heavily constrained both by the US Department of Defense and by the Organization's member states. Both the Clinton administration and NATO's Secretary General Javier Solana insisted that the campaign should be conducted by air only, partly to minimize casualties amongst NATO forces, and notwithstanding misgivings expressed by, amongst others, then-CIA Director G. Tenet and then-Chairman of the Joint Chiefs of Staff General Shelton (see J. F. Harris, 'Advice Didn't Sway Clinton on Airstrikes', *Washington Post*, 1 April 1999; 'Stealth Fighter "Shot Down" as Serbs Slaughter Hundreds', *Sunday Times*, 29 March 1999.)

does not confer similar immunity on those international organizations' officials whose decisions are relevantly connected to the plight of the very deprived.

### 3.4.2 Subsistence wars, poverty, and collateral damage

So far, I have argued that the very deprived have the right deliberately to kill affluent civilian wrongdoers only if the latter's individual actions or omissions relevantly contribute to the plight of the very poor. That view is compatible with the claim that some civilians who wrongfully contribute to their plight nevertheless are not liable to being killed (for example, because their contribution takes the form of voting for certain kinds of policies), though they might be liable to the infliction of non-lethal harm, either as a defensive move made on the assumption that war will ensue, or once the war itself has started. It is also compatible with the claim that the very deprived are permitted to kill those civilians foreseeably though unintentionally in the course of that war. In the remainder of this section I focus on the permissible infliction of collateral damage on those members of A who are not taking part at all in their community's war effort. More specifically, I focus on the appropriate weight which P's leaders and citizens should give, when deciding whether to go to war, to the risk that the war would create or worsen severe poverty for the following categories of A's population: the very young, the mentally disabled, but also (if A is governed by a ruthless dictator who uses mass killing as a tool for domestic law enforcement) those who are utterly unable to change A's policy. At first sight their case might seem particularly problematic for a cosmopolitan defence of subsistence wars. For according to cosmopolitan justice, individuals' entitlements to basic resources are independent of their membership in a political community. Were P to act in such a way as to cause or contribute to causing severe poverty for innocent A-civilians, would it not thereby illicitly attach greater importance to relieving severe poverty for its own members than on A-civilians' similar interests?

It is important to bear in mind that P contributes to causing severe, indeed life-threatening, poverty in A, and thus P is not charged with failing to provide assistance to A's members. The question is whether P justifiably infringes non-combatants$_A$' right not to be subject to severe poverty, or whether it violates it. Now, as we saw in Section 1.2.1, individuals, whether acting singly or as a community, are under a *prima facie* duty not to harm innocent bystanders for the sake of securing their own prospects for a minimally decent life. However, as we saw in Section 2.4, to claim that they may never inflict any harm at all on innocent bystanders would be paralyzingly demanding indeed, since (to reiterate) all wars necessarily inflict harm on some innocent bystanders. The question, then, is that of which kind of damage, and more precisely, how much poverty, P may collaterally inflict on A's innocent civilians.

Consider two ways in which P's decision to go to war can contribute to causing severe poverty for A's innocent civilians. First and most obviously, the war will in all likelihood destroy some of A's civilian infrastructures, such as electricity generators, communication lines, food supplies, and so on, which are vital to meeting individuals' basic needs. I see no reason to treat that case any differently from other instances of collateral damage which just belligerents may inflict (on cosmopolitan grounds) on the enemy's innocent civilians. If it is (sometimes) permitted to inflict *lethal* collateral damage on non-combatants$_A$ in the course of a war of defence against a military aggression, then it is (sometimes) permitted to inflict poverty-related collateral damage in the course of a subsistence war.

Second, for as long as A's regime refuses to surrender, it will use resources (material and human) for the prosecution of its (*ex hypothesi* unjust) war which could be used towards helping its (innocent) needy members. Intuitively, it would seem that P is not under a duty to take into account the deprivation-related harm which befalls those civilians as a direct result not of P's own destructive acts, but rather of a decision by A's regime to continue with its unjust war instead of diverting resources to help them. Suppose that the only way I can survive the lethal threat to which an attacker subjects me is by killing him; and suppose further that his death would cause very severe hardship to his dependent children. Ought I sacrifice my life for their sake? Surely not. Whilst I may not intentionally expose those children themselves to save my life (for example, by forcibly using them as shields against their father's attack), I am not under a duty to save them from a harm which is wrongfully inflicted on them by some other party, when saving them from harm would cost me my own life: notwithstanding the difficulties raised by intervening agency (to which I shall return in Section 7.3), there is a limit to what we may expect agents to do for the sake of others. To be clear, my point is not that we need never take into account the harm which innocent parties are likely to suffer at the hands of the targets of our own actions. Suppose that you take an heirloom from me which I legitimately inherited and which does not have much sentimental value for me. Suppose further that you will fight me for it through the courts at all costs—including your dependents' well-being (you are prepared to ruin their prospects for a minimally decent life, and so on). Whilst I would not wrong you by pursuing you through the courts, I ought not to do so, in the face of the harm which your stubbornness would cause to your children relative to the harm which losing that heirloom would do to me. In war, however, lives are at stake on both sides, and this is why, *in the case at issue here*, P need not take into account the deprivation-related harm which A's regime will inflict on its own innocent civilians in the prosecution of that war. At the very least (if the point is too strong), it need not confer on such harm as much importance as it ought to give to the collateral deprivation-related damage it *itself* inflicts on A's innocent civilians.

## 3.5 CONCLUSION

In Chapter 1 we saw that membership in a political community is morally irrelevant to individuals' rights to the resources they need for a minimally decent life. Accordingly, the very deprived have various rights against the foreign affluent that the latter not deny them access to those resources. An important question for cosmopolitans—which they have not fully addressed—is that of the responses which are available to the very deprived should the foreign affluent prove derelict in their duties of distributive justice. In this chapter I have argued that war is one such remedy, under certain conditions. Rather than summarize my arguments, let me highlight ways in which they should lead us to revise the just war tradition, and deal with some worries about the thesis defended here.

I claimed that severe deprivation constitutes a just cause for going to war not merely because it undermines states' political sovereignty and territorial integrity, but also because it harms the very deprived in their individual interests in leading a minimally decent life. By implication, then, the just cause requirement ought not to apply solely to collective goods but can also apply to individual goods. Moreover, in claiming that the very deprived have a right to go to war independently of their state, I have argued that we ought to broaden the scope of the requirement of legitimate authority.

Many will remain unconvinced, on diametrically opposite grounds. On the one hand, some will press that if my accounts of both the affluent's liabilities and the notion of reasonable chance of success are correct, then so few individuals are liable in subsistence wars, and those wars are so seldom just, that the issue is not worth addressing. I disagree. For a start, if I am right that subsistence wars are likely to loom larger on our global horizons than they currently do, then it does pay to inquire whether, and if so under what circumstances, they can be just. Moreover, once one brings into focus the similarities between rights violations which are said to provide a just cause for a traditional war (namely, rights to territorial integrity and political sovereignty) and violations of distributive rights, it is not obvious that subsistence wars are unjust. In such cases, as in other kinds of war which we will examine in subsequent chapters, the delivery of a verdict of 'just' or 'unjust' does require careful analysis.

Others, on the other hand, will claim that the thesis defended here paves the way for more wars still—wars which will harm primarily those for whom they are fought and who are already their chief victims: namely, the very deprived themselves. For war and the destruction it causes triggers, or worsens, poverty. Is more war not the very last thing which they need? Is it not, in fact, utterly self-defeating? Would it not be better for them to seek redress by some other means? Clearly so, *if* those alternative means are effective. It goes without saying that the world would be a better place if the affluent could be persuaded to set up just and democratic international institutions in which the governments of very deprived countries could have a decisive say on matters which affect them most, from trade agreements to conflicts over natural resources. It also goes without saying that if there turned out to be serious prospects for improvement on those fronts without the need to resort to military force, subsistence wars would be unjust, since they would breach the requirement of necessity. However, those conditional concessions are wholly compatible with the view that under certain conditions (such as those outlined in this chapter), revising just war theory in the light of a cosmopolitan ethics of assistance yields the controversial but defensible conclusion that subsistence wars can on principle be just. Moreover, those concessions are also compatible with the thought that one may (under certain conditions) wage war for the sake of protecting the fundamental rights of individuals even if some of those individuals—the intended beneficiaries of the war—will suffer considerable hardship as a result. We shall explore that issue in greater detail in Chapter 5, in the course of our normative study of humanitarian intervention. For now, it is time to address another kind of conflict altogether: civil wars.

# 4

# Civil wars

## 4.1 INTRODUCTION

The empirical literature on war standardly points out that there have been far
more intrastate wars, and higher numbers of casualties in those wars, since
1945, than there have been interstate wars in the same period. From Sierra
Leone to Rwanda, from Afghanistan to Iraq, from Yugoslavia to Somalia, from
Chechnya to the Sudan, from Lebanon to Zaire—to mention but a few
countries ravaged by internecine strife—the list of internal war theatres is
depressingly long and the number of victims, upward of 16 million individuals
since 1945, harrowingly high. My aim in this chapter is to set out and defend a
cosmopolitan account of a subset of intrastate violence: namely, civil wars.[1]

At first sight, that might seem an odd endeavour. On the one hand, if the
distinctiveness of cosmopolitanism as a moral and political theory lies in its
endorsement of the view that *transnational* borders are morally arbitrary, then
it is hard to see what it could possibly tell us about conflicts occurring *within*
borders. And yet, as I shall argue, cosmopolitanism does have something
interesting to say about civil wars, in at least two respects. First, some civil
wars are wars of self-determination. In so far as sufficientist cosmopolitanism
grants individuals a (limited) right to self-determination, it behoves its proponents to set out the conditions under which groups which do not collectively determine their own future (such as non-self-governing minorities

---

[1] See SIPRI, *SIPRI Yearbook 2010* (Oxford: Oxford University Press, 2010). The *Correlates of War
Project*, based at the University of Pennsylvania, has comprehensive datasets on all armed conflicts, both
interstate and intrastate, since the Napoleonic wars. See *Correlates of War* (http://www.correlatesofwar.
org/: 1963–present). For a useful and concise statement of the relevant facts, see, for example,
J. D. Fearon and D. D. Laitin, 'Ethnicity, Insurgency, and Civil War', *The American Political Science
Review* 97 (2003): 75–90, at 75. I use the words 'intrastate wars' or 'civil wars' more or less
interchangeably, against legal usage in fact. In the law of armed conflict, a war of national liberation
against a foreign occupier certainly counts as an intrastate war if it is conducted within the political
boundaries of the country at issue, but not as a civil war. As I note below, however, I see little reason in
principle to rule out wars of national liberation from the category of civil wars. For a clear account of the
evolution of legal classifications in that area, see E. Crawford, *The Treatment of Combatants and
Insurgents under the Law of Armed Conflicts* (Oxford: Oxford University Press, 2010), ch. 1.

within a state) may resort to force for the sake of enjoying that particular good. Second, the resort to and conduct of civil and interstate wars are standardly thought to be subject to different normative principles—not merely by lawyers but also by some philosophers. As we shall see, so to differentiate between state actors and insurgents is not tenable on cosmopolitan grounds: it is a central contention of this chapter that the geographical location of a conflict (as within, or across, borders) and the political status of its actors are irrelevant to the determination of the latter's rights, duties, and liabilities.

On the other hand, others might point out that civil wars do not properly belong to the intellectual field of just war theory, since the latter's main remit is to set out and defend principles for interstate wars. A cursory look at the philosophical literature on war and at the relevant body of international law seems to bear out the criticism. To give but two examples, civil wars are largely absent from Walzer's seminal *Just and Unjust Wars*, and the 1977 Second Protocol Additional to the Geneva Conventions, which tackles intrastate conflicts, is considerably shorter than the First Protocol, which deals with interstate wars. I suspect that for many, civil wars can be adequately approached through a theory of just resistance to illegitimate state action and, when the insurgents act impermissibly, through a theory of just law enforcement by lethal means. On that view, we can dispense with just war theory. This, however, would be a mistake. For a start, the very first codified set of rules for the conduct of armed forces in war—namely, the Lieber Code (1863)—has served as a model for subsequent international texts and yet was written (at President Lincoln's request) as a guide for the Union's army during the American *Civil* War.[2] This suggests that the moral norms which the Union deemed applicable to its domestic conflict are not as different from the norms of interstate conflicts as one might suppose. In any event, war, whether civil or interstate, is not akin to law enforcement: it is about killing as well as inflicting huge losses of property to one's enemy, in defence of some fundamental rights of one's own *qua* individual or *qua* group member. To the extent that just war theory seeks to provide an account of the permissibility of such actions, it is entirely appropriate that it should scrutinise the ethics of civil wars.

Roughly put, a civil war is (typically) a conflict between a group of individuals and the state which has *de facto* authority over them (though we shall return to terminological difficulties below.) Accordingly, a normative

---

[2] Not that the Union's army always abided by the Code—far from it. To give but one example, General Sherman, one of the main Union generals, was well known for advocating and implementing a policy of total war, including scorched-earth tactics, pillaging, and indiscriminate killing of civilians. See, for example, J. McPherson, *Battle Cry of Freedom: The Civil War Era* (London: Penguin Books, 1990), esp. 809ff.

account of civil wars must assess whether the fact of that special relationship together with the fact that one of the belligerents (to wit, the insurgent) is not a state-actor make any difference to the permissibility of the resort to war. I attend to both issues in Sections 4.2 and 4.3 respectively. In Section 4.2 I argue that if a given rights violation constitutes a just cause for an interstate war, it also constitutes a just cause for a civil war—though (as we shall also see) whether the war is inter- or intrastate may well have a bearing on the degree to which the war meets some of the other requirements of both the *jus as bellum* and the *jus in bello*. In Section 4.3 I revisit a thesis which I began defending in Section 3.3, to the effect that individuals in their private capacity may hold the right to wage war. I argue more fully than I did then that it is not a necessary condition for *all* wars to be just that they be waged by state-actors—which thus opens the door (contra some important strands within the tradition) for the view that a civil war can be just on the side of the insurgents. Finally, I close in Section 4.4 with a few comments on agents' liability to lethal harm in such conflicts.

Before I begin, a point of terminology. The *Oxford English Dictionary* defines a civil war as a war 'such as occurs among fellow-citizens or within the limits of one community', in contrast with wars such as occur between states. The contrast should not be drawn too sharply: a civil war can turn into an interstate war once one of the belligerents has become a state which the other belligerent (such as the state from which it seceded) refuses to acknowledge as legitimate. Moreover, some wars would normally be regarded as interstate wars even though they oppose co-citizens only—as when the army of political community A invades political community B, and when a dissident minority within A joins B's army but are the only individuals to resist A's aggression (for example, because members from B who have enlisted never get deployed to the front).[3] My focus will be on wars which occur within the borders of a political community.

The foregoing characterization of civil wars is deceptively simple, however. In particular, one must distinguish between a civil war on the one hand, and on the other hand, criminal violence, sporadic political violence, and genocide respectively. War violence is not the same as criminal violence: unlike the latter, it is directed towards political ends—typically, control of the state's institutions and policies. This is not to say that a regime cannot, by definition, be at war against criminal gangs. Indeed, it is a well-known fact that civil wars which are fought ostensibly for political ends often involve criminal gangs or/

---

[3] I owe this point to Kasper Lippert-Rasmussen.

and are partly funded by criminal activities (since insurgents cannot resort to taxation as a way to fund their war). More strongly still, some criminal gangs such as Latin American drug cartels seek to exercise political and social control over the territory within which they operate.[4] My focus, however, is on those cases where the ends of the conflict are clearly and avowedly political ends.

That said, the fact that an insurgent's ends are political is not enough to deem his or her action a war. Thus, when Timothy McVeigh detonated a truck bomb in front of a federal building in Oklahoma City in 1995, thereby killing 168 people, he was not taking part in a civil war against the US government, whatever he himself may have thought: the relatively low number of victims, together with the fact that his act did not prompt fellow sympathisers or members of the militia movement to emulate him, firmly place the bombing in the category of one-off terrorist acts. Finally, when the Nazi regime killed and imprisoned defenceless German Jews by the hundreds of thousands, they were not engaging in a civil war with that particular community, precisely because they were largely unopposed in their enterprise by their victims. By contrast, the 1994 Rwandan genocide, during which the Hutu government and its militia killed close to one million Tutsis and moderate Hutus in the scope of three months, took place within the context of a long standing conflict between the Tutsi-dominated Rwandan Patriotic Front and the Hutu-dominated regime. Similarly, the genocide of African populations carried out by Sudanese government-backed Arab militias (the *Janjaweed*) in Darfur in 2003–04 cannot be explained outside the decades-long civil war which served as its background. Though civil wars often lead to, or are motivated by the desire for, a genocide, a genocide on its own does not make a civil war.[5]

One must also bear in mind important distinctions between the following kinds of civil war: (a) civil wars fought for the sake of deciding which sub-

---

[4] See, for example, Kaldor, *New and Old Wars*; Munkler, *The New Wars*; D. Keen, 'The Economic Functions of Violence in Civil Wars', *Adelphi Papers 320* (1998).

[5] For an interesting study of the connections between war and genocide, see M. Shaw, *War and Genocide* (Cambridge: Polity Press, 2003). For a useful and concise account of the Darfur genocide, see R. Collins, 'Darfur: A Historical Overview', in S. Totten and E. Markusen (ed.), *Genocide in Darfur: Investigating the Atrocities in the Sudan* (New York: Routledge, 2006); S. Strauss, 'Darfur and the Genocide Debate', *Foreign Affairs* 84 (2005): 123–33. Whether or not the atrocities committed in Darfur by the *Janjaweed* did amount to a genocide in the legal sense of the term (as given by the 1948 Genocide Convention) was the focus of intense debate in the international community at the time. For good discussions, see S. A. Kostas, 'Making the Determination of Genocide in Darfur', in S. Totten and E. Markusen (ed.), *Genocide in Darfur: Investigating the Atrocities in the Sudan* (New York: Routledge, 2006) and J. Fowler, 'A New Chapter of Irony: The Legal Definition of Genocide and the Implications of Powell's Determination', in S. Totten and E. Markusen (ed.), *Genocide in Darfur: Investigating the Atrocities in the Sudan* (New York: Routledge, 2006).

community or group within the larger community will control the state's apparatus; (b) civil wars fought for the sake of founding or preventing the creation of a new state on part of the territory of that larger community; (c) civil wars between insurgents and their regime where the latter's authority over the territory is undermined by the presence of, and its collaboration with, unjust foreign occupiers; (d) civil wars between communal factions with the regime in power attempting to act as a mediator; (e) civil wars between communal factions in the face of the collapse of state institutions. 'Good' examples of the first kind of conflicts are the Lebanese civil war of 1975–90 between and within (sketchily put) Muslims and Christian factions, the Peruvian civil war of 1980–2000 between the Peruvian government and the Communist movement Shining Path, and the Spanish Civil War of 1936–39. The American Civil War and the break-up of Yugoslavia in the 1990s are paradigmatic examples of the second kind of conflict. The armed struggle between the French Resistance and the Vichy regime during World War II illustrates the third kind of conflict. The religious conflict between Protestant and Catholic factions in France in the *initial* stages of the long religious war which took place at the end of the sixteenth century illustrates the fourth kind of war (before the King sided with the Catholics); and the war which ravaged Sierra Leone in the 1990s provides a vivid and depressing example of the fifth kind.[6] In this chapter I shall focus on conflicts of the first three kinds, since the claim that one may go to war against one's state is more controversial than the claim that one may go to war against (unchecked) private wrongdoers within one's community.

Last, but not least, a recurrent difficulty in the empirical literature on civil wars pertains to the status of wars of national liberation against a foreign, colonial power. On some views, those wars are not civil wars proper even though they deserve the label of 'intrastate war', because they are fought against a state which does not have a legitimate claim to govern over the

<hr/>

[6] The literature on the examples I have cited so far is enormous. As first cuts, the following are good, accessible accounts: McPherson, *Battle Cry of Freedom*; P. Preston, *The Coming of the Spanish Civil War: Reform, Reaction and Revolution in the Second Republic*, 2nd edn. (London: Routledge, 1994); M. Wenger and J. Denney, 'Lebanon's Fifteen-Year War 1975–1990', *Middle East Report* 162 (1990): 23–5; C. McClintock, 'The Evolution of Internal War in Peru: The Conjunction of Need, Creed, and Organizational Finance', in C. J. Arnson and I. W. Zartman (ed.), *Re-thinking the Economics of War* (Washington, DC: Woodrow Wilson Center Press, 2005). For a good summary of the break-up of Yugoslavia, see Wheeler, *Saving Strangers*, ch. 8. On the French wars of religion, see P. Benedict, 'The Wars of Religion, 1562–1598', in M. P. Holt (ed.), *Renaissance and Reformation France* (Oxford: Oxford University Press, 2002). On Sierra Leone, see L. Gberie, *A Dirty War in West Africa: the RUF and the Destruction of Sierra Leone* (London: Hurst and Co., 2005). On the Vichy regime, see R. O. Paxton, *Vichy France: Old Guard and New Order, 1940–1944* (New York: Columbia University Press, 1972).

territory which they have colonized. The *OED* definition seems to support that view, in so far as the colonized and the colonizers cannot really be described as fellow citizens (since the former, unlike the latter, do not enjoy citizenship rights) nor even as fellow *community* members (since the latter are foreigners in relation to the former.) On other accounts, however, there is no reason not to treat a colonial war as a kind of civil war. As two commentators note, 'to drop such cases would be like dropping the current conflict in Chechnya as a civil war in Russia if the Chechens succeeded in gaining independence'—which is arguably counter-intuitive.[7]

Drawing together the various points raised by those definitional and typological complexities, I shall posit throughout this chapter that a civil war counts as such if it meets the following conditions: (a) the war is fought either between insurgents and the regime in place, or amongst factions within the community; (b) the war is fought for political ends; (c) the number of victims must exceed 500; (d) those casualties are inflicted over several months; (e) each side is genuinely in a position to inflict casualties on the other side.[8]

## 4.2 CIVIL WARS AND THE 'SPECIAL RELATIONSHIP'

Civil wars, it is standardly said, last longer and cause more devastation than interstate wars. Although the blood-soaked history of the twentieth century should make us hesitate before subscribing to that particular verdict, those wars do seem more intractable than their transnational counterparts, taking place as they do amongst groups linked by long standing rivalries and shared history and on territories which are often rich in natural resources. It is not surprising, therefore, that a good deal of the empirical literature on civil wars should seek to explain, *inter alia*, what motivates participants to subject others, and expose themselves, to such suffering. One of the key debates in that area is that which opposes proponents of the view that participants are motivated by deep political, religious, and cultural grievances, and advocates of the thesis that greed for the riches of the earth—diamonds, oil, and other natural resources—is the decisive explanatory factor for the onset, duration,

---

[7] Fearon and Laitin, 'Ethnicity, Insurgency, and Civil War', 76.

[8] The account I offer here is a combination of fairly standard definitions found in, and used by, for example, the online project *Correlates of War*. See also P. Collier and A. Hoeffler, 'Greed and grievance in civil war', *Oxford Economic Papers* 56 (2004): 563–95; Fearon and Laitin, 'Ethnicity, Insurgency, and Civil War'; N. Sambanis, 'What Is Civil War? Conceptual and Empirical Complexities of an Operational Definition', *The Journal of Conflict Resolution* 48 (2004): 814–58.

and ferocity of those wars. As one might expect, the truth seems to lie in the combination of those various and multifaceted demands.[9]

In any event, irrespective of participants' motives, our focus for now is on just causes for civil wars—in either the narrow or wide senses defined in Section 2.3.1. As we saw in Section 1.4, individuals are not under a duty to regard their regime's directives as binding if the latter fail to respect their fundamental human rights and do not enable them better to fulfil their moral duties than if those directives were not issued in the first instance. A genocidal or grossly negligent regime such as the Nazi and Soviet regimes is thus not to be deemed legitimate by its members (or anyone else, for that matter). However, that point alone—that such a regime is not legitimate—does not entail that its victims have a just cause for going to war—in other words, for subjecting its civilian and military officials to widespread and ongoing lethal threats. War consists, *inter alia*, in inflicting widespread damage to the life and limbs of considerable numbers of people to political ends—whether those ends are ends in themselves (as when the war is fought in defence of communal values) or means towards the protection of some further ends (as when the war is fought in defence of individual rights the protection of which requires political changes); and it is the infliction of such harms which stands in need of justification—on pains of being deemed unjust. For a group of German Jews to kill the SS soldiers who are sending them at gunpoint to Auschwitz is not to go to war against the regime. For them to kill not merely those soldiers but members of the SS in general as well as Wehrmacht soldiers, as part of a broader campaign aimed at stopping the genocide in the long term, is an act of war. In the most severe cases, stopping exactions will require overthrowing the regime which commits them. In less severe cases it will require winning a sufficiently comprehensive military victory so as to force the regime to effectuate radical reforms. Our task, at this juncture, is to discern when exactions committed against individuals by their

---

[9] The *locus classicus* for the greed thesis are P. Collier and A. Hoeffler, 'On Economic Causes of Civil War', *Oxford Economic Papers* 50 (1998): 563–73, and 'Greed and Grievance in Civil War'. For a philosophical account of the so-called 'resource curse', see Wenar, 'Property Rights and the Resource Curse'. For the view that ethnic grievances are a powerful explanatory factor in civil wars, see, for example, D. Horowitz, *Ethnic groups in conflict* (Berkeley, CA: University of California Press, 1985). The literature on the greed versus grievance thesis is enormous. For useful first cuts at the debate, see, for example, M. Berdal, 'Beyond greed and grievance—and not to soon . . .', *Review of International Studies* 31 (2005): 687–98; C. J. Arnson and I. W. Zartman (ed.), *Re-thinking the Economics of War* (Washington, DC: Woodrow Wilson Center Press, 2005); M. Berdal and D. M. Malone (ed.), *Greed and Grievance: Economic Agendas in Civil Wars* (Boulder, CO: Lynn Rienner, 2000). For a fascinating study of the interplay between macro-cleavages between groups taken as a whole, and micro-cleavages between individual participants in civil wars, see S. N. Kalyvas, 'The Ontology of "Political Violence": Action and Identity in Civil Wars', *Perspectives on Politics* 1 (2003): 475–94.

own regime constitute a just cause for war so conceived, as opposed to a justification for 'mere' self-defensive killing.

In the *inter*state case, the judgment that there is a just cause for war (understood as a military campaign to remove the aggressor's army from one's territory, for example, or forcibly removing the aggressor's regime and replacing it with a non-threatening one) presents relatively little difficulty. As we saw in Chapter 2, if sovereign state A violates the individual and jointly held rights of members of sovereign state V, either directly through the use or with the help of lethal force, then V has a just cause for going to war against A. The question, then, is whether those rights violations which provide their victims with a just cause for waging war against a foreign attacker[10] also provide them with a just cause for going to war against their own regime or fellow community members. More generally put, the question is whether the fact that victims stand in a special relationship with the rights violator (it is *their* regime after all) has any bearing on the determination of the rights violation as a just cause for taking up arms.

On one possible view, the fact of that relationship does make a crucial difference, as follows: individuals' *prima facie* duty to regard their state's directives as binding, which they owe to one another but not to foreign actors (or at least not to the same degree) forbids them to take up arms against the former, though they would have a just cause against the latter had it committed the same wrongdoings. From the standpoint of cosmopolitan justice, however, that view is not tenable. For to reiterate, a regime's directives are binding only if they do not violate the fundamental human rights of those who are subject to those directives, and if they enable individuals better to comply with their moral duties than they would otherwise. Accordingly, the claim that there is a such a duty cannot provide a basis for distinguishing between rights violations which provide a just cause (as occur across borders) and rights violations which do not (as occur within borders).

That said, individuals do have (limited) rights against their regime and compatriots which they do not have against foreign states. To use the terminology employed in Section 1.2.3, and as noted in Section 1.4, *qua* human beings they have a general right against the world at large (*in rem*) to the respect and promotion of their interests in communal goods such as political self-determination; *qua* members of a political community they have special rights against fellow citizens (*in personam*) that the latter not harm those interests in so far as the latter are furthered through that community's institutions. Those

---

[10] By which I mean here, a foreign regime which has neither *de jure* nor *de facto* jurisdiction over them.

special rights *in personam* are the instantiation of those general rights *in rem*. But one should not infer from that point the thought that a civil war cannot have, as a just cause, a kind of rights violations which an interstate war would have. As I shall now show through the example of the Spanish Civil War, the fact that rights are violated by the victims' regime is irrelevant to the determination of the just cause. Following its electoral victory in April 1931, the Spanish Left established the Second Republic and conducted a programme of religious, military, and agrarian reforms, with a view to turning Spain into a liberal democracy and to improving the disastrous social and economic situation of the landless rural workers. Although the Left lost the general elections of November 1933 to a centre-right government, it won again in 1936 under the label Popular Front. Convinced that the legalist route—working within the institutional, democratic framework of the Republic only to undermine it once in power—would not work, the Right, backed by most of the army and led by General Franco, rose against the Popular Front on 18 July 1936, thus starting a civil war which it finally won in 1939.[11]

Now, Spanish citizens who elected the Popular Front had a special right against fellow Spaniards who supported Franco that they accept the outcome of the elections, as well as a general right against foreign regimes that the latter not support the insurgents. In overthrowing the democratically elected and legitimate government, the insurgents acted unjustly. So did foreign supporters of Franco—most notably, Nazi Germany and Fascist Italy—who supplied him with weapons and military personnel; indeed, who on occasion took a direct part in the civil war (as when the German Luftwaffe bombed the Basque town of Guernica in April 1937.) *Both* Franquist insurgents and those foreign actors provided the Left with a just cause for going to war. They did so in different ways, of course: the former by refusing to accept the outcome of the election and thus by betraying the trust of their compatriots; the latter by agreeing to lend military support to an unjust end. However, the relevant consideration for deciding whether supporters of the Popular Front had a just cause against their compatriots is not the fact that Franco and the insurgents enjoyed co-citizenship with left-wing fellow Spaniards (or, indeed, that they had a *special* duty of obedience in respect of the democratically elected Popular Front). Rather, it is the fact that the insurgents violated fellow Spaniards' fundamental right (*in rem* and general) to political self-determination. Put differently, if a regime or a group within the state violates a fundamental and general right *in rem* of individuals (in that instance, the right to political self-determination) by

11 See Preston, *The Coming of the Spanish Civil War.*

infringing the special rights *in personam* which instantiate it, then its actions do provide victims with a just cause for waging a civil war, in just the same way as the violation of that very same fundamental right at the hands of a foreign actor would also provide those very same rights-bearers with a just cause for going to war against the latter.

That conclusion finds support in cosmopolitan principles of justice. As we saw in Section 1.3, membership in a political community is morally irrelevant to individuals' basic entitlements. As we also saw in Section 2.3.2, combatants who fight on the unjust side are not permitted—indeed, lack the right—to kill enemy (*ex hypothesi* just) combatants in defence of their comrades. *If* they decide to fight, they must side with the enemy. By implication, unjust combatants are liable to being killed at the hands of *their* comrades for unjustly killing the enemy. In other words, just as political membership is irrelevant to the conferral of fundamental rights, it is irrelevant to the imposition of liability to harm for violating rights. To claim otherwise is to claim, counter-intuitively, that Polish Jews had a just cause for waging war against Nazi Germany but that German Jews did not, even though both groups were victims of the Holocaust. The point also applies to violations of the right not to be subject to severe poverty. Take the case of the Ukrainian famine. From 1928 onwards the Soviet Government, aided by local party functionaries and armed urban cadres, began to seize crops, as well as seeds, from all over the country, with a view to funding rapid industrialization by exporting the grain. The Ukraine, which was one of the country's richest rural areas, was particularly affected. Predictably, as anyone at the time could have foreseen, famine set in, which in Ukraine alone killed several million people. It is still a matter of debate amongst historians whether the famine was intended by the Soviet authorities as a way decisively to weaken the Ukrainian peasantry (which was hostile to Moscow), or whether it was the result of culpable negligence, short-sightedness, and incompetence on the part of the authorities. On either view, it constituted a gross violation of human rights. If the conclusions reached in Chapter 3 are sound, the Ukraine clearly would have had a just cause for war against the Soviet regime had it remained a sovereign, independent state. According to cosmopolitan justice, however, it is equally clear that the fact that the Ukraine was a republic within a federal union did not deprive it of a just cause against Moscow. By the same token, insurgent movements which have taken up arms against their regime as a means to force the reforms necessary to alleviate severe, debilitating poverty had a just cause for so doing.[12]

---

[12] For a classic—if controversial—account of the Ukrainian famine, see R. Conquest, *The Harvest of Sorrow* (London: Hutchinson, 1986). A useful summary of the policy of collectivisation can be found in S. Fitzpatrick, *The Russian Revolution*, 2nd edn. (Oxford: Oxford University Press, 1994),

The foregoing points have interesting implications for wars of secession. Consider the following two cases:

*Interstate aggression.* Sovereign state A invades sovereign state V to appropriate part of the latter's territory.
*Secession.* Political community C (or a federation of such communities) within sovereign state A unilaterally decides to secede, and declares its independence. A sends in armed forces to block the secessionist move.

*If* V has, but C lacks, a claim to national self-determination, then A is committing an act of wrongful aggression in *Interstate aggression* but is legitimately defending the integrity of the state in *Secession*. The American Civil War is a case in point. Recall that a state is legitimate only if it respects the human rights of its members (as well as outsiders). By implication, not all cultures are worth protecting through the exercise of self-determination. A cultural or political group which is threatened in its common life by its own state thus does not have the right to defend itself pre-emptively by waging a war against it if its common life violates the central tenets of cosmopolitan justice. To illustrate, to the extent that the Confederate States of America regarded Abraham Lincoln's victory in the 1860 Presidential election as an indication of the North's resolve to undermine the institution of slavery, and to the extent that they regarded abolition as a justification for seceding, they did not in fact have a just cause for going to war against the North.[13] Suppose, however, that C *does* have a legitimate claim to secede from A—that is to say, a claim to become a sovereign independent state on the territory on which it currently lives and which is currently within A's jurisdiction.[14] In that case, C's declaration of independence is legitimate, and A's attempt militarily to thwart C's exercise of its right to national self-determination is wrongful. That

ch. 5. For the view that severe poverty is a just cause for civil war, see R. Gargarella, 'The Right of Resistance in Situations of Severe Deprivation', in T. Pogge (ed.), *Freedom from Poverty as a Human Right: Who Owes What to the Very Poor?* (Oxford: Oxford University Press, 2007). For the role of hunger in the Peruvian conflict, see McClintock, 'The Evolution of Internal War in Peru: The Conjunction of Need, Creed, and Organizational Finance'.

[13] For a magisterial account of the American Civil War and of the central role which slavery played in it, see McPherson, *Battle Cry of Freedom*, esp. chs. 7, 8, and 16.

[14] I say 'In addition' because (as we saw in Section 1.4) it is one thing to claim a right to govern oneself: it is another to claim a right to govern over a particular territory. In addition, it is one thing to claim a right to govern over a particular territory, but it is quite another to claim a right to take from another party land over which the latter has so far exercised jurisdiction in common with us and in which it has invested together with us. To use a standard analogy, it is one thing to grant spouses the right unilaterally to dissolve their marriage: it is quite another to grant them the right unilaterally to decide who, of the two, will keep the family home. The issue of secession thus raises specific territorial issues. See, for example, A. E. Buchanan, *Secession: The Morality of Political Divorce from Fort Sumter to Lithuania and Quebec* (Boulder, CO: Westview Press, 1991); M. Moore (ed.), *National Self-Determination and Secession* (Oxford: Oxford University Press, 1998).

being so, C has a just cause for waging a self-defensive war against A. In this case there is no difference, with respect to the just cause, between *Interstate aggression* and *Secession*.

Thus, grievous rights violations, backed by or carried out through the use of lethal force and of a kind as to provide their victims with a just cause for war against a foreign wrongdoer, also provide their victims with a just cause for war against their own, domestic, wrongdoer. Note, however, that the thesis is wholly compatible with the (plausible) view that a given rights violation is more likely to provide its victims with an all-things-considered justification for the war when the wrongdoer is a foreign state than when it is the victims' own regime. For a war is just not merely if it has a just cause: it must also be the option of last resort, the harms it causes must be outweighed by the goods it brings about, and it must stand a reasonable chance of success. A civil war waged against one's democratic regime is perhaps less likely to meet the condition of last resort than a war waged against a foreign regime, to the extent that the former is more likely to offer its members non-violent ways to express their grievances and respond to force. Likewise, a civil war as waged by groups which still (*ex hypothesi*) lack the full attributes and wherewithal of a state is less likely to succeed than an interstate war; it is also by that token perhaps less likely to meet the requirement of proportionality. Conversely (and the point bears stressing), it could be that victims of rights violations as committed by their regime have an all-things-considered right to go to war against the latter which they would not have had had the violations been committed by a foreign state. Whether those points hold depends on the facts of each case. In any event they do not undermine the conclusion that the violation of a fundamental right—a violation, in other words, which rights-bearers are not under any obligation to accept—which, if committed by a foreign state would provide them with a just cause for war against the latter, also provides them with a just cause for war against their own, culpable regime.

## 4.3 NON-STATE ACTORS AND
## THE RIGHT TO WAGE WAR

Let us assume, then, that some individuals within state A have a just cause for taking up arms against their regime. Let us assume further that war is the option of last resort, that it has a reasonable chance of success, and that there is good reason to think that it would meet the requirement of proportionality. According to orthodox just war theory, however, such a war would be unjust, precisely because its participants—on the insurgent side—do not meet what has become a fundamental *ad bellum* requirement for a just war: to wit, the requirement of legitimate authority. I took steps to reject the orthodox view in Section 3.3: there I argued that the very poor themselves have the right to go to war against the affluent if their own state is derelict in its own duties towards them. In this section I provide a fuller discussion of the requirement of legitimate authority. According to the deep morality of war, I argue, it is not necessary for a war to be just that it should be waged by the kinds of entity on which the right to go to war has traditionally been conferred: namely, state or quasi-state actors. Rather, an entity can hold the right to wage war if it is the best placed to put a stop to the wrongdoings which provide agents with a just cause for war. As we shall see, it might be that some just causes are best prosecuted by state actors whilst others can successfully be fought for by non-state belligerents. I first offer reasons to oppose the requirement of legitimate authority, before scrutinizing three objections against abandoning it.

### 4.3.1 Jettisoning the requirement of legitimate authority

The requirement, though central to medieval and modern interpretations of the tradition, has received less attention in the contemporary literature than other conditions for a just war. It stipulates who can judge whether the war is just (whether it has a just cause, would be a proportionate response, and so on), as well as who can act on the basis of that judgement. Those two stipulations need not coincide: it is entirely coherent on the one hand to say that anyone can reach a judgement on the justness of the war, and on the other hand to insist that only agents with specific features can resort to war. In fact, very few philosophers take the view that no one except legitimate war-wagers can judge whether the war is just. Accordingly, the requirement of legitimate authority usually applies to the right to wage war rather than the right to express a judgement about its moral status.

What counts as a legitimate authority is of crucial importance. As standardly interpreted in the modern European era, the requirement confers the right to wage war (in other words, the status of lawful belligerent) on states and coalitions of states—in other words, on sovereign political organizations with the power to enforce laws within a given territory. That view gained ascendancy, at least in Europe, over a long period of time lasting from about the fourteenth century to the end of the eighteenth century (prior to which the right to wage war was gifted, not merely to the sovereign, but to any prince who had the wherewithal to raise an army and buy its loyalty), and found its clearest expression in the writings of, amongst others, Augustine, Aquinas, and

Pufendorf. As the former avers in *Contra Faustum* (XXII, 74–5), war must be declared by a legitimate authority so that a soldier, acting as he does under orders from the Prince, does not violate God's proscription against killing. Likewise, Aquinas insists in *Summa Theologia* (II–II, Q. 40) that war should be waged by a legitimate authority—that is to say, the ruler—as a precondition for it to be a just war. In a similar vein, Pufendorf stresses in *On the Duty of Man and Citizen* that 'the right of initiating war in a state lies with the sovereign' (16–8).[15]

In the aftermath of colonial wars, the status of lawful belligerent has been conferred on political movements engaged in so-called 'wars of national liberation' which have typically been fought against oppressive foreign rulers.[16] Those non-state actors are thus treated as if they were states, on the twofold grounds that they defend 'state values' such as national sovereignty and territorial integrity from colonial powers, and that they are representative of the people on whose behalf they fight. Interestingly, a people need not be organized into a national liberation movement in order to be regarded as a lawful belligerent: the laws of war and orthodox just war theory confer legitimacy on a *levée en masse* of a people against its foreign conqueror. In so doing, however, the tradition does not depart from one of its central aims, which is to justify states' right to resort to violence in defence of their territorial integrity and political sovereignty. Rather, it strengthens the principle by widening its scope, since it now implies that colonial wars, fought as they are by national communities which are wrongfully denied the attributes of state sovereignty, ought to be regarded as a kind of interstate war.

The rationale for restricting the conferral of the right to wage war to public, sovereign authorities, is the following. Wars are normally fought in defence of communal, state interests, such as sovereignty and territorial integrity. Whether or not the community's resources—both material and human—should be deployed, at considerable and inevitable costs, for the defence of those interests is to be decided by the community's rulers, for they and they alone have the authority to decide what those common interests are and what

[15] Augustine, 'Contra Faustum', in M. W. Tkacz and D. Kries (ed.), *Augustine's Political Writings* (Indianapolis, IN: Hackett, 1994); Aquinas, *Summa Theologia*. ed. B. Bros. (Grand Rapids, MI: Online Christian Classics Ethereal Library, 1947); Pufendorf, *On the Duty of Man and Citizen*. ed. J. Tully. (Cambridge: Cambridge University Press, 1991). See also B. Coppieters, 'Legitimate Authority', in B. Coppieters and N. Fotion (ed.), *Moral Constraints on War* (Landham, MA: Lexington Books, 2002), pp. 41–4, and Coates, *The Ethics of War*, ch. 5.
[16] See articles 1(4) and 44(3) of the 1977 Protocol Additional to the Geneva Convention of 12 August 1949 Relative to the Protection of Victims of International Armed Conflicts. For an illuminating philosophical treatment of the orthodox view as applied to national liberation movements is C. Kutz, 'The Difference Uniforms Make: Collective Violence in Criminal Law and War', *Philosophy & Public Affairs* 33 (2005): 148–80.

their defence requires. As it happens, the status of lawful belligerent is now conferred on national liberation movements, on the grounds that the latter have a plausible claim to representing the peoples on whose behalf they act. By that token, on cosmopolitan grounds, the same legitimacy can easily be conferred on a people which rises up against its own, tyrannical state. For a cosmopolitan, the rights of state officials are derived from and constrained by the fundamental rights of the state's individual members. In so far as a tyrannical state, via its agents, fails to respect those fundamental rights, it has lost its claim that its victims not overthrow it by military force. More precisely, agents of that state not only no longer have the *de jure* power to govern: they no longer have a claim, qua such officials, not to be violently interfered with in the exercise of their *de facto* but illegitimate power.

Yet the troublesome question for cosmopolitanism is whether or not it is a necessary condition for an agent to have the right to wage war that he or she be an official of a state or quasi-state. I do not think that it is. On the contrary, on cosmopolitan grounds, groups of actors which act in unstructured, disorganized ways, as well as individuals themselves, can have the right to go to war. For consider. The force of the requirement of legitimate authority partly depends on the soundness of the view that war is the exercise of lethal force in defence of communal, political ends—paradigmatically so, national sovereignty and territorial integrity—which states, as agents of their community, are tasked with protecting. Clearly, as we saw in Chapter 2, a cosmopolitan can happily endorse that view, on the grounds that violations of V's political sovereignty and territorial integrity threaten its members' fundamental human rights. However—and this is crucial—not all such rights are rights to communal goods; most such rights, in fact, are rights to goods and freedoms the provision and protection of which are of central importance to individuals *qua* individuals. I argued in Section 3.2 that cosmopolitans have every reason to broaden the range of just causes for waging war so as to include violations of individual basic rights, as well as violations of collective, political rights. If that is the case, there is less reason to insist that war be waged (if it is to be just) by actors—states, or aspirants to statehood—whose task it is to promote and protect their members' *communal* political ends.

The requirement of legitimate authority traditionally understood is the weaker, thus, for that particular reinterpretation of the just-cause requirement. But there are further reasons for doubting its cogency. Consider the following example. Regime A is guilty of gross human rights violations against a religious group V. Its agents have closed all of V's churches, maintain surveillance operations on suspected religious leaders, and routinely carry out acts of killing and torture against V's members. Clearly, V has a just cause for using lethal force against A. But a cosmopolitan who insists that war, in order to be just, must also be waged by a legitimate authority such as a state, quasi-state, or supranational institutions, is committed to the view that V cannot wage a *just* war against A, but that it would have been able to do so had it been a (quasi) state-actor of some kind. And yet, so to deny V the status of a lawful belligerent is misguided, *on cosmopolitan grounds*. For cosmopolitanism claims that all human beings have human rights to the goods and freedoms they need in order to lead a minimally decent life—irrespective of residence, gender, race, and so on, since membership in those groups is irrelevant to their need for the goods and freedoms which those rights secure. As I argued in Section 3.3, the right to protect oneself from violations of one's human rights on the part of others is also a human right, in the sense that it is a right to a freedom (the freedom to defend oneself, without interference, against others) which we need in order to lead a minimally decent life. By extension, the right to wage a war in defence of one's human rights should also be conceived of as a human right. If that is so, the right cannot be denied to some groups of individuals on the grounds that they lack some characteristic or other, when lacking or possessing those characteristics is irrelevant to their fundamental interest in being able to protect their rights. Whether or not a group is a national liberation movement, a state, or organised into supranational institutions, is precisely one such characteristic. A cosmopolitan who would claim otherwise would commit herself to the two-pronged view (at least at first sight) that the conferral of the right not to be killed without just cause, or the right to worship as one wishes, or the right not to be subject to severe poverty, is not dependent on individuals' membership in a given political community rather than another, but that the conferral of the right to defend those very same rights is dependent on membership in a community of a particular kind. And that, it seems, is blatantly incoherent.

To recapitulate: it is not necessary for an actor to have the right to wage war that it be a group with *de facto* power or *de jure* authority coercively to enforce its decisions over a given territory. Still, some might insist that it be held, at the very least, by a *group*, however unstructured or disorganised. On that view, individuals acting alone cannot be regarded as lawful belligerents, and their war, therefore, cannot be regarded as just. The point is definitional as much as normative. For war, if we are to rely on the *Oxford English Dictionary*, is defined as 'Hostile contention by means of armed forces, carried on between nations, states, or rulers, or between parties in the same nation or state; the employment of armed forces against a foreign power, or against an opposing party in the state.' Admittedly, that definition seems to rule out the possibility that an individual can have the right to wage war, for the obvious reason that one person makes neither a party nor armed forces. Yet it is not entirely clear that war must, by definition, oppose armed *groups* of individuals. Suppose that one individual embarks on his own in a violent campaign to put an end to a grievously unjust institution in his own country—say slavery—when peaceful, democratic means have failed. He blows up armouries, kills slave-owners as well as the policemen who stand guard at slave auctions, and having evaded the police he does it again, and again, and again. It would seem odd to maintain that he is *not* committing acts of war.[17] In any event, the pressing question is whether, acting alone as he does, he can have the right to commit that act. Put more generally, the question is whether, *if* all other requirements of *jus ad bellum* are satisfied, the mere fact that one individual alone is destroying property and human life warrants the conclusion that his actions—call them war or not—are wrongful. That is a substantive, normative issue, which cannot be resolved by definitional *fiat*.

No war (to my knowledge) has ever been fought by one individual single-handedly. Yet the question is worth addressing, on two grounds. First, it is true that individuals acting on their own do not inflict the kind and scale of damage which are constitutive of war because they do not have the ability to mount kinetic large-scale attacks (with missiles, tanks, and guns); however, our increased reliance on computers, and vulnerability to their failure, correspondingly provides lone hackers with unparalleled destructive abilities. Granted, the fact that a large-scale computer attack on our transport systems or water delivery networks has not yet occurred suggests that breaching system firewalls is not as easy as popular TV series such as *Spooks* or *24* make it sound. Still, there have already been smaller-scale attacks—notably in 2000, when Hezbollah cyber-targeted a number of Israeli Internet companies.[18] It would be irresponsible to assume that individuals acting on their own will not at least attempt to do the same sooner rather than later.

Second, the issue here is whether individuals, in their private capacity as opposed to *qua* members of an avowedly political movement, have the right to wage war. The claim that they do finds support in the writings of both Vitoria

---

[17] I have in mind the abolitionist John Brown, who mounted several armed attacks, in the course of which some people died, against pro-slavery activists in the late 1850s. John Brown did not act alone but led a small group of men. My point, precisely, is that I do not see what difference his acting alone would have made to the characterization of his actions as 'of war'. I am grateful to Chrisantha Hermanson and Cheney Ryan for bringing my attention to this example. For a fascinating biography of Brown, see D. Reynolds, *John Brown, Abolitionist* (New York: Vintage Books, 2005). For a shorter argument to the effect that anyone with a just cause can have authority to declare war, see also Palmer-Fernandez, 'Cosmpolitan Revisions to Just War Theory'.

[18] R. Thornton, *Asymmetric Warfare: Threat and Response in the Twenty-First Century* (Cambridge: Polity, 2007), 61, and ch. 3 in general.

and Grotius. Thus, Vitoria claims that 'any person, even a private citizen, may declare and wage a defensive war'. When his act of war is a response to an imminent threat to his life or property, he need not obtain permission from a public authority. Similarly, Grotius argues that a private man may wage war against his own state if no legal recourse is available, as well as against a sovereign other than his own. This is not to say that Vitoria and Grotius see no important moral difference between private and public wars. According to Vitoria, for example, a commonwealth may, but a private individual may not, wage a punitive war. According to Grotius, when a war endangers the state itself, the sovereign authority alone has the right to start it. Still, the fact remains that, in principle, individuals may sometimes go to war absent permission from the sovereign and in defence of their fundamental interests in life and property. In an age—ours—where the primary targets of belligerents are civilians who can expect little, by way of protection, from their state, Vitoria's and Grotius's point is worth bearing in mind.[19]

Furthermore, the very reasons which tell against conferring the right to wage war solely on sovereign and independent states (or coalitions thereof) also tell against conferring it on groups only. To reiterate, and as we saw in Chapter 1, cosmopolitan justice holds that individuals' prospects for a minimally decent life ought not to be jeopardized for reasons which are beyond their control. Accordingly, conferring the right to wage war on groups only, and not individuals acting on their own, is to penalize the latter for something for which they are not responsible: to wit, not belonging to a group which, for example, has a just cause for going to war *qua* group, or is able and willing to go to war. Return to the case of Rwanda, and suppose that the Rwandan Patriotic Front, which eventually overthrew the genocidal Hutu regime in June 1994, had not existed; suppose in fact that no armed, organized, structured group had been able to come to the defence of the victims, and that the latter would have had no recourse but to fight on their own in a series of disconnected defensive moves without a clear chain of command. Suppose, finally, that they somehow would have been able to kill the regime's main officials and weaken the government to such an extent as to halt the genocide. Surely it would be incoherent to regard their war as *unjust* simply because they fought it in disparate rather than in organized ways. To be sure, if a single individual were to wage a war against a state on the grounds that the latter has violated his fundamental human rights, he would in all likelihood fall foul of the requirement that war should have a reasonable chance of success. Or he

---

[19] Vitoria, *On the Law of War*, Q.1, 2–3; Grotius, *The Rights of War and Peace*, Book I, chs. III–V.

would probably inflict far more harm, for the sake of redressing the injustice which gave rise to his just cause, than would be allowed by the principle of proportionality. In either case this would lead us to deny him the right to wage *that particular war*. But it would not, in and of itself, rebut the radical claim that he can hold the right to wage war in general. Nor, more generally, would it rebut the claim that individuals can hold that right in their private capacity.

To be clear, my claim is not that individuals acting alone have the authority to wage war against a foreign aggressor whenever her country is attacked, irrespective of what her own state might do. In fact, to the extent that they would be better off by transferring the meta-right to protect their human rights to an organization like the state, it is in their interest to do so. Should the state be derelict, however, the meta-right to protect fundamental human rights reverts back to individuals. On that account, and in line with the cosmopolitan account of state legitimacy which underpins this book, the state's right to wage war is one which it has precisely to the extent that it does a better job than individuals at protecting the latter's fundamental human rights through the use of lethal force. If the state is unable or unwilling to wage war on behalf of its individual members in those cases where there is an all-things-considered justification for it, the right to do so reverts to the latter.

### 4.3.2 Three objections

In the remainder of this chapter I rebut three objections against my claim that a war can be just even if it is not fought by a sovereign state, a coalition of states, or a national liberation movement, and in so doing qualify the view that the requirement of legitimate authority ought to be jettisoned. According to the first objection, private actors who go to war are more likely to act in breach of the principle of non-combatant immunity than states are when waging war against other states, and we thus ought to view the claim that non-state actors can rightfully wage war with extreme caution. The reasons why that is so are twofold.[20] First, individuals and private groups typically are weaker from a

---

[20] See Coates, *The Ethics of War*, 131–4. The objection under scrutiny here is not quite the same as another objection which has regularly been levelled against the view (which I defended in Sections 3.3 and 4.3.1) that individuals acting alone hold the right to wage war: namely, that I am in effect condoning terrorism. This objection invites the following response. Unless one is prepared to stipulate by definition that terrorism is morally wrong, to say that I am endorsing terrorism is no objection to my view. In so far as settling normative issues by definitional *fiat* is not a good idea, I propose to adopt here a value-neutral definition of terrorism, whereby an act of terrorism is an act of extreme violence carried out by non-state actors against innocent civilians with a view to furthering some social and political goal. On that definition, whether terrorism so defined is morally justifiable is

purely military point of view than the state which they are fighting (be it their own or not). As a result, they more often than not invoke the requirement of necessity (`we must do whatever is necessary to win the war`) to justify acts of killing against non-combatants which would not be necessary, and thus not permitted, in wars whose actors have comparable military strengths and weaknesses. Second, wars which are fought by private actors are more often than not justified by belligerents on the grounds that the whole order which they seek to overthrow is oppressive. That, in turn, leads them to identify as combatants anyone who acts for, and supports, that order, and who yet would be regarded as non-combatants in interstate wars.

We shall return to the ethical issues raised by military asymmetry in Chapter 7. Meanwhile, measured in millions of lives lost, it is unclear that more non-combatants have been killed in wars involving private actors than in interstate wars.[21] In any event, even if the objection's central claim is correct—namely, that private belligerents violate the principle of non-combatant immunity more often than states or supranational institutions do—its lesson is limited. For it merely suggests that we are more likely to arrive at the conclusion, in specific instances, that private belligerents in a particular case have breached the principle, and thus that their war was unjust, than we are to do so in cases where wars are fought by public belligerents. But it does not support the conclusion that the right to wage war should be conferred only on state actors.

A second (three-pronged) cosmopolitan objection might perhaps provide stronger support for that conclusion.[22] Individuals, it is sometimes argued, generally cannot take the law in their own hands whenever their regime wrongs them: instead, they should go through legal channels. Moreover, in so far as there is considerable disagreement as to what constitutes a right violation, what are the best ways of promoting rights, and when and how war can or should be waged, we need to defer to the judgement of a legitimate authority such as a political community—and preferably states or supranational institutions—when making such decisions. Finally, in so far as war can

---

a further question. *If* terrorism so defined is not permissible, then the objection does have a point, *provided* that my view of legitimate authority does indeed entail that killing innocent civilians is morally permissible. I do not think that it does—any more than the claim that a state has authority to go to war entails that its agents may kill innocent civilians.

[21] My point is compatible with the well-established fact that civil wars kill more civilians than they kill soldiers (see, for example, Kaldor, *New and Old Wars*). Death tolls in twentieth-century wars are a matter of dispute—not least because of the difficulties inherent in obtaining reliable data. For a list of available sources and death-toll estimates in post-1945 conflicts, see M. Leitenberg, 'Deaths in Wars and Conflicts between 1945 and 2000', *Occasional Papers*, no. 29 (2006), http://www.cissm.umd.edu/papers/display.php?id=153 (accessed 6 June 2011).

[22] See Caney, *Justice Beyond Borders*, 206, for the first and second prongs. See Rodin, *War and Self-Defense*, 174–88, for the third prong.

only be conceived of as an operation of law enforcement and punishment, and in so far as only legitimate authorities such as states or a union of states can enforce the law and punish wrongdoers, only legitimate authorities of that kind have the right to wage war.

This argument in favour of the principle of legitimate authority is cosmopolitan in that it need not, and in fact, as articulated by its proponents, does not, vest the right to wage war in states only, but also in supranational, democratic, institutions or, indeed, a global state, the legitimacy of which is in turn defended by appealing to their ability to protect and promote human rights. However, it remains unconvincing. To repeat, war is not an operation of law enforcement. At the very least, a defence of the right to wage war must account for the fact that war, if it is about anything at all, is about killing and inflicting serious harm on other people in self-defence or other defence. If that is correct, it will not do to reject the conferral of the right to wage war on private individuals by appealing to the importance of ensuring that norms be enforced solely by independent sovereign states or supranational institutions. Moreover, insisting that individuals go through legal channels rather than take the law in their own hands will not do when they do not have access to such channels in the first instance—as is the case when their regime is violating their fundamental rights or (in the case of so-called failed states) is simply powerless to enforce their rights against sub-state wrongdoers. Nor will it do when supranational institutions are unable or unwilling to take their case. Admittedly, if individuals could go through legal channels they would indeed lack the right to wage war against their state *in that particular instance*, since they would fall foul of the *jus ad bellum* principle of last resort. That, however, is not the same as to say that as individuals acting privately they can never have the right to wage war in general. Finally, to insist that individuals should entrust a legitimate authority with the right to decide on such controversial issues, such as how best to promote rights and when and how to wage war, will not do in cases where insurgents have good grounds for disagreeing with the existing state that it has authority over them. The point is particularly apposite in the case of secessionist and colonial wars, whose trigger is precisely the (plausible) denial by insurgents that the state which exercises *de facto* jurisdiction over them has the authority to make and enforce laws over its territory.

At this juncture I suspect that proponents of the requirement of legitimate authority will raise the following question (in effect, the third objection).[23] Let

---

[23] See, for example, O. O'Donovan, *The Just War Revisited* (Cambridge: Cambridge University Press, 2003), 25–7; L. McPherson, 'Is Terrorism Distinctively Wrong?', *Ethics* 117 (2007): 524–46, at 539–45.

us return to our earlier example of regime A's persecution of one of its religious minority V. Let us suppose that an individual member of V has the where-withal to wage a war, on his own, against A. Let us further assume (as per the conclusions reached in Section 2.2) that the violation of his and his fellow members' fundamental right to religious freedom, backed as it is with lethal force, provides him with a just cause for war. Notwithstanding the justness of his cause, the objection would go, this particular individual cannot hold the right to go to war against A (though he does have the right to kill specific individual officials from A if the latter subject him to a lethal threat of harm as part of their campaign of persecution.) For in so far as he would act on behalf of his fellow victims, he would, on their behalf, inflict significant damage, suffering, and death on some other individuals. Moreover, his actions would in all likelihood lead A to inflict greater harms on V for example, by way of reprisals. Even if the harm occasioned by this particular war would not violate the principle of proportionality, the objection would press, a lone individual does not have the authority, and thus lacks the right, to do either, at least without the consent of the individuals on whose behalf he acts—a consent which, as a lone individual, he is not in a position to secure.

This putative objection to the view defended here has intuitive force, not merely in the case of the lone individual, but also in the case of unstructured groups which take it upon themselves to fight on behalf of some 'constituents' and which do not appear to have a mandate for so doing. In fact, it is a standard criticism of terrorist movements such as Al Qaeda that they cannot make a plausible claim for acting on behalf the world-wide Muslim community. Correspondingly, it is a central tenet of many philosophical writings on civil war and, relatedly, revolutionary action, that its participants must be able to show that they have a mandate from those whom they claim to defend. The point might seem all the stronger both for the claim, which I defended in Section 1.2.2, that agents must be able to deny themselves the freedoms and resources to which they have a right, and for the claim, which I defended in Section 2.3, that collective political self-determination is a good the protection of which warrants resorting to force: for if it does have that kind of impor-tance, and if a community cannot be said to be collectively self-determining unless its members consent (directly or indirectly) to its major decisions, how can it be just to wage a war without such consent?[24]

And yet the objection ultimately proves too much. For to insist that any major decision affecting a community's future should be made with the

---

[24] I am grateful to C. Ryan for pressing me hard on this.

consent (direct or indirect) of the people as a condition for being just implies that the decision to constitute oneself into a self-determining community is *itself* unjust, since prior to that decision being made, the community is not (yet) self-determining.[25] Furthermore, if the objection applies to the view that individuals alone can have the right to wage war, then it must also apply to the view that a state alone can have that right. This is because any state which wages a war does so (or at least claims to do so) on behalf of its people, and in turn risks subjecting it to lethal retaliatory measures on the part of the enemy. Yet in many cases, states are not in a position to secure the consent of those on whose behalf they act. Ought we to insist, though, that they should do so on pain of lacking the relevant right? I submit that we ought to, but only in cases where it is not clear that there is a just cause. When it is unquestionably the case that a wrongdoing has been committed of the kind as to justify war, then (as I shall now argue) the consent objection does not succeed.

It is important to distinguish two variants of that particular objection to the conclusions reached here. On the first variant it is necessary for a war to be just that the decision to wage it is taken with the consent either of those on whose behalf it is fought or of their formally elected representatives. A *levée en masse* meets that condition, whereas a war waged by uncoordinated partisans with no clear chain of command or mandate from citizens does not. Unfortunately, however, the requirement that a belligerent should secure the consent of those on whose behalf it fights seems impossibly demanding, in so far as it would regard as unjust wars of which we surely would want to say that they are, or were, just wars. To be clear: if there are doubts as to whether or not there is a just cause, or whether the war would meet the requirement of proportionality or be the option of last resort, then it does make good normative sense to claim that the decision to wage it ought to be made by state officials. Thus, on 19 March 2003 the British House of Commons voted in support of Mr Blair's decision to go to war against Iraq alongside the United States, by 412 to 149 votes.[26] Had the House of Commons *not* voted for the war, the cause for which was of extremely dubious moral status, Prime Minister Blair and the Cabinet clearly would have been acting *ultra vires*. In other cases, however, we might hesitate before reaching such a judgement. Thus, in the immediate aftermath of the attack on Pearl Harbor by Japan, and Germany's own

[25] This is a variant of the familiar point that a decision to set up democracy cannot itself by democratic. For detailed exploration of that issue, see Fabre, *Social Rights under the Constitution*, section 4.3.

[26] For polls conducted in the UK—most notably by ICM—from January 2003 up to the invasion of Iraq in March 2003, which show how divided public opinion was, see http://www.icmresearch.co.uk (accessed 6 June 2011).

declaration of war against the United States, all members of the United States' Congress, bar one, voted in favour of formally declaring war against Japan, Italy, and Germany: in this case too this was a decisive victory for the administration in power—not least President Roosevelt—which, on this occasion, also had the support of the majority of the American people.[27] It would seem unreasonable to insist, however, that this particular war, as fought by the United States, would have been unjust had Roosevelt dispensed with the approval of Congress—indeed, with the approval of the American people. If any decision to go to war is to be deemed just, this one surely is.

The second variant of the objection avoids that criticism, by holding, not that the decision to go to war must be taken only by actors who are in a position to secure consent to the decision itself to wage war, but only that it must be taken by actors who are given a general, non-war-specific mandate by those on whose behalf they fight. Whether such defence takes the form of a war is for those actors to decide. On that view, had Roosevelt not been able to secure Congress approval, the war against Japan would not have fallen foul of the requirement of legitimate authority, since he had been democratically elected by the American people in 1940. By contrast, in so far as Al Qaeda has not been given any mandate by Muslims world-wide, whatever decision it makes to defend the latter's interests does fall foul of the requirement, and its war, *ipso facto*, can be deemed unjust on those grounds alone.

However, the difficulties with that argument are threefold. First, it implies that regimes which do not govern in virtue of their citizens' (valid) consent cannot be regarded as legitimate belligerents. But as we saw in Section 2.4, illegitimate regimes do have the right to take the steps necessary to defend their members' rights. Second, it delivers counter-intuitive results in some domestic conflicts where the regime in place had secured the consent of the people through its formally elected representatives, whilst the insurgents had not. General De Gaulle's refusal to submit to the French government's surrender to Germany in June 1940, and his decision to organize an insurgent movement—the Resistance—is a case in point. On 17 June 1940, with the German Army already in Paris and millions of French civilians fleeing its advance, the government of the day, which was deemed legitimate according to the constitution of the (Third) French Republic, agreed to have Marshall Pétain form a new government of national unity with a view to negotiating an armistice with Hitler. Pétain was granted full powers by the semi-democratically

[27] For a fascinating account of American public opinion regarding the United States' war against Nazi Germany, see S. Casey, *Cautious Crusade: Franklin D. Roosevelt, American Public Opinion, and the War against Nazi Germany* (Oxford: Oxford University Press, 2001).

elected National Assembly in July, and embarked on a systematic policy of collaboration with Germany from the administration's seat in the southern town of Vichy. On 18 June, General De Gaulle, who had been under-secretary for war in that government and had escaped to London, launched a radio appeal through the BBC to the French People to resist first the invasion, then the government-sanctioned German occupation of northern France. Now, in so far as French women did not have the right to vote in those days, the decision to grant full powers to Pétain was illegitimate on those grounds alone. That said, Pétain clearly had a greater claim (at least procedur-ally speaking) to represent the French people than De Gaulle. Yet it seems counter-intuitive to hold that the actions carried out by the French Resistance against German occupiers at the behest of General De Gaulle were unjust simply in virtue of the fact that De Gaulle had no mandate from the French (at least not in 1940, and probably not until the end of 1943[28]).

Third, and relatedly, civil wars, and the years of rights violations which precede them, usually do not afford propitious conditions for obtaining a clear mandate from one's 'constituents'. Individuals who are threatened with torture, death, and arbitrary imprisonment for daring to demonstrate against their regime are unlikely to have many opportunities for organizing them-selves into clearly identifiable opposition movements. By that token, indivi-duals who wish to take up arms against that regime are unlikely to be able clearly to discern how much support they elicit from those whom they wish to defend. Often, of course, they do: the ANC in South Africa, the PLO in Palestine, the NLF in French-dominated Algeria, and other similar move-ments, have been plausibly deemed to enjoy support, under extremely difficult conditions, from those they claimed to represent, which testifies to human beings' obdurate resilience in the face of brutal oppression. At the same time, the considerable obstacles encountered by partisans in German-occupied *eastern* Europe (where the occupation was infinitely more savage than in the west) also testify to the difficulties inherent in fighting an enemy which will stop at nothing to impose its will. That the Tutsis in genocidal Rwanda did have in the form of the Rwandan Patriotic Front a movement able to wage war on their behalf does not undermine the point, since the RPF was constituted and armed before the genocide started—at a time, in other words, where there still were interstices for the structured organization of armed resistance.

The problem at hand can be couched as follows: the more grievous the rights violations which provide their victims with a just cause for war, the less

---

[28] See Paxton, *Vichy France*, for a classic account.

likely it is that those victims will be able to meet the requirement of legitimate authority; by that token, the easier it is for them to meet the requirement, the weaker the justness of their cause. And therein lies, perhaps, the beginning of a tentative solution to the problem of authority—a solution which enables us to qualify the claim, defended in Section 4.3.1, that individuals can wage war in a private capacity. When conditions are not there under which victims of rights violations can give consent (indirect or not) either to the war itself or to institutions mandated with fighting the war, insurgents may take matters into their own hands, subject to two conditions: they have good reasons to believe that their fellow community members *would* consent if they could, *and* they put in place institutional mechanisms whereby those for whose sake they fight can hold them into account once the war is over. Put differently, the more grievous the rights violations, the less scope there seems to be for the issuing of a mandate, but the more reason there is to assume that victims presumptively consent to insurgents' decisions and to act on the basis of that presumption, and the more likely it is that such institutional mechanisms will be needed. Contrastingly, the less serious (though still a just cause for war) the rights violations and thus the more scope for authorization, the more reason there is to insist that insurgents not act without it. Analogously, doctors may operate on a patient who is in a coma and thus is not in a position to give consent to surgery, on the presumption that he would consent if he could—absent explicit instructions from him (such as a signed DNR order) to the contrary. If he is awake and of sound mind, doctors may operate only if he consents. It is in that sense—and in that sense only—that the requirement of legitimate authority ought to be rejected: just as a patient's consent is not *always* necessary for doctors permissibly to operate on him, the consent of victims of rights violations is not *always* necessary for insurgents permissibly to wage war on their behalf.

The point gains further strength still when one bears in mind that a war, from onset to victory, has different stages. Thus, whether or not the Rwanda Patriotic Front had a mandate from the Tutsis to fight the genocidal Hutu regime in late April 1994, when the latter was orchestrating killings in *the dozens of thousands*, frankly does not seem to matter, unless Tutsis had explicitly declined their help, which they had not. By killing Hutu militia-men and members of the regular Rwandese army in the opening weeks of the genocide, when those militia-men and soldiers were killing people with machetes, torturing opponents to death with screwdrivers, and eviscerating live pregnant women, the RPF, although a political movement acting for the sake of political ends, acted in defence of the Tutsis' fundamental right not to be killed wantonly—an act of war to be sure, but one which surely anyone can commit, irrespective of their political status. Overthrowing and replacing a regime, by contrast, is a clearly political act which cannot be committed by just anyone; thus, whether the RPF had a mandate to overthrow the Hutu regime, and to take its place, even as a transitional government, does matter rather more. These are not precise guidelines, of course: many insurgent movements have been torn by ferocious internecine fighting, which suggests that claims to authority made in the absence of formal, recognized, and accepted procedures are always likely to be disputed. (One need think only of the struggle into which the PLO and Hamas, both claiming truly to represent the Palestinian people, have been locked for more than twenty years). But they do at least lend support to the view that it is not absolutely necessary that an individual acting alone, or a group, be able to secure a mandate from those on whose behalf they go to war, in order for their war to be just. Rather, attention must be paid to the phase of the war in which they act, the severity of the human rights violations which provide them with a just cause in the first instance, the collateral damage which the war would cause as set against the restoration of those rights, and the extent to which there are procedures in place to generate such a mandate.[29]

## 4.4 KILLING IN CIVIL WARS

To recapitulate, I have argued that if a regime, A, violates the fundamental rights of some of its members—whether those rights are individual rights, for example, not to be killed, or to worship as one wishes, or jointly held rights to, for example, self-determination—those members have a just cause for going to war: with respect to the just cause, there is parity between domestic and transnational conflicts. Moreover, I have argued that it is not a necessary

---

[29] The argument I deploy here is broadly similar to that advanced by C. J. Finlay in a recent article on legitimate authority. Unlike myself, however, Finlay defends the orthodox variant of the requirement of legitimate authority. In Finlay's view, even though the moral status of the cause for the war does indeed affect the moral status of the war's constitutive acts of killing—so that combatants are not, at a deep level, on a moral par—there are good pragmatic reasons for endorsing the moral equality thesis and, further, for ensuring that the kind of violence carried out by non-state actors differs from criminal violence. To extend to such actors the authority to initiate a war would make it impossible to distinguish between those two kinds of violence; moreover, non-state actors are not able, on the whole, to claim that they act with the consent of those whom they claim to represent. I lack the space to discuss this two-pronged argument in full here, but let me simply note, first, that I can endorse the consent claim reasonably happily (with the *caveat* that explicit consent is not required to ward off immediate, mass violence), and second, that as my own inquiry into just wars is conducted through the lenses of the deep morality of war, his first claim is not relevant to it. See C. J. Finlay, 'Legitimacy and Non-State Political Violence', *Journal of Political Philosophy* 18 (2010): 287–312.

condition for all wars to be just that they be waged by a legitimate authority. However, to say that some individuals have a just cause against their regime and that they can hold the right to resort to war in prosecution of that cause even though they are not state-actors leaves open the difficult question of who may be killed in such a war. I now turn to this issue.

### 4.4.1 Killing non-combatants

Defenceless civilians are the chief victims of civil wars, subject as they are to being massacred, raped, or tortured, or to die as a result of civil-war-induced starvation and/or forced displacement. Whether their suffering and death are themselves war ends (as is the case in a genocide) or a means towards such ends such as secession (as is the case when they are terrorised into leaving their homes, thereby making way for their enemy to settle, or when they are killed in reprisals to deter others from taking sides in the war), their plight is a daily reminder of the degree to which participants in those wars deem themselves permitted to flout, again and again, that cornerstone of *jus bello*: the principle of non-combatant immunity.[30] Those acts cannot possibly be condoned from a cosmopolitan point of view: if communal membership is an arbitrary basis for anything at all, then surely it is a wholly arbitrary basis for the right not to be killed deliberately. Note that one need not be a cosmopolitan (sufficientist or otherwise) to endorse that view. Anyone who believes that the basis of liability to lethal harm lies in agents' contributory responsibility for unjustified and wrongful threat must reject those acts as beyond the pale—not merely when they are a war end in themselves (which end is clearly unjust), but also when they are a means to prosecute a just cause.

I shall return to the deliberate killing of the innocent in Section 7.2 when examining the ethics of violating the principle of non-combatant immunity under conditions of military asymmetry. For now, I focus on the liabilities of those actors who share responsibility for the wrongdoings which provide insurgents with a just cause, but who do not act in a combatting capacity— in other words, individuals who are not in a position to subject fellow compatriots to a lethal threat of harm but who support the regime and its policies. We encountered a similar case in Section 3.4, when we discussed the liabilities of affluent wrongdoers whose support for unjust distributive policies

---

[30] For a useful typology of violence against civilians in civil wars, see S. N. Kalyvas, *The Logic of Violence in Civil Wars* (Cambridge: Cambridge University Press, 2006). Although my focus is on killing, everything I say here applies to other atrocities such as rape, torture, or limb amputations (the latter being a widespread occurrence in, for example, the war in Sierra Leone; see Gberie, *A Dirty War in West Africa*, esp. ch. 6).

is a significant contributory factor to the plight of the very poor. There we saw
(drawing from the cosmopolitan account of justice sketched in Chapter 1)
that individuals are under a duty not to take part in or support unjust practices
and unjust policies which issue in the denial of other individuals' fundamental
rights. As we also saw, whether or not those agents are liable to being targeted
depends on whether their contributions to those practices and policies themselves constitute a wrongful harm when taken on their own, or are significantly causally related to the resultant human rights violations. The point
applies, *mutatis mutandis*, to the case of civil wars. To give but two examples,
devising on paper the regime's genocidal plan (even if one does not and will
not yield a machete oneself) might well make one liable. By contrast, the mere
act of supporting an illegitimate regime (for example, by voting in its favour)
does not suffice to make a citizen liable to attack. It might, however, make him
liable to incurring a harm lesser than death, and/or widely liable to being killed
foreseeably (albeit unintentionally) in the course of a just military mission
carried out by insurgents.

So far, I have focused on the deliberate killing of civilians. But what of their
collateral deaths? Assume, to be clear, that the war has a just cause and that
insurgents either have good reasons to presume that their compatriots would
consent to the war if given the opportunity (the civil war is meant to stop a
genocide), or that there is clear evidence of popular support for it. Interestingly, some might press, at this juncture, that the fact of the special relationship rears its head again: when an actor decides to resort to war, they might
argue, that actor must take into account the likelihood that civilians will die in
the war who nevertheless are not liable to being killed, but who will be caught
in the cross-fire. And (the argument might continue) it might seem that the
decision to resort to war in intrastate cases faces greater justificatory burdens
than a decision to go to war against a foreign state, precisely because the
civilians who will die are 'our own', to whom we stand in a special relationship, and to whom, thus, we have a greater duty of care than we do to foreign
civilians. Lest one should think that the point stands too glaringly at odds with
cosmopolitan justice to warrant scrutiny *here*, it would pay to note (the
argument would point out) that given the choice between saving innocent
civilians from their own community and saving innocent foreign civilians,
soldiers surely are justified—indeed, are under a duty—to do the former. By
that token, members of a political community are under a greater duty to
spare fellow members than they are to spare the distant strangers.[31]

---

[31] I am grateful to Cheyney Ryan for pressing me hard on this issue. Note that the question I raise
here differs from the problem of collateral damage as I tackled it in the context of defensive wars

What are we to make of that claim? For a start, even if it is true that soldiers are under the aforementioned duty, we are not thereby licenced to conclude that citizens are similarly duty-bound, for it may well be that the justification for the former's duty lies in the specific features of the contractual undertaking which binds soldiers to those who, in effect, are their employers—which features are not present in the ties of co-citizenship. Moreover, as we also saw in Section 1.3.1, there are rescue cases where it seems plainly wrong to hold individuals under a duty to save a co-citizen at the expense of a foreigner—as when, for example, I, being French, have a choice of rescuing from drowning either a fellow French person or (for example) a Sri Lankan. Many will find this point utterly unpersuasive in general, and particularly so in the present context: for there is a rather considerable difference, they might say, between saving a foreigner and thereby allowing a compatriot to die, and killing one's compatriots collaterally as opposed to killing foreigners. Undoubtedly so, but not in a way that yields the desired verdict of placing the former kind of killings under a greater justificatory burden than the latter. For we must distinguish between three categories of compatriot who might incur collateral damage as a result of our decision to wage war against our own regime: compatriots who are complicitous in the wrongdoing which furnishes us with a just cause, compatriots who are the intended beneficiaries of our decision, and compatriots who are neither (partly) responsible for our predicament nor beneficiaries of our war. With respect to the former, the question is whether we have a greater duty to them not to inflict collateral damage on them than we would do (in the case of an interstate war) if they were equally responsible for our predicament but members of a foreign state. As should be clear from the conclusion reached in Section 4.2 (where the special relationship makes no difference to the determination of rights violations as a just cause), the answer to that question is a resounding 'no'—as is the answer to the question raised by those compatriots of ours who are neutral third parties, as it were, in the conflict which opposes us to our regime (for to claim otherwise would be to say that political membership is decisive for the conferral on the innocent the right not to be killed—contra cosmopolitan justice.) Interestingly, however, a war in the course of which some of the war's beneficiaries will be killed collaterally might well be placed under a weaker justificatory burden than an interstate war in which (equal numbers of) foreign civilians will be killed

---

(Section 2.4). There I examined whether the combatants of an unjustly aggressed community V were permitted to give priority to their compatriots when faced with a choice between killing them (or letting them die) and killing non-combatants belonging to the aggressor. Here the issue is that of the weight which insurgents may and should attach to the lives of their compatriots in a civil conflict relative to the weight which they may and should confer on the lives of enemy non-combatants when locked in a conflict with a foreign aggressor.

collaterally, precisely because the former civilians are meant to benefit from the war in a way that the latter will not. Far from tightening constraints on the resort to war, the special relationship might well loosen them.[32]

### 4.4.2 Combatants' liabilities

Let us now turn to the case of (regular) combatants who fight insurgents on behalf of the regime. Interestingly, just as domestic and transnational conflicts are often thought to differ with respect to the just cause, they are thought by some similarly to differ with respect to principles for their conduct. At one end of the scale, and at the risk of anachronism, Plato tells us that Greek soldiers owed it to fellow Greeks, but not to non-Greeks, not to spoil, loot, and enslave them should they lose on the battlefield.[33] At the other end of the scale, some aver that insurgents ought to be denied rights and immunities standardly given to regular combatants in transnational states.[34] This, in fact, is the standard view, which flows straightforwardly from the tradition's insistence (in its orthodox variant) on the requirement of legitimate authority. As we saw in the previous section, the requirement pertains, in the main, to the decision to wage war, but it also has a crucially important role *in bello*: in orthodox just war theory, members or agents of a legitimate authority—typically, uniformed soldiers—may kill with impunity (provided they abide to the other requirements of *jus in bello*) once the war has started, and this precisely because they kill on behalf and at the behest of a legitimate authority. On the standard interpretation of the requirement, it is both necessary and sufficient, for soldiers to be allowed to commit acts of killing in the course of a war, that they belong to the army of a legitimate or representative authority, and this even if the particular war which that authority is waging is unjust at the bar of some other requirement(s) of *jus ad bellum*. Moreover, and crucially for our purposes here, it is also sufficient, for them to be *liable* to being killed by other uniformed combatants, that they bear arms and pose a threat to another combatant. The orthodox view thus yields the following account of the right to kill and the liability to being killed in transnational and domestic wars: in transnational wars, regular soldiers have the right to kill enemy uniformed

---

[32] I am assuming that the interstate war under scrutiny here is not an humanitarian intervention in the affairs of another state which is waged on behalf of that state's victims. I shall address those cases in the next chapter, especially in Section 5.5.2. The claim that the special relationship of co-citizenship creates weaker duties than are owed to distant strangers is not unique to war: for an interesting defence and application to other contexts, see Goodin, 'What Is So Special about Our Fellow Countrymen?'.

[33] See Plato, *Republic* ed. R. Waterfield (Oxford: Oxford University Press, 1993), V-470c-1e.

[34] For a good exposition of that view, see, for example, Kalyvas, *The Logic of Violence in Civil Wars*, 62–4.

soldiers and are liable to being killed by them, irrespective of the justness of their cause. In domestic conflicts, regular soldiers, who are employed by, and kill on behalf of, their regime have the right to kill insurgents and are not liable to being killed by them, whilst the latter not only are liable to being killed by their opponents but, in addition, lack the right to kill them—unless those insurgents belong to quasi-state groups such as national liberation movements which can plausibly claim to have the ability (*de facto*) to govern.[35]

It should be obvious that neither the account of cosmopolitan justice nor the account of defensive rights which I have defended throughout this book can accept either view. A cosmopolitan cannot accept the claim that one may treat foreign enemies more harshly than enemy members of one's community simply because they happen to be foreign; nor is my account of defensive rights compatible with the claim that insurgents lack a right which they would have if they were fighting a foreign regime, irrespective of their cause. On the contrary, if insurgents' cause is just, regular combatants unjustifiably subject them to a wrongful threat, and therefore lack the right to kill them in their own defence and are liable to being killed by them. More specifically still, it pays to distinguish between regular combatants who commit the wrongdoings which provide insurgents with a just cause for war, and regular combatants who block insurgents' attempts to stop those wrongdoings. Consider our earlier example of a regime which forbids one of its religious minorities to practice their faith, by (for example) arresting its priests, breaking up masses, sending the faithful to prison, killing and torturing community leaders, and so on. Those individuals clearly have a just cause against their regime. More specifically, on my account of defensive killings, officials—typically the police, the army, or para-military groups—are liable to being killed. Suppose now that members of that minority decide to take up arms against the state in defence of their faith. It is probable that, in the course of that war, they will kill soldiers who did not themselves commit the wrongdoing of enforcing religious persecution by lethal force. But to the extent that those soldiers interpose themselves between the insurgents and the persecuting regime, then they too are liable, on two grounds: as posing a lethal and wrongful threat of harm

---

[35] In transnational conflicts, regular, uniformed soldiers also have the right to kill enemy irregular combatants, such as mercenaries who fight for the enemy, but they are not liable to being killed by them: mercenaries, in other words, do not have the right to kill them, at least in the orthodox view. I shall take issue with that claim in Chapter 6. For a good discussion of the history of legal norms relating to the status of lawful versus unlawful combatants, with particular focus on intrastate conflicts, see K. Nabulsi, *Traditions of War: Occupation, Resistance, and the Law* (Oxford: Oxford University Press, 1999). For a rather different view from Nabulsi's, see T. Meisels, 'Combatants: Lawful and Unlawful', *Law and Philosophy* 26 (2007): 31–65.

to insurgents in the course of the war itself, and as significant accomplices in the regime's wrongful religious persecution of the latter.

So far, so simple. As we have seen, however, some civil wars take place under the shadow of a foreign occupier. A number of mainland European countries suffered precisely that fate during World War II, torn as they were by lethal, internal conflicts between supporters of collaboration with Nazi Germany and those who held the view that the war should go on. In some cases (such as Greece), the government which had been in place before the onset of the war had fled into exile, as a result of which the country was left without any institutions of its own and the civil war was fought unmediated, as it were, between groups of partisans with different post-war aims in mind (such as, in Greece, the restoration of the monarchy on the one hand, and the establishment of a communist regime on the other hand). In others (such as France), the civil war unfolded between the collaborationist regime and insurgents. From a cosmopolitan point of view, civil wars against a regime which collaborates with a foreign occupying army are of particular normative interest. For suppose that the occupation is unjust, and that the collaborationist regime thus acts unjustly when repressing those of its citizens who resist the occupation. More often than not, insurgents may well have to choose whether to target foreign occupying soldiers and fellow compatriots who have chosen to fight on behalf of the regime with the occupier (if only because resources are scarce and a war cannot always be fought on all fronts). For expository ease, let us imagine that a group of French Resistants face the following choice: blow up the headquarters of the local Gestapo (*Gestapo*), or blow up the headquarters of the local French police (*French Police*), many of whose agents assist the occupier with the task of arresting, torturing, and deporting Jews, homosexuals, Resistants, and so on. Let us further assume that either option would constitute a meaningful contribution to the war effort and would be proportionate. On what grounds compatible with cosmopolitan justice, if any at all, may those Resistants opt for *Gestapo* (killing German soldiers) rather than *French Police* (killing French policemen), or indeed, *vice versa*?

On limited grounds, I should like to suggest.[36] At first blush there is one argument which one might be tempted to invoke in favour of some form of

---

[36] With the *caveat* that as the issue of occupation is enormously complex, my account will be on the sketchy side, focusing as it does on the issue of patriotic preference or disfavour in such wars. There is, astonishingly,* a dearth of normative work on occupation. The only two philosophical articles I know of are J. McMahan, 'The Morality of Military Occupation', *Loyola International and Comparative Law Review* 31 (2009): 101–23; J. Rocheleau, 'From Aggression to Just Occupation? The Temporal Application of *Jus Ad Bellum* Principles and the Case of Iraq', *Journal of Military Ethics* 9 (2010): 123–38. (*I find this astonishing, considering, first, that the US and the UK have been occupying Iraq and Afghanistan for more than seven years, and second, that during World War II—

patriotic partiality, which proceeds in this way. Even in war, it might be said, thieves need arresting, 'ordinary' murders need solving, and laws (not all of which are unjust) need enforcing. And more often than not it is the collaborationist regime, when there is one, which must carry out those essential tasks of government. To target its officials *as opposed to* enemy combatants is thus to run the risk of making life under occupation, for ordinary citizens, even more precarious than it is already. Note, however, that Resistants could not invoke that argument in support of *Gestapo* if the alternative were to target members of the regime whose *sole* task is to assist the later—as was the case with the so-called French Milice, set up by the collaborationist Vichy regime to implement Germany's policy of racial supremacy on French soil and ruthlessly to pursue Resistants. In that particular case (*Milice*), given that there is nothing really to distinguish members of the Gestapo and members of the Milice—in that they all unjustifiably pose a wrongful threat of grievous harm to the innocent—the fact that the latter were French whilst the former were German ought not to have been a relevant consideration in support of *Gestapo*.

The case of police officers who help the Gestapo to enforce laws which not only have nothing to do with the prosecution of the war proper but in addition help promote citizens' rights (such as laws against theft, for example, or against ordinary murder) is slightly different. In Section 1.4 I noted that state officials have an interest, in that capacity, in not being interfered with when exercising their official power to change citizens' bundles of claims, duties, and powers. The question, then, is whether those officers' interest in enforcing laws is sufficiently important to be protected by such a claim (which would include a claim not to be killed), given that they *also* take part in grievous wrongdoings. It is unclear to me that it is: in domestic contexts, one would not (I think) regard a policeman as immune from being killed as he carries out a murderous attack on some innocent person on the grounds that, if alive, he would also arrest common murderers and in so doing assist the latter's victims in obtaining justice.[37] That said, there might well be good reasons for not systematically killing state officials (and thus for targeting

---

still so present in collective memories—most of mainland Europe was occupied at least once (by Germany), if not twice (first by Germany and then by the Allied)—as was Asia.)

[37] The case of police officers who do not help the Gestapo at all is difficult. On the one hand, there is a sense in which they are not to be regarded as *combatants* proper in the conflict which opposes the collaborationist regime (and its foreign counterpart) and insurgents, since they do violate the latter's fundamental rights. On the other hand, by helping the regime exercise *de facto* power over the territory of the community, they contribute to bolstering whatever claim it may think to have to govern—at the long-term cost (one might think) of making it much harder for insurgents to overthrow it. A full treatment of the ethics of killing under conditions of occupation would have to deal with this issue.

members of the Gestapo, in our example), as reside in the importance of ensuring that there be a sufficient number of officials to maintain some degree of protection for citizens' rights whilst the war is unfolding. Thus, the necessity of ensuring that essential tasks of government are carried out may provide a reason for the French Resistance to opt against *French Police* (but not *Milice*) and in favour of *Gestapo*. Crucially, however, those considerations dictate in favour of patriotic partiality, *not* in the sense that there is something of value to be preserved in that special relationship (co-citizenship) between Resistants and Vichy officials, but rather, in the sense that those individuals (police officers), in virtue of their membership in the French state, happen to be the most likely to carry out those tasks. If, as may well happen in other cases of civil wars, members of the occupying forces in fact carried out those tasks during or after the war, then this would constitute a reason not to target them, but instead to attack one's compatriots.

So much, then, for reasons in favour of *Gestapo*. Might there be, on the contrary, reasons for French Resistants to target their own compatriots, as opposed to German occupiers, precisely on grounds of co-nationality? I can think of three arguments which some might be tempted to adduce to that effect. The first holds that unlike German wrongdoers, French officials who assist the former with the task of rounding up other French individuals are guilty of betraying their fellow compatriots by collaborating with the enemy. Collaboration, in fact, is usually regarded as a particularly heinous crime—heinous enough, some might think, to justify targeting its agents rather than the enemy itself: though *ex hypothesis* both the Gestapo and the French Milice unjustifiably subject the innocent to wrongful threats of serious harm, the latter's wrongdoing is compounded by their co-nationality with their victims, which in turn might make them liable to a greater degree than the foreign occupier.

I do not find that putative argument persuasive. For a start, it does not justify opting for *Milice* in those cases where its members rounded up and tortured foreign Jews and captured British airmen. Moreover, on cosmopolitan grounds, French officials were not under a stronger duty than the German Gestapo not to violate the fundamental human rights of other French nationals.[38] This is not to deny, once again, that members of the same political community have special obligations to one another which foreigners do not have towards them. In the

---

[38] I do not wish to imply that one's general obligations to others—for example, not to kill, not to lie, not to deceive, amd so on—are never strengthened by our special relationships with them. Thus, killing someone without just cause is morally wrong; killing one's spouse or one's child without justification is infinitely worse. But my point here is that the relationship of co-citizenship does not make those particular wrongdoings worse. I am grateful to David Miller for pressing me on that point.

case at hand, however, the duties which are being violated by both French officials and the Gestapo are universal duties of justice which apply across borders, and which, in their violation, issue in similarly strong liability to attack.

That said, there are two further plausible justifications, compatible with cosmopolitan justice, in favour of *Milice/Police* rather than *Gestapo*. Targeting the enemy, which is obviously likely both to have superior military strength and fewer reasons to exercise restraint than the collaborationist regime, is more likely to result in reprisals against the civilian population; moreover, attacking collaborationists and thus disrupting law and order might in fact be a more effective way to help end the occupation than by directly attacking occupying forces, since the latter are reliant on the former to maintain the occupation. In both cases, however, the point is contingent on the facts of the case, so that if Milice men were more likely than foreign occupiers to retaliate towards civilians, or if attacking occupying forces were more effective, then insurgents ought to target them if given the choice (assuming, of course, that the likelihood of reprisals does not make it impermissible, all things considered, to engage in lethal acts of resistance).

## 4.5 CONCLUSION

In this chapter I have argued that what counts as a just cause for an interstate war also counts as a just cause for a civil war, and *vice versa*. *Pace* standard views within just-war theory, in other words, these two kinds of conflict should be treated on a par. As I also showed, and again *pace* the tradition, cosmopolitan justice dictates against the requirement of legitimate authority: more precisely, it is not a necessary condition for a war to be just that it be waged by such an authority. In fact, in some cases individuals alone can have the right to go to war, even though in other cases the latter should be prosecuted by actors with some degree of representativeness of, and authority over, the people and territory which they claim to govern. Finally, I sought to bring to bear some of the central tenets of cosmopolitanism on non-combatants' and combatants' liability to being killed. Throughout my inquiry I have argued that the individuals' political status is far less relevant to the conferral on them of the right to resort to war than is standardly thought. I shall further develop that thought in Chapter 6, when I tackle commodified wars—wars, in other words, in which the use of violence is in part outsourced to private economic actors. In the next chapter, however, I tackle a different kind of conflict, which is often triggered by civil wars: to wit, humanitarian intervention.

# 5

# Humanitarian intervention

## 5.1 INTRODUCTION

So far, this book has focused on wars fought by individuals and communities in defence of their own rights. In this chapter we turn to wars of humanitarian intervention, which are fought in defence of the rights of distant strangers. In the vast literature which this particular kind of conflict has generated over the last twenty years or so, much space is taken by defining what counts as humanitarian intervention.[1] I shall adopt throughout, and without defending it, the following definition: an agent (henceforth, IP—intervening party) can be described as waging a humanitarian war against a sovereign political community (henceforth, TP—target party) if (a) it uses large-scale military force against TP, (b) over which it has no *prima facie* jurisdiction, and if it uses such force (c) without the consent of TP's regime, (d) in order to stop ongoing human rights violations which that regime and its supporters carry out against some members of TP, or which factions within TP carry out due to the regime's unwillingness or inability to keep them in check. My concern in this book is with justifying the use of force via military means (and concomitant acts of killing and destruction), as distinct from alternative means of coercion such as economic sanctions. Furthermore, in keeping with standard usage, I do not use the label 'humanitarian' to describe wars which are fought by a regime to stop ongoing human rights violations within its own borders (such as, for example, the American Civil War, at least on those interpretation of the conflict which claim that the abolition of slavery was a primary motive of

---

[1] See, for example, Caney, *Justice Beyond Borders*, ch. 7; Wheeler, *Saving Strangers*, ch. 1; A. Bellamy, 'Motives, Outcomes, Intent and the Legitimacy of Humanitarian Intervention', *Journal of Military Ethics* 3 (2004): 216–33; T. Nardin, 'The Moral Basis of Humanitarian Intervention', *Ethics and International Affairs* 16 (2002): 57–70; 'Introduction', in T. Nardin and M. S. WIlliams (ed.), *Humanitarian Intervention: NOMOS XLVII* (New York: New York University Press, 2006); C. A. J. Coady, 'War for humanity: a critique', in D. K. Chatterjee and D. E. Scheid (ed.), *Ethics and Foreign Intervention* (Cambridge: Cambridge University Press, 2003); J. Donnelly, 'Human Rights, Humanitarian Crisis, and Humanitarian Intervention', *International Affairs* 48 (1993): 607–40. By IP (intervening party) I shall mean throughout IP's leaders and citizens.

the federal government's military intervention against Confederate states.) Rather, I focus on transnational humanitarian wars which breach the so-called non-intervention principle in virtue of which sovereign political communities are not permitted to aggress other such communities. For that reason, I also focus on cases where the intervention is carried out without the consent of the target regime, and where it is justified mostly on the grounds that the latter is unwilling or unable to protect the fundamental human rights of some of its individual members.

That very last point—on the justification for intervention—needs elaboration. For a start, I say 'mostly justified' as I do not believe that a war must be fought purely for altruistic reasons in order to count as humanitarian and thus to count as a *just* humanitarian war. Moreover, I surmise that many, when asked to cite examples of humanitarian intervention, will refer to cases where the intervention was carried out against a regime which was itself guilty of violating the fundamental human rights of some of its members, and thus without that regime's consent. The bombing of Serbia by NATO in 1999 is a paradigmatic example of such a war, since the latter was waged in defence of Kosovars, over whom Serbia did have jurisdiction and which its regime (it was alleged) had proceeded to exterminate. Two other examples, drawn from the 1970s, are the 1978–79 intervention by Tanzania into Uganda, whose regime, led by Idi Amin, was committing atrocities against real and imaginary opponents within its own borders, and the 1979 intervention by Vietnam against Pol Pot's murderous regime in Cambodia. However, there is no principled reason to exclude from the scope of this inquiry interventions against communities whose institutional apparatus is no longer capable of protecting their own members from serious wrongdoings at the hands of third parties (as was the case, it seemed, in Somalia in the 1990s), or against regimes who are negligently unwilling to do so.[2]

The foregoing remarks are definitional and do not settle the question of the legitimacy of intervention. In this chapter I argue that at the bar of cosmopolitan justice there is not only a moral right (Section 5.2), but also, under certain

---

[2] For a good discussion of the relevance, or lack thereof, of motives and intentions in determining the moral status of an intervention, see Pattison, *Humanitarian Intervention and the Responsibility to Protect*. For discussions of the NATO campaign, see, for example, A. Roberts, 'NATO's Humanitarian War over Kosovo', *Survival* 41 (1999): 102–23; H. Shue, 'Bombing to rescue?: NATO's 1999 bombing of Serbia', in D. K. Chatterjee and D. E. Scheid (ed.), *Ethics and Foreign Intervention* (Cambridge: Cambridge University Press, 2003); Wheeler, *Saving Strangers*, ch. 8. For a discussion of the intervention in Cambodia, see Wheeler, ibid., ch. 3. On the intervention in Somalia by UN-mandated US forces in 1992, see M. Berdal and S. Economides (ed.), *United Nations Interventionism, 1991–2004* (CAmbridge: Cambridge University Press, 2007), and Wheeler, ibid., ch. 6. On India's intervention in East Pakistan, see, Wheeler, ibid., ch. 2, and Tesón, *Humanitarian Intervention*, ch. 8. On the case of Uganda, see Wheeler, ibid., ch. 4, and Tesón, ibid.

conditions, a moral duty (Section 5.3) to wage a humanitarian war—in other words, to mount an aggression against the territorial integrity and political sovereignty of another country. Having made my case to that effect, I then turn to the issue of whose right and duty it is to do so, and seek to show that a multi-institutional and multilateral approach is the morally best, but not the only legitimate, option (Section 5.4). Finally, I provide an account of liability to attack in humanitarian war which is sensitive to the following two features of such a war: the fact that soldiers who defend their community from just aggression and are killed in the process often are not themselves responsible for the rights violations which provide IP with a just cause, and the fact that many non-combatants on behalf of whom the intervention is carried out will die or be severely maimed in the process (Section 5.5).

I must include three final comments before I begin. First, it pays to remember that humanitarian intervention and the controversies which it arouses are not a particularly modern form of warfare: whether it is appropriate to intervene in the internal affairs of a community for the sake of protecting some of its members is a question which, in the Western tradition at least, has been raised since Thucydides and has appeared on foreign policies agenda since then. That being said, I shall tend to refer to recent interventions when searching for examples.[3]

Second, here as throughout the book, I seek to inquire into the deep morality of war, not (or at least not primarily) its legality or the desirability of institutionalising its constituent rights. On the issue of desirability, I concede at the outset that if the implementation of a norm of intervention proves more damaging to cosmopolitan values than leaving the victims of severe human rights violations to their fate, then we should do the latter—on cosmopolitan grounds.[4] On the issue of legality, lawyers deeply disagree. At first sight, humanitarian intervention by one state into the internal affairs of another for the sake of protecting the latter's victims is illegal according to the UN Charter (as per article 2(4) and Chapter VII). Yet a number of scholars have argued—in the face of fierce opposition by other commentators—that

---

[3] See G. J. Bass, *Freedom's Battle: The Origins of Humanitarian Intervention* (New York: Alfred Knopf, 2008), and S. Chesterman, *Just War or Just Peace? Humanitarian Intervention and International Law* (Oxford: Oxford University Press, 2001), ch. 1, for fascinating studies of cases from the sixteenth to the nineteenth centuries.

[4] For an interesting argument to the effect that institutionalising a norm in favour of intervention risks proving very damaging to human rights, see, for example, A. J. Kuperman, 'The Moral Hazard of Humanitarian Intervention: Lessons from the Balkans', *International Studies Quarterly* 52 (2008): 49–80, and Chesterman, *Just War or Just Peace? Humanitarian Intervention and International Law*. I assume here that one can address the moral legitimacy of an intervention independently of its legality. For the opposite view, see M. Patrick, 'Humanitarian Intervention and the Distribution of Sovereignty in International Law', *Ethics & International Affairs* 22 (2008): 369–93.

there is a growing trend, in the relevant circles, towards widening the scope of the Charter so as to permit intervention.[5] I shall leave this particular inquiry to public international lawyers.

Third, the claim that there sometimes is a moral right—indeed, a duty—to wage a humanitarian war so as to protect the fundamental human rights of distant strangers has been attacked from many different quarters—from those who argue that, if institutionalized, the right would destabilize world order, to those who insist that the value of communal integrity is always overriding all things considered, to those who claim that humanitarian intervention never works anyway. Responses to those objections abound in the relevant literature. I shall ignore concerns as deployed by ethical particularists and realists and which a cosmopolitan clearly could not endorse as they are radically antithetical to her moral outlook. Instead, I shall address concerns which a cosmopolitan ought to bear in mind, such as the costs of intervention as well as its likelihood of success.[6]

## 5.2 THE RIGHT TO INTERVENE

To say that there is a right to intervene in the internal affairs of another political community is to say, first, that the latter is not wronged by the intervention and thus ought not to resist it, and second, that third parties are under a duty not to block IP's campaign (for example, by deploying their own forces in support of TP's army should TP decide to defend itself). According to the aforementioned principle of non-intervention, the burden of the argument ought to be borne by proponents of the right to intervene, since

---

[5] For the view that there is no legal right (let alone a legal duty) to intervene, see, for example, M. Byers and S. Chesterman, 'Changing the Rules about Rules? Unilateral Humanitarian Intervention and the Future of International Law', in J. L. Holzgrefe and R. O. Keohane (ed.), *Humanitarian Intervention: Ethical, Legal and Political Dilemmas* (Cambridge: Cambridge University Press, 2003); For the view that there is, see, for example, J. Welsh, 'Taking Consequences Seriously: Objections to Humanitarian Intervention', in Jennifer Welsh (ed.), *Humanitarian Intervention and International Relations* (Oxford: Oxford University Press, 2004); N. Wheeler, 'The Humanitarian Responsibilities of Sovereignty: Explaining the Development of a New Norm of Military Intervention for Humanitarian Purposes in International Society', in Jennifer Welsh (ed.), *Humanitarian Intervention and International Relations* (Oxford: Oxford University Press, 2004); Wheeler, *Saving Strangers*; Tesón, *Humanitarian Intervention*, esp. ch. 7.

[6] For useful reviews of the most common of objections to intervention, see, for example, Caney, *Justice Beyond Borders*; F. R. Tesón, 'The liberal case for humanitarian intervention', in J. L. Holzgrefe and R. O. Keohane (ed.), *Humanitarian Intervention: Ethical, Legal and Political Dilemmas* (Cambridge: Cambridge University Press, 2003); J. Welsh, 'Taking Consequences Seriously: Objections to Humanitarian Intervention', in J. Welsh (ed.), *Humanitarian Intervention and International Relations* (Oxford: Oxford University Press, 2004); Atack, *The Ethics of Peace and War*, ch. 9; Tesón, *Humanitarian Intervention*, chs. 2–4.

sovereign political communities are morally immune, at least *prima facie*, from foreign intervention. However, it might be tempting to think that from a cosmopolitan standpoint the burden of argument ought to be shouldered, on the contrary, by proponents of the principle. For as we saw in Chapter 1, a political regime has a claim to govern over a given territory only if it respects and protects the fundamental rights of its individual members. One might be tempted to think, thus, that proponents of the non-intervention principle cannot be cosmopolitan, and conversely, that the default cosmopolitan position is that there is a *prima facie* right to intervene—justifications for which TP must defeat (through its human rights record, for example) in order to retain its claim to govern. But that would be too quick: non-interventionists who defend the sovereignty of independent states are often concerned to protect universal values such as peace; conversely, cosmopolitans are concerned to ensure that individuals' jointly held rights are respected (subject to the proviso that those rights must not be exercised in violations of other fundamental human rights). A cosmopolitan thus need not deny that the presumptive case is against, not in favour of, aggression. What she does deny, however, is that there is any intrinsic value to attach to communal sovereignty which would always dictate against intervention.[7] As we shall also see, she assigns the status of a just cause for intervention to a greater range of human rights violations than non-cosmopolitans are willing to accept, even though she may well agree with the latter that, all things considered, humanitarian intervention is legitimate only in very few cases.

A standard argument for the right to intervene takes the following form: a regime which violates the fundamental rights of its members undermines the very rationale for its existence and for its claim to authority, and thus forfeits its immunity from interference in its conduct; by implication, foreign

---

[7] The doctrine of acts and omissions also provides support for the principle of non-intervention: for in so far as it holds that doing harm is worse other things equal than allowing harm to happen, it avers that harming some for the sake of preventing harm to others is worse than allowing harm to happen to the latter. A classic exposition and defence of the non-intervention principle is R. J. Vincent, *Nonintervention and International Order* (Princeton, NJ: Princeton University Press, 1974). For interesting remarks on the relationship between those two distinctions (cosmopolitans versus particularists, and interventionists versus non-interventionists), see P. B. Mehta, 'From State Sovereignty to Human Security (via Institutions?)', in T. Nardin and M. S. Williams (ed.), *Humanitarian Intervention: NOMOS XLVII* (New York: New York, 2006), and Tesón, 'The Liberal Case for Humanitarian Intervention'. Note, furthermore, that (as we saw in Chapter 1) the cosmopolitan also rejects what Allen Buchanan calls the discretionary association account of the state, whereby a state is just an instrument for the promotion of the interests of *its* citizens. The point bears stressing here because, as Buchanan shows, the discretionary association approach is not readily compatible with the view that a humanitarian intervention might be internally legitimate (legitimate, that is, from the point of view of the citizens of the intervening state.) See A. E. Buchanan, 'The Internal Legitimacy of Humanitarian Intervention', *Journal of Political Philosophy* 7 (1999): 71–87.

communities are entitled to intervene militarily on behalf of its victims, subject to the latter's consent and considerations of proportionality.[8] The argument is intuitively appealing from a cosmopolitan point of view, since it rests on the claim that state legitimacy wholly depends on respect for fundamental human rights. However, all that it establishes (and that is admittedly quite a lot) is that some actors in the target *regime* would not be wronged if the intervention were to take place. What it does not show is that intervening belligerents may indeed have the right to authorize some of their members— typically soldiers—to kill, maim, harm, and inflict widespread damage and destruction on TP's supporters and innocent non-combatants within TP's borders, for the sake of TP's victims. And yet it is precisely that which any plausible justification for intervention must show.

As a preliminary step towards offering such a justification, let me restate, first, the account of the right to wage a war of self-defence against a foreign community which I defended in Chapter 2, and second, the account of the right to self-defence against one's own regime which I defended in Chapter 4. In Chapter 2 I argued that the right to wage a war of self-defence consists in a right which agents have to kill in defence of their fundamental individual and jointly held rights, and which they hold both as individual agents, as members of a political community, and as soldiers entrusted with the task of prosecuting the war. As we also saw there, the right to wage war is not simply a right to kill in defence of one's rights: it is also a right to kill in defence of the rights of others which victims transfer to rescuers by way of a Hohfeldian power. On that account, due consideration is given to the special stake which victims have in blocking their attacker. Furthermore, as we saw in Chapter 4, individuals have the right to wage war in defence of their own rights against their own regime if the latter's agents (its leaders, its army, its police force, and so on) are unjustifiably posing a threat, backed by lethal force, to their fundamental rights. As I have taken pain to stress throughout, the reason why some agent V has the right to kill an attacker A in self-defence lies in the moral status of

---

[8] Tesón, *Humanitarian Intervention*, pp. 16–17, and ch. 6. See also Caney, *Justice Beyond Borders*, ch. 7; H. Shue, 'Limiting Sovereignty', in J. Welsh (ed.), *Humanitarian Intervention and International Relations* (Oxford: Oxford University Press, 2004); J. McMahan, 'The ethics of international intervention', in A. Ellis (ed.), *Ethics and International Relations* (Manchester: Manchester University Press, 1986). Incidentally, McMahan argues that there is a presumption against (non-consensual) intervention against legitimate states which can be overridden when a legitimate state conducts an extremely aggressive foreign policy. On his view, however (at least as articulated in this particular piece), a state is legitimate to the extent that it acts in the interests of its members and with their general approval. Given that state legitimacy is purely internal, a state can be legitimate in that sense and yet mistreats outsiders. Not so on my conception (as per Section 1.4), which is thus not open (at least on that count) to the view that an intervention against a legitimate state can be permissible.

the threat to which A subjects him—not in the fact that A is a member of the enemy.

These claims are wholly uncontroversial when the rights violator is a *foreign* regime: if some individuals who belong to political community V are attacked by regime A, they are entitled, via their regime, to defend themselves against A, but they also have the power to transfer that right to some other party, such as a foreign state. By that token, however, they also have the power to transfer their right to a foreign party when they are under threat from their own regime, or when the latter is unable to protect them within its own territorial borders. For in so far as *they*, and not their regime itself, ultimately have both the right and the power respectively to exercise lethal force and authorize its use, there is every reason, on cosmopolitan grounds, to extend the reach of the justification for rescue killing to internal conflicts. Consider individuals whose fundamental rights are violated by their own regime by way of lethal threat, or whose regime is unable or unwilling to protect them from attacks by third parties. It follows from the arguments deployed in Chapters 2 and 4 that those individuals have the right to kill their attackers in self-defence, as well as the power to transfer that right to potential rescuers. To claim otherwise is tantamount to conferring on membership in a given political community decisive weight when deciding who has the power to transfer their right to kill. Yet, in so far as communal membership is an arbitrary basis for conferring the right to kill in self-defence, it is also an arbitrary basis for conferring the power to authorize third parties to kill in our own defence: borders cannot acquire greater intrinsic relevance in the case of rescue killing than they do in the case of self-defensive killing.[9]

My case for the right to intervene thus proceeds by way of an argument in favour of victims' right to enlist third-party help, and rests on two analogies— between one-to-one private killings and the right to kill in war on the one hand, and between transnational and internal conflicts on the other hand. As stated, the case needs elaborating along two dimensions. Which rights violations warrant intervention? Is the consent of the agents on whose behalf the intervention is carried out a necessary condition for the latter to be just?

The first issue is one of the most contentious in the philosophical literature on intervention. On what one may call the minimalist view, only those acts

---

[9] The claim that borders are irrelevant for the right to intervene is made by, for example, Simon Caney (*Justice Beyond Borders*), and more comprehensively still, by Fernando Tesón ('The liberal case for humanitarian intervention'). For the claim that humanitarian intervention is deeply antithetical to war understood as an exercise in collective self-defence, see Rodin, *War and Self-Defense*, pp. 130–1. For a decisive rebuttal of Rodin's argument, see F. R. Tesón, 'Self-Defense in International Law and Rights of Persons', *Ethics & International Affairs* 18 (2004): 87–92, at 88–9.

which, in the now standard phrase, 'shock the conscience of mankind', such as genocide and mass enslavement, can provide IP with an all-things-considered justification for going to war against TP. On that view, violations of other civil and political rights cannot justify intervention, for even if those violations did provide a just cause for it, there are very good reasons (to do with effectiveness, cultural sensitivity, greater likelihood of success if liberal reforms come from the inside, and so on) to respect IP's sovereignty.[10] On a more demanding view, violations of civil and political rights can be part of a justification for intervention; on a more demanding view still, so can violations of socioeconomic rights.[11]

Now, it should be clear from the foregoing case in support of intervention that a cosmopolitan should endorse the most demanding view. Consider first the case of civil and political rights: as we saw above, it is in virtue of the fact that agents have a right to wage a war of self-defence that they have the power to transfer that right to third parties. In so far as violations of civil and political rights are a paradigmatic just cause for self-defensive wars, and to the extent that self-defensive wars for the sake of those rights meet other requirements such as reasonable chance of success and proportionality, victims of those particular violations have the right to go to war against wrongdoers. By that token they have the power to transfer it to intervening parties. The invasion of Pakistan by India in 1971 is a case in point. Following the partition of India in 1947, East Pakistan was dominated by a Bengali majority, whose aspirations to autonomy, in the face of systematic economic and political discrimination by the regime, were brutally crushed in the spring of 1971. In the resulting conflict, millions of individuals were killed, raped, or made refugees. India intervened in December of that year—partly in defence of those individuals, and partly to stem what it perceived as an unmanageable and destabilizing flow of refugees. One might think that only the atrocities carried out by the Pakistani army provided India with a justification for going in; yet the Bengali majority—or at any rate, the biggest single political party in East Pakistan (the Awami League) did have a clear platform of political autonomy short of

[10] See, for example, Coady, 'War for Humanity: a Critique', and M. Blake, 'Reciprocity, Stability, and Intervention: the Ethics of Disequilibrium', in D. K. Chatterjee and D. E. Scheid (ed.), *Ethics and Foreign Intervention* (Cambridge: Cambridge University Press, 2003). I agree with Blake that considerations such as reasonable chance of success might dictate against intervention for the protection of political rights. Unlike him, however, I do not believe that it is inherent in those rights (unlike the right not to be massacred) that such considerations will always apply.

[11] See, for example, Caney, *Justice Beyond Borders*; H. Stacy, 'Humanitarian Intervention and Relational Sovereignty', in S. Lee (ed.), *Intervention, Terrorism, and Torture: Contemporary Challenges to Just War Theory* (Dordrecht: Springer, 2006). On violations of political and civil rights as a just cause, see also G. Elfstrom, 'On Dilemmas of Intervention', *Ethics* 93 (1983): 709–25; and Luban, 'Just War and Human Rights'.

independence—a platform which India recognized as legitimate. If one believes that Bengalis in East Pakistan did have a case for autonomy, and that they did have the right to resist the regime's military aggression on their civil and political rights (as well as their basic right not to be killed, raped, and tortured), then, on cosmopolitan grounds, one must accept that they also had the power to authorize India to help them protect those very same rights.[12]

Likewise, the cosmopolitan accounts of subsistence and civil wars which I provided earlier in this book support the perhaps highly controversial view that violations of basic welfare rights also constitute a just cause for intervention and can form part of an all-things-considered justification for it. For consider. In Section 3.2 I argued that breaches of the right not to be subject to severe poverty provide the very poor with a just cause for going to war against the affluent. In Section 4.2 I showed, through the hypothetical example of the Ukrainian famine, that the very poor have the (*prima facie*) right to wage war against their own regime if the latter is negligently or culpably failing to secure their subsistence. Those points, combined with the foregoing account of the right to kill in defence of others, yield the conclusion that the very poor have the power to transfer their right to wage war to potential rescuers.[13]

Note, crucially, that my point is not that IP has the right to wage a humanitarian war whenever and provided that the agents on behalf of whom it intervenes themselves have the right to wage a war of self-defence. To reiterate, the judgement that, in a given scenario, an agent has the right to go to war is an all-things-considered judgement which must take into account not merely whether there is a just cause for the exercise of lethal force, but also whether the response would be proportionate, have a reasonable chance of success, and so on. Accordingly, one can imagine a state of affairs where the victims of rights violations would be more likely to succeed than outsiders; conversely, there might also be cases where they would be less likely to

---

[12] For a discussion of this particular case, see, for example, Walzer, *Just and Unjust Wars*; Wheeler, *Saving Strangers*.

[13] For an argument against intervention in defence of subsistence rights, see Tesón, *Humanitarian Intervention*, 123–6. Tesón's argument takes the following form: liberty trumps economic justice, as reflected in the fact that different majorities may yield different conceptions of justice on which there can be reasonable disagreement (whereas there can be no reasonable disagreement on the demands of civil and political rights.) Accordingly, one may not intervene militarily in the affairs of another community on the grounds that its chosen 'pattern of wealth distribution' is unjust, save in the case where the government of that community wilfully fails to take action to prevent the starvation or death by disease of the population.' (126.) Two points by way of reply: first, if liberty trumps justice, then by implication, the rationale for not intervening is that although they act unjustly they must be free to do so. But that is not the same as to say that they act justly though on the basis of a different conception of justice than that endorsed by the intervening party. Second, assuming that Tesón really does have in mind the latter claim, it should be clear that it ought to be rejected on cosmopolitan grounds.

succeed, in which case outsiders may, in that instance, have a right which they cannot exercise themselves. With respect to proportionality, account must also be taken of the use to which the resources could be put if the war were not waged: if the choice, therefore, is between rescuing 800,000 people from genocide and saving 18 million people from starvation, perhaps we should do the latter: as I noted in Section 2.4, our positive duties of justice to provide material assistance to the needy might sometimes trump our negative duties not to harm the innocent. Assume, then, that some members of political community V are victims of severe rights violations, either at the hands of their own regime or at the hands of third parties within the community which the regime is unable or unwilling to stop. Assume further that war is the option of last resort, a necessary means to obtaining redress, and a proportionate response to those violations. Under those conditions those individuals have the (*prima facie*) right to kill wrongdoers in defence of their rights, and the (*prima facie*) power to authorize potential intervening parties (IP) to wage war on their behalf.

The justification thus offered for the right to intervene seemingly implies that the victims' consent to the intervention is required in order for IP to have the right to act, since there can be no authorization without consent. To reiterate briefly a point made in Section 4.3.2 when discussing insurgents' claims to act on behalf of their community, the crucial question is whether victims' *explicit* consent is required or whether their presumptive consent suffices. Insisting on explicit consent clearly would be too demanding, in so far as it would deprive of protection individuals who are not in a position to give their consent. The problem is particularly salient in humanitarian conflicts, whose victims quite often are very young children (who are thus not morally able to give or withhold consent), or individuals who are subject to such severe hardship that they simply do not have the means (physical, psychological, and material) to make themselves heard. It seems natural, therefore, to claim that as long as IP has good reasons to presume that victims would consent to the intervention if they were in a position to do so, then it may act as if they had explicitly authorized it to put a stop to the rights violations.

The presumptive-consent claim draws support from a number of empirical cases. For example, it is not far-fetched to suppose that the millions of Bengalis who were subject to atrocities on the part of Pakistan's regime in 1970 and 1971 would have explicitly called for intervention had they been in a position to do so. It is even less far-fetched to make a similar assumption of the hundreds of thousands of Tutsis and moderate Hutus who were massacred or had to leave Rwanda, under unimaginable conditions, during the 1994 genocide, and whom the international community simply left to their fate as dismembered bodies were piling up throughout the country. Nor, finally, is there reason to deny that the Darfurians killed, raped, and mutilated in their thousands by government-backed *Janjaweed* militias in 2003–04 would have welcomed military action from the international community at least as much as fact-finding missions and carefully crafted arguments for, and, or against, the determination of their fate as genocide.[14]

Yet however intuitively appealing the point might be, the presumptive-consent claim is not without posing some difficulties. First, there might be cases where the majority of the population in TP is oppressed by TP's regime yet would not welcome interveners, and where TP's regime concurrently carries out atrocities against a minority.[15] Without wishing to deny that a great many numbers of Germans supported Hitler and his policies—including his genocidal policies—there is no doubt that their fundamental human rights were violated, as evidenced by the punishment meted out as early as 1933 to anyone who dared oppose the regime. And yet it is far from clear that the Germans would have wished to be liberated from the Nazis—whereas one can safely assume that those who were oppressed infinitely more savagely (such as Jews, gypsies, and the profoundly disabled) would have welcomed an early intervention. Any argument to the effect that presumptive consent is decisive must be able plausibly to identify those individuals about whom it can be presumed.

Furthermore, IP should be wary of always assuming that the existence of widespread rights violations is sufficient basis for presuming that the victims will welcome its forces. The case of Somalia, against whom the US intervened in 1992 with the backing of the UN, should serve as a reminder that even in a failed state riven by widespread famine and atrocities, it is possible to take peaceful, negotiation-based, small, but sure steps towards a resolution of the conflict, where a military intervention might well fail for encountering hostility on the part of (some of) the victims.[16]

---

[14] On the Rwandan genocide, see, for example, L. Melvern, *Conspiracy to Murder: the Rwandan Genocide* (London: Verso, 2006); P. Gourevitch, *We wish to inform you that tomorrow we will be killed with our families* (London: Picador, 1999); R. Dallaire, *Shake Hands with the Devil* (London: Arrow Books, 2004). On the international response to Darfur, see (in addition to the works cited in Chapter 4), A. Bellamy, 'Responsibility to Protect or Trojan Horse? The Crisis in Darfur and Humanitarian Intervention after Iraq', *Ethics & International Affairs* 19 (2005): 31–54; H. Slim, 'Dithering over Darfur? A Preliminary Review of the International Response', *International Affairs* 80 (2004): 811–28; A. De Waal, 'Darfur and the Failure of the Responsibility to Protect', *International Affairs* 83 (2007): 1039–54. Commentators note that the international community was not as slow, and certainly not in as much denial, in its treatment of Darfur in 2004 as it was in its handling of Rwanda in 1994.

[15] I am grateful to T. Meisels for raising this point.

[16] See, for example, Wheeler, *Saving Strangers*, ch. 6.

Still more problematically, there is a crucial difference between one-to-one cases and intervention. In the former, killing the attacker is sufficient (we may suppose) to secure the victim's right not to be killed. In the latter, whilst killing the direct perpetrators of the rights violations will put an end to victims' immediate plight, it is unlikely on its own to secure conditions under which those victims can enjoy longlasting prospects for a minimally decent life. For that reason, some authors who were initially sceptical of intervention beyond massacre prevention now concede that war ends must include, if necessary, toppling the regime which directed or failed to prevent severe rights violations, and replacing it with one whose claims to internal legitimacy will be, if not beyond dispute, at least markedly better from a humanitarian point of view.[17] But herein lies the rub. For whilst IP may have good reasons to presume that the agents on whose behalf it intervenes would explicitly consent to having the massacres stopped or the regime removed, it may well have far fewer reasons to presume that it would explicitly consent to IP's use of military force to help put in place and consolidate a new regime. In fact, the phrase 'we must prepare for what happens after the war', where the war is inaccurately thought to stop when human rights violations themselves stop, has become a truism. Preparing for after thus requires that IP have evidence of more than presumptive consent on the part of TP's population for its actions. The difficulty, of course, is that IP may end up intervening in an institutional vacuum: either there are no adequate procedures for delivering consent; or actors who claim to act on behalf of the victims either are not properly representative of the latter (such as warlords in Somalia and Afghanistan, male tribal elders in very hierarchical, women-oppressing cultures, and so on), or are themselves guilty of serious human rights violations (such as the Rwandan Patriotic Front, which is alleged to have committed atrocities during the Rwandan civil war in 1990–94), and therefore may not be presumed clearly to have the unambiguous backing of their 'constituents'. The problem is particularly acute in those cases where IP is perceived, rightly or wrongly, to have its own self-interested agenda for conducting a regime-changing intervention, since it is more likely still to encounter hostility on the part of the victims.[18]

It is beyond the scope of this book to tackle the issues of regime change and military occupation. The question at hand here is whether the difficulties

---

[17] See, notably, M. Walzer, 'The Politics of Rescue', in *Arguing about War* (New Haven, CT: 2004).

[18] The point is forcefully made in R. W. Miller, 'Respectable Oppressors, Hypocritical Liberators: Morality, Intervention, and Reality', in D. K. Chatterjee and D. E. Scheid (ed.), *Ethics and Foreign Intervention* (Cambridge: Cambridge University Press, 2003).

inherent in establishing whether IP can be said to have authorization for doing more than merely putting a stop to grievous rights violations are severe enough to undermine the claim that there is an all-things-considered right to intervene to put a stop to those violations as they are occurring. I do not think that they are—any more than similar difficulties undermine insurgents' right to wage a civil war—at least not if the alternative is to allow thousands, hundreds of thousands, or millions of people to be hacked to death, die of starvation, and be denied the essential necessities of life. Moreover, to say that IP does not have a right to intervene because it cannot be sure that its military presence and use of force in support of regime change will be welcome proves too much, for it imposes on IP epistemic requirements which no belligerent can hope to meet, even in cases of collective self-defence: the British government could not have known in 1939 whether the British public would have endorsed a six-year long war with all its attendant grief and deprivations. Lest one should think that Britain, unlike communities in the grip of a humanitarian war, did have the procedures and institutions which enabled it to gauge its citizenry's support for the war, it is worth noting that there were no general elections between 1935 and 1945. More appositely still, as we saw in Chapter 4, one cannot expect a national liberation or revolutionary move-ment to fulfil the internal procedural legitimacy requirements one can expect of a sovereign regime, as a condition for being seen as a legitimate belligerent: for the cost of such expectation is the denial, in effect, of the right to go to war in defence of individuals' rights, which is not acceptable. If, in other words, a liberation movement in an internal conflict need not be certain of its con-stituents' consent to the overthrow of the regime, IP need not have such certainty either when it acts on behalf of those individuals. That having been said, in so far as IP lacks intimate knowledge of the community into which it is stepping, it ought to be held to a higher threshold of evidence for presumptive consent than if it were conducting the war on behalf of its own people. In that respect, the case of humanitarian intervention differs from the case of collec-tive self-defence (whether transnational or intraborders), though not to such an extent as to undermine the claim that there is a *prima facie* right to intervene.

## 5.3 THE DUTY TO INTERVENE

Some cosmopolitans maintain that a commitment to the right to intervene logically implies a commitment to the duty to do so. One such argument proceeds as follows. Intervention is morally permitted, which in turn implies that there are considerable limits to the rightful exercise of sovereignty rights (since the target state cannot rightfully treat its subjects as it wishes, and cannot rightfully object to the intervention). But if one accepts that sovereignty rights can be drastically restricted, then one must impose limits not merely on target states' sovereignty rights, but also on the rights of potential interveners *not* to intervene. In other words, conditional and limited sovereignty within borders goes hand in hand with conditional and limited sovereignty outside borders.[19]

But this will not do. For the claim that internal sovereignty is limited to the point where, should TP violate the rights of (some of) its members, other communities may intervene, is tantamount to asserting that IP *may*, and has the right to, treat TP's victims on a par with their own members, and thus would not wrong TP's regime (and its actors) in so doing. This is not the same as to say that it must so act, and a separate argument is thus required towards the latter conclusion.

One important consideration in support of the view that intervention, whilst permitted, is not mandatory, relates to its costs and burdens. It is one thing to say that potential rescuers are morally permitted to incur those burdens, but it is quite another to hold that they must do so. I shall argue presently that cosmopolitan justifications for the duty of assistance, which do take costs into account, also support the duty to wage a humanitarian war, with appropriate qualifications. Meanwhile, it is worth scrutinizing another argument to the effect that a claim of permissibility entails a claim of mandatoriness. According to that argument, if there is a right to intervene, then by implication the war is just, since a war is just only if the costs to combatants and non-combatants of the intervening state are sufficiently low to be warranted; and if those costs are sufficiently low in that sense, then by implication there is a duty to impose them.[20]

Note first that the claim that IP has a right to intervene does not imply that the war is not unwarrantedly costly for its soldiers or citizens. For consider. It follows from the cosmopolitan account of political sovereignty which underpins this book that a political regime has the right to wage war to the extent that its members, either singly or taken collectively, also have that right. Now

[19] See, for example, J. Davidovic, 'Are Humanitarian Military Interventions Obligatory?', *Journal of Applied Philosophy* 25 (2008): 134–44; (although Davidovic, in the end, seems to favour a justification based on duties of Good Samaritanism); K.-C. Tan, 'The Duty to Protect', in T. Nardin and M. Williams (ed.), *Humanitarian Intervention: NOMOS LVII* (New York: New York University Press, 2006).

[20] J. Pattison, 'Whose Responsibility to Protect? The Duties of Humanitarian Intervention', *Journal of Military Ethics* 7 (2008): 262–84, 270.

suppose that a majority of IP's citizenry, via its regime, consents to supporting the war against TP, at some cost (C) to them. To say that IP, understood as IP's citizens taken on their own or collectively, has the right to intervene is to say, first, that it would not wrong TP by so doing, and second, that the costs incurred by those who do not or are not in a position to consent to the operation do not exceed that which may be imposed on them without their consent (whether those individuals are a dissenting minority within IP, or members of TP who, against a majority of their compatriots, would rather be left to their fate than be subjected to the intervention.) But that claim is entirely compatible with the thought that the costs accruing to those who support and prosecute the intervention may exceed that level provided that they consent to incur them. Put differently, IP may well consent in super-erogatory fashion to incurring costs C for the sake of distant strangers, which exceed the maximum costs—$C_m$—which it would be permissible to inflict on them absent their consent. This suggests that there can be a cost-related gap between the right and the duty to intervene.

Second, even if it were true that the costs attendant on the intervention are such that imposing them on IP's population and soldiers is permissible, it does not follow that the latter are under a duty to incur them. To see this, consider the view that in so-called situations of supreme emergency a just belligerent may deliberately target enemy innocent non-combatants so as to weaken their morale and, thereby, the enemy war effort—for example, by bombing densely populated areas. So construed, the view implies that it is permissible, under such circumstances, deliberately to impose on innocent non-combatants the costs attendant on winning the just war. But even if that is correct (a claim which I shall revisit in Section 7.2), it does not follow that those non-combatants are under a duty to act in such a way as to incur those costs. At the very least, if they can leave their city, thereby considerably blunting the impact of the bombing, they may do so. More strongly still, if they have the wherewithal to shoot down the bombers, they may do so as well.[21] Analo-gously, to claim that imposing C on IP's population and soldiers is permissible is entirely compatible with the claim that they are not under a duty to act in such a way as to incur C but, rather, are only under a duty (if they are at all) to act in such a way as to incur $C_m$.

---

[21] In Section 2.4 I argued that non-combatants who are under unintentional threat by a *tactical* bomber may defend their own lives by killing him. Here I claim that *if* terror bombing is permissible under a situation of supreme emergency, then the two scenarios should be regarded on a par with respect to what non-combatants may do to thwart the attack.

In sum, having established that there is a right to intervene is one thing, but showing that there is a duty to do so is another. In what follows, assuming throughout that IP already has the right to intervene, I offer an argument in support of the duty which appeals to some key tenets of the cosmopolitan ethics of assistance which I defended in Chapter 1. Note that there is another argument for the duty to intervene as grounded in considerations of reparative justice, whereby IP is under the duty because it is in part responsible for the predicament in which TP's victims find themselves. Whilst this is not a specifically cosmopolitan argument, it may well have a role to play in cosmopolitan justifications for the duty to intervene. If there are a number of victim communities, and if a potential rescuing regime is not in a position to help them all but is in part responsible for the predicament of one of them, the fact of its responsibility for those wrongdoing may well justify holding it under a duty to help that particular community rather than the others. I shall revisit some of these rectificatory considerations in Section 5.4.

In Chapter 1 I argued that all individuals, wherever they reside, have fundamental rights to the material resources without which one could not hope to live a minimally decent life. Those rights, which I have called subsistence rights and which are held against their fellow community members *and* foreigners, include the following: negative rights not to be interfered with when attempting to secure those resources as well as not to be subject to avoidable ill health and physical harms (what I called the human right not to be subjected to severe deprivation); and positive rights to be provided with the assistance they need to lift themselves out of their predicament (what I called the human right to receive help). One might think that the foregoing thesis straightforwardly extends to the provision of military assistance, via taxation, to distant strangers who do not enjoy fundamental human rights. If the affluent are under a duty to fund the delivery of food, medical supplies, engineering expertise, and so on, for the sake of helping distant strangers, then it would seem that they are under a duty to protect the latter from harm by way of a humanitarian intervention. There are different ways, in other words, in which to be a Good Samaritan.[22] And yet standard arguments in

---

[22] See, for example, Elfstrom, 'On Dilemmas of Intervention' for a Good Samaritan argument in favour of the duty to intervene. For a Kantian argument in favour of the duty to intervene as a perfect duty of justice, see C. Bagnoli, 'Humanitarian Intervention as a Perfect Duty: A Kantian Argument', in T. Nardin, and M. S. Williams (ed.), *Humanitarian Intervention: NOMOS XLVII* (New York: New York University Press, 2006). To the duty to protect victims, Bagnoli adds a duty to coerce wrongdoers. But she does not tackle the difficulties raised by the fact that fulfilling both duties requires acts of killing. In the paragraphs that follow I develop a justification for the duty to intervene which is sensitive to the fact that an intervention imposes different kinds of costs on interveners (notably, the financial costs attendant on funding the war, and the human costs attendant on actually

favour of duties to help the very poor do not, on their own, constitute an appropriate basis for arguing in favour of a duty to intervene. For they tend to assume, first, that the very poor's needs arise from natural causes, and second, that those who provide them with assistance do so *ex post* as a way to relieve an already existing need. However, the beneficiaries of humanitarian intervention are victims of someone else's wrongdoing. Moreover, intervening forces have to step in as the rights violations are ongoing, and in so doing must expose themselves to a risk of harm.

The foregoing remarks suggest that there are three kinds of cost which members of IP might have to incur as a result of waging a humanitarian war: the material costs attendant on financing the war; the costs, in terms of harm to life and limbs, to which members of IP might be subject were TP's regime decide to retaliate militarily against the intervention; and the costs for intervening soldiers of actually fighting the war. Accordingly, any argument to the effect that IP is under a duty to intervene must show that IP's members are under a duty to incur those particular costs. It must also show why they are under such a duty given that, *ex hypothesi*, the individuals whom they have been called upon to help are placed in their predicament as a result either of TP's direct wrongdoing or of its failure to protect them itself.

Let us turn first to the costs borne out by IP's residents, which consist of material—mostly financial—costs inherent in funding the war, as well as in the harm (to life and limbs) to which the war exposes them. Within borders, individuals are under a duty to help, via general taxation, those who are wrongfully harmed by others. If Blue attacks Red without any justification whatsoever, and if White can save Red's life at no cost to himself, surely he should do so. At least, the fact that Red is under threat from another agent, and not (for example) knocked unconscious by a falling branch, surely is irrelevant to establishing whether White must intervene. *Mutatis mutandis*, the fact that beneficiaries of an intervention suffer from rights violations at the hands of their state as opposed to (for example) from non-anthropogenic harm is irrelevant to establishing whether IP is under a duty to help them. Such a duty, moreover, does not depend on common citizenship: clearly, it would be wrong of a regime to cut down funding for the police on the grounds that the latter ought not to protect passing tourists from unwarranted attacks at the hands of citizens. Nor does the duty depend on there being no other duty-

fighting it). In an interesting article written shortly after NATO's 1999 bombing campaign of Serbia, David Luban insists on the importance of justifying those costs, but is sceptical of the claim that there is a duty to intervene (in the light of the aforementioned human costs). See D. Luban, 'Intervention and Civilization', in P. De Greiff and C. Cronin (ed.), *Global Justice and Transnational Politcs: Essays on the Moral and Political Challenges of Globalization* (Boston, MA: MIT University Press, 2002).

bearers: no less clearly, it is a requirement of justice that children whose parents are alive and are thus primary duty-bearers should receive assistance if their parents are derelict. Generally, and subject to costs and to considerations of allocative fairness, individuals can be held under a duty to step into the breach when primary duty-bearers are no longer able or willing to protect those whom they must protect.

At the bar of cosmopolitan justice, the duty extends across borders as well. Let us take for granted that members of community A are under a duty to provide the means, by way of taxation, of protecting from attack by one of their members a tourist from country V who happens to pass through A's territory. Let us assume further that they are under such a duty even if that tourist's friends or relatives, who could easily help him, flee the scene, and even if he is attacked by those individuals themselves. If that is the case, then (and subject to considerations of costs and feasibility) they also are under a *prima facie* duty to provide for similar protection if the tourist is attacked on the territory of his own community, either by his own regime or by someone else in the face of his regime's failure to protect him. To claim, *a contrario*, that the location of the wrongdoing on one side or other of the border or the wrongdoers' nationality make a difference to the imposition of the duty to help falls foul of cosmopolitan justice, particularly given that, *ex hypothesi*, IP has a right to intervene, which in turn implies that TP is not wronged by the intervention.

Some might be tempted to object to my argument as follows. A regime's right to govern is conditional on its ability to provide the basic necessities of life for those over whom it claims jurisdiction, *and* to protect them from wrongdoers. But as I myself argued in Section 1.4, the rationale for making its legitimacy conditional upon its fulfilment of the duty to protect lies in its special relationship with its members. *That* regime, rather than any other, has a claim to enforce compliance from *those* individuals as located on *that* territory if it does a better job at protecting those rights than individuals themselves would. Upstream, as it were, members of a territorially bounded political community may demand compliance from one another and authorize institutional actors to enforce it, provided that they give one another, via taxation, the means to protect their rights. Conversely—the objection would continue—it is precisely because individuals agree, explicitly or implicitly, to comply with the law and authorize that particular regime to enforce compliance that they are all under a duty to provide protection for all. However, no such special, broadly Lockean relationship exists between those individuals and foreign political communities. Accordingly, borders *are* relevant to the duty to protect individuals from wrongdoers.

Although the objection is intuitively appealing at first sight, I believe that it fails. For the claim (which lies at its heart) that legitimacy is conditional upon (*inter alia*) the fulfilment of the duty to protect individuals from wrongdoers is not the same as the claim (which lies at the heart of the case for mandatory intervention) that the justification for that duty lies in a more general duty to provide assistance to those in need. The reason why the affluent are under a duty to help the needy within their borders has got nothing to do with the fact that the needy will be more effective citizens and cooperative members of society.[23] Nor does it have anything to do with the need or desirability to secure their compliance with the law. Rather, it has everything to do with the fact that they are needy, period. By that token, as I stressed in Section 1.3.1, there is a cross-border duty to help those in need, when the notion of need is broadly construed (as it surely must be) to include deprivation of fundamental freedoms and essential resources as a result of some other party's dereliction of duty.

The foregoing argument supports a duty on the part of IP's members to divert material resources towards a humanitarian war. But note that its rationale also supports the claim that IP's members are under a duty to expose themselves to the risks attendant on waging that war, such as, for example, the risk that TP's army will retaliate against them. Those risks are very real indeed, particularly if IP and TP are neighbouring countries, so that it would be easy for TP's army to carry out lethal incursions into IP's territory. Yet it would be odd to think that agents are never under a duty to expose themselves to some risk, including a risk of death, for the sake of others: if R sees someone collapse across the street, with no other pedestrian in sight, R surely is under a duty to cross the road to come to her help, even if there is some traffic, and even if, thus, R is at risk of being run over. That said, as I argued in Section 1.2.1, agents are not under a duty to give assistance to strangers at the cost of their own prospects for a minimally decent life. Therefore, if the costs of support-ing, financing, or authorizing the war are so high as to undermine such prospects for IP's members, then they are not under a duty so to act. Note that the reason why that is so is not that those for whom the war would be waged are *distant* strangers: to claim that it is would breach the cosmopolitan requirement that political borders should be seen as arbitrary from a moral point of view with respect to individuals' fundamental human rights. Rather, it lies in the claim that there is a limit to the sacrifices which individuals may be expected to make for the sake of others, whether or not the latter are their compatriots.

---

[23] See Fabre, *Social Rights under the Constitution*, 62–4.

So much for the claim that IP's members are under a duty to provide assistance to victims of severe rights violations in TP by financing and authorizing a humanitarian war. Without soldiers to prosecute the war, however, IP is not in a position to fulfil its duty. Are soldiers, then, under a duty to fight for the sake of distant strangers? It is important to bear in mind that the duty consists, on the one hand, in a duty to kill, and on the other hand, in a duty to incur the costs and run the risks inherent in participation in military hostilities: the Belgian peacekeepers who were murdered by Hutu militias in the early days of the Rwandan Genocide are testimony to the fact that carrying out a humanitarian intervention is not merely about providing essential necessities to the victims (as recruitment films for the British Army sometimes seem to imply) but is also about killing and dying. Now, as I have argued elsewhere, agents sometimes are under a duty to kill attackers in defence of their victims, provided that they would not incur an unacceptable risk of jeopardising their own prospects for a minimally decent life in the course of the rescue attempt.[24] The duty is not a contractual obligation of the kind which agents incur when they decide to work for the police or, appositely here, sign up for the army. Rather, it is a general duty, owed to all others, to help them meet their need—here construed as a need for assistance in the face of severe rights violations at the hands of attackers. To the extent that the risks and costs of fighting a war of intervention are very likely to exceed that which one may legitimately impose on rescuers, a government may not conscript part of its citizenry to fight such a war—subject to the following qualification.[25] Humanitarian interventions, it is often and accurately said, are never waged solely out of concern for the victims; rather, interveners have their own, self-interested reasons for financing the war and exposing their troops to its risks. Normatively speaking, I do not believe that the presence of

[24] See 'Mandatory Rescue Killings', *Journal of Political Philosophy* 15 (2007): 363–84. This paragraph and the next summarize the article. See also Moellendorf, *Cosmopolitan justice*, 122ff. For a conclusion similar to mine, see D. Baer, 'The Ultimate Sacrifice and the Ethics of Humanitarian Intervention', *Review of International Studies* 37 (2011): 301–26. For the view that military conscription for the sake of waging a humanitarian war is permissible, see Tesón, 'The Liberal Case for Humanitarian Intervention'.

[25] I am sceptical of the claim that that humanitarian conscription is permissible if the war can be fought at very low, acceptable, costs to intervening forces—for example, by way of air bombardments, rather than on the ground (provided, of course, that it is waged justly). For even if it were possible for combatants to incur only acceptable costs (acceptable, that is, as a matter of duty), waging such a war requires that one learn the relevant skills and undergo extensive training, which can be done only within the army itself. This in turn would require that individuals be forced to become soldiers. At the bar of freedom of occupational choice, however, one cannot hold agents under a duty to do so for the sake of others—for exactly the same reasons adduced earlier in support of the view that agents are not under a duty to provide assistance at the cost of their own prospects for a minimally decent life.

self-interested motives is enough to taint a humanitarian war to such an extent as to make it impermissible. However, unless TP also threatens those collective self-interests in such a way as to provide IP with another just cause for war, the acts of killing committed by intervening soldiers in prosecution of that subsidiary cause, as part of the wider humanitarian conflict, are impermissible.

That said, there might be cases where IP has two just causes for waging war against TP—the defence of TP's victims on the one hand, and on the other hand some collective self-interest of its own. Thus, the threat which Pakistan's repression of autonomist parties in East Pakistan allegedly posed to India— uncontrollable influx of refugees, increasing levels of violence in the border region, and so on—was invoked by the latter as the main justification for its intervention in Pakistan in 1971. Let us assume, for the sake of argument, that India had a strong case for intervening, on grounds of self-defence as well as defence of others.[26] Let us further assume (to anticipate on a claim which I shall defend in Section 7.3) that conscription for collective self-defence is morally legitimate under specific conditions—that is, under those conditions, individuals are under an enforceable moral duty to serve in the army of their community for the sake of jointly securing the non-excludable good of collective security which they deem in their individual interest to preserve. Accordingly, sending conscripts to fight a war of humanitarian intervention is permissible (which suggests that there is a duty on the part of agents both to kill and to expose themselves to acceptable risks for the sake of distant strangers), but only if the following conditions obtain: (a) military conscription is legitimate, in principle, as a means to fight a collective war of self-defence; (b) the collective self-interests which in part motivate the decision to go to war are part of a just cause for the war; (c) in the course of their tour of duty, conscripts learn the skills required to wage a just humanitarian war at acceptable costs to their lives.

By acceptable costs, I have in mind the following. There are costs which agents may not be forced to bear, even for the sake of collective self-defence. Below that threshold $T_{CSD}$, collective self-defence costs are acceptable. There are also costs which they may not be forced to incur for the defence of others. Below *that* threshold, $T_{DO}$, those humanitarian costs are acceptable. Suppose now that the costs for combatants$_{IP}$ of defending their community's collective interests are higher than the costs of defending the interests of distant strangers, though below $T_{CSD}$. May they be held under a morally enforceable duty to incur them, through conscription, even though they would not

26 Wheeler, *Saving Strangers*, ch. 2.

(*ex hypothesi*) be under a moral duty to incur those very same costs were the latter attendant on a purely other-regarding intervention? I believe so. Crucially, the point is not that (in violation of cosmopolitan justice) IP's members are under a duty to their compatriots to give greater priority to their fundamental interests than to the fundamental interests of distant strangers *qua* distant strangers. Rather, the point is that if an agent stands to benefit from other agents' contribution to a joint public good, and if securing that public good requires of participants in the collective venture that they incur a given cost, then that agent can be made to incur it (subject to the aforementioned conditions) on the grounds that his failure to do so would be tantamount to (impermissible) free-riding.

Thus, if those two just causes obtain, and if IP's conscripts are properly trained, then in the course of fighting that war, they may be expected to incur costs which fall above $T_{DO}$ and below $T_{CSD}$. Absent the aforementioned conditions, the claim that political communities and their members are under a duty to TP's victims to intervene in their defence does not imply a duty to kill and to expose themselves to the risks inherent in actually fighting the war for their sake. It is, rather, a duty to fund, support, and direct a professional army of willing soldiers. It remains to be seen who, precisely, is under that duty.

## 5.4 WHOSE RIGHT? WHOSE DUTY?

The question of who is a legitimate intervener is central to the literature on intervention. For it is one thing to claim that there is such a thing as a general right or a general duty to intervene; but it is quite another to assign that right and that duty to specific parties. The question, in fact, raises two often conflated but distinct issues: that of who may or must *authorize* the war in order for the latter to be just, and that of who may or must *prosecute* the war. On the first count, some argue that a humanitarian war cannot be just unless it is authorized by a multinational organisation such as the UN, whilst others counter that any community, be it a single-state or a multistate organisation such as NATO, may resort to force to solve a humanitarian crisis. Others still aver that whilst multilateralism is preferable to unilateralism (for reasons to be set out below), in some extreme cases, of which an ongoing genocide is the paradigmatic example, unilateral intervention is permissible.[27] On the second

---

[27] For strong defences of multilateralism, see, for example, Coady, 'War for humanity: a critique'; Mehta, 'From State Sovereignty to Human Security (via Institutions?)'; Moellendorf, *Cosmopolitan justice*, 118ff. For the view that multilateralism is preferable thought not necessary, see, for example,

count, some scholars defend the creation of an international army, account-able to a multinational organisation such as the UN, and whose main task would be to intervene against human rights violators and secure the condi-tions under which stable, rights-promoting institutions could be set up.[28]

Now, recall that the right to wage war is a right held by individuals which they can transfer to institutional actors if doing so is a more effective way of protecting their fundamental human rights. Accordingly, whether an institu-tional actor has the right to wage war on behalf of the victims of rights violations is entirely dependent on its ability to carry out the task at hand. Domestically, citizens are (usually) better off entrusting the defence of their rights to the police—a publicly funded and appointed set of agents who are authorized by transparent, accountable, and impartial public institutions to use force against wrongdoers, and properly trained to do so. By parity of reasoning, victims of rights violations at the hands of their own regime are (usually) better off entrusting multinational institutions with the task of authorizing the quick deployment of an international army, since those institutions are more likely to be impartial and to reach their decision to use force in a transparent and accountable way than lone, unmandated interve-ners. Those institutions and their armed forces, which should be funded by all member communities in proportion to the latter's GDP, thus constitute the primary institutional rights-holders and duty-bearers when humanitarian intervention is at issue. Or so one might think.

And yet state institutions are not always transparent, fair, and impartial—far from it. To reiterate, when they are derelict in their duty to protect the fundamental rights of their citizens or are simply incapable of doing so, the right to authorize and wage war reverts to the latter. By that token, when multinational institutions are similarly derelict and cannot or will not mobilise forces and funds quickly enough to avert rights violations on a mass scale (as was the case during the Rwandan genocide), the right to wage war may be held by whoever is in a position to protect the victims: just as there is nothing intrinsically valuable in entrusting territorially-bounded states with the task of resorting to violence, there is nothing intrinsically valuable in entrusting

J. Boyle, 'Traditional Just War Theory and Humanitarian Intervention', in T. Nardin and M. S. WIlliams (ed.), *Humanitarian Intervention: NOMOS XLVII* (New York: New York University Press, 2006); N. Dobos, 'Is U.N. Security Council Authorisation for Armed Humanitarian Intervention Morally Necessary?', *Philosophia* 38 (2010): 499–515; M. Smith, 'Humanitarian Intervention: An Overview of the Ethical Issues', *Ethics and International Affairs* 12 (1998): 63–79. The works cited in footnotes 1 to 5 above, taken together, cover most of the issues tackled in this section. In addition, for a recent book-length treatment of the issue of who may and must intervene, see Pattison, *Humanitarian Intervention and the Responsibility to Protect*.

[28] See, for example, Caney, *Justice Beyond Borders*; Tan, 'The Duty to Protect'.

multinational institutions with the task of protecting individuals from rights violations at the hands of their own regime, or of factions within their own country which their regime is unable or unwilling to thwart.

Note that the approach defended here, which one may call 'heavily-qualified multilateralism', does not imply that the only parties who may wage a humanitarian war are rights-respecting communities. One might think that it does, in so far as a community which respects the rights of its own members is more likely, perhaps, to conduct the humanitarian war justly and to realize its just ends.[29] But although the point might hold in practice, in principle, the fact that an intervening regime is a dictatorship is not enough to condemn as unjust the war it conducts to stop a genocide—as was the case, for example, when Vietnam intervened in Cambodia in 1978 and overthrew Pol Pot's regime. More generally, as Nardin aptly puts it, 'a murderer is not forbidden to save a drowning child.'[30] What matters, rather, is that he should be able to swim and rescue the child effectively—and then hand her over to appropriate parties.

The foregoing points might seem to suggest that heavily-qualified multilateralism puts a premium on effectiveness and ability to protect victims above all other considerations, where effectiveness is defined as (or coming as close as possible to) bringing about the just ends of the intervention with the least amount of wrongful losses to lives and limbs on all sides.[31] But whilst effectiveness is paramount, other considerations come into play. In particular, a potential intervener who is unable or unwilling to carry out the intervention without infringing fundamental requirements such as non-combatant immunity cannot be regarded as a legitimate belligerent. Furthermore, considerations of fairness dictate that the costs of intervention be spread amongst potential rescuers based both on their ability to contribute and on the extent to which they already have contributed to previous interventions. The point applies not merely to the financial cost of the war but also to its human costs: a community which has already and recently provided troops for several humanitarian operations might thus have a very strong case for not doing so in the case at hand.

In addition, whether a potential intervener is partly responsible for the rights violations to which the intervention is a response might be thought relevant to the assignment of the duty to intervene. By way of example, it is

---

[29] See, for example, F. R. Tesón, *A Philosophy of International Law* (Boulder, CO: Westview Press, 1998), 59.

[30] Nardin, 'The Moral Basis of Humanitarian Intervention', 68.

[31] For the view that effectiveness is the main criterion for assigning the duty to intervene, see Pattison, *Humanitarian Intervention and the Responsibility to Protect*. I say 'wrongful losses' because those whose lives really matter in the proportionality calculus are those who are not liable to being killed in the first instance.

estimated that close to a million people—most of them Tutsis, others Hutu
opponents to the regime in power—died in the Rwandan genocide. It is also
widely alleged, with some evidence, that Belgium, Rwanda's former colonial
power, encouraged and fostered a climate of ethnic divisions and hatred
during its mandate. It is also alleged, again with archival and testimonial
support, that France, a long-term supporter of the extremist Hutu regime of
President Habyarimana, supplied the Rwandan regular army with weapons as
well as technical and strategic expertise not merely in the months leading up to
the genocide, but as the massacres had already started—this despite growing
evidence (which had long been gathered by UN observers and inside infor-
mants) that the deaths were not a 'by-product' of a raging civil war but rather
the intended outcome of a long-planned campaign of extermination.[32] Let us
assume, for the sake of argument but entirely plausibly, that France's and
Belgium's successive regimes were guilty of grievous wrongdoing towards the
Tutsi minority and those members of the Hutu majority who opposed President Habyarimana. In such cases it might stand to reason that France had a
primary responsibility to intervene in the genocide as early as April 1994—just
as it behoves me, out of all available rescuers, to help the child I negligently
pushed into the water. Having said that, here too effectiveness matters. Indeed,
as we saw in Section 5.2, a humanitarian war will not successfully fulfil its just
cause if it merely stops human rights violations in the short term: instead, it
must secure the conditions under which the rights of its beneficiaries are secure
in the long term. It is particularly important therefore that the interveners
should be able to gain and keep the trust of the local population. However, the
more serious the wrongdoing, the more likely it is that the intervention will be
met by its intended beneficiaries with scepticism and suspicions of wrong
motives and unjust ends—as was, in fact, the case in Rwanda, when the then
French government finally sent in French troops in June 1994.[33]

   This might seem to give rise to the following paradox of intervention: the
greater the degree of responsibility for rights violations, the weaker the case for

---

[32] See, for example, Melvern, *Conspiracy to Murder*; Wheeler, *Saving Strangers*, ch. 7, esp. 218–9
and 234–6; Gourevitch, *We Wish to Inform you that Tomorrow we will be Killed with our Families*. To
be clear, in this section I am not claiming that the French deliberately helped Hutu extremists of
carrying out the genocide; rather, my claim (which is supported by the evidence cited in those works)
is that they provided assistance to Habyarimana's regime for their own geopolitical aims,
notwithstanding the fact that the latter was known to have a genocidal 'project' and was more
than capable of bringing it to fruition. Bluntly put, the French were negligently unwitting abettors of
the genocide.
[33] For the claim that the French intervention—*Operation Turquoise*—was unjust, see Wheeler,
*Saving Strangers*. On the basis of the evidence provided by Wheeler, it is hard indeed to dissent. (See
also Melvern, *Conspiracy to Murder*, 246–51; Gourevitch, *We wish to inform you that tomorrow we
will be killed with our families*, 158–61.)

assigning the duty to intervene to wrongdoers. And yet there still is space for imposing on the wrongdoer a greater share of the burdens of intervention. Earlier, I distinguished between two components of the general duty to intervene: namely, the duty to fund and provide material support for the war and the duty to deploy one's own forces and actually prosecute the war. The risk that a wrongdoer's army might not be able successfully to conduct a just war of intervention might well dictate against, for example, France sending ground troops to Rwanda in the summer of 1994. But it does not dictate against France assuming the lion's share of supplying other armed forces with equipment, let alone of funding the war.[34]

To recapitulate, *modulo* wrongdoers' special responsibilities to their victims, the right to intervene, in its various specific components, ought to be held by whichever actor is best placed to meet the requirements of impartiality, transparency, and fairness when authorizing the war, and the requirement of reasonable chance of success (constrained by proportionality and necessity) when fighting, funding, and prosecuting it. The duty to intervene, meanwhile, ought to be borne by all other countries in proportion to their means when it comes to funding the war, and by the most effective army, which may well mean a multilateral international force, when it comes to fighting.

It might seem as if my account of who has the right or, as the case may be, the duty to intervene for the sake of distant strangers is tantamount to endorsing the following view of intervention, whereby the right to intervene constitutes not so much a right to kill in defence of the victims as a right to stop wrongdoers from violating universal norms. On that view, a humanitarian war is not a lethal conflict between soldiers who ought to be regarded as morally on a par: it is, rather, a police operation conducted by law-enforcers against criminals. And if that is the case (the view continues), there are three crucial differences between humanitarian intervention and 'standard' armed conflicts: soldiers on the intervening side are required *not* to shift harm, deliberately and knowingly, away from themselves and onto non-combatants; they must not inflict collateral damage on those non-combatants; and they must hand over prisoners of war after the war as a means to ensure that the latter are tried for their criminal activities (the criminal activities consisting of either directly committing the human rights violations which provided the intervening side with a just cause, or blocking the latter's attempts at stopping those violations.)[35]

---

[34] I prescind from addressing the many difficulties raised by a rectificatory approach to intervention.
[35] For good examples of the position described here, see G. R. J. Lucas, 'From *jus ad bellum* to *jus ad pacem*: Rethinking Just War Criteria for the Use of Military Force for Humanitarian Ends', in

The difficulty with the police-operation model is that it does not provide a satisfactory account of the right to *kill* in war: clearly, on that count, it is deficient as a framework for humanitarian interventions (just as it is lacking as a framework for understanding collective self-defence[36]). Moreover, the model's claims to superiority on the orthodox theory of armed conflicts, as expounded above, are not persuasive. For on the account of the right to kill in war which underpins my cosmopolitan theory of a just war, soldiers who contribute to the unjust initial attack(s) are regarded as wrongdoers. There is thus no reason so to distinguish between wars of self-defence and wars of humanitarian intervention. Moreover, it is not clear at all that in a humanitarian war, intervening forces may not shift harm, deliberately or unintentionally, to non-combatants. To this issue I now turn.


## 5.5 KILLING IN HUMANITARIAN WARS

In a humanitarian war the following categories of individuals are likely to be killed: intervening combatants, combatants who resist the intervention at TP's behest, and innocent non-combatants within TP. My aim in this section is to explore the permission and right to kill those agents in the course of an intervention. Before proceeding, however, a few reminders. An agent X has the *right* to kill Y only if the latter unjustifiably poses, or significantly contributes to the posing of, a wrongful threat of lethal harm either to X himself or to some other party Z. To say that X has the right to kill Y is to say that Y has made himself *liable* to being killed deliberately, and is under a duty not to retaliate in his own defence against X. If Y's contribution to a wrongful threat is not of a kind as to warrant the loss of his right not to be killed, he might nevertheless be liable to the deliberate infliction of a harm lesser than death; it might also be permissible to kill him unintentionally (though foreseeably). Finally, although materially innocent non-combatants on the unjust side are not liable to being killed, just combatants sometimes have a justification for killing them unintentionally—in other words, for justifiably infringing their right not to be killed. With those considerations in mind, we shall assess, in Section 5.5.1, whether combatants on either side of the humanitarian war are liable to being killed. In Section 5.5.2 we shall

D. K. Chatterjee and D. E. Scheid (ed.), *Ethics and Foreign Intervention* (Cambridge: Cambridge University Press, 2003); Kaldor, *New and Old Wars*, ch. 6.

[36] For a criticism of the norm-enforcement model which is directly focused on humanitarian intervention, see Mehta, 'From State Sovereignty to Human Security (via Institutions?)'.

examine whether combatants$_{IP}$ have a justification for killing TP's victims, given that the latter are not liable to being killed. I assume throughout that IP has the *prima facie* right to intervene in TP's internal affairs, whether this is so because TP's regime is guilty of severe rights violations against some of its members, or because it is unable to protect the latter from such violations as committed by third parties.

### 5.5.1 Killing combatants

I have maintained throughout this book that soldiers are not morally on a par once the war has started, and that, on the contrary, the justness of their war *ad bellum* has decisive weight when determining whether they have the right to kill enemy soldiers *in bello*. In the case at hand, some members of TP—extremist militias, some sections of the armed forces and the police, and so on—are responsible for violating the fundamental human rights of some of their compatriots—violations which are such, *ex hypothesi*, as to provide IP with a just cause for intervening. As a first rough cut at the issue of combatants' liability in a humanitarian war, those individuals clearly have lost their right not to be killed deliberately by combatants$_{IP}$, and are thus liable to being attacked. By that token, combatants$_{IP}$ have not lost their right not to be killed by those combatants.

Suppose, however, that other soldiers within TP, such as its regular army, are not taking part in those atrocities. Are they too liable to being killed by IP's forces as the latter advances through TP's territory? It is sometimes argued that intervening soldiers must exercise greater restraint in a war of humanitarian intervention against enemy combatants (even if the latter are deemed to be unjustly fighting) than in a conventional transnational war—for reasons examined above when dealing with the police-operation model of intervention. Thus, on one view, whereas a just belligerent's soldiers may seek comprehensively to defeat the enemy army and carry out the acts of killing necessary for that purpose, intervening soldiers must restrict themselves to preventing enemy combatants from committing atrocities against their compatriots (the regime's victims), or to preventing rebel armed groups and the regime's conventional forces from fighting one another in an all-out war—unless destroying the target country's infrastructure is necessary to prosecute the war successfully.[37] I am not convinced, however, that wars of intervention differ, with respect to the ethics of

---

[37] See Pattison, *Humanitarian Intervention and the Responsibility to Protect*, 106ff. More generally, for a thoughtful treatment of soldiers' liabilities in wars of intervention, see A. Leveringhaus, 'The Moral Status of Combatants during Military Humanitarian Intervention', *Utilitas* 24 (2012): 237–58.

killing enemy combatants, from conventional wars. For in the latter too, combatants are under an obligation to use only such force as is required by the successful prosecution of the just cause; moreover, if (as I argued in Section 5.2), ensuring that TP's regime stops carrying out human rights violations in the long term is a just cause for intervention, and if overthrowing that regime is the only way to bring about that end, then IP will need to secure a sufficiently comprehensive military victory as to make it impossible for TP's army to bolster their leaders' position.

Finally, and decisively, members of TP's army who resist IP's intervention are unjust combatants, and IP's soldiers thus have the right to kill them. Analogously, suppose that A is unjustifiably subjecting V to a wrongful lethal attack, and that R is coming to the latter's rescue. Suppose further that C, who is blocking the door of the room where A holds V captive, shoots at R as the latter approaches. It follows from the account of the right to kill offered in Section 2.2 that R has the right to kill C in self-defence, since the latter unjustifiably subjects him to a lethal threat which he has not done anything to warrant. Moreover, C is liable not merely for threatening R but also for contributing to V's predicament by assisting A. Suppose that V has a gun which she cannot use against A because the latter immobilises her arm, but that she can stop A by shooting at C. Given the significance of C's contribution to her being killed (he is, after all, blocking her only escape), V has the right to kill him and the power to transfer that right to R. R thus has the right to kill C in her defence. As applied to the case of war, TP's standing army, if it resists IP's intervention, occupies a similar role as C does towards R and V. By using lethal force to block combatants$_{IP}$' move to rescue TP's victims, combatants$_{TP}$ are making a highly significant contribution to the latter's predicament, who thus have the right to kill them in self-defence and the power to transfer that right to their rescuers; moreover, combatants$_{IP}$ also have the right to kill combatants$_{TP}$ in defence of their own right to life. Once those considerations are brought into view, it is far from clear that greater restraint is called in wars of humanitarian intervention than in conventional warfare.

These points need qualifying. As they stand, they are plausible only if combatants' right to kill in war depends solely on the moral status of a war *in toto*. As we saw in Section 2.3.2, however, a war which is just *in toto* may well have unjust phases, in which *ad bellum* just combatants take part in unjust missions; conversely, a war which is unjust *in toto* may have just phases in which *ad bellum* unjust combatants kill permissibly. The point is particularly relevant to wars of humanitarian intervention, in so far as they are unlikely to be fought solely out of concern for TP's victims, particularly if they are authorized and prosecuted, not by impartial multinational institutions and armed forces, but rather, by a political community acting on their own initiative (as France did in Rwanda.) To be sure, in some cases, the self-interested ends which partly motivate IP's decision to intervene might be part of an all-things-considered justification for war, so that the war would be justified even if TP's wrongdoing did not suffice on its own to justify it. In other cases, however, IP's self-interested ends cannot contribute to providing IP with an all-things-considered justification for waging war against TP. Consider the following cases.

*Stolen territory.* Forty years before IP's humanitarian intervention against TP, the latter's regime wrongfully annexed a largely empty part of IP's territory. Although TP's regime clearly violated IP's (collective) right to territorial integrity, forty years on there is a very strong chance that IP would be able to recover its territory via diplomatic means, or in a post-intervention settlement. IP, in other words, lacks a justification for waging war against TP as a means to obtain redress for the rights violations to which it was subject in the past. However, its leaders instruct the army to seize that territory by force in the course of the humanitarian intervention (for which the plight of TP's victims does provide a justification). In that particular phase of the war, combatants$_{IP}$ directly and intentionally subject combatants$_{TP}$ to a lethal threat at time $t_1$ and are met with equally fierce and lethal resistance at $t_2$.

*Diamond mines.* IP launches a military intervention against TP not merely in order to protect the latter's victims, but also with a view to seizing TP's diamond mines over which it has no rightful claim whatsoever. Its leaders deploy a number of their divisions towards the diamonds mine, and instruct those soldiers to take the latter by lethal force. In response, TP deploys some of its combatants to resist IP's expansionist aggression.

In both cases, combatants$_{IP}$ unjustifiably pose a wrongful lethal threat to combatants$_{TP}$, and the latter therefore may kill them in self-defence. Some might object, at this juncture, that combatants$_{TP}$ ought not to fight combatants$_{IP}$, even though the latter are wrongfully targeting them, but rather, ought to surrender. For by prolonging the fight over the stolen territory and the diamond mines, the objection might press, they weaken IP's army in its effort to stop the rights violations of which TP's members are victims, and in so doing, strengthen TP's regime. The objection has bite if combatants$_{TP}$ are given the option to surrender the territory or the mines without being killed, or, indeed, to join IP in its fight against TP's leaders. For under those circumstances they ought to take that option, even though, in the case of *Diamond mines*, they would thereby accede to the commission of a wrongdoing by IP against members of TP considered collectively. But if IP does not allow for the possibility of seizing either the stolen territory or the mines bloodlessly, and thus subjects combatants$_{TP}$ to an unprovoked and unwarranted lethal threat, then it is not clear at all that the latter may not defend their lives. Of course, by defending themselves they do help perpetuate the injustices of which their compatriots are victims. The alternative, however, consists in letting themselves be killed *wrongfully* for the sake of others. Even if, merely by swelling the ranks of the army, they have contributed to bolstering a rights violating regime, they have not (it seems to me) lost their right, *vis-à-vis* their compatriots, not to protect their own life from unjustifiable wrongful attack. Analogously, an armed member of a criminal gang who does not himself wrongfully kill innocent citizens and/or police officers has not lost his right not to be killed wrongfully by the latter in, for example, an illegal and massive 'street-cleaning operation': one cannot expect him to allow the police to shoot him wrongfully for the sake of weakening the gang's influence.

Note, however, that in *Stolen territory*, combatants$_{TP}$ are protecting land over which they, *qua* TP's members, have no collective claim. In *Diamond mines*, by contrast, they are protecting their rightful claim to property. This makes a difference with respect to those combatants' liability to harm. In *Stolen territory*, whilst they are not liable to being killed deliberately, they might well be liable to non-lethal force. Analogously, I may not kill you as a means to recover the invaluable family heirloom you have just stolen from me; but I may—indeed have the right to—deliberately twist your arm to get you to let go of my property (at least so long as the police is not on the scene, as I catch you red-handed, and so on). By contrast, combatants$_{TP}$ in *Diamond mines* are not liable to intentional harm at all, since they are not preserving an unjust allocation of resources by protecting the mines from IP's attack. Analogously, I certainly may not twist your arm to take from you a necklace which belongs to you.

Furthermore, the fact that in one case combatants$_{TP}$ protect a resource over which they have no claim, whilst in the other case they act rightfully by opposing IP, results in different verdicts with respect to the infliction of foreseen but unintentional lethal harm on combatants$_{TP}$, as will be seen if we combine and revise our two scenarios as follows. Suppose that TP has territory which it stole from IP decades ago, and diamonds mines over which IP has no claim. Suppose further that IP can weaken TP in either one of two ways: by carrying out missions which will have the effect either to kill (foreseeably but unintentionally) combatants$_{TP}$ stationed to protect the stolen territories, or to kill (foreseeably but unintentionally) combatants$_{TP}$ stationed to protect the mines. Other things equal, IP clearly ought to do the former, and not the latter: in so far as, in *Stolen territory*, combatants$_{TP}$ are guilty of wrongdoing, they have a much weaker claim than their *Diamond mines* colleagues not to be subjected to unintentional killing.

To conclude, combatants who do not themselves carry out the human rights violations which provide IP with a just cause may nevertheless be liable to harm in the course of the intervention, though whether they are liable to being killed will largely depend on the phase of the war in which they are engaged. None of this is to deny that in practice, combatants will have little choice as to where they are deployed—to capture, or as the case may be, defend, *Diamond mines* or *Stolen territory*, and that in practice we should treat both cases entirely similarly. According to the deep morality of war, however, the two cases are rather different, as we have just seen.

### 5.5.2 Killing non-combatants: collateral damage and harm-shifting in humanitarian wars

So far, so good. In Section 5.2, however, I argued that IP cannot simply presume, but instead must have good evidence, that its war of intervention would be welcomed by those for whom it is fought. The claim might seem all the stronger for the fact that although the war will benefit many of TP's victims, it will also inevitably harm some of them. This highlights yet another difference between one-to-one cases of rescue killings and humanitarian war: whilst V, it is assumed, will survive R's killing A, many non-combatants on whose behalf the intervention is carried out will die. Accordingly, any account of the right and duty to intervene must attend to the harms which combatants$_{IP}$ will inevitably impose on the intervention's intended beneficiaries. Moreover, combatants$_{IP}$ might also find themselves in a position to harm innocent non-combatants who are not TP's victims and who thus are not the beneficiaries of the intervention. There too we must assess whether they may so act. Finally, we must also discern whether combatants$_{IP}$ may shift onto those different categories of non-combatants some of the harm attendant on the intervention in order to protect themselves.

Let us begin with collateral damage. The issue first arose, you will recall, in the case of self-defensive wars, with one crucial difference (Section 2.4). Whereas, in that case, we needed to establish whether combatants$_V$ are permitted (foreseeably though unintentionally) to kill non-combatants$_A$ in defence of their own compatriots, here we need to establish whether combatants$_{IP}$ may (foreseeably though unintentionally) kill some non-combatants$_{TP}$ for the sake of protecting the *latter's* compatriots. More precisely still, we need to establish whether combatants$_{IP}$ may so act when victims' compatriots are also victims of the wrongdoing regime (for example, Tutsis or moderate Hutus at risk from the Hutu regime), and whether they may so act when victims' compatriots are not themselves TP's victims (such as Hutus who did not actively support yet were not targeted by the Rwandese regime.)

The justification for the right to kill in a war of humanitarian intervention which I offered in Section 5.2. appeals to victims' right to defend themselves against their attackers—a right which, I also claimed, they have the Hohfeldian power to transfer to their rescuers. Accordingly, to ask whether combatants$_{IP}$ have the permission or the right to harm some of non-combatants$_{TP}$ in the course of the intervention is tantamount to asking whether TP's victims have the transferrable permission and right to kill some of their compatriots (some of whom are also victims of TP's wrongdoings, others not) in self-defence. I shall argue in Section 7.2.2 that one may kill bystanders in self-defence deliberately only if this is the only way to avert a much greater evil, and subject to (relative) numbers of individuals saved and killed. If that is correct, it follows that combatants$_{IP}$ may, under those strict conditions, deliberately target non-combatants$_{TP}$ for the sake of winning the war of humanitarian intervention. I shall take the point as fixed in the remainder of this chapter and assess when they have the permission or right to kill them unintentionally.

In so far as non-combatants$_{TP}$ are *ex hypothesi* materially innocent of the wrongful threat to which victims are subject, they have not lost their right not to be killed. Consequently, they are at liberty to retaliate if V kills them (unintentionally), and V therefore does not have the right so to act *vis-à-vis* them, and nor do combatants$_{IP}$. And yet, V does (I believe) have a partiality-based justification for infringing their compatriots' right not to be killed unintentionally, whether or not the latter are also victims of rights violations at the hands of TP. To repeat, there are limits to the sacrifices which agents can be expected to incur for the sake of strangers, subject to proportionality considerations. The proviso is crucial: if the only way in which an agent can save his life is by detonating a bomb which will kill his attacker as well as 10,000 bystanders, he may not do so. But if the bomb kills only one innocent bystander, then I suggest that he may so act. The point applies not merely against the duty to die for the sake of *foreigners*, but also against a putative duty to die for the sake of one's compatriots: if (as I have argued throughout) one's fundamental rights and duties are not dependent on one's membership in a given political community, and if one is not under a duty to die for the sake of foreigners, one is not under a duty to die for the sake of one's compatriots (a point which we first encountered in Section 2.4).[38] V's justification lies in their own predicament: that of suffering grievous rights violations at the hands

---

[38] Note, incidentally, that the point is wholly compatible with the (sketchy) case I offered for humanitarian conscription in Section 5.3. There I argued that the collective self-interests which in part motivate the decision to go to war and which support the decision to conscript individuals into the army must be part of a just cause for the war. It might be, therefore, that TP's victims may legitimately expect of one another willingness to fight for the survival of their community when the latter is at stake (as was the case in the Rwandan genocide.) But even if that is correct, a duty to risk one's life by providing a military service is not tantamount to a duty to die for the sake of collective security.

of TP which can be stopped only by acts of whom non-combatants$_{TP}$' deaths are a foreseen though unintended side-effect. To ask, then, whether combatants$_{IP}$ may kill non-combatants$_{TP}$ in defence of victims$_{TP}$ is to ask whether the latter have the power to transfer to them their permission to do so.

It is at this juncture that the distinction between non-combatants$_{TP}$ who are not, and those who are, also victims becomes crucial. In the former case, victims$_{TP}$ face a choice between allowing themselves to continue to suffer grievous rights violations and killing (some of their) compatriots who do not themselves suffer from TP's actions. Their dilemma is structurally similar to that faced by just belligerents—whether combatants or those on whose behalf they fight—in wars of collective self-defence, who have to choose between allowing themselves to submit to a wrongful military aggression and cause lethal collateral damage on enemy (innocent) non-combatants. Combatants$_{V}$, I argued in Section 2.4, are permitted to confer greater weight on the interests of their compatriots than on the interests of non-combatants$_{A}$ precisely because, in so acting, they are defending *their* own (jointly held) rights to the territorial integrity and political sovereignty of their country—rights whose promotion is a constitutive element of a minimally decent life. The reason, therefore, why combatants generally may inflict collateral damage on innocent non-combatants as a means to save other innocent non-combatants lies in the importance of defending rights which combatants jointly hold with the latter. But if that is correct, then victims$_{TP}$' permission to confer greater weight on their own rights than on the rights of those of their compatriots who are not subject to TP's wrongdoing is not one which they may transfer to combatants$_{IP}$, since the latter do not fight in defence of such jointly held rights. Accordingly, the infliction of collateral damage on non-victims can be justified either by appeal to justifications relative to IP itself (as would be present if the war of humanitarian intervention has a self-interested as well as an altruistic just cause) or by appeal to agent-neutral considerations such as the importance of blocking a grave evil, or both. Suppose, then, that in April 1994 the Rwandan genocide could have been prevented if an intervening force had bombed the regime's headquarters and, in so doing, unintentionally killed ten Hutu infants in a nearby nursery. I believe that this particular act would have been permissible, but not just in virtue of Tutsi victims' personal prerogative so to act. It really does matter to know what does the justificatory work in such cases. As I noted in Section 2.2, rescuers who do not have a special relationship to the victim must confer greater weight than the latter on the interests of innocent bystanders when assessing whether their defensive move is a proportionate response to the wrongdoing which they would thereby block.

We now consider cases where some of TP's victims—let us call them $V_1$—face a choice between allowing themselves to die, and (unintentionally) killing some of their fellow victims—let us call them $V_2$—in self-defence. One might think that there too agent-neutral considerations (such the value *simpliciter* of getting rid of a genocidal regime) or considerations relative to IP (such as their own interest in getting rid of a foreign tyrant) must be brought to bear in defence of combatants$_{IP}$' permission to kill a subset of TP's victims. Yet in consenting (presumptively or explicitly) to the intervention, TP's victims consent to being put at risk of dying at the hands of the intervening forces: this is another way of saying that they transfer to intervening forces their permission to inflict collateral damage on one another.

If that is so, however—and herein lies a difficulty—both $V_1$ and $V_2$ have the power to transfer to combatants$_{IP}$ their permission to defend themselves against one another.[39] For $V_1$ and $V_2$ are morally symmetrical to each another, and there is therefore no reason to deny some of them a power granted to the others: since both are permitted to infringe the other's right not to be killed, it would be unfair to grant one, but not the other, the power to transfer that permission to interveners. And if *that* is correct, then the following objection arises: given that both $V_1$ and $V_2$ have the power to transfer their respective permission to infringe the other's right to combatants$_{IP}$, combatants$_{IP}$ are permitted to kill either $V_1$ or $V_2$ in defence of the other. In fact, given that $V_1$ and $V_2$ are morally symmetrical to each other, it seems that combatants$_{IP}$ have no greater reason to opt to save one rather than the other. Moreover, if $V_1$ are permitted to kill $V_2$ in self-defence, then it would seem that they are permitted to kill $V_2$'s rescuers in self-defence as well—and *vice versa*. And if *that* is correct, and if $V_1$ and $V_2$'s permissions to kill the other's rescuers are *also* transferrable to combatants$_{IP}$, it would seem that combatants$_{IP}$ would in turn be permitted not merely to kill, for example, $V_2$ in defence of $V_1$ or $V_1$ in defence of $V_2$, but also those of their comrades who have elected to come to $V_1$'s help or to $V_2$'s help. On that view, one ends up with an absurdly Hobbesian situation where victims and combatants$_{IP}$ are permitted to kill one another in self-defence and in defence of one another.[40]

[39] Contrastingly, they clearly lack the power to transfer it to combatants$_{TP}$—just as non-combatants$_A$ who are justifiably (because unintentionally) killed by combatants$_V$ in the course of the latter's war of defence against A lack the power to transfer their permission to defend themselves to their unjust combating compatriots (see Section 2.4.) As we shall see in Section 7.5, however, *ad bellum*-unjust combatants sometimes may defend their non-combatting compatriots from *ad bellum*-just combatants who violate those non-combatants' rights (for example, in breach of the principle of non-combatant immunity).

[40] For points along those lines, see McMahan, 'Self-Defense and the Problem of the Innocent Attacker', 283–4, and Davis, 'Abortion and Self-Defense'.

Fortunately, I believe that it is possible to rescue the partiality account from that objection. The worry seems threefold: (a) given that there is no moral asymmetry between $V_1$ and $V_2$, the partiality account does not provide a criterion for directing combatants$_{IP}$ since they may be permitted to kill either; (b) $V_1$ and $V_2$ are permitted to kill combatants$_{IP}$; and (c) the account thus also supports the view that combatants$_{IP}$ may kill one another in defence of either. In response to the first worry, the claim that combatants$_{IP}$ are permitted to an equal degree to kill either $V_1$ or $V_2$ simply means that they would not wrong either victim by choosing to save the other. But a permission does not constitute a reason for action. To criticize the partiality account for not providing combatants$_{IP}$ with a reason to choose to save one rather than the other is to criticize it for failing to do something which it is not meant to do. As for the second worry, it is not as deep as might appear. After all, combatants$_{IP}$ do pose a wrongful threat of harm to some of the victims, say $V_2$, on behalf of $V_1$. But if the former are permitted to defend themselves against $V_1$ should the latter, rather than combatants$_{IP}$, take action, then it is not absurd to permit them to defend themselves against $V_1$'s rescuers. I concede that by so acting, $V_2$ would contribute to undermining IP's rescue operation—as in fact would combatants$_{TP}$ who, whilst not committing atrocities themselves, nevertheless seek to repel IP's army. But whereas those combatants$_{TP}$ are derelict in their duty not to support their regime, and whereas combatants$_{IP}$ thus have the right to kill them in self-defence and other defence, $V_2$'s case is different, for, *ex hypothesi*, they are not subject to an attack (at the hands of combatants$_{IP}$) which they have warranted. And if the only way for them to survive is to kill combatants$_{IP}$, then (at the bar of the constrained partiality justification) they may do so.[41]

Finally, in response to the third worry, the partiality account is not committed to the view that combatants$_{IP}$ who come to $V_1$'s rescue may kill combatants$_{IP}$ who come to $V_2$'s rescue, and *vice versa*. Its central insight, which draws on the interest-based theory of rights, is that some interests of agents are so important that they warrant being protected, not merely by rights and permissions, but also by powers to transmit those rights and

---

[41] $V_2$'s situation *vis-à-vis* combatants$_{IP}$ is thus similar to that of innocent non-combatants$_A$ *vis-à-vis* just combatants$_V$ in a war of collective self-defence of V against A (see Section 2.4). Just as non-combatants$_A$ lack the power transfer their permission to kill combatants$_V$ to combatants$_A$ (as we saw there), $V_2$ lack the power to transfer their permission to kill combatants$_{IP}$ to combatants$_{TP}$. Note that in those examples, the fact that *one's* right not to be killed is under threat is what both supports the permission to kill one's attacker and blocks its transfer to third parties—in this instance, *ex hypothesi* unjust combatants. Accordingly, my argument in the text here is compatible with my earlier claim that combatants$_{TP}$ are permitted to kill combatants$_{IP}$ in *Diamond mines and Stolen territory* (for there *their* life was at stake).

permissions. However, the interest theory is compatible with the point that agents' interests, however important they are to them, nevertheless do not always warrant protecting. Thus (as we saw in Section 2.2), an unjust attacker who clearly *does* have an interest in surviving his victim's self-defensive move, nevertheless does not have the right to kill her in his defence. Likewise, the interest theory is compatible with the thought that even if an agent's interest is important enough to permit him to act in the relevant ways, it is not important enough to be protected by a power—as when conferring on the agent the power to transfer the permission would undermine some weightier interest of some other agents or would violate weightier agent-neutral considerations. In the case at hand, that weightier interest is one which combatants$_{IP}$ have in being able to rely on one another's compliance with the strategic option chosen through the chain of command as the best means to maximize their chances of surviving the war whilst promoting the latter's just ends. That interest is weighty enough, in fact, to be protected by a special right which combatants have against fellow combatants that the latter not turn their guns on them. This is not to say that combatants' special rights and duties *vis-à-vis* one another always trump their duties to others: quite the contrary, in fact, as we saw in Section 2.3.2. It is to say, though, that once combatants have adopted a course of action which does not violate the rights of the non-combatants who will die as a result, they must do their duty by one another as (just) combatants. Thus, once the decision has been made to carry out a particular mission, at the (*ex hypothesi* justified) cost of the lives of some victims, individual combatants$_{IP}$ may not suddenly decide to change tack and kill their comrades in defence of those victims—even though those victims themselves are permitted to kill them in self-defence.

To recapitulate, combatants$_{IP}$ are (sometimes) permitted to kill non-combatants$_{TP}$ in defence of (a subset of) TP's victims. Let us turn now to harm-shifting tactics as employed by combatants$_{IP}$ against some non-combatants$_{TP}$ with a view to minimize the costs, to them, of the intervention—focusing again on cases where the resulting deaths are a foreseen but unintentional by-product of the tactics. The question of the grounds upon which combatants are permitted to shift harms away from them to non-combatants arises in all conflicts, particularly (as we saw in Section 2.4) in wars of collective self-defence. But it is particularly salient in humanitarian wars, because those non-combatants are meant to benefit directly from the war whilst interveners do not (except in those cases, which I shall tackle briefly at the end of this section, where the intervention has an altruistic and a self-interested just cause). The historical case which is most often cited in the rather sparse discussions of harm-shifting is the 1999 NATO bombing of Serbia as a response to the mass-killings campaign carried out by the latter's regime against Kosovars. NATO, it is widely claimed, instructed its pilots to fly at high altitude in order better to avoid being hit by Serbia's anti-aerial missile defence system, even though it thereby blunted their ability to carry out precision bombing. The policy, it is also widely alleged, resulted in far greater civilian casualties but far fewer NATO casualties than would have been caused by low-altitude bombing.[42]

Now, as we saw above when discussing the police-operation model of intervention, some scholars argue that IP are under a duty to expose themselves to considerable risks for the sake of protecting civilians whose plight is central to the decision to intervene. Upon closer inspection, however, the rationale for forbidding combatants$_{IP}$ to shift harm away from them to the detriment of victims$_{TP}$ cannot be that the operation is meant to help the latter. In Section 2.4 I argued that combatants in a war of collective self-defence may sometimes shift harm onto their compatriots, who stand to benefit from the war, and away from innocent non-combatants who belong to either the aggressor community or from a neutral community. But harm-shifting away from combatants to those foreign non-combatants whom they are rescuing is also permissible. Suppose (for example) that you fall in a river and will drown unless I come to your rescue. Suppose further that I can rescue you either by breaking my leg or in such a way that your side will be bruised but my leg will remain intact. It does not seem wrong of me to choose the latter course of action, for the harm that you will suffer, relative both to what I shall incur if I choose to spare you from it and to the fate that will befall you if I desist altogether, seems rather minor. And if that is correct, then whatever reason there is for forbidding combatants$_{IP}$ to shift harm onto victims$_{TP}$ cannot appeal to the general claim that rescuers may never cause harm to the beneficiaries of their attempt for the sake of their own life and limbs. Rather, the reason lies in the magnitude of the harm which they inflict on the intended beneficiaries of the intervention. Suppose, therefore, that I can save you in either one of two ways: by lifting you out of the water in such a way that you will suffer no injury, whereas I shall inevitably break my leg; or by pulling you out in such a way that I shall emerge unscathed, but you will be paralysed from the neck down. It seems clear, here, that I may *not* do the latter.[43]

---

[42] See, for example, Shue, 'Bombing to rescue?: NATO's 1999 bombing of Serbia'; S. Economides, 'Kosovo', in M. Berdal (ed.), *United Nations Interventionism, 1991–2004* (Cambridge: Cambridge University Press, 2007); Roberts, 'NATO's Humanitarian War over Kosovo'; Wheeler, *Saving Strangers*, esp. ch. 8.

[43] I heard that example, or something like it, in a 2009 Oxford seminar on humanitarian intervention, though I cannot remember who actually supplied it.

So put, the argument is too rough. For a start, the thought that TP's victims may reasonably be expected to incur some of the costs attendant on rescuing them on the grounds that they benefit from the war relies on comparing two states of affairs: one in which combatants$_{IP}$ do nothing, and the other in which they act and as a result kill or maim some of those victims. If some of TP's victims stand a higher chance of chance of having their fundamental human rights protected as a result of the operation than they would have if no intervention took place, then it is appropriate to describe them as *ex ante* beneficiaries of the war, even if the latter turns out to make them worse off *ex post* (for example, if they die during the war).[44]

The foregoing remarks call for three further points. First, if the fact that one benefits from a rescue attempt provides rescuers with a justification for shifting harm away from them, one may wonder whether rescuers may shift harm on those of non-combatants$_{TP}$ who are not subject to TP's wrongdoing and who are not beneficiaries of the war. As I noted in Section 5.3, R may expose bystander B to some risk of harm in the course of rescuing V from A, provided that the costs or risks of costs to which B would be exposed as a result do not exceed that which she would be under a duty to incur were she to help V herself. I submit that R may so act with a view to lessen the risk which rescuing V poses to him: B, in such a case, can plausibly be regarded as contributing her share in the rescue attempt. Likewise, then, in the case of war. Note, however, that in so far as non-combatants$_{TP}$ do not benefit from the operation, the risks to which combatants$_{IP}$ may expose them are lower than would be permitted if they were beneficiaries.

Second, the fact that victims$_{TP}$ are *ex ante* beneficiaries of the war does not permit combatants$_{IP}$ always to shift harm onto them. Whether the latter may so act partly depends on the relative losses and gains of combatants$_{IP}$ and victims$_{TP}$. But it also depends on the absolute costs incurred by the latter, where costs include loss of life and limbs as well as risks thereof. Suppose that the costs incurred by combatants$_{IP}$ for rescuing $V_1$ are the maximum costs— $C_m$—which they can be held under a duty to incur for the sake of rescuing

---

[44] See McMahan, 'The Just Distribution of Harm Between Combatants and Noncombatants', 360–1—though McMahan couches the point in the context of discussing harm-shifting onto beneficiaries versus harm-shifting onto bystanders (such as neutrals.)

  To put my point differently: TP's victims taken together and as a group are both *ex ante* and *ex post* beneficiaries of the war; those who survive the war with better prospects for a minimally decent life than if it had not taken place are also *ex ante* and *ex post* beneficiaries as individuals; those who do not survive the war, or survive it but with worse prospects than if it had taken place are its *ex ante* beneficiaries as members of the group 'TP's victims', though they are not its *ex post* beneficiaries as individuals taken singly.

victims$_{TP}$.[45] If combatants$_{IP}$ can be held under a duty to incur $C_m$, it does not seem that they may kill or severely maim some of TP's victims ($V_2$) in order to incur a *lesser* cost $C_{m-1}$ whilst rescuing $V_1$. (That claim is compatible with the surely correct view that they need not incur $C_m$ if, by acting in such a way as to incur $C_{m-1}$, they can save $V_1$ without harming $V_2$.) Analogously, if I can reasonably be required to break my leg in order to save your life, be it as an act of Good Samaritanism or as a result of having accepted a contract to work as your bodyguard, I can reasonably be expected to incur that exact same cost even if I could avoid paying it by, for example, causing your friend to be permanently paralysed from the waist down whilst saving you.

Third, suppose now that the costs incurred by combatants$_{IP}$ for the sake of rescuing $V_1$ whilst at the same time avoiding harm to $V_2$ are in excess of what they are under a duty to incur—let us call them $C_e$—so that even if there is no other way to save TP's victims, the latter may permissibly be allowed to die at the hands of the *genocidaires*.[46] Suppose further that combatants$_{IP}$ can save $V_1$, though killing or maiming $V_2$ in the process, by incurring a cost which is lesser than $C_e$ but higher than $C_m$—let us call it $C_{m+n}$. Combatants$_{IP}$ are thus faced with three options:

(1) Do nothing and let $V_1$ die, as a result of which $V_2$ will survive;
(2) Save $V_1$ and spare $V_2$, at cost $C_e$.
(3) Save $V_1$ and in so doing kill or maim $V_2$, but only pay $C_{m+n}$.

*Ex hypothesi*, they are not under a duty to opt either for (2) or for (3): they may instead opt for (1). The question, then, is what they may or must do as between (2) and (3), *if* they decide to intervene. Two kinds of consideration support opting for (2) rather than (3). If numbers are a relevant consideration, then it seems that they may—indeed, perhaps must—opt for (2) rather than (3), since (2) results in a greater number of lives saved than (3). Furthermore, our task is to justify severely maiming and killing in war, on the understanding that there is a strong *prima facie* presumption against it, that, other things equal, maiming and killing are morally worse than letting comparable harm happen, and that deliberately maiming, killing, or letting comparable

---

[45] By costs, I mean both the harm itself which combatants$_{IP}$ will suffer, and the risk of suffering a given harm. Although I run them together *here*, the distinction is important for the imposition of the duty: for it may be that although agents are not under a duty to, for example, die for the sake of a stranger, they are under a duty to run a tiny risk of dying for her sake.

[46] As I have already noted, there is no general principle for determining what counts as an acceptable cost. But it seems, for example, that one cannot expect anyone to incur a more than 70 per cent risk of actually dying for the sake of saving a stranger from death. A professional soldier thus ought to be able to refuse an order to take part in such risky operations—without incurring sanctions for so doing.

harm happen is morally worse than unintentionally (but foreseeably) letting harm to happen. *If* combatants$_{IP}$ decide to do that which they are not under a duty to do (to wit, intervene), then it seems that they must do that against which the presumption is *prima facie* the weakest (not killing or not letting die): in other words, they must choose (2) over (3). Of course, it may well be that combatants$_{TP}$ would decide not to help $V_1$ at all, on the grounds that the costs of (2) are too high. In that case, $V_1$ would have no legitimate grievance against them were they to desist, since they are permitted to refuse to incur $C_e$.

I must make one final remark before concluding. Throughout our discussion I have pointed out that combatants$_{IP}$ are sometimes under a duty to incur some harm, or risk thereof, for the sake of victims$_{TP}$, and that there are limits to the extent to which they may shift some of those risks and harm onto the latter. It is worth noting that the degree of stringency of those limits partly depends on the kind of humanitarian intervention carried out by IP. Consider, first, an intervention of Good Samaritanism the justification for which simply lies in the victims' predicament at the hands of the *genocidaires*. And let us suppose that combatants in that war are under a duty to incur a given risk of harm, or harm *tout court*, for the sake of those victims. Consider, next, an intervention for which the justification is two-pronged, each of which would constitute a just cause for war: the plight of the victims on the one hand, and on the other hand the fact that IP's territorial integrity and/or sovereignty is under threat as a result of TP's actions. In this particular case, in so far as combatants$_{IP}$, in their capacity as citizens, obtain from the war the benefit of collective security, it would be fair to ask them to incur a greater share of the harm attendant on the war than if they derived no collective benefit from it.

## 5.6 CONCLUSION

Proponents of the right to intervene militarily in the affairs of another country standardly make their case by arguing that rights violating regimes have no claim not to be attacked. As I noted above, this argument does little to justify the right to kill individual members of those regimes. Proponents of the duty to intervene, meanwhile, all too quickly tend to assume that the grounds upon which one has the right to intervene are *ipso facto* grounds for being under a duty to do so. As I also noted, this move from the right to the duty is too quick, oblivious as it is to the difference which costs make to interveners' moral situation *vis-à-vis* the intended beneficiaries of their intervention. My aim in this chapter has been to construct a liberal cosmopolitan argument for both the right and the duty to intervene which is not vulnerable to those criticisms. I defended the right to intervene by appealing to the general thought that victims of severe human rights violations who have the right to kill in defence of their rights also have the Hohfeldian power to transfer that right onto the third parties. As for my argument for the duty so to act, it rested on the claim that a cosmopolitan ethics of assistance yield a duty to provide military help to those in need. Finally, I brought out some of the ethical issues raised by the killing of both combatants and non-combatants in the course of a just war of humanitarian intervention.

As I noted at various junctures in this chapter, wars of intervention tend to be fought by interveners who have a vested interest in doing so. Whilst this does not in itself call into question the justness of such a war, it draws our attention to the fact that the plight of victims calls for greater involvement on the part of potential rescuers than the latter are usually willing to show—largely for cost-related reasons. As a remedy for nation-states' refusal to send troops to protect the fundamental human rights of distant strangers, some have argued in favour of enlisting help from private military corporations. This in turn supposes that private soldiering, or mercenarism, is morally legitimate—or at the very least not too morally problematic as to being ruled out altogether. To this issue I now turn.

# 6

# Commodified wars

## 6.1 INTRODUCTION

In previous chapters I provided a cosmopolitan ethics of different kinds of war, and focused on the notions of just cause, legitimate authority, and liability to being killed. In this chapter I offer an account of wars in which private economic actors take on important roles alongside or in replacement of regular armed forces—or, as I shall call them, commodified wars. The growing role of so-called private military corporations (PMCs) such as Blackwater in recent military conflicts—particularly the Iraq war of 2003 and its aftermath—has elicited concern from many commentators. Those companies offer a wide range of services to states willing to pay for them, such as specialized training courses for members of standing armies, the provision of security details in war zones, logistical support by way of weapons and transport systems, and the deployment of combat troops. It is commonly estimated that by the end of 2006 there were about 20,000 euphemistically-called 'private contractors' in Iraq—about three times as many as regular British soldiers. Although states have relied on private firms and freelance mercenaries for military purposes for centuries, private military corporations, to a greater extent than ever, are taking over tasks and functions which used to be performed by the army itself.[1]

---

[1] Blackwater recently changed its name to Academi, but is still commonly referred to as Blackwater—a practice I shall adopt here. For accounts of the privatization of war, and new forms of warfare in general, see, for example, Duyvesteyn and Angstrom (ed.), *Rethinking the Bature of War*; Kaldor, *New and Old Wars*; Munkler, *The New Wars*. For typologies of PMCs and reviews of their activities in recent conflicts, see, for example, D. D. Avant, *The Market for Force: The Consequences of Privatizing Security* (Cambridge: Cambridge University Press, 2005); C. Kinsey, *Corporate Soldiers and International Security: the Rise of Private Military Companies* (London: Routledge, 2006); J. Scahill, *Blackwater: The Rise of the World's Most Powerful Mercenary Army* (London: Profile Books Ltd, 2007); P. W. Singer, *Corporate Warriors: The Rise of the Privatized Military Industry* (Ithaca: Cornell University Press, 2003). The estimate of the number of private contractors relative to the number of British soldiers in Iraq is quoted from Scahill, *Blackwater*, 161; see also Avant, *The Market for Force*, 2. For a thorough discussion of the role of PMCs in Iraq, see D. Isenberg, 'A Government in Search of Cover: Private Military Companies in Iraq', in S. Chesterman and C. Lehnardt (ed.), *From Mercenaries to Market: The Rise and Regulation of Private Military Companies* (Oxford: Oxford University Press, 2007). Note that in this chapter I deal with private

The prevalent normative view on the marketization of war is that it is morally wrong—for reasons to be found, in part, in the medieval condemnation of mercenarism. In this chapter, however, I argue that under certain conditions, mercenarism is morally legitimate. In Section 6.2 I expose a weakness in the most obvious justification for mercenarism, to wit, that which appeals to the value of freedom of occupational choice. I then deploy a less obvious yet stronger argument—one which is grounded in the importance of enabling just defensive killings. In Section 6.3 I rebut five moral objections to mercenarism;[2] and in Section 6.4 I argue that private soldiers do not markedly differ from public soldiers with respect to both their right to kill and their liability to attack.

Before I begin, I have five clarificatory remarks. First, it is worth explaining once more why the issue of mercenarism is worth addressing in this book. If my cosmopolitan accounts of both state legitimacy and the requirement of legitimate authority are correct, then there is more space in a cosmopolitan theory of war for the view that combatants who are not employed by states have the right to fight.

Second, the difficulties attendant on defining mercenarism are well-known. Typically, a mercenary is defined as a soldier who fights in a foreign war essentially out of financial motives.[3] Those two features—nationality and motivations—are standardly thought to distinguish a mercenary from a uniformed soldier of a political community's armed forces. Yet the nationality criterion is problematic, as it implies, somewhat counter-intuitively, that an American employee of Blackwater who fights in Iraq for the US government is not a mercenary. By mercenary, then, I shall mean an individual who offers his

military corporations rather than private security companies, to the extent that the former, unlike the latter, are deployed in war theatres.

[2] Whether or not using private military corporations and/or private soldiers is the best way (functionally) to conduct a war is a separate question which I shall not address here. Functional concerns include, for example, the practice by private actors of defaulting on their contractual duties when the military situation of their employers is deteriorating, or the fact that contractual relationships (which set out fixed rights and duties) are not suited to the conduct of war (which requires flexible and quick decisions under changeable circumstances.) See, for example, Avant, *The Market for Force*, M. N. Schmitt, 'Humanitarian Law and Direct Participation in Hostilities by Private Contractors or Civilian Employees', *Chicago Journal of International Law* 5 (2005): 511–46; E. Krahmann, 'Transitional States in Search of Support: Private Military Companies and Security Sector Reform', in S. Chesterman and C. Lehnardt (ed.), *From Mercenaries to Market: The Rise and Regulation of Private Military Companies* (Oxford: Oxford University Press, 2007). Krahmann focuses on functional concerns as arise in transitional states such as Bosnia and Croatia. For the view that functional concerns are largely without basis, see, for example, D.-P. Baker, *Just Warriors, Inc.* (New York: Continuum, 2010), esp. ch. 6.

[3] See Article 1 of the 1989 International Convention against the Recruitment, Use, Financing, and Training of Mercenaries, and Article 47 of the 1977 Geneva Protocol I Additional to the Geneva Conventions of 1949. For discussions of those definitional difficulties, see, for example, S. Percy, *Mercenaries: The History of a Norm in International Relations* (Oxford: Oxford University Press, 2007), ch. 2; Coady, *Morality and Political Violence*, ch. 10; H. C. Burmester, 'The Recruitment and Use of Mercenaries in Armed Conflicts', *The American Journal of International Law* 72 (1978): 37–56.

military expertise to a state against payment outside the latter's military recruitment and training procedures, either directly to a party in a conflict or through an employment contract with a private military corporation. Unless otherwise stated, I shall use the word 'mercenarism' to refer to both kinds of private soldier. For reasons to be outlined below, I leave open the question of motivations.

Third, my defence of marketized soldiering does not take the pragmatic form adopted by those who worry about mercenarism but claim that, since it has always existed and always will, regulation is more efficient than prohibition—a view which is non-coincidentally similar to arguments in favour of the regulation of prostitution.[4] Rather, I shall defend the view that all three parties (individual private soldiers, private military corporations, and political communities) sometimes have the moral right, in the threefold sense of a liberty, a claim, or a power, to contract with one another for the purpose of waging a war. For stylistic convenience, and unless specified otherwise, when I say that they have the right to enter into a mercenary contract, I shall say that they have a liberty, a claim, and a power to do so.

Fourth, whilst political communities are the most likely of all belligerents to hire private soldiers, other actors, such as the UN and NGOs, are known to have done so—in the former case as a remedy to member-states' unwillingness or inability to commit their own troops to peace-keeping operations, and in the latter case as a remedy to their status as a private belligerent. In this chapter I shall make my case specifically by reference to sovereign political communities, for whilst my argument in support of the view that mercenary contracts are legitimate apply to all such belligerents, some objections to mercenarism are specifically targeted at sovereign states.

Finally, nothing I say in this chapter is meant to support the use to which political communities such as the US put private soldiers and private military corporations in conflicts such as the Iraq war. Nor is my argument for mercenarism in any way meant to support the well-documented exactions which have been perpetrated by private soldiers in various conflicts.[5] To express it

[4] I say 'non-coincidentally' because mercenaries are often referred to as 'whores of war' (on the grounds that, like prostitutes, they do for money what should be done for 'nobler' reasons). See, for example, W. G. Burchett and D. Roebuck, *The Whores of War: Mercenaries Today* (London: Penguin, 1977).
[5] See, for example, evidence of abuse perpetrated by so-called private contractors (as well as US soldiers) at the Abu Ghraib Prison in Iraq in 2003. The report on the official investigation into such abuses can be found at http://fl1.findlaw.com/news.findlaw.com/hdocs/docs/dod/fay82504rpt.pdf (accessed 23 February 2009). See also reports of killings of civilian bystanders killed in Iraq by private contractors, in a February 2007 memorandum prepared for the Oversight Committee of the US Congress House of Representatives (http://www.c-span.org.pdf/blackwater100207/pdf accessed 8 June 2012).

emphatically, my claim is that, under strict conditions (which current practices do *not* meet), the marketization of war is not morally wrong. Those conditions are drawn from the account of the right to kill in war which I offered in Chapter 2. On that account, one has the right to kill in war only if the war or phase of war in which one takes part has a just cause. In addition, one's acts of killing must also respect the principles of proportionality, necessity, and (to anticipate Section 7.2) non-combatant immunity. These various conditions hold irrespective of the status—public or private—of combatants, and it is only if they are met that marketized soldiering is morally legitimate.

## 6.2 IN DEFENCE OF THE (LIMITED) MARKETIZATION OF WAR

Arguments for or against the marketization of war must deal with the following questions:

(1) On what grounds, if any, does an individual have the right to offer his services (to kill, or to assist in killing) under the terms of a private contract (either directly between him and a state, or between him and a corporation)?
(2) On what grounds, if any, does a state have the right to hire mercenaries or PMCs to protect its interests?
(3) On what grounds, if any, does a PMC have the right to act as an intermediary between a state and individual soldiers willing to offer their services?

A negative or positive answer to one of these three questions will sometimes, but not always, yield a correspondingly negative or positive answer to the other two—whether liberties, claims, or powers are at issue. Thus, the claim that hiring oneself to kill others is morally wrong (for example, on the grounds that one should never kill for gain) does not commit its proponents to the view that hiring a private soldier is morally wrong: for although it does make the recruiter complicitous in the soldier's wrongdoing, the need for the latter's service might be so great as to provide him with a justification (and not merely an excuse) for so acting. Likewise, one can coherently claim that a private soldier is acting permissibly by killing for gain, but that his employers are guilty of (for example) exploiting his need to make a living or treating him merely as a killing machine rather than a human being. With these preliminary considerations in hand, I now turn to defending mercenary contracts.

### 6.2.1 Freedom of occupational choice

An agent enjoys the contractual freedom to earn a living if she is able to exchange services, money, or both with some other party with a view to benefitting financially from the transaction. This supposes, at the very least, that there should be no legal ban on the provision of the relevant specific services or financial resources. Compare the following scenarios:

A.  Blue decides to enlist into the standing professional army of his home state. He knows that he might be deployed anywhere in the world as thought fit by his superiors, and that he will kill some other human being(s).

B.  White finds a job with a PMC which has successfully won a number of government contracts. He knows that he might be deployed anywhere in the world as thought fit by his employers and that he will kill some other human being(s).

C.  Red sets up a business as a freelance mercenary. He hires himself out to different kinds of political communities for different tasks, from participating in active combat to training professional soldiers for specialized roles on the front line. Unlike White, he has considerable control over where he is deployed and for what purposes.

In all three cases the soldier will either kill or be complicitous in acts of killing, and will be paid for doing precisely that. The only difference between Blue on the one hand, and White and Red on the other hand, is that Blue is formally part of the state's military apparatus, whereas the latter two are not. At first glance this difference seems irrelevant. As we saw in Section 1.2.1, individuals have a fundamental interest in framing, revising, and pursuing a conception of the good. To most people, the occupation which they pursue, thanks to which they can earn a living, are part and parcel of such conception—which may well include killing other individuals by enlisting in the army. If one believes that pursuing this particular conception of the good is morally permissible (as one must on pain of being a radical pacifist—a position which I ruled out at the outset of this book), it is hard to see why one is morally permitted to exercise it in the formal service of a state but neither as an employee of a private corporation nor as a freelance soldier. By the same token, if Blue's interest in joining the army is important enough to be protected by a claim, the same applies to White's and Red's.[6] Similar considerations apply to employees of PMCs. A private military

---

[6] For an argument along those lines, see F. Suarez, *De Bello*, in J. B. Scott (ed.), *Selections from Three Works of Francisco Suarez, S.J: De Triplici Virtute Theologica, Fide, Spe, et Charitate (1621)* (Oxford: Clarendon Press, 1944).

corporation, as we have seen, acts as an intermediary between political communities on the one hand, and individuals willing to offer their lethal services on the other hand. It advertizes for openings, recruits employees, trains them, offers them logistical support, oversees their career, monitors their performance, and so on. These tasks are carried out by lawyers, human resources personnel, advertising personnel, administrative assistants and accountants, in just the same way as the tasks which enable individuals to join and effectively perform in a regular army are carried out by lawyers, human resources personnel, and so on. At the bar of freedom of occupational choice, then, if someone's interest in earning a living by, for example, working as a recruiter for the army ought to be protected by a claim and a liberty, so should her interest in working as a human resources adviser for a PMC. And so on.

As should be clear, however, a political community, *qua* political community, is not properly to be regarded as engaging in activities which would enable it to make a living. Consequently, the foregoing argument cannot support the conferral on political communities of a right to enter a mercenary contract, from which it follows that freedom of occupational choice cannot, on its own, support mercenary contracts. For on the account of rights which I espouse, X has a right in respect of an interest of his if that interest warrants protection. In so far as freedom of occupational choice is not an interest of a political community, the latter cannot be granted a right—and therefore a power—to enter in a mercenary contract on the grounds that this particular value warrants promoting. Freedom of occupational choice, therefore, may well support mercenaries' and PMCs' liberty and claim to do so; but in so far as it cannot support political communities' similar power and as it is a necessary condition, for A to have the power to make a transaction with B, that B also has that power, it cannot support mercenaries' and PMCs' *power* to enter into a contract with the former. Suppose that A and B agree that A will sell B his car for £5,000. Assume that A's interest in being able to divest himself of his property is important enough to confer on him a power to change his and others' relationship to it, by selling it. However, A cannot have the power to transfer his car *to B* in exchange for *B's* £5,000 if B does not herself have the power to transfer £5,000 to A in exchange for his car. Accordingly, any argument to the effect that the transaction ought to be regarded as valid must show that both A and B have the power to enter into that kind of contract—and, by implication, that some interest of both A and B is important enough to be protected by the relevant power.[7] As we have just seen, freedom of occupational choice is not an interest

---

[7] Generally it is not a necessary condition for a change in A and B's moral/legal relationship validly to take place that both A and B have the relevant power (if A gives G to B, A thereby changes their

of political communities. Therefore, in order to defend the view that mercenary contracts as between a political community and mercenaries (or PMCs) are legitimate, we shall have to identify some interest(s) of political communities which can be protected by the relevant powers.

## 6.2.2 Just defensive killings

The foregoing considerations should not be taken to imply that freedom of occupational choice has no role to play in justifying political communities' right to enter mercenary contracts. Indeed, it might be in the interest of a political community—call it C—that *individuals'* freedom of occupational choice, which they exercise by hiring themselves out as mercenaries or by working in a PMC, be respected. In such a case, though, the interest which justifies C's right is, ultimately, that which is fulfilled by respecting individuals' freedom of occupational choice. To illustrate: suppose that White's employer wins a government bid to send a number of (private) soldiers to help fight a justified humanitarian war against a genocidal tyrant. White, in that war, might be assigned to combat duties or to a security detail for the protection of some high-ranking official, with license to kill if necessary. Or suppose his employer wins a bid to help a foreign government fight a war of national self-defence against an unjust aggression. In all those cases, White kills in defence of others: in defence of those whose lives are threatened by their own genocidal government; in defence of the high-ranking official; and in defence of the collective interests of the political community whose government hired his company.

In Sections 2.2 and 2.3 I argued that the right to kill in war is not merely a right to kill in self-defence: it is also a right to kill in defence of others—a claim which I developed in Section 5.2 when discussing humanitarian intervention. The question at issue here, then, is whether he can make the transfer of that right (to him) conditional upon payment, outside the institutions of the state. Now, I take it for granted that one is permitted and has a claim, at least *prima facie*, to exercise one's freedom of occupational choice by offering goods and services (against pay) in justified defence of other people's lives and of other political communities' economic or national interests. Thus, a group of food producers surely can sell food to whatever organization will then distribute it to the starving. A doctor surely can offer his medical services, against pay, and via the state-based health system and/or medical insurance companies, to

moral relationship in respect of G, without B having to exercise the same power.) Here, however, I focus on exchanges.

those who need them as a matter of life and death. An IT technician surely can offer her services to a company who is particularly vulnerable to hackers. And so on. If that is correct, as it surely is, then White too can become a private soldier in defence of third parties' fundamental interests.

To be sure, unlike White, those agents contribute to saving the lives or protecting the interests of others without thereby contributing to killing someone else. It is hard to see, however, why that should make a difference to the issue at hand. Consider the case of weapons manufacturers, who sell guns to those who need them so as to defend their life or protect the national interest: if they can do so even though the assistance which they provide involves a contribution to an act of killing, then private soldiers and PMCs can (respectively) offer and procure killing services.[8]

I have argued that individuals can hire themselves out for killing services, as well as procure such services, in so far as they thereby provide some other party with the resources it needs rightfully to defend itself against an unjust threat. The point also provides a justification for conferring on political communities the right to hire mercenaries—here understood as a collective right held by community members as such. For political communities need armies and weapons, not only for the purpose of collective self-defence (to point out the obvious), but also for the purpose of defending distant strangers when called upon to wage a war of intervention. Note, on that very last point, that the argument from just defensive killing, when constrained by cosmopolitan justice and applied to the case of wars of humanitarian intervention, does not and cannot imply that hiring (willing) foreign nationals is morally appropriate as a means to spare the lives of one's own soldiers—or at least to the extent that the claim is tantamount to viewing the lives of foreign private soldiers as less valuable, *per se*, than the lives of one's fellow citizens–soldiers.[9] Rather, the argument holds that political communities need the wherewithal to have acts of killing carried out in their name and with their authorization, in self-defence as well as in defence of others. And if a political community is at liberty to buy guns from private manufacturers for the aforementioned purposes—as it surely is—then it is also at liberty to buy soldiering services from those willing to provide them, irrespective of the latter's nationality.

---

[8] As I argue elsewhere, giving a gun to someone who needs it in self-defence and killing (for free) that person's attacker are relevantly analogous. The argument applies, *mutatis mutandis*, to the act of selling a gun and the act of killing against payment. See Fabre, 'Mandatory Rescue Killings'. Incidentally, I am assuming that White is not otherwise under a duty to provide the needed assistance.

[9] For a positive assessment of the role which PMCs might be able to play in a war of humanitarian intervention, see Baker, *Just Warriors, Inc.*, chs. 8–9. For a critical assessment, see Pattison, *Humanitarian Intervention and the Responsibility to Protect*, ch. 7.

Moreover, if a political community has a right to pay for a standing army—as it surely does—then it also has a right to pay for a private army. Finally, recall my earlier point, to the effect that an individual's interest in working as a private soldier ought to be protected by rights that neither PMCs nor political communities be interfered with when hiring him, and that third parties recognize his employment contract with them as legally binding. Likewise, political communities' interest in hiring a private army ought to be protected by similar rights as pertain to private soldiers and PMCs.

In sum, whereas the argument for freedom of occupational choice failed to provide a justification for political communities' power to enter in a mercenary contracts (and thereby for mercenaries' and PMCs' similar power), the argument from just defensive killings can do so. That said, whilst the view that political communities are at liberty to hire mercenaries is relatively straightforward, the view that they have a claim and a power to do so needs unpacking. As I noted in Section 1.2.2, to say that X has a claim to do $p$ is to say that third parties are under a duty not to interfere with his doing $p$. Moreover, to say that he has the power to do $p$ is to say that by doing $p$ he changes his moral relationship to others by transferring to them some of his claims, liberties, powers, and immunities, and/or acquiring new ones. A contract whereby X hires Y for a particular service against a certain fee is a paradigmatic example of the exercise of a power, whereby X loses his entitlement to that sum of money but acquires claims over Y's use of his time and skills to the ends specified by the contract. For X to have that power thus requires that third parties recognize it as a valid transaction, in order that either X or Y could seek redress through some institution in cases of dispute.

Standardly, the third party which is under the relevant duty not to interfere (when a claim is at issue), or to recognize a transaction as valid (when a power is at issue) is, more often than not, the political community, via the state. Accordingly, when a political community is said to have claims and powers, identifying who exactly is supposed not to interfere or to recognise the transaction as valid, is of the utmost importance. Therefore, a community's claim to do $p$ (for example, to buy weapons for the purpose of fighting a just war) is held against those of its individual members who might wish to stand in the way of its doing $p$ (such as radical pacifists who destroy its military factories.) Likewise, a political community's power to enter into a contract with some other party (for example, a contract for the delivery of ammunition) ought to be recognized as valid by those of its individual members who might wish to reject the new distribution of claims, privileges and powers (by, for example, refusing to accept that the political community is now the legitimate owner of the ammunition.) Crucially for our present purposes, however, political communities' claims and powers are also held against other political communities. To say, then, that a political community A has a claim to hire mercenaries to fight just wars is to hold other political communities—such as C—under a duty not to interfere with the transaction—for example, by preventing mercenaries from joining in. It is also to say that C ought to recognize as valid the employment contracts passed by A and the mercenaries or PMCs.

None of this is to deny, of course, that C might have countervailing and important interests which would be harmed by A's decision to contract with mercenaries—particularly if those mercenaries are citizens of C. In that case, C's interests might take precedence over A's, so that it would not be under a duty not to interfere with the latter's decision. Note, however, that the same considerations might well apply, *mutatis mutandis*, to A's decision to increase the size of its regular standing army—for example, by setting up in its midst foreign regiments akin to the Ghurkhas or the French Foreign Legion. In that case too one might draw the conclusion that C is not under the relevant duty to A. The point remains, then, that *if* A's interest in obtaining what they need for their collective self-defence or for the defence of others is important enough to be protected by a right to set up a standing army, then it should also be protected by a right to contract with private parties.

To recapitulate, I have argued that political communities, PMCs, and individual soldiers have the right to contract with one another. Note that my argument and its conclusion are compatible with the widely held view that it is better, on the whole, that political communities should have their own standing army than resort to private forces—that there is something to be gained (for example, with respect to national cohesiveness) by having one's national interests defended by one's compatriots. My point is simply that the reasons which are routinely thought to support the conferral of the moral right to enter a commercial contract when some fundamental interests are at stake extend to mercenary contracts—*unless* one can show that soldiering somehow differs, morally speaking, from other kinds of activities.[10]

---

[10] My argument for mercenarism, which appeals to the value of enabling just-war killings, raises the interesting issue of the extent to which a PMC's contractual obligations to state A may be allowed to override a non-contracting state B's urgent need for military manpower. Should the PMC be allowed to default on the contract it made with A at time $t_1$, so as to help B whose needs at time $t_2$ are more pressing? Or should it be held to its contractual obligations to A? Of course, the issue arises, not merely in the context of mercenarism, but whenever private actors are allowed to contribute to helping those in need: if a company is under contract with hospital H1 for the delivery of medical equipment, should it be allowed to default on its contract for the sake of supplying H2, which is facing an unexpected shortage in surgical instruments? And so on. I lack the space to deal with those complications here. Some of the concerns which they raise are ethical, whilst others are more functional.

I shall examine some arguments to that effect presently, and show that they fail. Meanwhile, it is worth emphasizing what this chapter is *not* claiming: that is, it is not claiming that one can choose to make a living however one wishes. An argument for unbridled freedom of occupational choice would lead to the absurd conclusion that Luca Brazzi, Don Corleone's top henchman, has the moral right to offer his killing services to the latter against shopkeepers who refuse to pay protection money, or that the Mafia has the right to procure killing services to corrupt politicians who wish to eliminate their political opponents. That conclusion would be absurd simply because, in those two examples, the acts of killing are straightforwardly impermissible. Analogously, as we saw in Chapter 2, whether or not individuals may offer or procure killing services to political communities depends on the justness of the war. So does political communities' right to contract with private soldiers. If the war is unjust, parties' interests in, respectively, freedom of occupational choice and getting the means to kill in self-defence or other defence, are *not* important enough to be protected by liberties, claims, and powers. By implication, if the contracting political community wages a just war, and if individuals' interest in joining the army is important enough to be protected by a right, then individuals' similar interest as exercised outside army structures ought also to be protected by a right.

## 6.3 FIVE OBJECTIONS TO MERCENARISM

I have defended the right to enter a mercenary contract by appealing to the importance of enabling just defensive killings. I have also argued that uniformed soldiers and mercenaries should be treated on a par—and that what matters, for deciding whether a combatant has the right to kill, is not the nature (political or economic) of the organization by which he is employed, but rather whether he abides by the principles of the just war. In this section I examine and reject five objections to mercenarism, the first three of which bring to bear on the issue of war familiar worries on the encroachment of market norms on hitherto largely public spheres of activities: the motivational objection, the objectification objection, the profiteering objection, the loss-of-control objection, and the neutrality objection.[11]

---

[11] Important accounts of the moral limits of markets include E. Anderson, *Value in Ethics and Economics* (Cambridge, MA: Harvard University Press, 1993); M. J. Radin, *Contested Commodities: The Trouble with Trade in Sex, Children, Body Parts and Other Things* (Cambridge, MA: Harvard University Press, 1996); M. Sandel, "What Money Can't Buy: The Moral Limits of Markets," in

## 6.3.1 The motivational objection

The claim that mercenaries act wrongly because they fight for financial gain rather than out of loyalty to their political community and/or commitment to a just cause has a very long pedigree in the intellectual and legal history of warfare. It draws on the traditional stipulation that a war is just only if belligerents wage it with the right intentions (defined as wanting to redress the wrong which justifies the war), and applies the requirement to the individuals who actually fight in the war. The condition of right intentions is ambiguous, requiring as it does either that belligerents and soldiers act from the right motives or that they wage, and kill in, a war towards just ends. As applied to mercenaries, it is usually interpreted as pertaining to agents' motives; accordingly, it is this particular interpretation which I shall target here.[12]

As has been often noted, any argument for or against a particular act which appeals to the agent's motivations is vulnerable to two criticisms: (1) discerning what those motivations are is not as easy as it might seem; (2) motives are irrelevant to the permissibility of actions. For what it is worth, I do not find either claim persuasive. And so assuming, for the sake of argument, that the motivational objection's fundamental premises are correct (to wit, motives are discernable and do matter), it is nevertheless vulnerable to the following criticisms. For a start, there is no reason to suppose that a member of regular armed forces *by definition* is not motivated mostly by financial gain and the social benefits which go with it, or is mainly motivated by loyalty to her political community and/or to a just cause. In fact, joining the army is, for many youngsters in many countries, a way out of poverty. It is also, for many of them, a way to channel aggressive tendencies, or to cater for a psychological need for a highly structured and hierarchy-based way of life. Contrastingly, there is no reason to suppose that a mercenary is, *by definition*, motivated mostly by the lure of financial gain. On the contrary, evidence suggests that a number of private soldiers take up jobs with PMCs after being made redundant by the army or after retirement from combat

---

*Tanner Lectures on Human Values* (University of Utah Press, 1998); D. Satz, *Why some Things should not be for Sale: The Moral Limits of Markets* (Oxford: Oxford University Press, 2010).

[12] For the distinction, in this context, between right motives and just aims (or, as he calls them, intentions), see Pattison, 'Just War Theory and the Privatization of Military Force'. For a comprehensive review of the motivational objection to mercenarism, see Percy, *Mercenaries*, esp. ch. 5. See also F. H. Russell, *The Just War in the Middle Ages* (Cambridge and New York: Cambridge University Press, 1975), ch. 6. Two classical thinkers who condemn mercenaries on motivational grounds are Machiavelli, *The Prince*, ed. G. Bull (London: Penguin Books, 1981), ch. XII, pp. 77–8, and Grotius, *The Rights of War and Peace*, Bk. II, Ch. XXV, §six, p. 1164. For a powerful rebuttal of the motivational objection along the lines deployed in this and the next two paragraphs, see T. Lynch and A. J. Walsh, 'The Good Mercenary?', *Journal of Political Philosophy* 8 (2000): 133–53.

duties, and that they see themselves as continuing to act for the defence of their country's interests.[13]

The foregoing points are definitional. So let us suppose, for the sake of argument, that a mercenary, unlike a regular soldier, just *is* someone who is essentially motivated by money. The crucial question is whether those definitional points have any bearing on the right to enter a mercenary contract. Two claims are usually made to the effect that they do. First, it is said that soldiers have the right to kill only if they are motivated to fight by the belief that the war is just. In so far as mercenaries by definition do not have those motives, mercenarism is condemned for being morally dubious—whether from the standpoint of mercenaries themselves or of those who procure or hire them. However, even if motives are decisive for the permissibility of actions, and thus even if mercenaries are guilty of wrongdoing, it does not follow that they lack a claim or a power to contract with political communities: conceptually speaking, there can be such a thing as a claim or a power to act wrongly. Accordingly, the motivational objection can successfully reject the conferral on mercenaries and PMCs of the relevant claim and power only if it can provide an independent justification for the view that this particular wrongdoing ought not to be protected by the law.[14] Suppose, for example, that White becomes a mercenary because he really enjoys killing. If motives are decisive to the permissibility of actions, White is acting wrongly. But that is not enough to show that White ought not to have the right to work as a mercenary—any more than the fact that someone becomes a surgeon because he becomes sexually aroused by cutting into the flesh of anaesthetized patients is enough to warrant legally preventing him from being a surgeon. Rather, it seems that one would have to show that his perverse motives lead him to provide sub-standard medical care to his patients. Analogously, unless one can show that mercenarism so defined harms more fundamental interests of third parties (a point to which I shall return below), it seems that mercenaries and PMCs' interests are, in fact, important enough to warrant such protection. After all, individuals do all sorts of things out of mostly financial motivations. They often choose a particular line of work, such as banking or consulting, rather than others, such as academia, largely because of the money. They often decide to become doctors rather than nurses, partly for similar reasons. Granting that their interest in making such choices, however condemnable

---

[13] See Scahill, *Blackwater*, esp. ch. 5. Suppose that uniformed soldiers in a given country decide to leave the army *en masse*, unless their pay is significantly raised. Would it be morally wrong of them to do so? I owe this point to Alan Hamlin.

[14] I deploy a structurally similar argument regarding organ sales, prostitution, and surrogate motherhood, in Fabre, *Whose Body is it Anyway?*, chs. 6–8.

their motivations, is important enough to be protected by a claim (against non-interference) and a power (to enter the relevant employment contracts), it is hard to see how one could deny similar protection to mercenaries. *Mutatis mutandis*, the point applies to executives and owners of PMCs, who procure, rather than directly offer, lethal services.

I noted above that the harms accruing to third parties as a result of mercenarism counts as a good reason against conferring on mercenaries, PMCs, and political communities the right to contract with one another. Appositely, the second normative worry about mercenarism is that mercenaries, precisely because of their desire for money, are much more likely to fight for unjust ends and to commit offences against the laws of war than are members of regular armed forces, who are motivated by the belief that their cause is just.[15] However, that claim is less persuasive than may appear at first sight. In the light of the long list of exactions committed against civilian populations by regular forces, precisely on the grounds that their cause was just, the suggestion that armed forces are more likely to abide by the laws of war than are mercenaries seems somewhat optimistic. One need only think of the Wehrmacht and the Red Army during World War II, the French Army in Algeria during the War of Independence (1954–62), the US Army in Japan in August 1945, and the British Air Force in Germany during that war. It is equally unclear—again judging on the basis of recent interstate wars—that regular armies are more likely than mercenaries to pursue just aims when making strategic decisions as to the target, which kind of infrastructures to destroy, and so on. The conflict in Iraq is a case in point: US soldiers, no less than private contractors, have killed non-combatants in the heat of battle and on the basis of questionable evidence as to the threat which their victims posed.[16]

In any event, those points about unjust aims and exactions are vulnerable to the charge that one may act out of wrong motives but nevertheless have just aims, or conduct oneself justly. More precisely, it is not inherent in the act of offering one's killing services in exchange for money that it should lead the agent to commit atrocities against civilians and to pursue unjust aims. Finally, it is worth noting that the freelance soldier, in so far as he has greater control over the conditions under which he will be deployed, is in a better position than the corporate fighter *or the professional soldier* to ensure that he will not be

---

[15] In other words, to advert to the aforementioned distinction between two interpretations of the requirement of just intentions, the worry is that precisely because they have the wrong motives, mercenaries are more likely to act in pursuit of wrongful aims. See J. Pattison, 'Just War Theory and the Privatization of Military Force', *Ethics and International Affairs* 22 (2008): 143–62, esp. 147 and 150–2.

[16] Baker, *Just Warriors, Inc.*, 48–52.

made to fight for unjust ends or in unjust ways. On that count, making oneself available for hire on a freelance basis might be less morally risky than joining the army and running the risk of having to obey an unjust order on pain of being dishonourably discharged.

Although the motivational objection's main target is mercenaries and PMCs (for obvious reasons), it might nevertheless be thought to apply to political communities as well, as follows: (a) to hire mercenaries to fight one's war is to countenance a wrongdoing, and (b) to countenance a wrongdoing is itself a moral wrongdoing of a kind which should not be protected by either a claim or a power. Assuming for the sake of argument that mercenarism is wrong as per the motivational objection, I shall not take issue with (a). Claim (b), however, is too strong—certainly in those cases where the political community which hires mercenaries simply could not conduct its (just) war otherwise, and particularly when its sovereignty and/or territorial integrity are at stake. Perhaps we have here a case of dirty hands, where a leader has to choose between the wrongdoing of hiring mercenaries and that of allowing the defeat of one's community by an unjust attacker.[17] Be that as it may, even if hiring mercenaries under those circumstances is morally wrong (albeit the lesser of two wrongdoings), this would not in itself count as a reason to deny a political community the claim and the power so to act. Here again, absent countervailing arguments, a political community's interest in fighting a just war surely is important enough to be protected by a right to enter mercenary contracts. Consider the following analogy. Even if it is wrong (*arguendo*) for someone to enter the medical profession mostly out of financial motives, and even if it is wrong for a patient to hire him, surely the patient's interest in surviving is important enough to grant him a right to do so. The alternative would be to subject him to criminal sanctions, or to deny him the protection of the law if the doctor breaches the contract (for example, by not providing the medical treatment which the patient paid for). Likewise, the alternative, for a political community, would be to be denied the protection of its own laws if the mercenaries or PMCs it has hired default on their contracts, as well as protection from interference, on the part of other political communities, with its attempt to secure its own survival. And yet, just as the patient's interest in remaining alive surely deserves the twin protection of a claim and a power, so does the political community's interest in its own survival.

---

[17] Coady, *Morality and Political Violence*, 218–9.

## 6.3.2 The objectification objection

The motivational objection—the most familiar of those deployed against mercenarism—focuses on mercenaries rather than their employers. By contrast, the objectification objection targets the latter and holds that hiring mercenaries is morally wrong because it consists in treating individuals as little more than both killing machines and cannon fodder. As Kant puts it, 'the hiring of men to kill or to be killed seems to mean using them as mere machines and instruments in the hands of someone else (the state), which cannot easily be reconciled with the rights of man in one's own person.'[18] Similar arguments were raised in Britain at the time of the American War of Independence, when Britain had to decide whether or not to recruit German mercenaries to its cause.[19] Interestingly, the objection is sometimes made against PMCs—with the further twist that those companies, motivated as they are by the search for greater profits, are also alleged to disregard their employees' welfare. It has thus been claimed by the families of the four Blackwater employees who were ambushed, killed, and dismembered in Fallujah on 31 March 2004, that their employers had assigned them to a highly dangerous mission with hardly any protection.[20]

Although the objectification objection is not always meant to condemn mercenarism while endorsing standing armies, it is nevertheless tempting to suppose that political communities are less likely to treat their own uniformed soldiers as killing machines and cannon fodder—particularly democratic political communities whose rulers are accountable to citizens, and particularly in an age where body bags bring home the true horrors of wars fought in far-flung

[18] Kant, I., 'Perpetual Peace: A Philosophical Sketch', in I. Kant, *Political Writings*, H. Reiss ed. (Cambridge: Cambridge University Press, 1991) 95. (See also Burchett and Roebuck, *The Whores of War: Mercenaries Today* for a similar objection in the context of the use of mercenaries in Africa in the 1970s.) According to Kant, the important difference is not between private and standing armies, but rather, between both kinds of army on the one hand, and occasional citizens' armies on the other hand. Standing armies should be abolished, he claims, because 'they constantly threaten other states with war by the very fact that they are always prepared for it.' (ibid., 94.)

Incidentally, and as Tamar Meisels pointed out to me, treating one's uniformed soldiers with undue caution might in fact lead to serious violations of civilians' rights (in so far as one thinks that priority should be given to one's own soldiers over enemy civilians. For a recent example of this view, see A. Kasher and A. Yadlin, 'Military Ethics of Fighting Terror: An Israeli Perspective', *Journal of Military Ethics* 4 (2005): 3–32). By that token, using mercenaries might enable one to do better at the bar of the *jus in bello*.

[19] The signatories of the American Declaration of Independence charge King George III for (*inter alia*) using foreign mercenaries in the War of Independence in the following terms: 'He is at this time transporting large Armies of foreign Mercenaries to compleat the works of death, desolation, and tyranny, already begun with circumstances of Cruelty & Perfidy scarcely parallelled in the most barbarous ages, and totally unworthy of the Head of a civilized nation.'

[20] See Percy, *Mercenaries*, 152–3 and 160, for the case of Britain, and Scahill, *Blackwater*, chs. 5 and 13, for the case of Blackwater.

corners of the world. The point, however, should not be overstated, for two reasons. First, non-democratic regimes are not noted for their respect for the lives of their soldiers: the objection thus applies to those regimes as well as to the use by political communities of private armies, and there is nothing distinctively wrong, with respect to the objectification of soldiers, about the latter.

Second, the objectification objection works best against practices which are concomitant to the hiring of private armies—such as the practice of not taking due care with mercenaries' lives. But it does not weaken the claim that political communities have the right to turn to private soldiers, or, for that matter, the claim that PMCs have the right to procure private armies. By analogy, the claim that men who visit prostitutes are likely to treat them in abusive ways does not entail that buying sexual services *per se* ought to be criminalized; nor does it entail that prostitutional transactions ought to be regarded as null and void. In fact, all that the objectification objection does (and that is in fact quite a lot, if off target) is support the view that political communities have a duty of care to the private soldiers whom they hire—just as they have a duty of care to their armed forces. More specifically, they have a duty to deploy them in accordance with the *jus in bello* requirements of proportionality (whereby the harms done by a particular tactical decision must not exceed the goods it brings about) and necessity (whereby political communities should risk soldiers'—and civilians'—lives if and only if it would serve their (just) ends.) Political communities which fail in that duty lack the power to contract with private soldiers if they fail to set out the ways in which they will discharge their duty of care to the latter, and are morally liable for their negligence. By contrast, political communities which abide by their duties to the private soldiers whom they hire cannot be charged with moral wrongdoing simply for recruiting forces outside state structures. Similar considerations apply to PMCs: those which treat their employees as little more than profit-making and fungible entities lack the right so to employ them, and, thereby, the right to contract with political communities for their use. However, those who fulfil their duty of care to their employees are left untouched by the objectification objection.

### 6.3.3 The profiteering objection

A third objection to mercenarism invokes the fact that individual mercenaries and PMCs live off the suffering of others. More recently, PMCs have been criticized for profiteering from the devastation brought about by war: they make a profit by sending out private armies who will cause considerable damage and destruction; they then make further profits by offering their protection services to the multinational corporations which are then entrusted by political communities with the task of reconstructing the country. Put bluntly, they get paid vast amounts of money for assisting in the reconstruction of countries which they were paid similarly vast amounts of money to help destroy. And even if they do not contribute to causing such destruction in the first instance, they nevertheless profit from the injustices which war victims suffer.

Here again, the objection may well have a point in so far as it targets current practices by political communities and PMCs, particularly in Iraq.[21] Its point is limited, however, for although it is true that PMCs do benefit from war and its attendant unjust practices, so too do weapon manufacturers and firms which supply armies (whether regular or private) with food and protective clothing. In fact, a vast range of private firms benefit from other people's suffering, such as companies which manufacture medical equipment, private medical practices, firms which provide the means (helicopters, life-saving equipment, engineering skills, and so on) for humanitarian relief, and so on. Indeed, many professions would not exist *but* for the fact that injustices have been committed—foremost amongst which is the legal profession. Yet to claim that those private firms therefore lack the right to contract with political communities for those goods and services seems rather extreme. By the same token, the fact that PMCs benefit from the suffering and destruction wrought by war cannot alone render their activities morally impermissible. In order to succeed, the objection would have to show that there is something *constitutively* wrong about PMCs' profiteering, which lawyering or manufacturing medical equipment lack. Yet it is not clear how it could establish that. The most obvious move which the objection could make, at this juncture, would be to insist that there is something inherently wrong about making a profit from killing, or helping kill, others. By contrast (it might say), a factory which manufactures surgical instruments helps save people's lives without thereby contributing to the deaths of others as a means to do so; likewise, there is nothing inherently unjust in helping people seek rightful redress through the courts. However, that putative move would fail. For surely, a firm which knowingly sells surgical instruments to doctors who practice surgical experiments on non-consenting patients lacks the right to do so; likewise, a corrupt lawyer who helps his mobster clients defraud the political community out of millions of pounds in owed taxes is not acting within his rights. In just the same way, a PMC lacks the right to hire private soldiers and offer their services

21 This, in effect, is the thrust of Scahill's critique of Blackwater's activities. See *Blackwater*, esp. ch. 13.

to a contracting political community if the war in which it fights is unjust. However, if the war is just, and if the deaths thus caused are not wrongful deaths, there is no reason for concluding on the aforementioned grounds that the medical factories and lawyers have the right to operate while PMC do not.

### 6.3.4 The loss-of-control objection

The fourth objection to mercenarism applies neither to individual mercenaries nor to PMCs but, rather, to states as the institutional apparatus through which political communities govern themselves. It avers that by contracting with either kind of agent, but especially PMCs, states lose exclusive control over the decision to use violence, as well as over the agents by which it is used. And yet, the objection claims, there are good reasons for granting states that kind of control. For in so far as they represent as well as articulate their members' interests, states are more likely to resort to, and control, violence for the sake of the common good rather than in defence of private interests. But when a state entrusts a PMC with the task of fighting its wars or assisting in the prosecution thereof, it is vulnerable to be unduly influenced by the corporation over the conduct of the war. It is also unable effectively to control the behaviour of the corporation's employees, since the latter are accountable to the corporation and not to the state itself: by contrast, a regular soldier is liable to being court-martialled if, for example, he commits exactions against enemy civilians. Finally, a state which routinely appeals to PMCs as a means to resolve military conflicts is in danger of becoming over-reliant on such firms at the expense of its own forces, which in turn might undermine its ability to promote its own interests when the latter conflict with PMCs' profit-driven goals. Although the objection can in principle be raised against both private and state actors, it has more bite against the latter, in so far as it invokes a moralized understanding of the Weberian account of state authority in virtue of which political commu-nities *should* retain a monopoly over the decision to resort to violence. By hiring private armies, in other words, a state fails to do its duty, which is to ensure that violence is used abroad only for the sake of the common good and in compliance with the laws of war. In so doing, it is guilty of a wrongdoing—and one of such magnitude that its interest in so acting can be protected neither by a power to contract with PMCs nor by a claim to do so.[22]

---

[22] For a study of the ways in which PMCs have been able to influence US foreign policy, see Avant, *The Market for Force*, esp. ch. 4, and D. Shearer, *Private Armies and Military Intervention* (Oxford: Oxford University Press, 1998), 34ff. For worries about the loss of accountability attendant on states' decisions to use PMCs, see, for example, Singer, *Corporate Warriors*, ch. 10; Pattison, 'Just War Theory and the Privatization of Military Force', 150ff; S. Percy, 'Morality and regulation', in

The objection draws considerable strength from the ways in which, in practice, political communities such as the US are alleged to have given private military corporations such as Blackwater some input into American foreign policy. In that vein, one of the last orders issued by Paul Bremner before leaving his post as head of Iraq's provisional civilian government removed private contractors suspected of war crimes from Iraqi jurisdiction (CPA Order 17). Although the order allowed the US to prosecute those contractors (as does the Military Extraterritorial Jurisdiction Act 10 USC §3261 (2000)), no such employee was prosecuted for crimes committed in Iraq until December 2008.[23] By contrast, while PMC employees enjoyed immunity, members of the US armed forces were facing prosecution for war crimes. Such decisions have done little to assuage the worries of opponents to mercenarism. However, proponents of the objection should beware the risk of overstating their case: any potential belligerent, including sovereign states, must seek advice from military and security experts when deciding whether or not to resort to war—if only because those experts, whether members of the army or civilians, have a better claim to know whether a particular military course of action has a reasonable chance of success. Including those actors other than elected leaders into the design of security policy is therefore essential.[24] What the objection must show, therefore, is that *private* military contractors acquire undue influence over decisions which are the political community's alone to take. Whether they do so is entirely contingent on the facts of the case. As a result, the objection is vulnerable to the counter-claim that proper regulation might succeed in mitigating the problems arising from political communities' loss of control over the transnational use of force. Such regulatory measures might

S. Chesterman and C. Lehnardt (ed.), *From Mercenaries to Market: The Rise and Regulation of Private Military Companies* (Oxford: Oxford University Press, 2007); M. Walzer, 'Mercenary Impulse: Is there an Ethics that Justifies Blackwater?', *New Republic*, 12 March 2008, http://www.tnr.com/article/mercenary-impulse.

[23] See, for example, http://www.nytimes.com/2005/09/28/national/28england.html, http://www.nytimes.com/2005/01/28/international/middleeast/28abuse.html, and http://www.nytimes.com/2008/12/06/washington/06blackwater.html?_r=1 (sources consulted 22 February 2009). The US War Crimes Act (18 USC §2441 (1996 and 2004)) provides that any American national or member of the US armed forces who commits a war crime is liable to prosecution: it would thus apply to American, but not foreign, PMC employees. In December 2008, US federal prosecutors charged five Blackwater guards for a shooting which killed at least seventeen civilians in a crowded Baghdad square. In December 2009 the case was dismissed by federal judge Ricardo Urbina, on the grounds that the prosecutors had compelled the accused men to testify against themselves, in violation of the US Constitution's Fifth Amendment. See M. Apuzzo, 'US judge throws out Blackwater case, citing missteps', *The Independent*, Friday, 1 January 2010.

[24] See, for example, A. Leander, 'Regulating the Role of Private Military Companies in Shaping Security and Politics', in S. Chesterman and C. Lehnardt (ed.), *From Mercenaries to Market: The Rise and Regulation of Private Military Companies* (Oxford: Oxford University Press, 2007), for a thoughtful discussion of that issue.

include, *inter alia*, clear rules for what constitutes an acceptable mercenary activity (a point to which I shall return in Section 6.4), licensing regimes similar to those which already regulate the arms trade, adequate provision for the prosecution and sanction of actors who fail to comply with those measures, as well as publicly funded electoral campaigns so as to deprive corporations of means of leverage over presidential candidates. Moreover, account should be taken of the fact that PMCs, like all other major corporations, are global in scope, which in turn requires a transnational regulatory framework. Under those conditions it is hard to see on what grounds one can deny political communities a right to hire a private army.[25]

Moreover, the objection supposes that political communities have compliant and effective armed forces at their disposal. Quite often, however, they do not, and are at the mercy either of their own soldiers or of armed rebel groups which operate within their borders, more often than not with the assistance or complicity of other political communities. In such cases, a political community's decision to hire a private army will help strengthen its control over the use of violence rather than undermine it. Thus it is often argued that Sierra Leone, which was blighted by civil war in the 1990s, was able to end the war only once they had brought in Executive Outcomes. Likewise, it is also argued that Croatia, when under attack by Serbia, was able to obtain some military successes in 1995 after entrusting Military Professional Resources Inc. with the task of training and restructuring its troops. Under those conditions, and to reiterate a point made earlier against the motivational objection, when a state can defend itself only with the help of private soldiers, denying it and its people the right to hire a private army is tantamount to denying it the right to avail itself of the resources it needs for collective self-defence. To insist on doing so *simply* on the basis of the status of such resources is a piece of fetishism.[26]

---

[25] For examples of ways in which to regulate PMCs, see, for example, Avant, *The Market for Force*, ch. 4, K. A. O'Brien, 'What Should and What Should Not be Regulated?', in S. Chesterman and C. Lehnardt (ed.), *From Mercenaries to Market: The Rise and Regulation of Private Military Companies* (Oxford: Oxford University Press, 2007); Krahmann, 'Transitional States in Search of Support: Private Military Companies and Security Sector Reform'; Singer, *Corporate Warriors*, ch. 15, and Baker, *Just Warriors, Inc.*, ch. 7.

[26] See Percy, *Mercenaries*, 218–9; O'Brien, 'What Should and What Should Not be Regulated?'; Avant, *The Market for Force*, ch. 4; Shearer, *Private Armies and Military Intervention*; M. Caparini, 'Domestic Regulation: Licensing Regimes for the Export of Military Goods and Services', in S. Chesterman and C. Lehnardt (ed.), *From Mercenaries to Market: The Rise and Regulation of Private Military Companies* (Oxford: Oxford University Press, 2007); J. Cockayne, 'Make or Buy? Principal-agent Theory and the Rregulation of Private Military Companies', in S. Chesterman and C. Lehnardt (ed.), *From Mercenaries to Market: The Rise and Regulation of Private Military Companies* (Oxford: Oxford University Press, 2007); L. A. Dickinson, 'Contract as a Tool for Regulating Private Military Companies', in S. Chesterman and C. Lehnardt (ed.), *From Mercenaries to Market: The Rise*

## 6.3.5 The neutrality objection

At various points in this chapter I have argued for a duty not to interfere with a decision by a mercenary or a PMC to, respectively, offer or procure lethal services, as well as a duty not to interfere with a political community's decision to hire them. If two political communities are at war against each other, other parties—typically, political communities—ought not to make it a criminal offence for a PMC to operate from within its territory, or for their own individual members to offer their military services to either belligerent. In addition, third-party political communities ought to recognize as valid under the relevant statute the employment contracts passed between individual mercenaries and PMCs.

The neutrality objection takes issue with that view. It claims that in a war between (say) political communities A and B, C not only may interfere with its own members, PMCs, and thereby A, but also that it ought to do so, on the grounds that failure to thwart mercenary activities is tantamount to breaching the principle of neutrality. According to the principle, political communities ought to remain neutral between those whom they have not explicitly undertaken to assist. For C to allow some of its members to offer their military services to A in the latter's war against B is to fail to remain neutral. So would C's decision to let PMCs take side in that war, from within C's territory. If the objection is correct, then neither freelance mercenaries nor PMCs have a right to offer or procure lethal services— services which political communities themselves do not have the right to buy.

Although the objection can (here again) be deployed, *mutatis mutandis*, against non-state actors, it tends to target state actors. Indeed, historically, the norm against mercenarism evolved partly as a result of rulers' awareness of the risks which their subjects' mercenary activities abroad posed to national interests.[27] However, the neutrality objection is both too narrow and too

---

*and Regulation of Private Military Companies* (Oxford: Oxford University Press, 2007); A. Bearpark and S. Schulz, 'The Future of the Market', in S. Chesterman and C. Lehnardt (ed.), *From Mercenaries to Market: The Rise and Regulation of Private Military Companies* (Oxford: Oxford University Press, 2007). See Singer, *Corporate Warriors*, chs. 1, 7, and 8 for discussions of the cases of Croatia and Sierra Leone. None of this is to deny, of course, that weak states which pay PMCs with, for example, mining concessions, risk jeopardizing their long-term ability to function without PMCs' continuous presence on their territory (if only because those mining concessions themselves will require protection which the client state is unable to provide). A sensible approach consists in setting up an international fund for paying those companies. For a good account of the tight and problematic connections between weak states in Africa, PMCs, and mining conflicts, see, for example, A. McIntyre and T. Weiss, 'Weak Governments in Search of Strength: Africa's Experience of Mercenaries and Private Military Companies', in S. Chesterman and C. Lehnardt (ed.), *From Mercenaries to Market: The Rise and Regulation of Private Military Companies* (Oxford: Oxford University Press, 2007).

[27] See, for example, J. E. Thomson, *Mercenaries, Pirates, and Sovereigns: State-building and Extraterritorial Violence in Early Modern Europe* (Princeton: Princeton University Press, 1994), esp. ch. 3.

broad. It is too narrow in so far as it fails to target the practice by a political community of hiring its own nationals as mercenaries. To be sure, if merce-narism just consists in hiring *foreign* nationals, then it is vulnerable to the objection. As we saw in Section 6.1, however, this definitional move is not convincing, since (to repeat) it implies that an American employee of Black-water who fights in Iraq is not a mercenary. Moreover, the objection is too broad, in so far as it also rejects, by implication, the enlistment by individuals into the army of a foreign state. Admittedly, a number of international conventions (such as the 1907 Hague Convention regarding the Rights and Duties of Neutral Powers) and domestic laws (such as the British Foreign Enlistment Act 1870) bar individuals from so doing. The difficulty, though, is that by the same token, France and Britain, to name but those two, would have been entitled—indeed, would have been under a duty—to block enlist-ment by their own nationals into the International Brigades during the Spanish Civil War. For reasons to be considered presently, that pushes the requirement of neutrality too far.

The neutrality objection, then, only works, if it works at all, against some but not all kinds of mercenarism. In any event, it does not work. It assumes, first, that political communities ought to remain neutral, and second, that they are accountable for the activities of their individual members as well of the corporate entities which act from within their territory. Both assumptions are problematic.[28] Take the latter. Although political communities have sometimes, and quite appropriately so, been held responsible for the conduct of private actors (when the latter were authorized to act by political commu-nities), an act of killing carried out by a national of a political community does not automatically implicate that state. If a British citizen residing in Germany murders a German for political motives, the UK will not be deemed responsi-ble by the German government for that act simply in virtue of the murderer's nationality. That such acts may occur in the context of war should make no difference on that particular count.

The objection's first assumption does not fare much better. The view that a political community may never take sides in a war unless bound by a prior treaty is tantamount to claiming that someone may never take side in a conflict opposing two individuals unless bound by a prior promise, even when one of them is under a lethal threat at the hands of an unjust attacker.

---

[28] Burmester, 'The Recruitment and Use of Mercenaries in Armed Conflicts', 41–7. For a good discussion of states' responsibilities for the conduct of their private members under international law, see C. Lehnardt, 'Private Military Companies and State Responsibility', in S. Chesterman and C. Lehnardt (ed.), *From Mercenaries to Market: The Rise and Regulation of Private Military Companies* (Oxford: Oxford University Press, 2007).

But if a victim of an attack has a right to kill her unjust attacker in self-defence, then (as we saw in Chapters 2 and 5) she also has the (Hohfeldian) power to secure third-party assistance. And if that is the case, then the latter may come to her help. By analogy, then, if A is under an unjust threat from B, and if it is entitled to wage a war of self-defence against the latter, *prima facie* it is also entitled to call for C's help. One way in which C may act in defence of A (for example) is by not forbidding its own members to offer their services to A, and by allowing PMCs to operate within its territory.

The foregoing points imply that C ought not to come to A's assistance, even in those limited ways, if A's war is unjust. This suggests that the neutrality objection ought to be recast as the claim that a political community may not facilitate the commission by (some of) their members of wrongdoings against another state—in that instance, B.[29] However, the objection so recast does not undermine mercenarism itself so much as the wrongful uses to which its actors sometimes put it. As such, it is wholly compatible with the view which I have defended throughout this chapter: namely, that *if* the war is just, then there is little reason to deem marketized soldiering morally unjustifiable in principle.

## 6.4 KILLING IN COMMODIFIED WARS

None of the five most commonly deployed moral objections to marketised soldiering work. It remains to be seen whether private soldiers have the right to kill in war in the same way and under the same circumstances as uniformed soldiers, and whether they are liable to being killed, in war, in the same way, and on the same grounds, as the latter.

On the orthodox account of war-killings, uniformed combatants may intentionally kill other soldiers without being liable to punishment (subject to considerations of necessity and proportionality.) Should they be captured by the enemy they must be regarded as prisoners of war and be treated as stipulated by the 1949 Geneva Convention Relative to the Treatment of Prisoners of War. By implication, civilians, who are not themselves legitimate targets, may not kill soldiers (unless the latter wrongfully target them, in which case their acts of killing are justifiable acts of self-defence). If they do so, they are to be treated as murderers and tried accordingly; and in addition,

---

[29] Burmester, 'The Recruitment and Use of Mercenaries in Armed Conflicts', 44.

should they be made prisoners by the enemy they do not have the rights and privileges normally extended to prisoners of war.

There are exceptions to the principle, of course. Thus, articles 1(4) and 44 (3) of the 1977 Protocol Additional to the Geneva Convention of 12 August 1949 Relative to the Protection of Victims of International Armed Conflicts extend the protection enjoyed by soldiers to members of national liberation movements. However, the international law of armed conflicts does not confer the legal status of a soldier to mercenaries. Under the International Convention against the Recruitment, Use, Financingm and Training of Mercenaries (1989), 'a mercenary, as defined in Article 1 of the present Convention, who participates directly in hostilities or in a concerted act of violence, as the case may be, commits an offence for the purposes of the Convention' (Article 3.1). According to international law, then, mercenaries are neither civilians nor soldiers: they belong to the grey category of unlawful combatants, who are liable to being killed with impunity (precisely in so far as they are combatants) but are denied the rights and privileges of soldiers (precisely in so far as they are not members of regular armed forces and thus do not satisfy the *in bello* requirement of legitimate authority as discussed in Section 4.4.2). By contrast, private contractors are usually treated as civilians rather than combatants (whether lawful or unlawful). Interestingly, and as we saw in Section 6.3.4, employees of PMCs who are currently operating in Iraq enjoyed, for a long time, *greater* rights and privileges than did US soldiers. Indeed, the label under which they are commonly designated—'private contractors'—seems to suggest that they ought to be regarded as civilians rather than combatants, and that they are not, therefore, legitimate targets.

Yet my arguments in support of the bestowal on private individuals of the right to hire themselves out for killing purposes also support the thesis (which I call the moral parity thesis) that private soldiers, whether free-lance mercenaries or PMC employees, should be treated on a par with uniformed soldiers, with one exception.[30] If the status (economic or political) of mercenaries'

---

[30] Note that in this section I shall consider only private soldiers' right to kill and liabilities to being killed. The issue of punishment is a matter for *jus post bellum*, to be tackled elsewhere. For interesting discussions of differential liabilities for uniformed soldiers and mercenaries, see Pattison, 'Just War Theory and the Privatization of Military Force', and Coady, *Morality and Political Violence*, pp. 226ff (though Coady is sceptical of the legitimacy of mercenarism). For discussions of the legal status of mercenaries and employees of PMCs, see, for example, L. Cameron, 'Private Military Companies: Their Status under International Humanitarian Law and its Impact on their Regulation', *International Review of the Red Cross* 88 (2006): 573–98; K. Fallah, 'Corporate Actors: the Legal Status of Mercenaries in Armed Conflict', *International Review of the Red Cross* 88 (2006): 599–611; E.-C. Gillard, 'Business goes to War: Private Military/Security Companies and International Humanitarian Law', *International Review of the Red Cross* 88 (2006): 525–72; L. Doswald-Beck, 'Private Military Companies under International Humanitarian Law', in S. Chesterman and

employers is irrelevant to the issue of the former's right to offer their services in war, it should also be irrelevant to the issue of their liabilities, rights, and privileges during war. To claim otherwise is tantamount to conferring on membership in a given group (here, a state army or a private corporation) decisive weight when granting or denying individuals rights to kill and not to be killed—which would contradict central tenets of cosmopolitan justice. Note, incidentally, that the claim is compatible with the (plausible) view that there are differences between armies' and private companies' duties and permissions before the war starts—such that (for example) the army is under a collective duty to go to a just war as ordered by its (civilian) political leaders, but a private company is not under a duty to accept a government's contract to fight in that war.

At first sight it would seem that the foregoing points apply only to mercenaries—free-lance or otherwise—who directly take part in combat operations, and not to those who offer training and protective and logistical support to regular forces. In so far as PMCs do not usually deploy personnel in a combating capacity but, rather, assist combat units, it would seem that the vast majority of their employees should be categorized as civilians rather than combatants. But that would be too quick, for armies are not made up solely of fighting soldiers: they also employ personnel who provide support to front-line units. Now, as I argued in Section 2.3.2, an agent is liable to being killed in war only if he contributes in certain ways to an unjust threat of serious harm to other agents (whether or not they are combatants) only if, in other words, he can be described as a direct participant in hostilities. Taking part in an armed attack or counter-attack clearly does, which includes in the category of legitimate targets Blackwater employees who, alongside US soldiers, fired at a crowd of protesters (some of them armed) from the occupation headquarters in Najaf, Iraq, in April 2004.[31] Whether or not assisting in attacks and counter-attack also counts as direct participation in hostilities is harder to determine. Whilst bringing ammunition to regular forces is plausibly regarded as such, providing security for military headquarters may not. Whilst providing training to jetfighters during the war itself can also plausibly count as participation in the latter's subsequent attacks, merely guarding military installations may not. And so on. These are difficult issues, but the

---

C. Lehnardt (ed.), *From Mercenaries to Market: The Rise and Regulation of Private Military Companies* (Oxford: Oxford University Press, 2007). For a book-length defence of the claim that, all other things equal, mercenaries are no better and no worse than uniformed soldiers, see Baker, *Just Warriors, Inc.*

[31] See Scahill, *Blackwater*, ch. 8.

crucial point is that they arise in just the same way for regular forces: some soldiers take a direct part in fighting, while others 'merely' provide logistical support to combat units. Accordingly, the moral parity thesis applies to those cases as well. *If* uniformed soldiers who do not directly take part in combat are not legitimate targets, on the grounds that they are not themselves posing an ongoing or imminent lethal threat to the enemy, mercenaries who provide logistical assistance to combat units ought not to be killed either.[32]

So far, I have focused on individual mercenaries. Yet the status of PMCs themselves is also at issue. If their employees are liable to being killed, are their executives similarly liable, and are their company headquarters legitimate targets for destructive bombings? Not necessarily. As we saw in Sections 2.3.2 and 3.4, individuals whose acts constitute a contribution to the war only by virtue of being connected to other agents' acts often escape liability precisely because their individual contributions are not significant enough, or are not of the relevant kind. By that token, of course, they can also meet either condition, which does make them liable to being killed. Moreover, even if they are not liable to direct attack, their contribution to the (unjust) war or (unjust) phase of war might still be significant enough to render them liable to the imposition of a lesser harm. Note, however, that those points apply to uniformed soldiers as well: in virtue of the moral parity thesis, a uniformed soldier whose individual contribution does not meet the relevant conditions is not liable either—at least, not at the bar of the neo-classical account of the right to kill in war.

It might be objected to the parity thesis that it fails to take into account a crucially important difference between public and private soldiers: to wit, that the latter are subject to the authority of the state and are under a *prima facie* duty to obey their leaders' order to wage war, whereas the former are not under a duty to contract with the state. As a result, some might press, private soldiers can only fight in wars which are clearly just, and (in addition) can only fight at the behest of legitimate states. No such restrictions apply to uniformed soldiers, who may fight in any war (or at least, in any war which is not manifestly unjust) and who may also fight at the behest of illegitimate states.[33] The objection need not deny that there is a morally relevant difference between uniformed soldiers who fight in unjust wars and those who fight in

---

[32] For a recent and illuminating discussion of direct participation in humanitarian law, see ICRC, 'Interpretive Guidance on the Notion of Direct Participation in Hostilities under International Humanitarian Law', *International Review of the Red Cross* 90 (2008): 991–1047. For a discussion of the issue in connection with private military contractors, see Cameron, 'Private Military Companies'.

[33] See J. Pattison, 'Deeper Objections to the Privatisation of Military Force', *Journal of Political Philosophy* 18 (2010): 425–47, at 429–33.

just wars. In particular, it need not deny that the latter have a justification for participating and killing in war which the former lack; nor need it deny that just combatants are not liable to attack whilst unjust combatants are liable. Rather, it claims that other things equal, unjust uniformed combatants may have an excuse for participating and killing in unjust wars which unjust private soldiers lack—on the grounds that the latter may never surrender their private judgement as to the justness of the war, whereas the former may do so, at least in those cases where the war is not manifestly unjust.

As should be clear, however, on the account of the right to kill in war which I have defended throughout this book, the objection misses the point. For even if a soldier has an excuse for participating in an unjust war, it does not follow that he has the right to kill just enemy combatants; nor does it follow that he is not liable to attack. Accordingly, even if the objection rightly gives uniformed soldiers an excuse which it denies private soldiers, it does not yield the conclusion that the former, unlike the latter, have the right to kill just enemy combatants and are not liable to being killed. In any event, it is not clear at all that uniformed and private soldiers differ in the way just suggested. It is true, of course, that the army is under a *prima facie* collective duty to obey a just order to go to war, and that its individual members are under a *prima facie* duty to obey a just order to fight; by contrast, a PMC is not under a duty to contract with the government, and some of its individual members may refuse the latter's request for their services without having to resign. Thus, whereas General Mike Jackson, head of the British Army in February 2003, could not possibly have remained in post *and* refused to deploy the troops to Iraq when explicitly ordered to do so by the British government, Erik Pringle, CEO of Blackwater, could have refused to contract with the US government without losing his job. Crucially, however, it does not follow that uniformed soldiers (of whatever rank) are morally permitted to stay in the army and wage the unjust wars to which private contractors are morally forbidden to contribute. Thus, if the Iraq war was an unjust war, and if that alone is a reason for denying Blackwater soldiers the permission and right to fight it, then that alone should also be a reason for withholding that very same right and permission from uniformed soldiers. Nor, finally, does it follow that uniformed soldiers may fight for the unjust states which private soldiers are morally prohibited from supporting. It is sometimes alleged that some PMCs did give consideration to working for Rwanda's genocidal regime in the spring of 1994.[34] Had they done so, their soldiers clearly would have acted

---

[34] Singer, *Corporate Warriors*, p. 225. See also Pattison, 'Deeper Objections to the Privatisation of Military Force', 432.

unjustly. But so did the regime's own soldiers, and so would have other uniformed soldiers from any other state(s) had they been deployed to fight against Tutsi forces.

Before concluding, recall that the parity thesis admits of one exception. In Section 2.4 I argued that combatants who defend their community's political sovereignty and territorial integrity from an unjust aggression by a foreign aggressor may inflict collateral and lethal damage on innocent enemy non-combatants precisely because, and to the extent that, their individual *and jointly held* fundamental rights are under attack. If that is correct, then combatants who are not members of V but who help V fight its war of collective self-defence—in other words, foreign mercenaries or foreign volunteers—cannot invoke patriotic partiality as a justification for causing the deaths of non-combatants$_A$. Their justification for so acting would have to take the form of an agent-neutral reason such as, for example, the importance of ensuring that political communities and their officials do not take the view that aggression can go unchecked. But as I noted in Section 2.2 in my account of the permissibility of killing in defence of others, those combatants would have to confer greater weight on the lives and interests of non-combatants$_A$ than combatants$_V$ would, precisely because they themselves would not have an agent-relative prerogative to kill in that particular conflict. To be sure, once they accept the mission their lives are under threat at the hands of combatants$_A$, and they thus acquire an additional reason to kill the latter in their own defence. In so doing they also acquire a victim-centred justification for unintentionally killing non-combatants in the course of defending their lives. But unlike combatants$_V$, they do not have a self-directed just cause for taking part in that war—which, I suggest here, has a particular bearing on what they may do in it, and in particular on the degree to which they may unintentionally kill non-combatants in defence of the rights of contracting belligerents (as distinct from in defence of their own right to life). With respect to collateral damage, in other words, the status of private soldiers who fight in a war of other-defence is similar to that of intervening forces who fight a war of humanitarian intervention.

## 6.5 CONCLUSION

I have argued that if the war is just, individuals have the right to hire themselves out for military services, political communities have the right to contract with them for those purposes, and private military corporations have the right to act as intermediaries between them. Under those conditions, mercenarism, whether it involves freelance mercenaries and political communities or takes the form of a triangular relationship involving PMCs, is morally legitimate. As I have also noted, however, once the war has started, private soldiers and PMCs should be treated on a par with uniformed soldiers and public military organizations.

I should like to end by sketchily addressing four worries concerning the chapter's conclusion.[35] The first worry is that extending the right to fight in war to private actors would in all likelihood increase the range of actors who take part in unjust conflicts, since PMCs and mercenaries are likely not be too concerned with the justness, or lack thereof, of the cause for which they are hired: more generally put, the more actors are allowed to kill in war, the greater the incidence of unjust violence in the world. Now, I agree that if, as a matter of fact, the use of PMCs and mercenaries to fight on the same terms as uniformed soldiers were to lead to increased levels of violence, then that would provide the international community with a good reason, all things considered, to outlaw them. By that token, however, the international community should also impose similarly harsh sanctions on the use by political communities of their own armies to further unjust ends. If aiming at decreasing levels of unjust violence justifies narrowing the range and number of military actors (as it surely does), then this applies to all (and only) those actors who engage in such violence, whether or not they are uniformed soldiers fighting in regular armies, or private military actors. In other words, faced with that particular worry one should uphold the moral parity thesis (whereby mercenaries ought to be treated in exactly the same way as regular uniformed soldiers), not jettison it.

And yet the second worry is that the moral parity thesis trivializes the case for mercenarism. Put differently, once constrained by the requirements of a just war, mercenarism is not a distinctive institution, and providing a justification for it is not such an important task after all. Perhaps. But in the light of the standard *moral* objections raised against mercenarism, it is worthwhile to show that, under those conditions at least, it is morally justified.

The third worry is that my argument for mercenarism implies that a vast range of tasks which, we normally think, should be performed only by state actors can in fact be outsourced to private actors—such as adjudicating disputes between citizens, administering prisons, policing our neighbourhoods, and so

---

[35] All four were raised, in one way or another, at the various fora where I presented this chapter. I am grateful to an anonymous referee for the *BJPolS* for pressing me on the first point, which also arises in connection with the claim, which I defended in Chapter 4, that private individuals as such are sometimes permitted to go to war in defence of their rights.

on. By way of reply, let me simply make the following observation: even if the arguments from freedom of occupational choice and the ethics of assistance which I deploy here support the privatization of other essential services, there might nevertheless be some disanalogies between public and private provision in those cases such that the latter lacks justification, all things considered. For example, it might be that the right to punish is different from the right to kill in such ways that privatizing the latter does not commit us to privatizing the former. And so on.

Finally, some might worry that, on the view that I have defended here, the wholesale commodification of war is permissible—or, to put it differently, that there is no reason for a political community to fund a regular army whose members are, in effect, civil servants. I am not convinced that this is so, for three reasons: first, it might well be that effective regulation of private armies as sketched here requires that private soldiers work alongside uniformed, regular soldiers; second, functionalist considerations (for example, concerning combat effectiveness) might well dictate in favour of maintaining a regular army; and third, and more importantly, there are good reasons to ensure that a political community should not be solely dependent for its security on the willingness or ability of one kind of institutional actor to deploy soldiers as and when required.

# 7

# Asymmetrical wars

## 7.1 INTRODUCTION

In the Introduction to this book, as well as at various junctures in the ensuing chapters, I took issue with standard interpretations of the principle of discrimination, according to which combatants, who pose a lethal threat, are legitimate targets whereas non-combatants, who do not participate in hostilities, are not. I argued that only those combatants who are causally responsible for grievous rights violations are liable to being killed, and that those non-combatants who are similarly responsible are also liable. By implication, many non-combatants are not legitimate targets. However, as we have also seen throughout, most notably in Chapters 3 and 4, some belligerents cannot successfully prosecute their just cause unless they resort to tactics which are prohibited by the laws of war—notably when they are faced with an opponent whose military might is vastly superior to theirs. Those tactics include, *inter alia*, the deliberate targeting of non-combatants, the use of non-combatants as shields, the use of deceptive tactics such as ambushes, or the practice of blending into the civilian population in order to lead the enemy to believe that one is harmless, and thus to make him more vulnerable to attack.[1]

None of those tactics are new—nor is the general problem of asymmetry between belligerents. However, addressing the ethics of asymmetrical warfare is particularly pressing for my account of the just war, since the latter regards as just causes rights violations which can be blocked only by resorting to the aforementioned means, and confers the status of legitimate belligerents on

---

[1] See, for example, Duyvesteyn and Angstrom (ed.), *Rethinking the Nature of War*; R. Geiβ, 'Asymmetric Conflict Structures', *International Review of the Red Cross* 88 (2006): 757–77; F. Hampson, 'Winning by the Rules: Law and Warfare in the 1980s', *Third World Quarterly* 11 (1989): 31–62; M. Kaldor, *New and Old Wars* (2nd edn., Cambridge: Polity, 2006), and Munkler, *The New Wars*. Although this chapter focuses on asymmetrical tactics as used by belligerents with weak conventional capabilities, one should not forget that those tactics are also used by military strong actors. Terrorism, in particular, is not the weapon of the weak exclusively, however it is defined. The point is a familiar one, but is pithily put by Uwe Steinhoff in his recent treatment of terrorism. See Steinhoff, *On the Ethics of War and Terrorism*, ch. 7.

*Asymmetrical wars*

actors (such as non-state actors) who can win their war only by so acting. The account thus faces the following dilemma, nicely set up by David Rodin: either it denies the weak (W) the right to resort to those means, which is tantamount to denying them the right to go to war, or it grants them that right, in which case it weakens standard protections afforded to non-combatants.[2]

My aim, in this final chapter, is to tackle this dilemma by focusing on three such tactics. Two of those—the deliberate targeting of non-combatants and the use of human shields—directly expose non-combatants to harm. The other—the use of deceptive tactics such as pretending to be a non-combatant in order safely to approach the enemy—does not do so, but instead relies on the latter's unwillingness to breach the principle of non-combatant immunity—as does the use of shields, in fact.

I proceed as follows. In Section 7.2 I argue that deliberate targeting is wrong unless as a means to avert a greater evil, where evil is understood as qualitatively different, in some sense to be explained therein, from mere moral badness. In Section 7.3 I offer a qualified argument in support of the use of human shields. In Section 7.4 I address the use of deceptive tactics and claim that resorting to them is wrongful to non-combatants only if the latter suffer greater harm, as a result, at the hands of the enemy than is generally required of them to incur. I also argue that such tactics are not wrongful to the enemy itself. Finally, in Section 7.5 I consider what non-combatants who are subject to wrongful harm at the hands of combatants$_W$ may do in their own defence.

Throughout the chapter, the following set of assumptions and *caveat* ought to be borne in mind. First, I posit that W's cause is just and that its powerful enemy P is unjust. As we saw in Chapter 2, combatants' right to kill (largely) depends on the justness of their cause.[3] If W's cause were unjust, their acts of war in prosecution of that cause would be unjust *irrespective of the form they would take*, which would render the problem of asymmetry uninteresting from an ethical point of view. Relatedly, I also assume that the fact that W's cause is just does not entail that W may do whatever is necessary to pursue it: if the end always did justify the means, asymmetrical tactics, as used by W, would be equally uninteresting. I take it for granted that the end does not justify the means, and thus focus on the task of exploring *which* means it allows.

[2] D. Rodin, 'The Ethics of Asymmetric War', in R. Sorabji and D. Rodin (ed.), *The Ethics of War: Shared Problems in Different Traditions* (Aldershot: Ashgate, 2006).

[3] Only largely so, because, as we saw in Section 2.3.2, a war has different phases, some of which are just, and others of which are unjust; and within a just phase, some combatants who fight in prosecution of their just cause might nevertheless at the same time commit unjust acts of killing, in which case they might be liable to attack.

Second, and relatedly, I assume that the use of those tactics is a necessary condition for W to stand a reasonable chance of success. In the present context the criterion might be thought to rule out such tactics at the outset, on the grounds that they make it impossible for enemies to trust each other and turn war into a rule-less fight to the death where belligerents inflict untold suffering on one another. As we saw in Chapter 3, winning the war does not simply mean getting the enemy to surrender: it means getting them to surrender under conditions such as to obtain redress for the wrongdoing(s) which gave rise to a just cause and to secure prospects for a durable peace. Broken trust and memories of atrocities on both sides are unlikely to win W its war, and for W to use those tactics is therefore unjust. Or so some might argue. Now, I agree (and indeed, who would not?) that *if* the deliberate targeting of non-combatants, their forcible use as shields, and the resort to deception do have those effects, then they should be ruled out as unjust. But here my aim is to assess whether they are also unjust on the assumption that their employment may furnish W with a reasonable chance of winning the war.

Third, my focus is not on cases where belligerents are merely unequal in conventional military power, but rather, on cases where they use qualitatively *different* tactics—one resorts to conventional air, land, and naval power (tanks, missiles, submarines, and so on), whilst the other resorts to non-conventional methods.[4] Moreover, I do not tackle all possible such methods. A full normative account of asymmetrical warfare would need to address, *inter alia*, the ethics of deception and the ethics of resorting to WMDs, as well as the ethics of so-called information warfare (which consists in targeting the enemy's information systems via the Internet, thus exploiting its economic, social, political, and military dependence on those systems.) Here I restrict my inquiry to modes of warfare which consist in harming, or pretending to be harming, non-combatants, and which give rise to the dilemma described at the outset of this chapter.

Finally, I do not tackle the vexed question of the ethics of using asymmetrical tactics against an enemy which itself does so impermissibly. Nor do I consider in any depth whether powerful *just* belligerents may use asymmetrical tactics against their weaker unjust opponents: if the thesis defended here is sound (namely that the weak, when their cause is just, may sometimes use asymmetrical tactics against the powerful in prosecution of a just war) then it applies to that particular case *a fortiori*.

---

[4] For a descriptive account of various forms of asymmetry in contemporary warfare, see, for example, Thornton, *Asymmetric Warfare*.

## 7.2 DELIBERATE TARGETING

In contemporary conflicts, the deliberate targeting of non-combatants is often—though not exclusively—a tactic employed by non-state actors against powerful military forces which are typically deployed by states and which they cannot overcome by resorting to conventional modes of warfare. Such acts are carried out for a variety of reasons: to instil fear in the enemy population with the hope that the latter will pressurize their regime into ending the war, to terrorize enemy civilian populations into not joining the war effort, and so on.[5] Attacks on civilians by separatist, nationalist, or political–religious factions in Northern Ireland, Palestine, Sri Lanka, and Iraq are paradigmatic examples of the kind of asymmetrical warfare at issue in this section, though what I shall say about them will apply to interstate as well as intrastate conflicts. They are also paradigmatic examples of a type of conduct which is prohibited by the laws of war and which the overwhelming majority of people condemn as morally repugnant. Non-combatants, it is said, are materially and causally innocent of the war, and belligerents therefore ought not treat them as legitimate targets, as to do so is an act of murder.

Note that the principle of *non-combatant* immunity is compatible with the view that some *civilians*—such as the civilian leader of a country at war, or civilian weapons manufacturers—are sometimes liable to being targeted. That view, in fact, is often deployed by supporters and practitioners of terror bombing, who argue that all civilian citizens are complicitous either by deed or omission in their state's initial wrongdoing, and thus are legitimate targets.[6] In Chapter 3, however, we saw that civilians who are responsible for the rights violations suffered by the very poor are not, on the whole, legitimate targets, since their contribution to the wrongdoing is not of a kind to warrant killing them deliberately (though it might warrant conducting military missions which will foreseeably but unintentionally result in their death). By that token, citizens who fail to stop their state P's unjust policies towards W are not liable to deliberate targeting either. *A fortiori*, civilians who are wholly innocent (morally and causally) of the wrongdoing which gave W their just

---

[5] For a very interesting account of violence against non-combatants as a tool for deterring the latter from joining the war, see Kalyvas, *The Logic of Violence in Civil Wars*, especially ch. 5.

[6] For views along those lines as advanced by leaders of groups which resort to terrorist tactics (such as the Chechen leader Shamil Basayev and Osama bin Laden), see, for example, L. Richardson, *What Terrorists Want: Understanding the Terrorist Threat* (London: John Murray, 2006), pp. 21–2, 36. For discussions of those views, see McMahan, *Killing in War*, ch. 5, and Kamm, 'Failures of Just War Theory: Terror, Harm, and Justice'.

cause or of the retaliatory war which P are waging against W (and who can thus be described as non-combatants) have not lost their right not to be killed either.[7] In fact, there is something particularly objectionable about such killings: to wit, the fact that they target individuals who are not in any way responsible for the harm to which W are subject, as well as the fact that they are (usually) defenceless in the face of such attacks. It is not merely that they lack the means to counter-attack W's combatants; it is also that they have few means to protect themselves from the latter's moves. (Such shelters as there might be are often not adequate protection; they might not have the option to leave the area under fire, or can do so only at the enormously high cost of being exposed to further attacks whilst on the move, or of having to leave friends and family behind, and so on.) It is no coincidence, in fact, if they, rather than P's armed combatants, are under threat: W, in other words, not only kills them as a means to prosecuting its just cause, but also exploits their vulnerability. And that, I think, is deeply problematic—so much so, in fact, as to be *prima facie* unacceptable.

To some, however, that might be too quick, for as we saw in Section 2.4, one sometimes has a justification for subjecting someone to a wrongful harm—a harm, that is, which they nevertheless have a right not to incur. There, I argued that Tactical Bomber$_V$ who targets a weapons factory and in so doing foreseeably but unintentionally kills innocent civilians might have a justification for doing so if he fights in a just war. Now, it would be tempting to think that a just cause can provide a justification for a rights infringement only if the latter is unintentional—albeit foreseen. If that were true, then W would not be justified in targeting non-combatants$_P$. As Feinberg's well-known 'blizzard' example suggests, however, one sometimes has a justification (in that instance, escaping death by frost and starvation) for deliberately infringing someone else's right (in that instance, their property right over their cabin, into which I knowingly and intentionally break without their permission, to seek temporary refuge from the blizzard in which I became lost[8]). The question at issue here, then, is whether W, who *ex hypothesi* have a just cause for war, have a justification for deliberately infringing the right of non-combatants$_P$ not to be killed, on the assumption that they cannot win their war in any other way. As this book seeks to articulate and defend a cosmopolitan theory of the just war, I shall not scrutinize justifications for

[7] I thus reserve the label 'non-combatants' to refer to civilians who do not take part in hostilities. For extensive discussions of the uses and misuses of the labels 'civilians' and 'combatants', see, for example, Coady, *Morality and Political Violence*, 110–16.

[8] J. Feinberg, 'Voluntary Euthanasia and the Inalienable Right to Life', *Philosophy & Public Affairs* 7 (1978): 93–123, at 102.

breaching the principle of non-combatant immunity which claim that we do not have any obligation of justice to foreigners. Instead, I shall first reject the view that patriotic partiality alone provides W with a justification for so acting. I shall then offer a heavily qualified argument in favour of relaxing the principle of non-combatant immunity.

## 7.2.1 The patriotic partiality argument

As we saw in Section 1.3, sufficientist cosmopolitanism is compatible with some degree of patriotic preference for fellow citizens: in particular, individuals, *qua* group members, may allocate amongst themselves the benefits which result from their mutual cooperation once they have met their obligations of justice towards foreigners. In addition, one might think that patriotic partiality permits them to act in such a way as to protect their community from total destruction *qua* community, so that when the very survival of a political community is under threat from some other community, the former may deliberately target non-combatants within the latter. The reason, in turn, why one might think that their justification is one of justice is that in protecting their community from destruction they are protecting their own and their fellow members' rights—in particular, their collective right to associate with one another, as well as their individual rights not to be tortured, killed, raped, and so on—all those rights which are likely to be violated by this particular kind of enemy (an enemy, in other words, who threatens their community's very survival *qua* community). One might also think, finally, that the justification is all the stronger when it applies to W's leaders, since, *qua* leaders, they have special duties to protect their compatriots from wrongful harm.

Note that the argument might be thought to justify not merely terror bombing, but also the act of deliberately killing non-combatants as a means to deter others from joining in the war. Some philosophers endorse that view. By way of example, Michael Walzer, whose discussion of the supreme emergency exemption from the principle of non-combatant immunity has generated considerable controversy, argues that *if* deliberately bombing German cities had indeed been the only way to defeat Nazism, then Britain would have been justified in so acting. In a similar line, Saul Smilansky—no apologist of terrorism in general—concedes that the principle of non-combatant immunity may be breached for the sake of stopping a genocide.[9] Suppose, thus, that

---

[9] See Walzer, *Just and Unjust Wars*, ch. 16; S. Smilansky, 'Terrorism, Justification, and Illusion', *Ethics* 114 (2004): 790–805; G. Øverland, 'Killing Civilians', *European Journal of Philosophy* 13 (2005): 345–63, and 'Contractual Killing', *Ethics* 115 (2005): 692–720. For a limited justification of

the Rwandan Patriotic Front had been in a position to save the lives of close to 1 million (innocent) mostly Tutsis—a just cause if there is one—by deliberately killing 500 innocent Hutus—say, the young children of Hutu extremists. On Walzer's and Smilansky's view, even if those 500 children had not lost their right not to be killed, the RPF may well have had a justification for deliberating infringing it.

To be fair, Walzer does not characterize the deliberate killing of non-combatants as justified: rather, he presents it as a case of dirty hands, where leaders acting on our behalf have to commit a moral wrongdoing in order to avert a much greater disaster.[10] Moreover, both Walzer and Smilansky claim that one may not deliberately kill non-combatants if one's predicament cannot plausibly be regarded as a supreme emergency: some causes, however just they might be, are not weighty enough to permit such killings. I shall offer some considerations in support of their view in Section 7.2.2. Meanwhile, however, I do not think that patriotic partiality alone can do the required work. In particular, I do not think that appealing to leaders' obligations to their people will succeed—for the same reasons I adduced in Section 2.4 when dealing with a similar argument in support of the infliction of collateral damage on enemy non-combatants. For a start, this putative move in defence of relaxing the principle of non-combatant immunity can apply only to actors who have the authority to act on behalf of their community: it cannot support combatants$_W$' targeting of non-combatants$_P$ in those cases where they act of their own initiative in the absence of an organized (and authorized) resistance to P's war. By implication, then, it cannot support deliberate targeting in civil wars fought by unauthorized actors. Furthermore, and more damningly so from a cosmopolitan perspective, framing the issue as specific to leaders will not do, in so far as the rights and duties of a government stem from its citizens' rights and duties. If W's citizens are not permitted to target non-combatants$_P$, then neither are their leaders: that they may have authorized the latter to do so on their behalf is neither here nor there. Finally, commitment to the doctrine of acts and omission sits uneasily with the claim that W has a justification for deliberately targeting non-combatants$_P$. For in so acting, W kills them,

direct targeting (and terrorism in general) see Steinhoff, *On the Ethics of War and Terrorism*, ch. 7. For a very interesting critique of self-defence-based justifications of the supreme emergency exemption, see D. Statman, 'Supreme Emergencies Revisited', *Ethics* 117 (2006): 58–79.

[10] Interestingly, proponents of that view generally do not claim that the leader is acting permissibly: rather, she is 'dirtying her hands' and is faced with a tragic choice between two wrongdoings, and must choose the lesser of the two. For classic accounts of the dirty hands problem, see, for example, M. Walzer, 'Political Action: The Problem of Dirty Hands', *Philosophy & Public Affairs* 2 (1973): 160–80, and Shue, 'Torture'. For a discussion of supreme emergency and the tragic choices faced by leaders, see Orend, *The Morality of War*, 148ff.

whereas in desisting they would 'merely' allow their compatriots to die. If killing is worse than letting die, other things broadly equal, one would have to show why patriotic partiality can tilt the balance in favour of killing—and in this case, of deliberate killing. In Section 2.4 I argued that combatants may (sometimes) unintentionally though foreseeably kill innocent non-combatants who belong to the enemy, and in so doing confer priority on the lives and interests of their compatriots, to the extent that their doing so is a necessary means to protect the rights (to political sovereignty and territorial integrity) which they jointly hold with the latter. Deliberate killing is another matter altogether. Consider the following variant of a one-to-one case which we examined earlier. Carl throws an incendiary bomb on a house which André and Bernard jointly own and currently occupy—with a view to forcing them to relinquish their joint rights over it to him. Suppose now that the only way in which André can defend their lives and property is by deliberately killing bystander Werner. Whereas killing Werner unintentionally might perhaps have been permissible, killing him deliberately clearly is not. It is a fixed point in our moral thinking, I take it, that an agent may not deliberately kill another morally and causally innocent person as a means to defend his rights or, indeed, the rights which he holds jointly with another person. If the deliberate killing of bystanders is not permissible in one-to-one, or one-to-two, cases, then arguments in support of such an act are likely to appeal to the importance and relevance of numbers of lives saved versus numbers of lives destroyed. I now turn to this issue.

### 7.2.2 The argument from numbers

All human beings, wherever they are, have fundamental human rights such as the right not to be killed unwarrantedly, the right not to be tortured, and the right not to suffer death by starvation—which act as constraints on other parties' conduct. The question is whether we may relax such constraints by targeting innocent non-combatants as a means successfully to win our just war. The absolutist claim that we may never do so is often criticized for failing to account for the intuition that we should, and so may, minimize the occurrences of those acts which deontological morality condemns as wrong—in the case at hand, human rights violations.[11] I believe that there is something

---

[11] Caney, *Justice Beyond Borders*, p. 210ff. See also R. Young, 'Political Terrorism as a Weapon of the Politically Powerless', in I. Primoratz (ed.), *Terrorism: The Philosophical Issues* (Basingstoke: Palgrave, 2004). Sen's rights-based consequentialism is best set out in A. K. Sen, 'Rights and Agency', in S. Scheffler (ed.), *Consequentialism and Its Critics* (Oxford: Oxford University Press, 1988). See also T. Scanlon, 'Rights, Goals, and Fairness', *Erkenntnis* 11 (1977): 81–95, and P. Pettit,

to be said for that intuition. I shall presently not so much offer a direct defence of it as draw attention to the fact that rejecting it comes at the very high cost of condemning all wars as unjust. Note for now that the intuition is only contingently related to considerations pertaining to communal member-ship.[12] Of course, it is likely that W will have a greater chance to win their war by killing $x$ number of non-combatants$_P$ than the same number of non-combatants$_W$, since P's regime is more likely to sue for peace if its own members are killed. Strictly speaking, however, the argument from numbers, when combined with cosmopolitan constraints on patriotic partiality, sup-ports the claim that W may kill $x$ number of their *own* non-combatants if that is the only way it can win its war against P and, in so doing, ensure that more individuals enjoy fundamental rights than would do were P successful. Suppose, for example, that W are waging a just war of self-defence against P. W's leaders have incontrovertible evidence that some of W's members are collaborating with P's forces, and that more such individuals might be tempted to follow the same path, with disastrous consequences for W's ability to win their (just) war. Suppose further that W get hold of those individuals and decide (without seeking proof) to make an example of them by killing them in public, so as to deter as-yet innocent non-combatants from siding with P. In so acting, W's regime would deliberately kill a small number of its own, formally innocent members as a means to secure the rights of a greater number of its own people. Or suppose (in a slight modification of the example) that W are waging a war of humanitarian intervention against P, that their leaders believe that some of their own members are supporting P's genocidal regime, and that a policy of reprisals against those individuals would have the desired effect of weakening that regime. However wrongful W's particular act might be, cosmopolitan justice cannot condemn it on the grounds that W's regime chose to kill the 'wrong' people.

That said, if the foregoing defence of direct targeting is to comport with the central tenets of sufficientist cosmopolitan justice, it must show that the following two-pronged view is internally coherent: (a) W do not have a justification for targeting non-combatants$_P$, *simply* because the latter belong to political community P (as we saw in Section 7.2.1); (b) W do have a justification for targeting a certain number of non-combatants (who happen to belong to P) if they thereby save the life of a greater number of other

'The Consequentialist Can Recognise Rights', *The Philosophical Quarterly* 38 (1988): 42–55. For other criticisms of absolutist prohibitions on deliberate targeting, see Kamm, 'Failures of Just War Theory: Terror, Harm, and Justice'.

[12] As Walzer himself stresses. See Walzer, *Just and Unjust Wars*, 260.

individuals (who happen to be fellow members.) In affirming (b), however, the cosmopolitan confers considerable weight on membership in a particular group—to wit, the larger, or smaller, group—since individuals' prospects for survival depend on which of those two groups they belong to. She must thus show why group-size membership is not a morally arbitrary basis for deciding who gets to live or die.

Here is one argument which some cosmopolitans might find appealing—though as I shall presently suggest, it does not in fact succeed. Political membership—or, for that matter, gender, skin colour, sexual orientation, and so on—are characteristics which though unchosen nevertheless serve to identify their bearers as the persons they are. Group-size membership, on the other hand, does not. In saying 'we will give her food because she is British, just like us', we confer on this special feature, Britishness, a moral significance in relation to the distribution of food which it cannot possibly have. By contrast, group-size membership does have significance for resource distribution, as when we are faced with a choice between giving a life-saving resource to members of a group of five and giving such a resource to members of a different (and non-overlapping) group of ten. In such cases, it does not seem to wrong those who are in the smaller group, as individuals, to give the drug to the ten.[13] Let us posit, thus, that we are under a *prima facie* duty to give equal amounts of life-saving resources to those in equal need, and that under conditions of scarcity, where we will not be able to save everyone, we have to get as close as we can to bringing about equality. Let us further accept (as per Section 1.2.1) that we are under a duty to help those in need, and that not giving the life-saving resource to anyone is therefore not an option. Giving the resource to the five is a better approximation of the egalitarian ideal than giving it to the one, because it is a step closer to a world where everyone has equal shares of life-saving resources.[14] This is why membership in groups of

---

[13] *Pace* J. Taurek, 'Should the Numbers Count?', *Philosophy & Public Affairs* 6 (1977): 293–316. Taurek's article has generated a voluminous literature. See, *inter alia*, F. M. Kamm, *Morality, Mortality*, vol. 1 (Oxford: Oxford University Press, 1993), ch. 6, and *Intricate Ethics: Rights, Responsibilities, and Permissible Harm* (Oxford: Oxford University Press, 2007); T. Scanlon, *What We Owe to Each Other* (Cambridge, MA: Harvard University Press, 1998), ch. 6; M. Otsuka, 'Skepticism about Saving the Greater Number', *Philosophy & Public Affairs* 32 (2004): 413–26; J. T. Sanders, 'Why the Numbers Should Sometimes Count', *Philosophy & Public Affairs* 17 (1988): 3–14.

[14] Here I borrow from N.-H. Hsieh, A. Struder, and D. Wasserman, 'The Numbers Problem', *Philosophy & Public Affairs* 34 (2006): 353–72. One might wonder why a sufficientist cosmopolitan ought to find egalitarian considerations such as these appealing. For if justice requires that each have opportunities for a minimally decent life, why not say that saving the five as opposed to the one is preferable as the course of action which enables more people to have such prospects? Equality, on that view, need not come into play (or so an anonymous referee for Oxford University Press suggested to me). However, as I noted in Section 1.2.1, 'sufficientists claim that individuals should have *equal*

different size is not an arbitrary basis for choosing between lives in those cases in so far as it yields a better approximation of the ideal of saving all. With those points in hand we are in a position to construct an argument for the deliberate targeting of non-combatants$_P$ along these lines: on the assumption that we are under a duty to all to respect and promote their right not to die unwarrantedly, and given that we cannot fulfil our duty to all, we must, and so may, fulfil it to as many individuals as we can, thus advancing one step closer to a world in which all individuals enjoy equal rights not to die unwarrantedly, even though this can only be brought about by deliberately killing a (smaller) number of non-combatants.[15]

I shall, in a moment, qualify the claim that we must so act. Meanwhile, the defence thus offered of relaxing the principle of non-combatant immunity, though appealing, is nevertheless seriously problematic, because the choice between giving to one and giving to five is fundamentally different from the choice (at issue here) between deliberately killing one in order to save five and desisting from killing one as a result of which five will die. In overlooking that distinction, one seemingly condones acts of killing in cases where one ought to reject them. Suppose that a victim V and her son are under a lethal threat at the hands of attacker A, and that the only way she can save both her son's life and her own is by deliberately killing bystander B. To reiterate, it is a fixed point of our moral thinking that V may not kill B, however high the cost, to her, of desisting (in that instance, her life and that of her son[16]). Yet if approximating equality justifies the deliberate killing of *n* numbers of

chances of having enough, and thus ground their principles of justice in a principle of fundamental equality whereby individuals have equal moral worth and should treat one another with equal concern and respect.' (20) The question at issue here is whether group-size membership is an arbitrary reason for deliberately depriving someone of the chance to survive and, thereby, of the chance to have a minimally decent life. (Taurek and others might insist that we ought to flip a coin, on purely egalitarian grounds. But my concern is with plausible egalitarian arguments in favour of saving the greatest number.)

[15] For a similar and much discussed argument, see V. Held, 'Terrorism, Rights, and Political Goals', in R. G. Frey and C. W. Morris (ed.), *Violence, Terrorism, and Justice* (Cambridge: Cambridge University Press, 1991), at pp. 80–1. For criticisms of her argument, see, for example, I. Primoratz, 'The Morality of Terrorism', *Journal of Applied Philosophy* 14 (1997): 221–33, and U. Steinhoff, 'How can Terrorism be Justified?', in I. Primoratz (ed.), *Terrorism: The Philosophical Issues* (Basingstoke: Palgrave, 2004).

[16] Perhaps some will counter that one may kill the innocent in defence of one's son. If so, may one kill a prospective heart-donor in order to save one's son who will certainly die unless he receives a heart within a week? I very much doubt it. The classic case is, of course, the 'Man on the Bridge' variant of the Trolley problem, whereby the only way to rescue some people from dying in a collision with a runaway train is to throw some other person onto the track, thereby stopping the train. I am not convinced that one may so act in order to save five people who would die otherwise; but I am reasonably convinced that one may so act in order to save 5 million people. See, for example, Foot, 'The Problem of Abortion and the Doctrine of the Double Effect'; Thomson, 'Killing, Letting Die and the Trolley Problem', and 'Turning the Trolley', *Philosophy & Public Affairs* 36 (2008):

non-combatants$_P$ for the sake of saving the lives of $n + x$ members of W, then, pending further argument to the contrary, it must also justify the deliberate killing of one bystander for the sake of saving two lives—which killing, we have just seen, is not permissible.[17]

An obvious move in favour of relaxing the principle of non-combatant immunity whilst maintaining that V may not kill B appeals to thresholds. On threshold-based views, whether numbers matter in the present context depends on the absolute size of W's group, the absolute size of the group of non-combatants$_P$ whose targeting is at issue, and the relative sizes of those two groups. One might say, therefore, that deliberately killing one non-combatant$_P$ to save fifteen members of W is not justified; that deliberately killing one non-combatant$_P$ to save 1.5 million members of W is justified; but that deliberately killing 1 million non-combatants$_P$ to save 1.5 million members of W is not justified. In a similar vein, and as we saw in Section 7.2.1, those who advocate relaxing the principle of non-combatant immunity usually give as paradigmatic examples of a 'supreme emergency' genocide, mass starvation, mass enslavement, and so on—situations, in other words, where the fundamental human rights of very large numbers of people are under threat.

Yet although appeals to large-number thresholds appear intuitively plausible in general, they do not offer an easy path for sufficientist cosmopolitanism; and it pays to see why. For the notion of a threshold conflicts with the plausible egalitarian requirement (which is at the heart of cosmopolitan justice) that the life of one individual should count for no more and no less than the life of any other individual. That requirement yields what one may call the number neutrality thesis, whereby, other things equal, the moral significance of the difference between $n$ versus $n+1$ individuals suffering a given harm or being saved from a given harm is the same for any whole number $n$, including the number 0.[18] As applied to the moral significance of individuals suffering a given harm (here, death) for the sake of saving others from a similar harm, NNT holds that the moral significance of the difference between killing 1 and killing 2 for the sake of saving, for example, 10,000, is

359–74; F. M. Kamm, 'The Trolley Problem', in *Morality, Mortality* (Oxford: Oxford University Press: 1996).

[17] A utilitarian cosmopolitan will have few qualms about that. See, for example, J. Harris, 'The Survival Lottery', *Journal of Philosophy* 50 (1975): 81–7. For arguments to the effect that the deliberate targeting of non-combatants is incompatible with treating agents as ends in themselves, see, for example, Nagel, 'War and Massacre', and Quinn, 'Actions, Intentions, and Consequences: The Doctrine of Double Effect'.

[18] There are different kinds of number neutrality. Here I discuss only one. I am grateful to Krister Bykvist, Mike Otsuka, and Nic Southwood for helpful discussions of the points made in the next paragraphs.

the same as the moral significance of the difference between killing 111 and killing 112 for the sake of saving those 10,000. As applied to the moral significance of individuals being saved from death at the cost of killing some others, NNT holds that the moral significance of the difference between saving 9,998 and saving 9,999 by killing 1 is the same as the moral significance of the difference between saving 253 and saving 254 by killing 1.

But now consider the appeal to thresholds. As applied to how many people we may deliberately kill for the sake of saving (a constant number of) the many more, the threshold thesis (TT) says: 'Let K stand for the number of people who will be killed for the sake of a constant number of people, and T stand for the permissibility threshold. We may so act only if K$\leq$T.' As applied to how many people we may save from death by deliberately killing (a constant number of) the few, TT says: 'Let S stand for the number of people we will save at the cost of a given number of lives, and T stand for the permissibility threshold. We may so act only if S $\geq$T.' To give a rough example, a typical proponent of TT might thus say that it is not permissible deliberately to kill 5,000 in order to save 10,000, but that it is permissible deliberately to kill 100 (the threshold) or fewer, in order to save 10,000. She might also say that it is not permissible deliberately to kill 1 in order to save 2, but that it is permissible deliberately to kill 1 in order to save 5,000 (the threshold) or more.

Proponents of TT face the familiar challenge of being able non-arbitrarily to identify a threshold at and below which we may deliberately harm the few to save (a constant number of) the many, and a threshold at and above which we may save the many at the cost of deliberately killing (a constant number of) the few. Once the number neutrality thesis is brought into view, the challenge appears all the more formidable. For according to NNT, the moral significance of the difference between $n$ versus $n+1$ individuals suffering a given harm or being saved from a given harm is the same for any whole number $n$. It follows, then, that the moral significance of the difference between deliberately killing 101 and deliberately killing 102 for the sake of saving 10,000 is the same as the moral significance of the difference between deliberately killing 100 and deliberately killing 101 to that very same end. But this contradicts the threshold thesis, which (on the assumption that the threshold stands at 100) holds that the move from deliberately killing 101 to deliberately killing 100 renders the act permissible, whereas the move from killing 102 to killing 101 has no such morally transformative effect. By parity of reasoning, NNT holds that the moral significance of the difference between deliberately killing 1 for the sake of saving 4,998 versus deliberately killing 1 for the sake of saving 4,999 is the same as the moral significance of the difference between deliberately killing 1 for the sake of saving 4,999 versus deliberately killing

1 for the sake of saving 5,000. But this contradicts the threshold thesis (on the assumption that, in this case, T stands at 5,000) according to which the move from killing 1 to save 4,999 to killing 1 for the sake of saving 5,000 makes the act permissible—unlike the move from killing 1 to save 4,998 to killing 1 to save 4,999.

It seems, therefore, that we cannot endorse both the number neutrality and the threshold theses—or rather, and at the very least, that commitment to the latter implies rejecting the strongest variant of the former, where it applies to any number $n$, in favour of a weaker variant, where it applies to any number $n$ *except* when $n$ = T−1, T, and T+1. I concede that rejecting strong number neutrality for the sake of the weaker variant might somewhat *ad hoc*, for if lives really are to count equally relative to one another (some might object), then they ought not to count for less, or more, depending on how close they are to the threshold. However, the alternative is to reject thresholds altogether. The costs of that particular move are very high indeed, for the number neutrality thesis (in either variant) applies not merely to the deliberate killing of a few to save the many: it also applies to their foreseen and unintended killing. If lives truly are to count equally relative to one another, then there is no reason to affirm on the one hand that the moral significance of the difference between deliberately killing 101 versus killing 102 is the same as the moral significance of the difference between deliberately killing 100 and killing 101, and on the other hand to *deny* that the moral significance of the difference between unintentionally killing 101 versus unintentionally killing 102 is the same as the moral significance of the difference between unintentionally killing 100 and unintentionally killing 101. And yet thresholds play a crucial role in justifications for foreseen and unintended killings. To claim (as I did in Sections 2.4 and 5.5.2) that agents may confer greater weight on their lives than on the lives of the innocent at the bar of partiality and so may unintentionally cause the latter to die, *subject to proportionality considerations*, is to say that there is a threshold below which we may unintentionally harm the few to save (a constant number of) the many, and a threshold above which we may save the many at the cost of unintentionally killing (a constant number of) the few. On the reasonable assumption that no war can be fought without causing people to die, to reject appeals to thresholds for the sake of preserving strong number neutrality is to embrace absolutist pacifism. The costs of endorsing that view are unacceptably burdensome, since it would commit us to rejecting the claim that we may, at least sometimes, confer greater weight on our lives than on the lives of the innocent.

A non-pacifist defender of strong number neutrality might be tempted to block the foregoing move by restricting the scope of number neutrality to the deliberate killing of the innocent and by relaxing it in the case of unintentional killing. Such restriction strikes me as more damningly arbitrary than the adoption of weak number neutrality. For although killing foreseeably though unintentionally is not as bad as killing deliberately, other things roughly equal, this moral difference between those modes of killing does not seem so profound as to yield the conclusion that deliberately killing 1 to save 1 billion is impermissible, whilst foreseeably but unintentionally killing 10,000 to save 1 billion is permissible. Rather, it seems more plausible to accept thresholds (and reject strong number neutrality) in both cases, and to insist on differential thresholds. On the differential threshold view, the threshold below which one may deliberately kill the few to save (a constant number of) the many is lower than the threshold below which one may unintentionally kill the few to save (a constant number of) the many; conversely, the threshold above which one may save the many at the cost of deliberately killing (a constant number of) the few should be higher than the threshold above which one may save the many at the cost of unintentionally killing (a constant number of) the few.

When, then, is it permissible deliberately to target non-combatants? In prosecution of a just cause, I submit, and only if the ongoing rights violations which the act of killing seeks to prevent constitute a far worse evil than deliberate targeting itself. By evil, I do not mean morally bad *simpliciter*, but rather, the qualitatively different kind of wrongness at play when, without either justification or excuse, large numbers of individuals are killed or enslaved—in other words, lose all their rights. The act of killing an innocent person—which infringes his right not to be killed and thereby extinguishes all his other rights—cannot be justified unless as a way to avert the greater evil of far greater numbers of individuals suffering a similar loss, or a violation, of all rights. By implication, violations of the right to collective self-determination alone do not justify deliberately targeting innocent non-combatants. To return, then, to the argument from patriotic partiality which I presented in Section 7.2.1, we must distinguish between a war in which W, as a political community, is under threat of destruction *qua* such community in the sense that P would take full control of its institutions if successful, and a war in which W is under threat of destruction *qua* community via a genocide (be it carried out by acts of killing or mass starvation) or the mass enslavement of its individual members. In the latter case, but not in the former, there is some justification, on the part of W's leaders, for ordering the deliberate targeting of (considerably fewer) innocent non-combatants as the only way to stave off the threat.

That said, whilst the view that the evil of genocide warrants deliberate targeting might seem utterly plausible, the claim that mass enslavement does as well warrants explaining. In Orlando Patterson's phrase, enslavement is a form of social death which all too often leads to its victims' actual physical death: it is a condition in which individuals are alienated from all and any relationships which would give them a distinct identity other than of a tool for their masters' ends, where such alienation takes the form of a complete denial of all of their moral rights over and *vis-à-vis* their body, their person and their kin, and is enforced by the constant threat of extreme coercion. Whilst the focus of Patterson's magisterial study is slavery as an essentially private, individualized relationship of domination between individual slaves and individual masters, enslavement can also take a public form, as when a whole people is collectively enslaved without its (informed) consent by its foreign conqueror (which arrogates property and sovereignty rights over its individual members) or, indeed, by a domestic tyrant. It is only to avoid that evil— whether it consists in the forcible transformation of free individuals to slaves *à la antebellum* American South, or in the forcible imposition of totalitarianism—in addition to the prevention or thwarting of a genocide—that the deliberate targeting of non-combatants is permissible.[19]

The foregoing claim admittedly has a troublesome implication: namely, that deliberate targeting is permitted if a sizeable share of the population would otherwise be under threat of a genocide or mass enslavement, but not if minority groups are. Suppose, counterfactually, that the deliberate targeting of innocent civilian German populations was a necessary step towards avoiding Britain's defeat by Germany during World War II. Suppose further that Britain's defeat would not have led to the genocide or mass enslavement of the British people (a plausible assumption to make, in fact, judging by the fate of Western Europe, including the Channel Islands, under German occupation[20]). Nor would it have led to the deaths of millions more innocent people. It would, however, have led to the mass killing of the relatively small (in

---

[19] See O. Patterson, *Slavery and Social Death: A Comparative Study* (Cambridge, MA: Harvard University Press, 1982), esp. ch. 2. Patterson's conception of social death, focusing as it does on processes of exclusions of slaves from the community, is slightly different from the way in which I use the label here. On genocide and mass enslavement as two processes the halting of which warrants deliberate targeting, see, for example, Smilansky, 'Terrorism, Justification, and Illusion'. I am assuming here that one cannot deliberately kill an innocent person for the sake of averting minor harms to many more others. I will not defend that assumption here, though I accept, of course, that some deontologists as well as consequentialists might be tempted to reject it. For explorations of this question, see, in addition to the works mentioned in footnote 13, M. Otsuka, 'Saving Lives and the Claims of Individuals', *Philosophy & Public Affairs* 34 (2006): 109–35, and A. Norcross, 'Comparing Harms: Headaches and Human Lives', *Philosophy & Public Affairs* 26 (1997): 135–67.

[20] For a brilliant and recent account of the occupation of France, see R. Gildea, *Marianne in Chains: Daily Life in the Heart of France during the German Occupation* (New York: Picador, 2002). For the occupation of the Channel Islands, see M. Bunting, *The Model Occupation: The Channel Islands under German Rule*, 2nd edn. (London: Pimlico, 2004).

relative terms) minorities of Jews, gypsies, and homosexuals. On my account, the deliberate targeting of innocent civilians in Germany by Britain would not have been permissible under those circumstances, though it would have been (*prima facie*) permissible had a majority of people been under such threats. This, I concede, is not a palatable view to defend—any more than it is palatable to say that we may, or indeed must, desist from saving an agent who happens not to be grouped with anyone and whom we would save if he happened to be part of a sufficiently large group. It seems to me, however, to be an unavoidable consequence of taking the principle of non-combatant immunity as seriously as we ought to do. Put differently, if the principle is to retain any bite at all, and if we also accept that, other things roughly equal, killing is morally worse than letting die, we have no choice but to accept that in many cases we must allow an evil to happen (here, the extermination or enslavement of a small minority), as opposed to bringing about evil ourselves (here, the deliberate killing of large numbers of innocent people.)

To recapitulate, I have argued that although appeals to number-based thresholds are problematic inasmuch as they contain strong elements of arbitrariness, rejecting such considerations in favour of strict neutrality between numbers of lives saved and sacrificed leads to absolutist pacifism. Since I reject the latter position at the outset, I conclude that one may relax the principle of non-combatant immunity under the very strict conditions described here. In further support of this conclusion, I also noted that one may—indeed, must—bring about a world in which all individuals enjoy equal rights not to die unwarrantedly and not to be enslaved. But now a qualification is in order. In Section 2.4 I argued that agents are permitted to kill a justified Tactical Bomber in self-defence, whilst in Section 5.5.2 I argued that victims of a tyrannical regime against which an intervention is carried out have the permission to kill fellow victims unintentionally if the latter are themselves posing a lethal threat to them. In both cases I appealed to an agent-relative prerogative not to sacrifice themselves for the sake of others. The point also holds in the case of deliberate targeting: if one is not under a duty to allow oneself to be killed unintentionally for the sake of third parties, and if deliberate killing is *prima facie* morally worse than unintentional though foreseen killing, and thus constitutes a worse infringement of the victim's right not to be killed, then *a fortiori* the latter is not under a duty to allow herself to be killed as a means only. In this case the stakes are very high indeed, since they consist (*ex hypothesi*) in averting a very grave evil. To some, this might well constitute a very powerful reason to demand such a sacrifice. On that view, *if* (contrary to what I argued above) it was permissible for the British air force deliberately to target innocent German civilians in 1940 as the *only way* to forestall a land invasion of Britain, then the latter would have acted impermissibly by shooting down British bombers, even if that had been the *only way* in which they could save their lives. However, if it is true that agents can be expected to die in virtue of the more general imperative of avoiding a much greater evil, then it would seem that they can be expected to remain in the line of fire, at the cost of their lives, if they could thereby achieve similar ends—for example, by standing as shields in front of combatants$_W$ in order to protect the latter from combatants$_P$, or by taking an active part in seeking to overthrow their own regime irrespective of the dangers involved. And yet I do not know of anyone who would argue that ordinary German or Soviet citizens were under a moral duty to die for the sake of resisting Hitler or Stalin. To be sure, there is a difference between preserving one's life by not participating in a movement of resistance, and preserving it by killing a justified attacker. However, we have already seen that killing a justified attacker in self-preservation is *prima facie* justified—in other words, that agents generally may not be expected to sacrifice their wrongfully threatened life for the sake of others. If that point is correct, and if it is also the case that innocent agents are not under a duty to die for the sake of averting a greater evil, then they may kill a justified attacker even though the latter is in the process of combating a great evil, if that is the only way to save their lives.

## 7.3 HUMAN SHIELDS

In this section I examine W's use of non-combatants as shields. Human shields are a depressingly familiar feature of contemporary wars. Here are some examples. In May 2002 the Israeli Defence Force invaded the Palestinian refugee camp of Jenin on the West Bank as part of its Operation Defensive Shield campaign. According to the Israeli authorities, intelligence suggested that the camp was used as a base by Palestinian terrorists to launch attacks on Israeli villages. During and after the battle, allegations were made by both parties, and documented by Human Rights Watch and Amnesty International, that Palestinian civilians had been used as shields—for example, by being forced to stand in front of soldiers while the latter shot at their enemy, or by being forced to remain in their houses while the latter were used as shooting bases. Similarly, testimonies from the conflict between the Sri Lankan authorities and separatist Tamil Tigers, ending in 2009, suggest that the latter also used civilians as shields. The Rwandan conflict provides yet another example of such tactics. According to a number of sources, Hutu militias, which had been defeated in the 1994 civil war, used refugee camps in

Zaire between 1994 and 1997 as bases for launching attacks into Rwanda—departing from the camps and returning after fighting, in the knowledge that their opponents would hesitate to pursue them precisely because of the risks which fighting within the camps would pose to refugees. During the US-led Operation Iraqi Freedom of 2003, the then-Iraqi regime and military authorities were widely reported to have used civilians as shields—for example, by ordering their soldiers to drive next to civilian cars as soon as coalition helicopters appeared. Finally, during the US, British, and French and air forces' bombing campaign against Colonel Gadhafi's regime in the spring and summer of 2011, coalition forces expressed worries that Gadhafi had deliberately moved some of his troops into densely populated areas. Those practices are prohibited by the laws of war—most notably by Article 51(7) of the 1977 Protocol I Additional to the 1949 Geneva Conventions.[21] They also elicit near-universal moral condemnation. Yet a cursory look at the contemporary literature on the use of human shields reveals that scholars focus on the legitimacy of targeting shields, and take for granted that using them is morally wrong.[22]

[21] See also Article 28 of the Fourth Geneva Convention, and a 2005 decision by the Israeli Supreme Court (HCJ 3799/02) (2005). For a good summary of the legal position, see, for example, R. Lyall, 'Voluntary Human Shields, Direct Participation In Hostilities And The International Humanitarian Law Obligations Of States', *Melbourne Journal of International Law* 9 (2008): 1–21. Empirical sources for the examples adduced in this opening paragraph are the following: Amnesty International, Gaza: military tactics on both sides endangering civilians (2009) (accessed 10 September 2009); Human Rights Watch, Israel/Occupied Territories: Jenin War Crimes Investigation Needed (2002) (accessed 10 September 2009); Human Rights Watch, Israel: Decision to Stop Use of 'Human Shields' Welcomed (2002) (accessed 10 September 2009). A recent UN report into human rights abuse by both Israel, Hamas, and the Palestinian Authority into the Occupied Territories reports similar incidents. See United Nations, Human Rights in Palestine and Other Occupied Territories: Report of the United Nations Fact Finding Mission on the Gaza Conflict (2009) (accessed 17 September 2009). Amnesty International, Sri Lanka: UN Security Council must demand immediate access and accountability (2009) (accessed 10 September 2009); C. Braeckman, 'Zaire at the end of a reign', *New Left Review* 222 (1997): 129–38; H. W. French, 'Zaire Government Is Arming Hutus, Making Human Shields of Refugees', *New York Times*, 19 February 1997. A similar tactic was apparently used by Vietcong fighters during the Vietnam War. For discussion, as part of a point on asymmetrical tactics, see Orend, *The Morality of War*, p. 89. For good examples of the difficulties posed to regular soldiers by insurgents who hide amongst civilian populations, see Kalyvas, *The Logic of Violence in Civil Wars*, ch. 4. See also M. N. Schmitt, 'Precision Attack and International Humanitarian Law', *International Review of the Red Cross* 87 (2005): 445–66, at 458 (and footnote 45).

[22] See, for example, D. H. Fischer, 'Human Shields, Homicides, and House Fires: How a Domestic Law Analogy Can Guide International Law Regarding Human Shield Tactics in Armed Conflict', *American University Law Review* (2008): 479–522; E. Gross, 'Use of Civilians as Human Shields: What Legal and Moral Restrictions Pertain to a War Waged by a Democratic State against Terrorism', *Emory International Law Journal* 16 (2002): 445–524; T. J. Koontz, 'Non-Combatant Immunity in Walzer's *Just and Unjust Wars*', *Ethics & International Affairs* 11 (1997): 55–82; Øverland, 'Killing Civilians'; M. Skerker, 'Just War Criteria and the New Face of War: Human Shields, Manufactured Martyrs, and Little Boys with Stones', *Journal of Military Ethics* 3 (2004): 27–39; N. J. Wheeler, 'Dying for "Enduring Freedom": Accepting Responsibility for Civilian

My aim in this section is to provide a qualified defence of the use of shields. The examples I have just given suggest that there are broadly three ways in which combatants use non-combatants as shields: by forcibly positioning the latter in the line of fire, by positioning themselves close to individual non-combatants when the enemy approaches, or (most commonly) by hiding amongst civilian populations. Combatants resort to those tactics for two reasons. Either they offer shields as targets for bullets which were initially aimed at them, or they use them as deterrent, relying on the fact that the enemy will want to (be seen to) respect the principle of non-combatant immunity and will desist from shooting, and thus depriving itself of a number of strategic options. Both cases raise the issue of the grounds upon which, if any, combatants may shift harm away from them by using non-combatants in certain ways. In both cases, moreover, the question is not, in the main, whether combatants may kill (whether deliberately or merely foreseeably) non-combatants as a means to minimize harm to themselves. Rather, the question is whether combatants may expose non-combatants to incurring harm (or risk thereof) at the hands of the enemy.[23] Those common features notwithstanding, shields-as-targets and shields-as-deterrents differ in one crucial respect. In shields-as-targets, combatants use the body of non-combatants physically to block an ongoing threat; in shields-as-deterrents, by contrast, they expose them to a risk of harm which, they hope, the enemy will not be willing to inflict, and they do so precisely for that reason. In this section I argue, controversially, that combatants$_w$ may sometimes use (unwilling) human shields, either as protection from ongoing fire or as a deterrent force, whether or not those non-combatants belong to their political community. I first outline and reject a basic objection against the use of shields, and then

Casualties in the War against Terrorism', *International Relations* 16 (2002): 205–25; J. T. Johnson, 'Maintaining the Protection of Non-Combatants', *Journal of Peace Research* 37 (2000): 421–48, at 436ff.

   [23] For a useful discussion of the advantages gained in those ways by the Taleban in Afghanistan over the US-led coalition in 2002 (and of similar issues raised by the NATO campaign in Kosovo), see, for example, B. Kashnikov, 'Target Approval Delays Cost Air Force Key Hits', *Journal of Military Ethics* 1 (2002): 125–8; O'Donovan, *The Just War Revisited*; T. Ricks, 'Target Approval Delays Cost Air Force Key Hits', *Journal of Military Ethics* 1 (2002): 109–13; M. Schmitt, '"Target Approval Delays Cost Air Force Key Hits": Law, Policy, Ethics and the Warfighter's Dilemma', *Journal of Military Ethics* 1 (2002): 113–25; T. Westhusing, '"Target Approval Delays Cost Air Force Key Hits": Targeting Terror: Killing Al Qaeda the Right Way', *Journal of Military Ethics* 1 (2002): 128–36. On a point of terminology, some might argue that using the word 'non-combatants' to refer to shields is inapposite, since those individuals, when used as shields, are in fact participants in hostilities (which non-combatants, by definition, are not). The question at issue in this section, however, is whether individuals who are not part of the hostilities can be turned into participants. For that reason I shall keep referring to them as non-combatants, unless they share contributory responsibility for the war (in which case I shall refer to them as 'civilians').

construct a qualified defence of that tactic. I shall not discuss the case of voluntary shields, as their consent is free and fully informed, and belligerents do not wrong them by using them.

Here is the basic objection. Suppose that someone, A, subjects another person, V, to an unjust lethal threat. Suppose further that a third party, S, is at the scene, and is neither related to V nor contractually bound to protect her. Suppose, finally, that S will die if he shields V from A. Surely S is not under a moral duty either to step or to remain in the line of fire. For to require of S that he should take either of those courses of action would be to treat him merely as a means to someone else's ends. That requirement, in turn, is entirely out of place in a morality based on the requirement that agents should respect one another as ends in themselves. Moreover, in the light of that requirement, V may not grab S and forcibly place him in front of her—any more than she may kill an innocent bystander as a means to defend herself. True, S dies at the hands of the attacker (if the latter persists in attempting to kill V), and not at the hands of V. But both attacker and victim treat S merely as means to their ends: the former displays utter indifference to her fate, and the latter uses her purely as an instrument to her survival. Both thus act wrongly towards her. To be sure, the fact that V 'merely' (forcibly) uses S as a shield whereas A kills him (in some cases) is relevant to judgements about their relative degrees of responsibility and culpability for S's death. Thus, if A is morally innocent (for example, deeply psychotic), one might conclude that V bears a greater degree of moral responsibility for S's death than him. Be that as it may, it remains the case that V does act wrongly when using S as a shield.[24]

If the foregoing points are sound, non-combatants, whether they belong to W or to P, seemingly are not under a duty to shield combatants$_W$ from combatants$_P$, which implies that combatants$_W$ seemingly do not have a right against them that they so act. By the same token, combatants$_W$ seemingly do not have a justification for forcing those non-combatants to stand in front of their tanks; nor, it seems, are they justified in choosing as a battlefield densely populated refugee camps and in preventing refugees from leaving those camps; nor, finally, are they justified in forcibly marching those non-combatants into close proximity to military objectives. For in so acting—the basic objection goes—they would treat those non-combatants as means only to their own (admittedly just) ends, which is impermissible. To be clear: sometimes just

---

[24] The argument I describe here relies on the oft-made claim that treating people *merely* as a means is especially wrong, and that the special wrongness of such treatment explains many of our intuitions about the wrongness of harming some as a means to save others. Though I reject the argument in so far as it applies to the use of shields, I endorse that oft-made claim. For recent dissent, see D. Parfit, *On What Matters* (Oxford: Oxford University Press, 2011), ch. 9.

combatants have no choice but to fight in densely populated areas—when, for example, their enemy takes the fight there. The point is not that they may not do so (unless their decision to fight results in vast numbers of deaths). Rather, the point is that they may not deliberately draw their (unjust) enemy into those areas. In other words, Palestinian fighters may not have much choice but to fight from the streets of Gaza; but they do have a choice as to where to station their missile launchers (the roof of a hospital versus a civilian-free slot.)[25]

The basic objection is too quick. For it rests on the general point that agents are not under an enforceable moral duty to die or suffer serious injury for the sake of others: that is why S is not under an enforceable duty to stand or remain in the line of fire between A and V. However, S's case might be thought to differ in one crucial respect from the case of human shields, at least when the latter belong to W. For in that case, non-combatants$_W$ are asked to incur high risks of harm, not for the sake of some strangers, but for the sake of prosecuting a war in the success of which they, as members of W, have a strong interest. And in some cases, it *is* appropriate to hold individuals under an enforceable moral duty to take part in a war of national self-defence. As I shall now show, the argument for conscription also applies to shields.

A standard (and, it seems to me, plausible) case for the duty to fight in a war of collective self-defence appeals to the moral prohibition on free-riding—a prohibition which rests on the so-called principle of fairness. Broadly put, the principle stipulates (*inter alia*) that agents are under a moral duty to contribute to the costs and burdens attendant on the joint production of non-excludable public goods—goods, in other words, such that they are necessarily enjoyed by all agents within the group whether or not those agents contribute to them—particularly if they themselves wish to continue to enjoy those goods in the long-term. An agent who willingly enjoys the benefit of a public and non-excludable good and who is in a position to contribute to its production but does not do so is guilty of the wrongdoing of free-riding.[26]

---

[25] I owe this example to Tamar Meisels.

[26] For formulations and defences of the principle of fairness, see, for example, Hart, 'Are There Any Natural Rights?', esp. p. 183; Rawls, *A Theory of Justice*, pp. 108–14; G. Klosko, *The Principle of Fairness and Political Obligation* (Lanham: Rowan and Littlefield, 1992); R. J. Arneson, 'The Principle of Fairness and Free-Rider Problems', *Ethics* 92 (1982): 616–33; R. Dagger, 'Membership, Fair Play, and Political Obligation', *Political Studies* 48 (2000): 104–17. For accounts of military conscription in the history of political thought, see, for example, M. Walzer, 'The Obligation to Die for the State', in *Obligations: Eessays on Ddisobedience, War, and Citizenship* (Cambridge, MA: 1970); A. Carter, 'Liberalism and the Obligation to Military Service', *Political Studies* 46 (1998): 68–82; I. Z. Baron, *Justifying the Obligation to Die: War, Ethics, and Political Obligation with Illustrations from Zionism* (Lanham, MD: Lexington Books, 2009). For a justification of conscription which circumscribes it to the protection of fundamental values such as liberty and

The principle of fairness has been criticized on a number of grounds, the most common of which is that it licences the imposition of contributory costs upon anyone who benefits from a collective venture, irrespective of her consenting to receiving such benefits and of the moral status of the venture.[27] Furthermore, as applied to the duty to fight, the principle cannot, *ex post*, justify holding under that duty individuals who die on the battlefield, since they will not benefit from the good of collective self-defence. Faced with the first objection, proponents of the principle have sought to qualify it in the following ways: the collective venture must be just, and the benefits it provides must be important enough that whether or not one consents to receiving them is irrelevant to the determination of one's obligations. In response to the second objection, and to reiterate a point made in Sections 2.4 and 5.5.2 when addressing harm-shifting, the principle ought to stipulate that agents must stand a higher chance than not of having prospects for a minimally decent life as a result of the collective venture. As applied to collective self-defence, the principle of fairness thus generates an obligation to contribute only if the war is just.[28]

If there is a moral duty to contribute to the war effort, as the case for wartime military conscription suggests, then there is a moral duty to contribute as a shield. Some might object to that claim on the grounds that acting as a shield, unlike giving time and money, is not properly regarded as a contribution. However, such a move should be rejected. Shields, it is true, do not need to do anything, at least not in those cases where combatants$_W$ move in their vicinity as the enemy approaches, or deliberately take the fight to where they live. All they need to do is stay where they are. Still, whether or not staying where one is can be properly seen as a contribution, it does not strike me as conceptually incoherent to hold that this is something which can be the subject of a duty. Suppose that three of us are trekking. Joe falls badly, and breaks his ankle. We agree that you will go in search of assistance and that I shall stay with Joe, because my mere presence calms him down and will make it more likely that the rescue helicopter will spot us. If I have enough to eat and drink, and if there is a very good chance that rescue services will find us

---

rights, see, for example, Rawls, *A Theory of Justice*, pp. 380–1; A. Gewirth, *Human Rights* (Chicago: University of Chicago Press, 1982), 251–3.

[27] See, for example, R. Nozick, *Anarchy, State, and Utopia* (New York: Basic Books, 1974) esp. 93; D. McDermott, 'Fair-Play Obligations', *Political Studies: Journal of the Political Studies Association UK* 52 (2004): 216–33; A. J. Simmons, 'The Principle of Fair Play', *Philosophy & Public Affairs* 8 (1979): 307–37.

[28] These points imply that holding individuals under *fighting* duties is permissible only if those conditions are met. This does not strike me as problematic.

within two hours, surely I am under a duty to stay. There is no reason on principle to rule out the possibility that such duty might be supported, in some cases, by arguments similar to those adduced in support of a duty to take part in collective self-defence.

Note that the conscription argument is less likely to work in the case of shields-as-targets than in the case of shields-as-deterrents. For as we saw earlier, agents are under an enforceable moral duty to contribute to national self-defence only if they stand a higher chance than not of having a minimally decent life after the war. If combatants$_P$ start shooting at combatants$_W$ and if the latter literally stand behind non-combatants$_W$ as a means to protect themselves, given that those non-combatants are (*ex hypothesi*) defenceless, it is unlikely that they would stand a higher chance of surviving and thus of having such a life than not. But if they are used as deterrents instead of targets, and if combatants$_P$ do indeed desist from shooting in order to avoid killing them, it may very well be that the risk of harm which they would incur would be lower than the risk of harm to which they would be exposed if they were armed combatants. And if, moreover, that risk turned out to be lower than the risk which combatants are under a duty to incur for the sake of national self-defence, then it would seem that non-combatants$_W$ are under a duty to serve as shields, from which it would seem to follow that combatants$_W$ may use them in that particular way.[29]

Suppose now that combatants$_W$ use enemy non-combatants as shields. Such tactics are more likely to succeed than the use of non-combatants$_W$, since combatants$_P$ might be more reluctant to kill their compatriots in prosecution of this war (though of course, from a cosmopolitan point of view, they ought to treat enemy non-combatants in the same way as their own). In that particular case, of course, arguments in favour of the duty to participate in a war of collective self-defence cannot support the claim that non-combatants$_P$ are under a moral duty to serve as shields.[30] But other

---

[29] Note that this putative argument in favour of the claim that W acts permissibly when using shields does not simply say that non-combatants are under a duty to act as shields; it also supposes that for them to refuse to do so—in violation of their duty—is not something which they have the right to do. That assumption is necessary to the success of the argument: the claim that non-combatants act wrongly is compatible with the claim that they have a right to do so, correlating into a duty on W's part not to use them in those ways.

[30] Unless, of course, W wage a war of humanitarian intervention against P's regime in defence of the latter's population. As we saw in Section 5.5.2, it might well be permissible, at least in some cases of HI, for the intervening party to impose on those non-combatants some of the costs attendant on rescuing them—in which case, using them as shields to protect combatants$_W$ might sometimes be permissible. Note, however, that in so far as, in that case, P's regime and army are indifferent to the plight of its own non-combatants (*ex hypothesi*), they are not likely to desist just because the latter are interposed in the line of fire. Whether W may use those non-combatants as shields is tantamount to

considerations, drawn from distributive justice, might well do so. One might say, in particular, that agents are under a duty of justice to provide assistance, in the form of personal services, to those in need, irrespective of borders. On that view, it would seem that non-combatants$_P$ may well be under a duty to act as shields for the sake of combatants$_W$ as well as of W's members generally, again subject to risks—and thus that combatants$_W$ act permissibly when so using them, particularly if the (acceptable) risks to which they are thereby exposed are lower than the (*ex hypothesi* acceptable) risks incurred by combatants themselves.

The view that agents are sometimes under a duty to contribute to a just war by shielding combatants from unjust harm will undoubtedly strike many as utterly repugnant. Here is an objection which they might be tempted to press—and which is particularly appealing in so far as it relies on intuitions which also support the principle of non-combatant immunity. Individuals who are made to fight are given the means to defend themselves from enemy attacks. Shields, by contrast, are not, whether they serve as conscripts on their own (W) side, or are enlisted by the latter against their own regime (P). Indeed, that is the main rationale for using them as deterrents, since their defencelessness, W hope or anticipate, will provide combatants$_P$ with a strong *dis*incentive to fire at combatants$_W$, thereby narrowing their range of options and, in turn, strengthening W's hand. Let us return to our one-to-one case, where A subjects V to a wrongful lethal threat of harm. Suppose that if S were to stand in the line of fire whilst unarmed, A would desist, as a result of which no one would be killed. Suppose further (to make the case closer to a war of self-defence) that S would benefit from the attack being stopped. Is S under a duty so to act? If he knows *for sure* that A will stop, perhaps. But in the event that he does not know for sure, the objection will press, then we could not hold him under a duty to step in unarmed—a duty, in other words, not merely to expose himself to the risk that A will not be deterred but, in addition, to deny himself the means to protect his own life should A carry on attacking. By that token, V may not deprive S of whatever weapon he might be carrying in order to maximize her chances that A will be deterred from fighting. And if those points are correct, then non-combatants are not under a moral duty to offer themselves as shields for combatants$_W$, whether or not they belong to the same community. As should be obvious, the claim is even stronger in the case where the rationale for so using them is not to deter combatants$_P$, but rather, to shift harm away from combatants$_W$.

---

asking whether they may expose them to a very high risk of dying for the sake of their own liberation—an issue which I addressed above.

Note that the defencelessness objection need not deny that the risks attendant on serving as a defenceless shield might be lower than the risks attendant on serving as an armed combatant. Nor need it deny that the latter risks (those incurred by armed combatants) are within the morally acceptable range. Nor, finally, need it deny that the risks to which shields are exposed might be lower than the risks of suffering lethal collateral damage which non-combatants (on either side) incur when caught in a bombing campaign. Its central point, rather, is this: the risks to which individuals are exposed in the course of a battle are based on the likelihood that the enemy will shoot at them, together with their chance of being able to thwart the attack. Shields, whose defencelessness is necessary to the realization of combatants$_W$' ends, are not in a position to protect themselves from enemy combatants. To hold non-combatants under a duty to offer themselves as shields without the means necessary to defend or preserve their lives should P decide to shoot at them violates the Kantian requirement that we ought not treat others as means only to our ends in a way that exposing *armed* combatants to a higher risk of severe harm does not (provided, of course, that the higher risk does not exceed a certain level: being given a weapon is not enough to justify one's being conscripted to fight). That claim is most obvious in shields-as-targets, but it also applies to shields-as-deterrents. In the former case it is hard to see how one could ever hold anyone under a moral duty to take a bullet for the sake of someone else without being able to defend oneself; in the latter case, it is equally hard to see how one could ever hold anyone under a moral duty to run the risk—however minute—of receiving a bullet without being able to either to kill their attacker or, more weakly still, effectively dodge the bullet.

As I suggested a couple of paragraphs ago, the objection appeals to the powerful thought that there is something deeply wrong about exposing defenceless and vulnerable people to harm. It goes further in suggesting that requiring those people to *remain* defenceless for the sake of others is particularly problematic from a moral point of view. And yet, the objection does not succeed. It holds, in effect, that requiring of defenceless non-combatants that they should incur a given risk of death *r* is itself morally wrong, whilst requiring of armed combatants that they should incur a higher risk of death is not morally wrong if the risk is within a certain range. But it is hard to see why defencelessness per se can be given such decisive moral weight irrespective of the overall level of risk to which non-combatants are exposed, whereas the overall level of risk to which combatants are exposed has decisive weight when deciding whether to hold them under a duty to fight. On the contrary, what matters is what chances agents would have to enjoy prospects for a minimally decent life given their personal circumstances. If one may require of agents that they fight and thus incur a given risk of having no such prospects, most clearly if they were to die—when that risk is calculated by taking into account the fact that they can block the threat—then one may require of agents that they serve as shields and thus incur a similar or lower risk—when that risk is calculated by taking into account the fact that they are defenceless, that the enemy might desist, and so on.

Non-combatants, therefore, are sometimes under a moral duty to act as shields. Suppose that this is wrong. Still, the claim that non-combatants are not under a duty to act as (defenceless) shields is compatible, strictly speaking, with the claim that combatants$_W$ have a justification for so using them—in particular, a justification which appeals to the importance of protecting the rights of W's members. For a start, two (possibly overlapping) categories of civilians$_P$ might well be liable to being used as shields by combatants$_W$—to wit, those non-combatants who share contributory responsibility for the wrongdoings which gave W their just cause for war, and those who share contributory responsibility for the fact that their community chose to wage war against W instead of putting a stop to those wrongdoings.[31] As I noted in Section 2.3.2, those civilians' contributions to an unjust war are sometimes such as to warrant the loss of their right not to be attacked. In some cases, of course, those contributions are not such as to justify the deliberate killing of their authors, but they might be such as to justify deliberately subjecting them to a lesser harm than death (such as, for example, the partial destruction of their houses during an intense bombing campaign), or to justify exposing them to a foreseeable though not intentional risk of death. That point (which we encountered at various junctures in this book) has obvious implications for the case at hand. Suppose that P could not prosecute its unjust war against W without the support of some civilians. Suppose further that their contribution to P's unjust war is not significant enough to warrant the loss of their right not to be killed deliberately. Still, they might be liable to incurring other costs—such as the costs attendant on running a risk of dying in the ensuing crossfire. Now return to our earlier, one-to-one case, where V uses S as a shield to protect herself from A at $t_2$, and suppose that S had culpably exposed V to A's attack at $t_1$ (for example, by luring her under false pretence to his house knowing that A was lying in wait). I believe that V may kill S in self-defence as a means to stop A (particularly if she would stand a better chance of surviving the attack than by attempting to kill A directly). And if that is correct, then

---

[31] In this paragraph I use the label 'civilian', as opposed to 'non-combatants', to denote the fact that those individuals are not wholly innocent either of the initial wrongdoings(s) or of P's subsequent unjust war.

V would not wrong S by using him as a shield, even if S is defenceless, at least if using him in that way is highly likely to cause A to desist (for example, because S is A's partner and A does not want to shoot through him, and so on). *Mutatis mutandis*, then, combatants$_W$ may use *those* civilians$_P$ as shields in prosecution of their just war.

Clearly, however, many non-combatants are not liable to being used in this way. By analogy, V may not forcibly grab S and position him in front of her as a means to stop A's bullets from hitting her if S's prospects of dying are higher than is morally acceptable to inflict on her—as is likely to be the case here. Nor, for that matter, may she deliberately draw A into S's house knowing that S is still there and prevent him from arming himself or from leaving the house in the hope that A will, as a result, stop shooting—again if S's prospects of dying are too high. Likewise, then, with the case of war.

Those two cases are relatively easy. Suppose, by contrast, that V draws A into S's house knowing that S is defenceless, but does not prevent S either from leaving or from procuring a gun. Is she acting impermissibly? Likewise, do combatants$_W$ act impermissibly when they deliberately withdraw, whilst pursued by the enemy, into refugee camps filled with defenceless women, children, and elderly people, even though they do not prevent refugees from leaving or do not make it impossible for them to obtain weapons? Not necessarily. Of course, there is a sense in which combatants$_W$ exploit the vulnerability of those individuals. Suppose that S simply cannot leave his house (for example, because he is disabled), or that his leaving the house is not a morally acceptable option (for example, because he would have either to leave his children behind or to take his children with him, thereby exposing them to further, much greater risk.) Or suppose that he simply does not have access to weapons. V, under those circumstances which are similar to those faced by hundreds of thousands of war refugees throughout the world, would be taking advantage of S's desperate situation. That seems wrong in some way, not simply in cases where S would not benefit from V's actions (as non-combatants$_P$ do not benefit from W's decision to use them as shields), but also in cases where S would stand to benefit (as non-combatants$_W$ might benefit from W's decision to use them as shields in a war of national self-defence). However—and this is crucial—I have argued at various junctures in this book (most notably in Section 2.4) that it is permissible unintentionally to kill innocent and defenceless non-combatants in the course of prosecuting a just cause, subject to meeting the requirements of necessity and proportionality. If that is correct, then it is hard to see how one can reject the view that it is permissible to use those non-combatants as shields. For a start, the claim that the infliction of lethal collateral damage is permissible subject to the aforementioned conditions goes through irrespective of the degree to which non-combatants are in fact able to vacate the area prior to the bombing: *prima facie*, then, the same can be said of the use of shields. Moreover, in the case of collateral damage, combatants$_W$ themselves kill non-combatants; in the case of shields, by contrast, they 'merely' expose them to a risk of dying at the hands of combatants$_P$. If killing is generally worse than contributing to causing someone to die at the hands of third parties, and if the former is in fact permitted, then the latter is *prima facie* permitted as well.

Admittedly there is an important difference between the two cases. When they inflict collateral damage, combatants$_W$ unintentionally subject non-combatants to a risk of death and thereby of the destruction of their prospects for a minimally decent life: in fact, they could successfully pursue their mission even if the non-combatants were not there. By contrast, in the case of shields, combatants$_W$ deliberately expose non-combatants to that risk, and indeed rely on their very presence, as defenceless agents, as decisive to the success of the mission. This, I suspect, will strike many as a crucially relevant difference between collateral damage and the use of shields, such as to issue in the verdict that the latter is impermissible even though the former is justified. However, remember an earlier point, made when discussing the claim that non-combatants might be under a duty to serve as shields. There, we saw that what matters is non-combatants' overall prospects for a minimally decent life when those prospects are assessed by taking into account the fact that they are defenceless, as compared with combatants' similar prospects when the latter are assessed by taking into account the fact that they are armed. I argued that if subjecting combatants to a given risk of having those prospects destroyed is permissible, then so is using them as shields when the risk is the same, and *a fortiori* lower. This helps us with the case at hand. True, the fact that combatants$_W$ deliberately expose shields to risk makes some difference; then again, so does the fact that third parties, in this case, do the killing. I am not entirely sure as to the degree to which the latter fact compensates for the former from a normative point of view. Thus, it might be that the fact that the exposure is deliberate imposes on combatants$_W$ an obligation to use non-combatants as shields only if the risks which the latter thus incur is much lower than the risk which they incur when caught in the bombing of (for example) a munitions factory. Conversely, it might be that the fact that combatants$_P$ are ultimately responsible for shields' deaths permits combatants$_W$ to expose those non-combatants to the same risks which they incur in the case of collateral damage. But whichever judgement one reaches on those two points, it seems that if non-combatants stand an overall very good chance of a minimally decent life—much better, in fact, than if they are subject to permissible collateral damage—then using them in this way might well be permissible.

## 7.4 DECEIVING THE ENEMY

In Sections 7.2 and 7.3 we assessed the permissibility of using civilians as a way to prosecute a just war against an enemy whose superior conventional military strength is such that one could not hope to defeat it otherwise. In this section I focus on the practice of deceiving one's enemy by pretending that one is a harmless party, such as a civilian or a member of neutral medical staff, so as to approach him safely and kill him. Examples of such tactics abound in the history of warfare, but particularly so in contemporary conflicts. Armed forces in highly developed industrial societies have satellite-based technologies which enable them to spot and identify enemy troop movements in real time at an unprecedented level of detail, which then allows them to strike swiftly and decisively. Under those circumstances their foes have little option but *not* to appear as combatants and, instead, to pretend to be harmless. Thus, in conflicts as diverse as the wars in Iraq and Afghanistan and the civil war in Somalia, reports are rife of combatants driving civilian vehicles in civilian attire, only to blow themselves up once in close proximity to the enemy, thereby causing many casualties. Likewise, combatants in various war zones have been reported to wear the emblems of the Red Cross or the UN as a way to disguise their real status.[32]

Such tactics are prohibited under the laws of war. According to Article 37 of the First Protocol Additional to the Geneva Conventions 'it is prohibited to kill, injure, or capture an adversary by resort to perfidy. Acts inviting the confidence of an adversary to lead him to believe that he is entitled to, or is obliged to accord, protection under the rules of international law applicable in armed conflict, with intent to betray that confidence, shall constitute perfidy.' The laws of war do not prohibit a soldier from wearing civilian clothes as a way to ensure that he will not be killed, but they do prohibit him from doing so as a means to kill.[33]

---

[32] For accounts of such incidents, see, for example, N.-I. S. A. Force, 'NATO News release', in *ISAF soldiers neutralise vehicle-borne suicide bomber attack* (2009); Amnesty International, 'Iraq: Soldiers' civilian disguise likely to rebound on civilians' (Amnesty International: 2003); E. Sanders, 'In Somalia, troops for peace end up at war', *Los Angeles Times*, 29 August 2009; Schmitt, 'Precision attack and international humanitarian law', 463ff. For a case drawn from the 2003 war in Iraq, see Gross, *Moral Dilemmas of Modern War*, 36.

[33] Perfidious tactics also include wearing the enemy's uniform in order to lead him to believe that you are a friend, and raising a white flag to signal—falsely—that you are seeking a truce. In those two cases the deceiver does not pretend that he is not a combatant; rather, he pretends to be a different kind of combatant than he really is—to wit, a comrade in arms, or an enemy combatant who no longer wishes to fight. Both tactics are prohibited under the law. In so far as my focus in this chapter is on asymmetrical warfare which trades on the enemy's reluctance to breach the principle of *non-combatant* immunity, I shall prescind from addressing them.

Not only are those tactics legally prohibited; they also elicit widespread moral condemnation, on two distinct grounds. First, combatants who pretend to be what they are not act perfidiously *vis-à-vis* their enemy, and perfidious behaviour, vitiative of trust as it is, generally does not warrant a laudatory response. In the context of war, as I noted at the outset, it is thought particularly wrong in so far as it destroys trust between belligerents—the kind of trust necessary, in particular, to end wars and negotiate just settlements *post bellum*.[34] Second, according to the laws of war, at least as traditionally construed, combatants may not kill enemy non-combatants. It is thus crucial both to their ability to respect the principle of non-combatant immunity and to defend themselves from enemy combatants that they should be able to determine who is a combatant and who is not. Faced with an enemy who makes it impossible for them to reach such a judgement, they must choose between not defending themselves lest they should risk killing non-combatants, at the cost of their lives, and killing individuals who appear not to be combatants lest they should risk dying at their hands, at the cost of their moral integrity.

However, in the case at hand, which pits just combatants$_W$ against unjust combatants$_P$, it is not clear that the former are acting wrongly—at least, not towards the latter. *Ex hypothesi*, W has a just cause and its combatants thus have a *prima facie* right to kill combatants$_P$. By that token, the latter have forfeited their right not to be killed, as well as their right to kill combatants$_W$ in self-defence. The question, then, is whether they have also forfeited their right not to be killed through the use of deception. At first sight, it would seem that they have. For consider. By, for example, driving a truck which appears to be a civilian truck right through a check-point manned by combatants$_P$, combatants$_W$ are relying on the likelihood that their enemy will take the truck at face value and will not be ready to fire back once combatants$_W$ start shooting. Deception, therefore, is an effective means by which to deny P the means and opportunity to defend themselves effectively. As we saw in Section 2.3.2, those combatants do not have the right to defend themselves against W's own defensive steps anyway, precisely because their cause is unjust. Consequently, acting in such a way as to deny them the means to do so, when they are engaged in the task of violating W's rights and show no sign of stopping, does not wrong them.[35] Compare this with ambushes, which

[34] For a good account of those criticisms in the context of asymmetrical wars, see Gross, *Moral Dilemmas of Modern War*, 109–11.
[35] Walzer seems to dissent, at least when those tactics are used by an insurgent group (in his example, French resistance fighters in Wolrd War II) against an occupying force (German troops) with whom the government of the occupied country has negotiated a truce. I say 'seems to' because

are another kind of deceptive tactic and which are generally not condemned as wrong. According to Aquinas, whose views on tactics seem to inform much of the tradition, laying an ambush is not morally wrong, because one is not under a duty not to hide one's plans and purposes from the enemy. Accordingly, one is not under a duty to disclose to one's enemy that one will attack him in a seemingly quiet wood clearing.[36] And yet, if the rationale for permitting ambushes lies in the absence of a duty to disclose one's intention, it would seem, by that token, to justify hiding the fact that one is not a non-combatant.

Some might reply to the foregoing that ambushes differ from the case under study in that ambushed soldiers are in a position to shoot at the very first sign that something is untoward: by contrast, they must exercise extreme caution when approached by individuals who appear to be non-combatants, and behave as far as possible as if those individuals really are what they seem to be, since they are under a duty to abide by the principle of non-combatant immunity. In other words (the reply might proceed), they are doubly defence-less, materially speaking, as is the case with ambushes, and morally speaking, as is not the case with ambushes. However, the objection will not do, for the simple reason that in a conflict opposing just W and unjust P, the latter are also morally defenceless against the former, since they are not permitted to kill them. The distinction thus drawn between ambushing the enemy and pre-tending to be a civilian collapses.

Before concluding that W do not wrong their targets by deceiving them, we must address two objections which are often levelled against such tactics—to wit, that they constitute an unacceptable breach of faith and that they violate the principle of fair play. Let us first address the breach of faith objection. Whilst some kinds of military deception are permissible (the objection goes, in dissent from the strict Kantian prohibition on lying), those which violate shared expectations amongst belligerents are not. On that view, ambushes are permissible because there is no shared expectation amongst soldiers that they will not meet enemy fire when marching through war zones; by contrast, they can and usually do expect not to be attacked when faced with an individual who is clothed as someone who, conventionally, is not to be regarded as a combatant. And the reason, in turn, why it is imperative to behave as stipulated by shared expectations is that acting otherwise damages the kind of mutual good faith without which belligerents could never be motivated to

his position is not entirely clear: on the one hand he labels such act an 'assassination'—which is hardly a term devoid of moral condemnation; on the other hand he suggests that assassination might sometimes be permissible. See Walzer, *Just and Unjust Wars*, ch. 11, esp. 183.

[36] Aquinas, *Summa Theologiae*, II-II, q. 40, art. 3.

place limits on the war, end it, and negotiate a lasting and just peace. In so far as a war is just only if it is fought with a view to achieve a lasting peace, it cannot both be just and be fought in a way which would make it impossible to bringing about that end.[37]

Note that the objection is compatible with my claim that combatants$_W$ do not wrong combatants$_P$ when they use those tactics. At its heart is the thought that all belligerents must strive to end the war on pain of committing a wrongdoing against its innocent victims—irrespective of the latter's communal membership. It is hard to disagree with that. Accordingly, if W has good reasons to believe that P would be willing to negotiate a just peace, and if breaching P's faith were to harden P's stand beyond the point of no return, then W ought to desist. However, in the cases which occupy us in this chapter, W cannot win the war *other than* by exploiting P's reluctance to target non-combatants. *Ex hypothesi*, P is not willing to negotiate a just peace—one in which W would obtain redress for the wrongdoing which gave them a just cause for war. In so far as the rationale for maintaining good faith is not present, the claim that W ought not to deceive P into believing that they are not under threat remains unsupported. Moreover, and relatedly, the objection holds only in those cases in which P is the kind of enemy with whom one could be reasonably expected to want to make peace. But not all belligerents are of that ilk. Some—genocidal tyrants, leaders whose appetite for wars of conquest seems limitless, and so on—are guilty of such grievous wrongdoing that nothing but their complete and unquestioned defeat will do.[38] Given that these are not the kinds of regimes or leaders whose good faith one needs to preserve, it is hard to see why defeating them by deceiving their soldiers in ways which exploit the latter's reluctance to target non-combatants (a reluctance, incidentally, which in those cases will not be shared by their leaders) is morally wrong.

A second, standard objection to deceitful tactics as used by militarily weak belligerents against their conventionally more powerful foes is that they are unfair to the latter. By dressing up as civilians, combatants$_W$ (it is objected)

---

[37] See J. M. Mattox, 'The Moral Limits of Military Deception', *Journal of Military Ethics* 1 (2002): 4–16, for a contemporary argument to that effect. Classical sources for the good-faith objection can be found in (for example) Kant's *Perpetual Peace*, first section, article 6, and Vattel's *Le Droit Des Gens*, book III, ch. 10. See Kant, 'Perpetual Peace: A Philosophical Sketch', and Vattel, *Le droit des gens, ou, Principes de la loi naturelle appliqués à la conduite et aux affaires des nations et des souverains*.

[38] Which is not the same as the misguided claim that one can fight with a view to get them to surrender unconditionally: no one—not even Hitler or Pol Pot—can be expected to accede to terms such as, for example, making all their fellow female citizens available for gang rape at the hands of the victorious soldiers, or handing over the whole of their country's monetary and gold reserves without material compensation of any kind in return.

impose on combatants$_P$ the burden of not being able to defend themselves and benefit from their compliance or, as the case may be, costly (to combatants$_P$) non-compliance with the principle of non-combatant immunity. At the same time, they themselves refuse to shoulder that burden. As critics of asymmetrical tactics sometimes put it, W is not 'fighting fair', or 'free-rides' on P's respect for the moral restraints on war. In Churchill's memorable words, spoken to the British Cabinet in the early stages of the war and recorded in his memoirs, 'It would not be right that the aggressive power should gain one set of advantages by tearing up all laws, and another set by sheltering behind the innate respect for law of its opponent.' Replace 'aggressive powers' with 'weak powers', and you produce the fair-play objection to asymmetrical tactics.[39] The objection is not deployed merely against deceitful tactics, but also against the deliberate targeting of non-combatants and their use of civilians as shields. In the remainder of this section I focus on its appropriateness for deception, though my points apply *mutatis mutandis* to its appropriateness for shields and for those very rare cases where deliberate targetting is permissible.

The objection draws support from the widely shared intuition that free-riding is morally wrong, and conceives of war as if it were a sporting contest in which the following three conditions obtain which together generate an obligation to abide by the rules of the contest: (a) the *equality condition*, whereby no player has a greater claim than other players, before the game has even started, to win or lose; (b) the *consent condition*, whereby by taking part in the contest, both players consent to playing by the rules; and (c) the *mutual benefit condition*, whereby the rules operate to the advantage of both players. If no football team has a greater claim to win the tournament than any other, if all players willingly take part, and if the rules operate to the advantage of all, then all must obey the rules of the game such as, for example, not handling the ball, not playing off-side, and so on.

Note that there are two ways in which players can be said to benefit from compliance with the rules. If the rules are constitutive of the game, players enjoy the benefit of playing *that* game so defined (thus, the no-hand-on-the-ball rule is constitutive of football in the sense that if all players handled the ball, the game played would not *be* football). If the rules are regulative of the game, they enjoy the benefit of playing a game with, for example, minimal risk of injury (through respecting the no-kicking-down-your-opponent rule), good compromise between scoring opportunities and defensive play (through the off-side rule, and so on). The rules of war are clearly regulative—not

---

[39] W. Churchill, *The Second World War, Vol 1: The Gathering Storm* (London: Cassell, 1948), 432–3. See also Meisels, 'Combatants: Lawful and Unlawful'.

constitutive: a so-called total war, which is characterized by the absence of compliance with most rules, remains a war.[40] Now, on the orthodox account of the moral status of soldiers, it may well make sense to see war, for all its atrocities, as relevantly similar to a game. For on that view, once the war has started, soldiers are equally at liberty to kill one another (subject to the requirements of proportionality and necessity), and are under an equal obligation not to kill non-combatants (condition (a)). By consenting to take part in the war, belligerents signal their consent to abide by the rules of war, and in particular the principle of non-combatant immunity—which are different from the rules of, say, policing (condition (b)). Finally, the rules work to the advantage of both parties in so far as compliance with them minimizes the damage and destruction caused by the war (condition (c)). According to the fair-play objection, by resorting to tactics which blur the distinction between combatants and non-combatants as a means to blunt P's effectiveness, combatants$_W$ subvert this mechanism and place combatants$_P$ at a serious disadvantage (in breach of (a)). They participate in the war yet do not respect its rules (in breach of (b)), and they benefit from combatants$_P$' willingness to abide by the rules whilst placing them at a serious disadvantage, so that (*pace* (c)), the advantage of compliance clearly is not mutual. In so doing, the objection maintains, combatants$_W$ are acting wrongly towards their enemy.

However, those three conditions do not obtain in the kinds of conflict at issue here.[41] Consider first the equality condition. As I argued in Section 2.3.2, soldiers are *not* morally on a par once the war has started, and thus do not have an equal claim to kill one another. Rather, whether or not they are permitted to kill other soldiers depends (in large part) on the justness of their war *ad bellum*. This point constitutes a decisive reply to the fair-play objection, for in so far as

---

[40] For a classic account of the distinction between constitutive and regulative rules, see J. Searle, *Speech Acts: An Essay in the Philosophy of Language* (Cambridge: Cambridge University Press, 1969). For a useful discussion of the distinction in the context of adversarial ethics, see A. I. Applbaum, *Ethics for Adversaries: The Morality of Roles in Public and Professional Life* (Princeton, NJ: Princeton University Press, 1999), ch. 5.

[41] My critique of the orthodox conception of war as a sporting contest differs from McMahan's. McMahan argues that, *pace* the sporting context analogy, it does not follow from the fact that combatants consent to participate in the war that they consent to being killed by enemies whose war is unjust (whereas someone who takes part in, for example, a boxing match clearly consents to being hit). I wholly agree with him, but my focus here is not on whether W consent to being killed by P, but whether they consent to respecting the principle of non-combatant immunity. See McMahan, *Killing in War*, 51–7. See also Coady, *Morality and Political Violence*, 128ff, for criticisms of the sporting contest model in the context of unequal war. For expositions of the sporting analogy (with reference to boxing), see, for example, Benbaji, 'A Defence of the Traditional War Convention', at 487–8, and T. Hurka, 'Liability and Just Cause', *Ethics and International Affairs* 21 (2007): 199–218, at 210.

unjust combatants lack a claim to win the war, they are not owed a duty by just combatants to be placed on an equal footing.

Some might be tempted to object that agents are under an obligation to abide by the rules of a contest even if they have a greater claim to win than their opponents. Suppose, for example, that T has an affair with his friend B's wife and that they decide to settle their conflict via a fist fight. Even though B has a greater claim than T to win the fight, he is still bound not to fight dirty.[42] However, it is not clear to me that this is always the case. If they explicitly undertake to abide by the Queensberry rules, then B owes it to T to do so, even though the latter wronged him. But if they do not enter such an agreement, then B may fight dirty, at least within limits (he may not, for example, try to bite off T's ear, on the grounds that T's wrongdoing does not warrant this kind of bodily injury, and so on). Analogously, in the conflicts at issue here, combatants$_P$ lack a claim against combatants$_W$ that the latter abide by the rules of conventional warfare, precisely because P's leaders and combatants committed the wrongdoing of violating some important rights of W's members. If combatants$_W$ (with their leaders' permission) explicitly and unambiguously undertake not to use tactics such as deceiving the enemy by pretending to be non-combatants, then they are under a duty to abide by the terms of their undertaking. Absent such undertaking, however, they do not owe it to P not to act in those ways (a point which is entirely compatible with the claim that they owe it to *non-combatants* not to use or target them in those ways).

So much, then, for the equality condition. The consent condition, whereby agents are bound by the rules of the contest (subject to the equality and mutual benefit conditions) if they consent to taking part, does not fare much better. In the case at hand, it yields the following point: in so far as W consent to take part in a war against P, whose conventions rule out the use of asymmetrical tactics, then W must not use those tactics. As we have just seen, I conceded that if W *explicitly* commit not to resort to asymmetrical means of warfare, then their combatants may not do so. Note, however, that the concession does not imply that the consent condition obtains in asymmetrical wars. It is true, of course, that W may be deemed to consent to fight P. However, the alternative to waging the war is to (continue to) suffer a wrongdoing which is severe enough, *ex hypothesi*, to constitute a just cause for war. In the light of that fact, W's consent to taking part in the war cannot be read on its own as implying that W consent to the war's conventions. Consequently, it cannot be deemed to generate, even when joined with the

---

[42] I owe this example to Mike Otsuka.

other two fair-play conditions, an obligation *to that enemy* to expose their combatants to the risk of suffering further wrongdoing by fighting a superior unjust enemy on terms which systematically disadvantage them.

Finally, although adversaries in sports clearly benefit from each other's compliance with the rules of the game, in a war where one party is vastly superior in conventional power to the other, it is not clear at all what the latter gains by observing the rules of war in general and those pertaining to non-combatant immunity in particular. W's leaders benefit from instructing their combatants to observe the principle, it might be thought, in so far as they are more likely to minimize non-combatant deaths in so doing: for example, if combatants$_W$ use deceptive tactics it is likely that combatants$_P$ will come to regard anyone dressed and behaving as a civilian as a potential combatant, and end up killing genuine non-combatants$_W$. However, whether asymmetrical tactics such as deception have tended to erode belligerents' willingness to respect the principle of non-combatant immunity (to their own detriment) remains an open question. For W has three options: (1) fight solely by conventional means, in which case (*ex hypothesi*) it will lose the war, and its members will continue to suffer severe rights violations, both as individuals and as group members; (2) not go to war against P in the first instance, knowing that it cannot win by resorting to conventional means of warfare, in which case too its members will remain victims of the severe, ongoing rights violations which provided it with a just cause; or (3) fight the war on asymmetrical (as opposed to unequal) terms, in which case (*ex hypothesi*) it will win the war and stop—and perhaps even obtain redress for—the wrongdoings suffered by its members. If W decides to fight its war by asymmetrical means, it can be said not to gain from its decision to violate the rules only if the loss of non-combatant lives from its side (resulting from its use of such tactics) is disproportionate in relation to the just cause, and in particular if W would have been better off either not waging the war in the first instance or waging the war on P's terms. Whether that is so is entirely contingent on the facts of the case. By that token, it is only contingently the case that W and P *both* gain by observing the principle of non-combatant immunity, and it is thus only contingently the case that a war displays the third feature of the sporting contest model which is at the heart the fair-play objection to asymmetrical tactics. Accordingly, even if (contrary to what I have in fact argued) W's war against P meets the conditions of equality and consent, in those cases where W does not stand to gain by observing the principle of non-combatant immunity, it is not under an obligation *to P* not to use those tactics.

That said, the foregoing points might be thought to suggest that W, in so doing, wrongs its own non-combatants, since it exposes them to the risk either that P might decide deliberately and knowingly to violate the principle, in retaliation for W's own violation (as, in fact, Britain did throughout World War II when bombing German cities), or that they might be led to take less care when attempting to discriminate between combatants and non-combatants. One of the most interesting and least studied questions raised by the conduct of war is precisely that of what counts as an acceptable distribution of risks between combatants and non-combatants from the same side, in prosecution of a just cause. I suggested in Section 7.3 that combatants may (under certain conditions) press non-combatants into service as shields precisely as a way to spread the burden of fighting the war. By the same token, subject to the same conditions which constrain such use, W may use deceptive tactics at the risk that its non-combatants will suffer at the hands of combatants$_P$.

## 7.5 JUST COMBATANTS, UNJUST TACTICS

As we saw in Sections 2.2 and 2.3, one's unjustifiable contribution to a wrongful killing warrants the loss of one's right not to be attacked, at least if that contribution is significant enough. As we also saw there, the fact that a belligerent's war is just *ad bellum*—particularly the fact that it has a just cause—does not establish that all of its combatants' acts of killing are just. Put differently, a combatant might be an *ad bellum* just combatant and, in discrete cases, an *in bello* unjust attacker. Were combatants$_W$ deliberately to target non-combatants$_P$ though not in order to avert a greater evil, or deliberately to use them or non-combatants from their own side as shields even though the latter would stand a higher chance of dying as a result than if left alone, they would act unjustly. In the former case they would unjustifiably subject those non-combatants to a wrongful threat of harm; in the latter case they would unjustifiably expose them to a risk of suffering such a harm, either at their own hands or at the hands of the enemy. The question, then, is whether this is the kind of act which makes *them* liable to attack—even though their war is just overall.

To be absolutely clear: the issue here is that of whether combatants, on either side, may or have the right to kill *ad bellum*-just-but-*in bello*-unjust combatants (whereas at the close of Sections 2.4 and 7.2.2 I considered the question of whether (unjust) combatants$_A$ may kill just combatants$_V$ in defence of the non-combatants whose rights the latter are justifiably infringing.) Now, it seems pretty clear that the non-combatants whom they deliberately target have the right to kill them in self-defence. It also seems plausible to hold that if non-combatants who are wrongfully used as defenceless shields suddenly acquire means of defence which they can only use against combatants$_W$, then they have the right so to use them. That said, if non-combatants have a choice between killing combatants$_W$ and combatants$_P$ in self-defence, they should do the latter: for it is morally preferable to defend one's life by killing *ad bellum* unjust combatants (which P are) than to kill *ad bellum* just combatants. (Strictly speaking, if they are armed, those non-combatants cease to be non-combatants and become participants in the conflict—but I set aside that terminological difficulty here.)

Whether *other* combatants have the right to kill combatants$_W$ in defence of those non-combatants is less straightforward. Suppose that V deliberately kills bystander B in self-defence against A, on the grounds that, as B is related to A, B's death will cause A to stop attacking her. Suppose further that another party, R, who has no particular tie to either A, V, or B, happens to be on the scene. What may or must R do? His options are the following:

1. Helping A by killing V.
2. Helping V by killing A.
3. Helping B by killing V.
4. Helping B by killing A.

It goes without saying (I hope) that R may not opt for (1), and (*if* he is to intervene[43]) ought to favour (2) or (4) over (3)—though which of those latter two options he should prefer over the other, if he has to choose between them, is an interesting question which I set aside here. Let us imagine, however, that neither (2) nor (4) are available. May he opt for (3)? Clearly, it would be better if he could kill A in defence of B since A, after all, is responsible for initially forcing a choice between lives. But if that option is not available to him, and given that B is subject to a wrongful threat to which V significantly (and wrongfully) contributed, it would seem that V has lost her right not to be killed and, by implication, that R may help B, at the cost of V's life. R, in other words, may opt for (3).

Yet we cannot let matters rest here. For in our stylized example, R has no particular tie to either victims, bystanders, or attackers. Not so in war, quite obviously. I imagined in Section 7.3 that combatants$_W$ use some non-combatants as shields; sometimes they do so wrongfully, by exposure to too high a risk of dying at the hands of combatants$_P$. Those two variables—the group memberships of shields-users and shield-killers, as it were—are constant. In Section 7.2 I imagined that combatants$_W$ deliberately attack non-combatants$_P$: in this case, the group membership of attackers and victims

---

[43] Whether he is under a duty to intervene is a question I need not address here. My aim here is to assess whether R *may* intervene in that particular conflict, and if so, what he must do.

remains constant as well. But in both cases, other variables must be taken into account. In the case of shields we must turn to the respective group memberships of the shields themselves and of their potential rescuers. In the case of deliberate targeting only the latter changes (for W has no reason at all to kill its own non-combatants deliberately). Let us assume that rescuers cannot be drawn from external actors such as multinational peace-keeping forces or other intervening parties, and instead belong either to P or W. Combatants$_W$ who use shields wrongfully are liable to being killed in defence of the latter—if they are liable to being killed at all—only at the hands of fellow combatants$_W$ who do not themselves use shields, or of combatants$_P$ who do not themselves kill the latter. Similarly, combatants$_W$ who deliberately target non-combatants$_P$ are liable to being killed in defence of the latter—if they are liable to being killed at all—either by fellow combatants$_W$ who object to those tactics, or by combatants$_P$ who wish to protect their compatriots.

Now, whether or not combatants who use shields wrongfully are liable to being killed by combatants, whether from W or P, who are not themselves wrongfully killing or using shields, might be thought to depend on the group membership of the shields. Compare and contrast the following scenarios:

A. Combatants$_W$ kill fellow combatants$_W$ in defence of shields$_W$.
B. Combatants$_W$ kill fellow combatants$_W$ in defence of shields$_P$.
C. Combatants$_P$ kill combatants$_W$ in defence of shields$_W$.
D. Combatants$_P$ kill combatants$_W$ in defence of shields$_P$.

In the case of deliberate targeting, the group membership of rescuers is what matters, as follows:

E. Combatants$_W$ kill fellow combatants$_W$ in defence of non-combatants$_P$
F. Combatants$_P$ kill combatants$_W$ in defence of non-combatants$_P$

The claim that (as per A) combatants$_W$ are liable to being killed by fellow community members for the sake of protecting other such members does not seem particularly controversial. The difficulty resides (some might think) in the other three kinds of scenarii. Let us start with cases (at B and E) where combatants$_W$ are liable at the hands of their own comrades for the sake of *enemy* non-combatants. I surmise that for many, to say that such acts of killing are permissible is to deny the importance, weight, and value of special duties which community members owe to one another. In particular (some might be tempted to say), combatants from the same side owe it to one another not to kill one another in defence of the enemy. We encountered a similar point in Section 2.3.2. But as I pointed out then, combatants do not have an obligation to other combatants *qua* compatriots to desist from killing them when, *ex hypothesi*, they are liable to being killed in general by virtue of wrongfully contributing to a wrongful threat against some distant strangers. Lieutenant Thompson, I argued, acted justifiably when threatening to kill fellow American soldiers if the latter kept shooting at Vietnamese civilians in the My Lai massacre. The same can be said, I think, of the case where combatants$_W$ kill fellow combatants$_W$ in defence of non-combatants$_P$ who are wrongfully used as shields.

Perhaps some will object that the claim trades on the thought, in this example, that the US did not have a just cause for war in Vietnam, or that they could not possibly have justified killing innocent Vietnamese villagers as a necessary means to achieve a military objective. By contrast, the objection might continue, combatants may display patriotic partiality when their cause is just *and* when deliberately harming non-combatants serves some military objectives which would not be achieved otherwise. If that is correct, then (the objection might proceed) combatants$_W$ may not kill fellow combatants$_W$ in defence of shields$_P$. I remain unconvinced. Let us take it as fixed that W may not deliberately target non-combatants$_P$ in prosecution of its just cause, and may not use them as shields (when those non-combatants' contributions to the war are not particularly significant, taken on their own, to warrant such treatment). Suppose, however, that W's leaders order their soldiers to do so. The latter pose to non-combatants$_P$ a threat to which they are not liable, and do so by way of an unjustified action. Suppose now that some combatants within W decide to intervene in the conflict which pits their comrade bombers and non-combatants$_P$: they can either help the former by (for example) taking part in the bombing themselves, or by killing those of non-combatants$_P$ who are trying to block the bombers' attacks; or they can help non-combatants$_P$ by killing their comrades. To claim that combatants$_W$ may take either one of the former two courses of action is tantamount to claiming that they may kill innocent non-combatants in defence of unjust attackers, on grounds of patriotic partiality, and simply because their cause is just. But if it is not permissible deliberately to kill non-combatants in prosecution of a just cause in the first instance, then it is hard to see on what grounds it could be permissible to kill non-combatants$_P$ in defence of one's comrades when the latter unjustifiably breach the principle of non-combatant immunity. If that is correct, and notwithstanding the problems raised by intervening agency, combatants$_W$ who use non-combatants$_P$ as shields are sometimes liable to being killed by other combatants$_W$ for so doing; and so are combatants$_W$ who deliberately target those non-combatants.

So far, so good. Cases where combatants$_P$ kill combatants$_W$ in defence either of their own non-combating compatriots or (in the case of shields) of non-combatants$_W$ are far less straightforward. For combatants$_P$, let us not forget, are fighting an *ad bellum* unjust war, and thus share responsibility for their regime's wrongdoing towards W. More precisely, they share responsibility for the fact that W are in a position where they have no choice (*ex hypothesi*) to resort to those means if they are to win their war. In the light of that fact, there are two related reasons which some might be tempted to adduce against the view that combatants$_P$ may kill combatants$_W$ in defence of those non-combatants. First, one might think that combatants$_P$ ought to surrender altogether, instead of contributing to the continuation of the *ad bellum* unjust war which their leaders are waging: given that there is a case for thwarting combatants$_W$' wrongful threats towards those combatants, and that surrendering is one way to do so, it is surely the morally preferable option. Second, by killing combatants$_W$, combatants$_P$ make it even more difficult for the latter to win the war which *they* (combatants$_P$) wrongfully started. On both counts, one might think, therefore, that even if (as we saw earlier) combatants$_W$ act unjustifiably, and even if they are liable to being killed for so doing by some other party, combatants$_P$ cannot possibly be that party.

The argument is strong in the case of shields, since all that combatants$_P$ need to do here is to desist from shooting. To be sure, in so acting, they will signal to W that the (wrongful) tactics are working and will thus provide them with an incentive to continue to use it. Still, given that they would risk killing shields (albeit unintentionally) if they were to shoot, it is best that they should desist. In the case of deliberate targeting, by contrast, there are countervailing and more powerful reasons for resisting the conclusion that combatants$_P$ may not kill combatants$_W$ in defence of non-combatants. For a start, and as we saw in Section 3.3, the fact that an agent commits a wrongdoing does not deprive him of the right to kill in defence of others, even though those victims are under threat partly as a result of that particular wrongdoing. Suppose (to return to a familiar Mafia example) that a Mafia Don and his men set up a lethal confrontation with some police officers, and that the latter will not survive unless they kill the Don's children or, indeed, use them as shields. Suppose further that the police officers do not give the Mafiosi the option of surrendering: theirs is a fight to the death. It is not clear (at least to me) that the gangsters may not kill those officers in defence of those children. It is even less clear to me that they may not so act in defence of children to whom they are not related. Indeed, the fact that they are partly responsible for the children's predicament might give them a justification, at the bar of rectificatory morality, to come to their help by killing the police officers who, at this point, ought to be regarded as unjust attackers. By that token, combatants$_P$ may well have a rectificatory reason for killing combatants$_W$ who, at this juncture, are *in bello* unjust though *ad bellum* just combatants.

To simplify matters I have stipulated that surrender is not an option. In the example of police versus gangsters, one can plausibly modify the example and suppose that if the latter surrender, the former will stop threatening innocent children. In war, however, surrender will serve its purpose (stopping an unjust war) only if a sizeable number of combatants choose that course of action, and choose it at the right time. Had a surrender order by the German High Command before the bombing of Hamburg in late July 1943 and early August 1943 lead to Bomber Harris ordering the bombers back to Britain, then the surrender would have been the morally required course of action. But if surrender will do nothing to block the wrongful threat which *ad bellum* just combatants unjustifiably pose to non-combatants, killing the former in defence of the latter does seem permissible, even if the threat is triggered by rescuers' overall wrongful endeavour and is the only way for the victims of that wrongful endeavour to win their (overall just) war.[44] Moreover, even if P ought to have surrendered a week before W's deliberate targeting of non-combatants but did not do so, the fact that they acted wrongly does not deprive them of a right to kill combatants$_W$. Thus, it may well be that Japan ought to have surrendered on 1 August 1945. That they did not do so does not entail that they would have acted impermissibly had they gunned down the US pilots who were on their way to Hiroshima and Nagasaki on 6 and 9 August respectively—and this *even if*, having thus prevented the US from using nuclear weapons, they would have made it impossible for the latter to win its war (a war which Japan started without just cause—or at least let us so assume for the sake of argument). The general point at issue here is that wrongfully starting a lethal process is not a sufficient reason to desist at any time: the costs of extrication (in the case at hand, surrender) for third parties (particularly innocent third parties) must be taken into account as well.[45] Sometimes, wrongdoers must, or at least may, continue to act wrongly (by

---

[44] I am stipulating for the sake of argument that Britain and the Allies could not have won the war without terror bombing. For a thoughtful discussion of strategic versus terror bombing in World War II, see R. A. C. Parker, *The Second World War: A Short History* (Oxford: Oxford University Press, 1989), ch. 10. I have chosen the bombing of Hamburg rather than the better-known example of the bombing of Dresden in February 1945, because Dresden was left virtually undefended by the German authorities. See F. Taylor, *Dresden: Tuesday, February 1945* (London: Bloomsbury, 2004). (Incidentally, Taylor's book-length study takes issue with the prevailing view that Dresden, one of Germany's finest cities, was an essentially open city of no strategic importance to the Allies, whose decision to bomb it could thus be explained only by the desire to terrorize civilians. Not so, according to Taylor, who describes Dresden as an important armament centre for Germany's Western Front operations. If his assessment is correct, it does somewhat complicate the standard view—though it falls short of justifying the bombing.)

[45] For insightful remarks on what he calls 'extrication morality', see C. A. J. Coady, 'Escaping from the Bomb: Immoral Deterrence and the Problem of Extrication', in H. Shue (ed.), *Nuclear Deterrence and Moral Restraint* (Cambridge: Cambridge University Press, 1989).

prolonging the war for which they have no just cause) for the sake of saving innocent lives from unjust attackers—although, of course, they must stop acting wrongfully as soon as those lives are saved. The right course of action for Germany and Japan would have been to gun down the bombers, thereby saving dozens of thousands of lives, and *then* to surrender. Likewise, under some circumstances, the right course of action is for combatants$_P$ to kill combatants$_W$ in defence of either non-combatants$_W$ or non-combatants$_P$, and then to surrender.

## 7.6 CONCLUSION

I have argued that militarily weaker belligerents may not deliberately target enemy non-combatants, unless as a means to avert a greater evil. I then showed, more controversially, that those belligerents sometimes may use non-combatants of either sides as shields, and that they sometimes may resort to deceitful tactics. In neither of those latter two cases, I finally claimed, do W wrong Ps' combatants and leaders, unless they have explicitly undertaken not to resort to such tactics. At the outset of this chapter, and following David Rodin's characterization, I described the problem of asymmetrical warfare as a dilemma: either we deny the weak the right to resort to unconventional means, which is tantamount to denying them the right to go to war; or we grant them that right, in which case we weaken standard protection afforded to non-combatants. As should be clear, taking seriously the rights which, I claimed throughout this book, are worth defending by force leaves us with little choice but to accept the second horn of the dilemma.

# Conclusion

My aim in this book was to articulate and defend an egalitarian, liberal, cosmopolitan account of the just war. More precisely, I sought to show when, and under what conditions, war is justified, if one takes as one's starting point the following two key claims, for which I provided a defence in Chapter 1 and in the first section of Chapter 2. First, all human beings, wherever they reside, are the fundamental locus of moral concern, are owed equal concern and respect, and have fundamental human rights as a matter of justice to the freedoms and resources which they need in order to lead a minimally decent life. Those rights, in turn, impose duties on all other human beings, wherever they reside. Borders, in other words, are morally irrelevant to the conferral of those rights; however, they become relevant once every one has those rights, at which point individuals, who all have the freedom to associate with whomever they wish, may allocate amongst themselves the benefits which result from their mutual cooperation. Second, as rational and moral agents whose fundamental human rights depend not on the groups to which they belong but, rather, on what they do, individuals are liable to defensive force only if they contribute in relevant ways to states of affairs in which the fundamental human rights of others are under serious and unjustified threat. Critically, they are sometimes liable to being killed for threatening not merely the life and limbs but also important fundamental rights of fellow human beings. The two assumptions are related, in that an egalitarian cosmopolitan simply could not consistently regard an individual's membership in a group in general, and in an army at war in particular, as a sufficient reason for killing him as a matter of right. By contrast, as we saw, orthodox accounts of war tend to regard group membership in general, and membership in a given political sovereign community in particular, as decisive for the conferral of rights and allocation of obligations as well as for the permission to kill enemy combatants in self-defence.

I noted in the Introduction that of all the traditional conditions which a war must meet if it is to be just, the requirement of just cause, the requirement of legitimate authority, the requirement of proportionality (particularly in its *in bello* version), and the principle of discrimination between combatants and non-combatants are the most likely to need revising if one adopts those two claims. Consider first the just-cause requirement. In the just-war tradition, armed aggression (be it ongoing or imminent) against a state's or political community's to territorial integrity and/or political sovereignty by another state or such community is regarded as a just cause for waging a war of self-defence—indeed, as the only just cause. Surprisingly, perhaps, my cosmopolitan sufficientist account also makes space for the right to wage a war of collective self-defence. However, it reaches that conclusion through a somewhat different route. Traditional just war theory and liberal nationalism justify that right by appealing to the non-instrumental value of the collective goods of national self-determination and territorial integrity. On my account, by contrast, the values of self-determination (which is not necessarily conceived of in national terms) and territorial integrity are largely instrumental to individuals' prospects for a minimally decent life. In looking for a just cause for self-defensive wars one must thus look to the rights which protect those prospects. If that is correct, then (as we saw), just causes for transnational self-defensive wars include violations of individual rights not to be killed or grievously maimed, of jointly-held rights to political self-determination and territorial integrity, and (more controversially) of rights to the material resources without which one cannot lead a minimally decent life. Moreover, the point applies not merely to transnational conflicts, but also to civil wars. For if political membership is morally irrelevant to the conferral of fundamental rights, and if the right to use force in defence of those rights is itself a fundamental human right, then what counts as a just cause for a self-defensive cannot depend on the existence or absence of a special political relationship between wrongdoers and victims.

Self-defence—whether individual or collective—is not the only just cause for war, of course. As we also saw, my cosmopolitan sufficientist account of justice yields the conclusion that individuals, via their own institutions, have the *prima facie* right to authorize, finance, and wage wars of intervention in the affairs of other political communities when the latter's members violate the fundamental human rights of their own members. On that account too, political borders have far less relevance than is standardly thought. To be sure, the claim that defence of others is a just cause for war is not unique to cosmopolitanism—far from it. But whereas non-cosmopolitans can validly argue in favour of non-intervention, cosmopolitans must not only claim that the resort to military force in defence of distant strangers is morally permitted: in virtue of their more general view that we have duties of assistance to one another across borders, they must also hold that it is sometimes mandatory.

So much, then, for the just cause requirement. The requirement of legitimate authority, meanwhile, also needs revising. According to the just war tradition, a war, if it is to be just, must be fought by actors who are deemed to have the relevant authority or competence. In its strictest formulation, the principle holds that it is both a necessary and sufficient condition for an actor to have the authority to wage war, that it should have *de jure* legal power to govern over a given territory; in its somewhat less restrictive interpretation, the principle holds that belligerents must at the very least have a strong claim to hold that power, as when they fight a war of national liberation against a colonial power. Moreover, although the requirement pertains to the *ad bellum* decision to wage war, it has a crucially important role *in bello*: in the tradition, members or agents of a legitimate authority—typically, uniformed soldiers—can kill with impunity (provided they abide by the other requirements of *jus in bello*) once the war has started, and this precisely because they kill on behalf, and at the behest, of such an authority.

In this book, however, I have argued that a state is legitimate only if and to the extent that its agents have the morally justified power to govern over a given territory. Whether they do have that power in turn depends on the degree to which those who are subject to its directives do better at the bar of their fundamental human rights by complying with those directives than they would otherwise do. It might seem tempting to infer from this account of state legitimacy that only legitimate states so conceived can be deemed competent to wage war. As we saw, however, this is not so. For a state might be illegitimate, all things considered (in that its officials routinely violate members' and outsiders' fundamental rights), and yet enable its members better to defend their fundamental rights against a foreign unwarranted invasion or from internal factions within the community than they would be able to do otherwise. However, by that token a state which does not meet that condition cannot be deemed competent to wage that war, whether or not it has the *de jure* legal power to govern over the community's territory. In other words, having a legal or morally justified power to govern is not a sufficient condition for having the authority to wage war.

Nor is it a necessary condition. At the bar of cosmopolitan morality, you will recall, all human beings have human rights to the goods and freedoms they need in order to lead a minimally decent life—irrespective of residence, gender, race, and so on. Put differently, individuals ought not to be denied those goods and freedoms on the grounds that they belong to a particular group, race, or gender, when their membership in the latter is irrelevant to their need for such goods and freedoms. Moreover, the right to protect oneself from violations of one's human rights on the part of others is itself a *human* right, in the sense that it is a right to a freedom (that is, the freedom to defend oneself, without interference, against others) which we need in order to lead a minimally decent life. By extension, the right to wage a war in defence of one's human rights should also be conceived of as a human right in that sense. If that is so, however, it cannot be denied to some groups of individuals and conferred on other groups on the grounds that the former lack, but the latter have, some characteristic or other, when lacking or possessing those characteristics is irrelevant to their fundamental interest in being able to protect their rights. Whether or not a group is a state or quasi-state is precisely one such characteristic. Likewise, if conferring the right to wage war on states only, and not on other groups, is to penalize the latter for something for which they are not responsible—to wit, not being or aspiring to become a sovereign state—then conferring the right to wage war on groups only, and not individuals, is to penalize the latter for something for which they are not responsible—to wit, not belonging to a *group* which has, as a group, a just cause for going to war, or is able or willing to go to war. In sum, on cosmopolitan grounds, individuals *qua* individuals can be deemed competent to go to war in prosecution of a just cause—subject, however, to considerations of proportionality, last resort, and reasonable chance of success. Finally, it is precisely because states' normative grip on the right to wage and fight a war is not as tight as mainstream just war theory claims that mercenaries can on principle be regarded as just combatants.

This leaves us with the principle of discrimination. According to the principle traditionally understood, (lawful) combatants may kill one another, on the grounds that they pose a threat to one another, but they may not kill non-combatants deliberately, on the grounds that the latter do not take part in the war. Killing non-combatants is permissible only as a foreseen and unintended side-effect of one's just mission. In this book, however, I have challenged this interpretation of the principle from three directions, which yields some revisions to the requirement of proportionality. First, I have argued that whether combatants may kill enemy combatants largely depends on the moral status of the war which they are fighting, and particularly on the moral status of the cause for the war. If their cause is unjust, then they lack the right to kill enemy combatants, unless the latter in turn carry out unjustified killings. This flows from the thesis that individuals are liable to defensive force only if they contribute in relevant ways to states of affairs in which the fundamental human rights of others are under a serious and unjustified threat. On that view, whether combatants are liable to being killed does not depend on the mere fact that they pose a lethal threat, let alone on the mere fact of their membership in the enemy's army. If this is correct, then in deciding how to weigh the lives of combatants on our side against the lives of enemy non-combatants, we should be guided by the criterion of contributory responsibility for a wrongful threat, and certainly not by the thought that 'their' combatants count for less than 'ours' precisely because they are 'theirs.'

Second, some civilians do in fact make a significant or relevant contribution to the wrongdoing which gives rise to a just cause. Moreover, in a handful of cases (involving the necessity of forestalling a grave evil), civilians are legitimate targets. In the latter respect my cosmopolitan account of the ethics of killing in war does not differ from a more traditional account. However—and this is crucial—it makes room for the thought that what matters when deciding whether or not to target civilians is not the latter's membership in our community, the enemy's, or indeed a neutral third party's; rather, it is the degree to which the attack will succeed in forestalling that evil. *Pace* Churchill, we ought not to have attacked German civilians just because they are Germans; we ought to have attacked them (if at all) just in so far as their being German would have made it contingently more likely that the Nazis would have given in. Furthermore, my cosmopolitan account also makes room for the thought that combatants may sometimes deliberately expose non-combatants to a risk of death (by bombing densely populated areas, for example, or by using non-combatants as shields) as a means to share the burdens of the war. Here too, however, communal membership does not matter in and of itself; it matters only to the extent that it maximizes or minimizes just combatants' and belligerents' chances of winning their just war justly. Furthermore, and once again, if the thesis defended here is sound, considerations of enemy civilians' responsibility for wrongful lethal threat should matter heavily in the proportionality calculus: the life of a civilian who does contribute should count for less than the life of an innocent civilian.

Third, I have conceded that the infliction of collateral damage in wars of self-defence is particularly problematic if borders in general and political membership in particular are deemed morally irrelevant, in the main, both to the conferral of human rights and assignment and duties, as well as to the kind of considerations which one may invoke to justify infringing those rights. For if political membership is irrelevant in that way, then it really is not clear at all how combatants can justify killing foreign non-combatants (albeit unintentionally) in the course of saving their own compatriots. I argued that collateral damage is in fact sometimes justified by appealing to combatants' and their compatriots' legitimate personal prerogative (as sharply distinct from a duty which some argue they do have—and which I rejected—to provide greater assistance to one another, *qua* compatriots, than to distant strangers). I then brought that argument to bear on the infliction of collateral damage in which the rights at issue are not held jointly by combatants—such as wars of intervention and wars fought by foreign mercenaries—and argued that there is correspondingly lesser moral latitude *vis-à-vis* non-combatants in those cases than there is in cases of collective self-defence. As I also showed, however, the claim that combatants may under certain conditions inflict collateral damage on enemy non-combatants is compatible with the following two views: first, in some cases, they may not inflict collateral damage as a means to alleviate their own burdens; second, they may sometimes inflict damage on their compatriots as a means to spread more fairly the burden of fighting the (just) war. The first view is tantamount to claiming that 'our' combatants' lives do not always matter more than 'their' non-combatants' lives; and the second view is tantamount to claiming that in some cases the lives of 'our' non-combatants can count for less than the lives of 'their' non-combatants, precisely because they are 'ours'.

My defence of the rights to wage war, and to kill in war, rests on the view that political borders have far less moral weight than is standardly assumed in the just war tradition. More deeply still, it is rooted in the thought that groups and institutions do not really matter *per se*, and that it is individuals' acts and suffering which stand in need of justification. This may seem blindingly obvious, but the fact that there still is fierce resistance to many of the theses defended here suggests that it is not. I began by quoting from *War and Peace*—arguably the greatest war novel of the Western canon—and from *Dulce et Decorum Est*—arguably one of its most powerful war poems. Let me end with some words from George Eliot's novel *Felix Holt the Radical*—an admittedly unlikely source in this context:[1]

We see human heroism broken into units and say, this unit did little—might as well not have been. But in this way we might break up a great army into units; in this way we might break the sunlight into fragments, and think that this and the other might be cheaply parted with. Let us rather raise a monument to the soldiers whose brave hearts only kept the ranks unbroken, and met death—a monument to the faithful who were not famous, and who are precious as the continuity of the sunbeams is precious, though some of them fall unseen and on barrenness.

Not just to soldiers, but to all of war's victims, irrespective of borders.

---

[1] G. Eliot, *Felix Holt the Radical*, ed. D. Thorold (London: Wordsworth, 1997), p. 158.

# Bibliography

Abizadeh, A., 'Cooperation, Pervasive Impact, and Coercion: On the Scope (not Site) of Distributive Justice', *Philosophy & Public Affairs* 35 (2007): 318–58.

Altman, A. and Wellman, C. H., *A Liberal Theory of International Justice* (Oxford: Oxford University Press, 2009).

Amery, H., 'Water Wars in the Middle East: A Looming Threat', *The Geographical Journal* 168 (2002): 313–23.

Amnesty International, 'Iraq: Soldiers' civilian disguise likely to rebound on civilians', in *Iraq: Soldiers' civilian disguise likely to rebound on civilians* (Amnesty International: 2003).

Amnesty International, *Gaza: military tactics on both sides endangering civilians* (Amnesty International, 2009).

Amnesty International, *Sri Lanka: UN Security Council must demand immediate access and accountability* (Amnesty International, 2009).

Anderson, D. L. (ed.), *Facing My Lai* (Lawrence, KS: University Press of Kansas, 1998).

Anderson, E., 'What Is the Point of Equality?', *Ethics* 100 (1990): 287–337.

—— *Value in Ethics and Economics* (Cambridge, MA: Harvard University Press, 1993).

Anscombe, G. E. M, 'War and Murder', in G. E. M. Anscombe, *The Collected Philosophical Papers: Ethics, Religion and Politics* (Oxford: Blackwell, 1981).

Applbaum, A. I., *Ethics for Adversaries: The Morality of Roles in Public and Professional Life* (Princeton, NJ: Princeton University Press, 1999).

—— 'Legitimacy without the Duty to Obey', *Philosophy & Public Affairs* 38 (2010): 215–39.

Apuzzo, M., 'US judge throws out Blackwater case, citing missteps', *The Independent*, Friday, 1 January 2010.

Aquinas, Thomas, *Summa Theologia*, ed. B. Bros. (Grand Rapids, MI: Online Christian Classics Ethereal Library, 1947).

Arneson, R., 'The Principle of Fairness and Free-Rider Problems', *Ethics* 92 (1982): 616–33.

—— 'Equality and Equal Opportunity for Welfare', *Philosophical Studies* 56 (1989), 77–93.

—— 'Luck Egalitarianism and Prioritarianism', *Ethics* 110 (2000): 339–49.

Atack, I., *The Ethics of Peace and War: From State Security to World Community* (Edinburgh: Edinburgh University Press, 2005).

Attaran, A., 'How do Patents and Economic Policies Affect Access to Essential Medicines in Developing Countries?', *Health Affairs* 23 (2004): 155–66.

Augustine, 'Contra Faustum', in M. W. Tkacz and D. Kries (ed.), *Augustine's Political Writings* (Indianapolis, IN: Hackett, 1994).

Avant, D. D., *The Market for Force: The Consequences of Privatizing Security* (Cambridge: Cambridge University Press, 2005).

Baer, D., 'The Ultimate Sacrifice and the Ethics of Humanitarian Intervention', *Review of International Studies* 37 (2011): 301–26.

Bagnoli, C., 'Humanitarian Intervention as a Perfect Duty: A Kantian Argument', in T. Nardin and M. S. Williams (ed.), *Humanitarian Intervention: NOMOS XLVII* (New York: New York University Press, 2006).

Baker, D.-P., *Just Warriors, Inc.* (New York: Continuum, 2010).

Baron, I. Z., *Justifying the Obligation to Die: War, Ethics, and Political Obligation with Illustrations from Zionism* (Lanham, MD: Lexington Books, 2009).

Barry, B., 'Humanity and Justice in Global Perspective', in B. Barry, *Liberty and Justice: Essays in Political Theory, vol. 1* (Oxford: Clarendon Press, 1991).

Bass, G. J., *Freedom's Battle: The Origins of Humanitarian Intervention* (New York: Alfred Knopf, 2008).

Bearpark, A., and Schulz, S., 'The Future of the Market', in S. Chesterman and C. Lehnardt (ed.), *From Mercenaries to Market: The Rise and Regulation of Private Military Companies* (Oxford: Oxford University Press, 2007).

Beitz, C. R., *Political Theory and international Relations* (Princeton: Princeton University Press, 1980).

—— 'Rawls's Law of Peoples', *Ethics* 110 (2000): 669–96.

—— *The Idea of Human Rights* (Oxford: Oxford University Press, 2009).

Bellamy, A., 'Motives, Outcomes, Intent and the Legitimacy of Humanitarian Intervention', *Journal of Military Ethics* 3 (2004): 216–33.

—— 'Responsibility to Protect or Trojan Horse? The Crisis in Darfur and Humanitarian Intervention after Iraq', *Ethics & International Affairs* 19 (2005): 31–54.

Benbaji, Y., 'The Doctrine of Sufficiency: A Defence', *Utilitas* 17 (2005): 310–32.

—— 'The Responsibility of Soldiers and the Ethics of Killing in War', *Philosophical Quarterly* 57 (2007): 558–72.

—— 'A Defence of the Traditional War Convention', *Ethics* 118 (2008): 464–95.

Benedict, P., 'The Wars of Religion, 1562–1598', in M. P. Holt (ed.), *Renaissance and Reformation France* (Oxford: Oxford University Press, 2002).

Berdal, M., 'Beyond Greed and Grievance—and not to soon . . .', *Review of International Studies* 31 (2005): 687–98.

—— 'The "New Wars" Thesis Revisited', in H. Strachan and S. Scheipers (ed.), *The Changing Character of War* (Oxford: Oxford University Press, 2011).

—— and Economides, S. (ed.), *United Nations Interventionism, 1991–2004* (Cambridge: Cambridge University Press, 2007).

—— and Malone, D. M. (ed.), *Greed and Grievance: Economic Agendas in Civil Wars* (Boulder, CO: Lynn Rienner, 2000).

Bilton, M. and Sim, K., *Four Hours in My Lai* (Harmondsworth: Penguin Books, 1992).

Black, S., 'Individualism at an Impasse', *Canadian Journal of Philosophy* 21 (1991): 347–77.

Blake, M., 'Distributive Justice, State Coercion, and Autonomy', *Philosophy & Public Affairs* 30 (2001): 257–96.

—— 'Reciprocity, Stability, and Intervention: the Ethics of Disequilibrium', in D. K. Chatterjee and D. E. Scheid (ed.), *Ethics and Foreign Intervention* (Cambridge: Cambridge University Press, 2003).

Boyle, J., 'Traditional Just War Theory and Humanitarian Intervention', in T. Nardin and M. S. Williams (ed.), *Humanitarian Intervention: NOMOS XLVII* (New York: New York University Press, 2006).

Braeckman, C., 'Zaire at the End of a Reign', *New Left Review* 222 (1997): 129–38.

Brock, G., *Global Justice: A Cosmopolitan Account* (Oxford: Oxford University Press, 2009).

Buchanan, A. E., *Secession: the Morality of Political Divorce from Fort Sumter to Lithuania and Quebec* (Boulder, CO: Westview Press, 1991).

Buchanan, A. E., 'The Internal Legitimacy of Humanitarian Intervention', *Journal of Political Philosophy* 7 (1999): 71–87.

—— 'Rawls's Law of Peoples: Rules for a Vanished Westphalian World', *Ethics* 110 (2000): 697–722.

—— *Justice, Legitimacy, and Self-Determination: Moral Foundations for International Law* (Oxford: Oxford University Press, 2003).

Bunting, M., *The Model Occupation: The Channel Islands under German Rule*, 2nd edn. (London: Pimlico, 2004).

Burchett, W. G. and Roebuck, D., *The Whores of War: Mercenaries Today* (London: Penguin, 1977).

Burmester, H. C., 'The Recruitment and Use of Mercenaries in Armed Conflicts', *The American Journal of International Law* 72 (1978): 37–56.

Buzan, B., *People, States and Fear: An Agenda for International Security Studies in the Post-Cold War Era*, 2nd edn. (Hemel Hempstead: Wheatsheaf, 1991).

Byers, M., and Chesterman, S., 'Changing the Rules about Rules? Unilateral Humanitarian Intervention and the Future of International Law', in J. L. Holzgrefe and R. O. Keohane (ed.), *Humanitarian Intervention: Ethical, Legal and Political Dilemmas* (Cambridge: Cambridge University Press, 2003).

Cameron, L., 'Private Military Companies: Their Status under International Humanitarian Law and its Impact on their Regulation', *International Review of the Red Cross* 88 (2006): 573–98.

Caney, S., *Justice Beyond Borders: A Global Political Theory* (Oxford: Oxford University Press, 2005).

Caparini, M., 'Domestic Regulation: Licensing Regimes for the Export of Military Goods and Services', in S. Chesterman and C. Lehnardt (ed.), *From Mercenaries to Market: The Rise and Regulation of Private Military Companies* (Oxford: Oxford University Press, 2007).

Carter, A., 'Liberalism and the Obligation to Military Service', *Political Studies* 46 (1998): 68–82.

Casal, P., 'Why Sufficiency Is Not Enough', *Ethics* 117 (2007): 296–326.

Casey, S., *Cautious Crusade: Franklin D. Roosevelt, American Public Opinion, and the War against Nazi Germany* (Oxford: Oxford University Press, 2001).

Cavanaugh, T. A., *Double-Effect Reasoning: Doing Good and Avoiding Evil* (Oxford: Oxford University Press, 2006).

Ceadel, M., *Thinking about Peace and War* (Oxford: Oxford University Press, 1987).

Chesterman, S., *Just War or Just Peace? Humanitarian Intervention and International Law* (Oxford: Oxford University Press, 2001).

Christopher, P., *The Ethics of War and Peace: An Introduction to Legal and Moral Issues* (Upple Saddle River, NJ: Prentice Hall, 1999).

Churchill, W., *The Second World War, Vol. 1: The Gathering Storm* (London: Cassell, 1948).

Coady, C. A. J., 'War for Humanity: A Critique', in D. K. Chatterjee and D. E. Scheid (ed.), *Ethics and Foreign Intervention* (Cambridge: Cambridge University Press, 2003).

—— *Morality and Political Violence* (Cambridge: Cambridge University Press, 2008).

—— 'The Status of Combatants', in D. Rodin and H. Shue (ed.), *Just and Unjust Warriors* (Oxford: Oxford University Press, 2008).

Coates, A. J., *The Ethics of War* (Manchester: Manchester University Press, 1997).

Cockayne, J., 'Make or Buy? Principal-agent Theory and the Regulation of Private Military Companies', in S. Chesterman and C. Lehnardt (ed.), *From Mercenaries to Market: The Rise and Regulation of Private Military Companies* (Oxford: Oxford University Press, 2007).

Cohen, G. A., 'On the Currency of Egalitarian Justice', *Ethics* 99 (1989): 916–44.

—— 'Where the Action Is: On the Site of Distributive Justice', *Philosophy & Public Affairs* 26 (1997): 3–30.

—— *Rescuing Justice and Equality* (Cambridge, MA: Harvard University Press, 2008).

Collier, P. and Hoeffler, A., 'On Economic Causes of Civil War', *Oxford Economic Papers* 50 (1998): 563–73.

—— 'Greed and Grievance in Civil War', *Oxford Economic Papers* 56 (2004): 563–95.

Collins, R., 'Darfur: A Historical Overview', in S. Totten and E. Markusen (ed.), *Genocide in Darfur: Investigating the Atrocities in the Sudan* (New York: Routledge, 2006).

Conquest, R., *The Harvest of Sorrow* (London: Hutchinson, 1986).

Copp, D., 'The Idea of a Legitimate State', *Philosophy & Public Affairs* 28 (1999): 3–45.

Coppieters, B., 'Legitimate Authority', in B. Coppieters and N. Fotion (ed.), *Moral Constraints on War* (Landham, MA: Lexington Books, 2002).

*Correlates of War*, http://www.correlatesofwar.org/: 1963-present.

Crawford, E., *The Treatment of Combatants and Insurgents under the Law of Armed Conflicts* (Oxford: Oxford University Press, 2010).

Crisp, R., 'Equality, Priority, and Compassion', *Ethics* 113 (2003): 745–63.

Dagger, R., 'Membership, Fair Play, and Political Obligation', *Political Studies* 48 (2000): 104–17.

Dallaire, R., *Shake Hands with the Devil* (London: Arrow Books, 2004).

Dannreuther, R., *International Security: The Contemporary Agenda* (Cambridge: Polity Press, 2007).

Davidovic, J., 'Are Humanitarian Military Interventions Obligatory?', *Journal of Applied Philosophy* 25 (2008): 134–44.

Davis, N., 'Abortion and Self-Defense', *Philosophy & Public Affairs* 13 (1984): 175–297.

De Waal, A., 'Darfur and the Failure of the Responsibility to Protect', *International Affairs* 83 (2007): 1039–54.

Dickinson, L. A., 'Contract as a Tool for Regulating Private Military Companies', in S. Chesterman and C. Lehnardt (ed.), *From Mercenaries to Market: The Rise and Regulation of Private Military Companies* (Oxford: Oxford University Press, 2007).

Dinstein, Y., *War, Aggression and Self-Defence*, 3rd edn. (Cambridge: Cambridge University Press, 2001).

Dobos, N., 'Is U.N. Security Council Authorisation for Armed Humanitarian Intervention Morally Necessary?', *Philosophia* 38 (2010): 499–515.

Donnelly, J., 'Human Rights, Humanitarian Crisis, and Humanitarian Intervention', *International Affairs* 48 (1993): 607–40.

Doswald-Beck, L., 'Private Military Companies under International Humanitarian Law', in S. Chesterman and C. Lehnardt (ed.), *From Mercenaries to Market: The Rise and Regulation of Private Military Companies* (Oxford: Oxford University Press, 2007).

Dower, N., *The Ethics of War and Peace: Cosmopolitan and Other Perspectives* (Cambridge: Polity Press, 2009).

Draper, K., 'Rights and the Doctrine of Doing and Allowing', *Philosophy & Public Affairs* 33 (2005): 253–80.

Duffield, J., 'The North Atlantic Treaty Organization: Alliance Theory', in N. Woods (ed.), *Explaining International Relations since 1945* (Oxford: Oxford University Press, 1996).

Duyvesteyn, I. and Angstrom, J. (ed.), *Rethinking the Nature of War* (London: Frank Cass, 2005).

Dworkin, R., 'What is Equality? Part One: Equality of Welfare', *Philosophy & Public Affairs* 10 (1981): 185–246.

—— 'What is Equality? Part Two: Equality of Resources', *Philosophy & Public Affairs* 10 (1981): 283–345.

—— *Law's Empire* (London: Fontana Press, 1986).

Easterly, W., *The White Man's Burden: Why the West's Efforts to Aid the Rest have done So Much Ill and So Little Good* (Oxford: Oxford University Press, 2006).

Economides, S., 'Kosovo', in *United Nations Interventionism, 1991–2004*, ed. M. Berdal (Cambridge: Cambridge University Press, 2007).

Edmundson, W. A., 'Legitimate Authority without Political Obligation', *Law and Philosophy* 17 (1998): 43–60.

Elfstrom, G., 'On Dilemmas of Intervention', *Ethics* 93 (1983): 709–25.

Eliot, G., *Felix Holt the Radical*, ed. D. Thorold (London: Wordsworth, 1997).

Emerton, P. and Handfield, T., 'Order and Affray: Defensive Privileges in Warfare', *Philosophy & Public Affairs* 37 (2009), 382–414.

Fabre, C., *Social Rights under the Constitution: Government and the Decent Life* (Oxford: Clarendon Press, 2000).

—— 'Global Distributive Justice: An Egalitarian Perspective', *Canadian Journal of Philosophy (Supplementary)* 31 (2005): 139–64.

—— *Whose Body is it Anyway? Justice and the Integrity of the Person* (Oxford: Oxford University Press, 2006).

—— 'Mandatory Rescue Killings', *Journal of Political Philosophy* 15 (2007): 363–84.

—— 'Guns, Food, and Liability to Attack', *Ethics* 120 (2009): 36–63.

—— 'Permissible Rescue Killings', *Proceedings of the Aristotelian Society* 109 (2009): 149–64.

—— 'Cosmopolitanism and Wars of Self-Defence', unpublished typescript.

Fallah, K., 'Corporate Actors: the Legal Status of Mercenaries in Armed Conflict', *International Review of the Red Cross* 88 (2006): 599–611.

Fawcett, L., 'Rivalry over Territory and Resources and the Balance of Peace and War: the 20th century', in G. Lundestad and O. Njølstad (ed.), *War and Peace in the 20th Century and Beyond* (New Jersey: World Scientific, 2002).

Fearon, J. D. and Laitin, D. D., 'Ethnicity, Insurgency, and Civil War', *The American Political Science Review* 97 (2003): 75–90.

Feinberg, J., 'Voluntary Euthanasia and the Inalienable Right to Life', *Philosophy & Public Affairs* 7 (1978): 93–123.

Finlay, C. J., 'Legitimacy and Non-State Political Violence', *Journal of Political Philosophy* 18 (2010): 287–312.

Fischer, D. H., 'Human Shields, Homicides, and House Fires: How a Domestic Law Analogy Can Guide International Law Regarding Human Shield Tactics in Armed Conflict', *American University Law Review* 57 (2008): 479–522.

Fitzpatrick, S., *The Russian Revolution*, 2nd edn. (Oxford: Oxford University Press, 1994).

Fletcher, G. P. and Ohlin, J. D., *Defending Humanity* (Oxford: Oxford University Press, 2008).

Foot, P., 'The Problem of Abortion and the Doctrine of the Double Effect', in P. Foot, *Virtues and Vices* (Oxford: Clarendon Press, 1978).

Fowler, J., 'A New Chapter of Irony: The Legal Definition of Genocide and the Implications of Powell's Determination', in S. Totten and E. Markusen (ed.), *Genocide in Darfur: Investigating the Atrocities in the Sudan* (New York: Routledge, 2006).

Frankfurt, H., 'Equality as a Moral Ideal', *Ethics* 98 (1987): 21–43.

French, H. W., 'Zaire government is arming Hutus, making human shields of refugees', *New York Times*, 19 February 1997.

Fried, C., *Right and Wrong* (Cambridge, MA: Harvard University Press, 1978).

Frowe, H., 'A Practical Account of Self-Defence', *Law and Philosophy* 29 (2010): 245–72.

Gans, C., *The Limits of Nationalism* (Oxford: Oxford University Press, 2003).

Gargarella, R., 'The Right of Resistance in Situations of Severe Deprivation', in T. Pogge (ed.), *Freedom from Poverty as a Human Right: Who Owes What to the Very Poor?* (Oxford: Oxford University Press, 2007).

Gberie, L., *A Dirty War in West Africa: the RUF and the Destruction of Sierra Leone* (London: Hurst and Co., 2005).

Geiß, R., 'Asymmetric Conflict Structures', *International Review of the Red Cross* 88 (2006): 757–77.

Gewirth, A., *Human Rights* (Chicago: University of Chicago Press, 1982).

Gildea, R., *Marianne in Chains: Daily Life in the Heart of France during the German Occupation* (New York: Picador, 2002).

Gillard, E.-C., 'Business goes to War: Private Military/Security Companies and International Humanitarian Law', *International Review of the Red Cross* 88 (2006): 525–72.

Gleick, P. H., 'Water and Conflict: Fresh Water Resources and International Security', *International Security* 18 (1993): 79–112.

Godwin, W., *An Enquiry Concerning Political Justice* (London: 1793).

Goodin, R. E., 'What Is So Special about Our Fellow Countrymen?', *Ethics* 98 (1988): 663–86.

—— *What's Wrong with Terrorism?* (Cambridge: Polity, 2006).

Gourevitch, P., *We wish to inform you that tomorrow we will be killed with our families* (London: Picador, 1999).

Green, L., *The Authority of the State* (Oxford: Oxford University Press, 1988).

Griffin, J., *On Human Rights* (Oxford: Oxford University Press, 2008).

Gross, E., 'Use of Civilians as Human Shields: What Legal and Moral Restrictions Pertain to a War Waged by a Democratic State against Terrorism', *Emory International Law Journal* 16 (2002): 445–524.

Gross, M. L., *Moral Dilemmas of Modern War: Torture, Assassination, and Blackmail in an Age of Asymmetric Conflict* (Cambridge: Cambridge University Press, 2010).

Grotius, H., *The Rights of War and Peace*, ed. R. Tuck. (Indianapolis, IN: Liberty Fund, 2005).

Hampson, F., 'Winning by the Rules: Law and Warfare in the 1980s', *Third World Quarterly* 11 (1989): 31–62.

Harris, J., 'The Survival Lottery', *Journal of Philosophy* 50 (1975): 81–7.

Harris, J. F. 'Advice didn't sway Clinton on airstrikes', *Washington Post*, 1 April 1999.

—— 'Stealth Fighter "Shot Down" as Serbs slaughter hundreds', *Sunday Times*, 28 March 1999.

Hart, H. L. A., 'Are There Any Natural Rights?', *The Philosophical Review* 64 (1955): 175–91.

Held, D. 'Violence, Law and Justice in a Global Age', no. (2001), http://www.theglobal-site.ac.uk/press/112held.htm.

Held, V., 'Terrorism, Rights, and Political Goals', in R. G. Frey and C. W. Morris (ed.), *Violence, Terrorism, and Justice* (Cambridge: Cambridge University Press, 1991).

Hills, A., 'Defending Double Effect', *Philosophical Studies: An International Journal for Philosophy in the Analytic Tradition* 116 (2003): 133–52.

Hohfeld, W. N., *Fundamental Conceptions as Applied in Judicial Reasoning* (New Haven, CT: Yale University Press, 1919).

Homer-Dixon, T. F., 'On the Threshold: Environmental Changes as Causes of Acute Conflict', *International Security* 16 (1991): 76–116.

—— 'Environmental Scarcities and Violent Conflict: Evidence from Cases', *International Security* 19 (1994): 5–40.

Honderich, T., *After the Terror* (Edinburgh: Edinburgh University Press, 2002).

—— *Terrorism for Humanity: Inquiries in Political Philosophy* (London: Pluto Press, 2003).

Horowitz, D., *Ethnic Groups in Conflict* (Berkeley, CA: University of California Press, 1985).

Hsieh, N.-H., Struder, A., and Wasserman, D., 'The Numbers Problem', *Philosophy & Public Affairs* 34 (2006): 353–72.

Human Rights Watch, *Israel: Decision to Stop Use of 'Human Shields' Welcomed* (Human Rights Watch, 2002).

Human Rights Watch, *Israel/Occupied Territories: Jenin War Crimes Investigation Needed* (Human Rights Watch, 2002).

Hurka, T., 'Proportionality in the Morality of War', *Philosophy & Public Affairs* 33 (2005): 34–66.

—— 'Liability and Just Cause', *Ethics and International Affairs* 21 (2007): 199–218.

Hurrell, A., *On Global Order: Power, Values, and the Constitution of International Society* (Oxford: Oxford University Press, 2007).

Husak, D., 'The Costs to Criminal Theory of Supposing that Intentions are Irrelevant to Permissibility', *Criminal Law and Philosophy* 3 (2009): 51–70.

Huseby, R., 'Sufficiency: Restated and Defended', *Journal of Political Philosophy* 18 (2010): 178–97.

ICRC, 'Interpretive Guidance on the Notion of Direct Participation in Hostilities under International Humanitarian Law', *International Review of the Red Cross* 90 (2008): 991–1047.

International Security Assistance Force, 'ISAF soldiers neutralise vehicle borne suicide bomber attack' (2009), http://www.nato.int/isaf/docu/pressreleases/2009/01/pr090102-005.html.

Isenberg, D., 'A Government in Search of Cover: Private Military Companies in Iraq', in S. Chesterman and C. Lehnardt (ed.), *From Mercenaries to Market: The Rise and Regulation of Private Military Companies* (Oxford: Oxford University Press, 2007).

Johnson, J. T., 'Maintaining the Protection of Non-Combatants', *Journal of Peace Research* 37 (2000): 421–48.

Jones, C. D., *Global Justice: Defending Cosmopolitanism* (New York: Oxford University Press, 1999).

Jones, P., 'Group Rights and Group Oppression', *Journal of Political Philosophy* 7 (1999): 353–77.

Kagan, S., *The Limits of Morality* (Oxford: Oxford University Press, 1989).

Kaldor, M., *Global Civil Society: An Answer to War* (Cambridge: Polity Press, 2003).

—— *New and Old Wars*, 2nd edn. (Cambridge: Polity, 2006).

Kalyvas, S. N., 'The Ontology of "Political Violence": Action and Identity in Civil Wars', *Perspectives on Politics* 1 (2003): 475–94.

—— *The Logic of Violence in Civil Wars* (Cambridge: Cambridge University Press, 2006).

Kamm, F. M., *Morality, Mortality*, vol. 1 (Oxford: Oxford University Press, 1993).

—— 'The Trolley Problem', in F. M. Kamm, *Morality, Mortality*, vol. 2 (Oxford: Oxford University Press, 1996).

—— 'Grouping and the Imposition of Loss', *Utilitas* 10 (1998): 292–319.

—— 'Failures of Just War Theory: Terror, Harm, and Justice', *Ethics* 114 (2004): 650–92.

—— *Intricate Ethics: Rights, Responsibilities, and Permissible Harm* (Oxford: Oxford University Press, 2007).

Kant, I., 'Perpetual Peace: A Philosophical Sketch', in I. Kant, *Political Writings*, ed. H. Reiss (Cambridge: Cambridge University Press, 1991).

Kaplan, L., *NATO Divided, NATO United* (Westport, CN: Praeger, 2004).

Kasher, A. and Yadlin, A., 'Military Ethics of Fighting Terror: An Israeli Perspective', *Journal of Military Ethics* 4 (2005): 3–32.

Kashnikov, B., 'Target Approval Delays Cost Air Force Key Hits', *Journal of Military Ethics* 1 (2002): 125–8.

Keen, D., 'The Economic Functions of Violence in Civil Wars', *Adelphi Papers 320* (1998).

Kinsey, C., *Corporate Soldiers and International Security: The Rise of Private Military Companies* (London: Routledge, 2006).

Klare, M., *Resource Wars: The New Landscape of Global Conflict* (New York: Henry Holt and Co., 2002).

—— *Blood and Oil* (London: Penguin, 2005).

—— *Rising Powers, Shrinking Planet* (Oxford: Oneworld Publications, 2008).

Klosko, G., *The Principle of Fairness and Political Obligation* (Lanham: Rowan and Littlefield, 1992).

Kolers, A., *Land, Conflict, and Justice: A Political Theory of Territory* (Cambridge: Cambridge University Press, 2009).

Koontz, T. J., 'Non-Combatant Immunity in Walzer's *Just and Unjust Wars*', *Ethics & International Affairs* 11 (1997): 55–82.

Kostas, S. A., 'Making the Determination of Genocide in Darfur', in S. Totten and E. Markusen (ed.), *Genocide in Darfur: Investigating the Atrocities in the Sudan* (New York: Routledge, 2006).

Krahmann, E., 'Transitional States in Search of Support: Private Military Companies and Security Sector Reform', in S. Chesterman and C. Lehnardt (ed.), *From Mercenaries to Market: The Rise and Regulation of Private Military Companies* (Oxford: Oxford University Press, 2007).

Kramer, M. H., 'Rights Without Trimmings', in M. H. Kramer, N. E. Simmonds, and H. Steiner, *A Debate Over Rights* (Oxford: Oxford University Press, 1998).

—— 'Getting Rights Right', in M. H. Kramer (ed.), *Rights, Wrongs, and Responsibilities* (Basingstoke: Palgrave, 2001).

Kuperman, A. J., 'The Moral Hazard of Humanitarian Intervention: Lessons from the Balkans', *International Studies Quarterly* 52 (2008): 49–80.

Kutz, C., *Complicity: Ethics and Law for a Collective Age* (Cambridge and New York: Cambridge University Press, 2000).

—— 'The Difference Uniforms Make: Collective Violence in Criminal Law and War', *Philosophy & Public Affairs* 33 (2005): 148–80.

Lackey, D. P., *The Ethics of War and Peace* (Upper Saddle River, NJ: Prentice Hall, 1989).

Lazar, S., 'Responsibility, Risk, and Killing in Self-Defense', *Ethics* 119 (2009): 699–728.

—— *War and Associative Duties,* Oxford D. Phil thesis, 2009.

—— 'The Responsibility Dilemma for *Killing in War*: A Review Essay', *Philosophy & Public Affairs* 38 (2010): 180–213.

—— 'The Morality and Law of War', in A. Marmor (ed.), *Routledge Companion to the Philosophy of Law* (London: Routledge, forthcoming).

Leander, A., 'Regulating the Role of Private Military Companies in Shaping Security and Politics', in S. Chesterman and C. Lehnardt (ed.), *From Mercenaries to Market: The Rise and Regulation of Private Military Companies* (Oxford: Oxford University Press, 2007).

Lefkowitz, D., 'Partiality and Weighing Harm to Non-Combatants', *Journal of Moral Philosophy* 6 (2009): 298–316.

Lehnardt, C., 'Private Military Companies and State Responsibility', in S. Chesterman and C. Lehnardt (ed.), *From Mercenaries to Market: The Rise and Regulation of Private Military Companies* (Oxford: Oxford University Press, 2007).

Leitenberg, M. 'Deaths in Wars and Conflicts between 1945 and 2000', *Occasional Papers*, no. 29 (2006), http://www.cissm.umd.edu/papers/display.php?id=153.

Leverick, F., *Killing in Self-Defence* (Oxford: Oxford University Press, 2006).

Leveringhaus, A., 'The Moral Status of Combatants during Military Humanitarian Intervention', *Utilitas* 24 (2012): 237–58.

Lichtenberg, J., 'Negative Duties, Positive Duties, and the "New Harms"', *Ethics* 120 (2010): 557–78.

List, C. and Pettit, P., *Group Agency: The Possibility, Design, and Status of Corporate Agents* (Oxford: Oxford University Press, 2011).

Locke, J., *Two Treatises of Government*, ed. P. Lasled (Cambridge: Cambridge University Press, 1960).

Luban, D., 'Just War and Human Rights', *Philosophy & Public Affairs* 9 (1980): 160–81.

—— 'Intervention and Civilization', in P. De Greiff and C. Cronin (ed.), *Global Justice and Transnational Politcs: Essays on the Moral and Political Challenges of Globalization* (Boston, MA: MIT University Press, 2002).

—— 'Unthinking the Ticking Bomb', in C. R. Beitz and R. E. Goodin (ed.), *Global Basic Rights* (Oxford: Oxford University Press, 2009).

Lucas, G. R. J., 'From *jus ad bellum* to *jus ad pacem*: Re-thinking Just War Criteria for the Use of Military Force for Humanitarian Ends', in D. K. Chatterjee and D. E. Scheid (ed.), *Ethics and Foreign Intervention* (Cambridge: Cambridge University Press, 2003).

Lyall, R., 'Voluntary Human Shields, Direct Participation In Hostilities And The International Humanitarian Law Obligations Of States', *Melbourne Journal of International Law* 9 (2008): 1–21.

Lynch, T. and Walsh, A. J., 'The Good Mercenary?', *Journal of Political Philosophy* 8 (2000): 133–53.

Machiavelli, Niccolò, *The Prince*, ed. G. Bull (London: Penguin Books, 1981).

Mason, A., 'Special Obligations to Compatriots', *Ethics* 107 (1997): 427–47.

—— *Levelling the Playing Field: The Idea of Equal Opportunity and its Place in Egalitarian Thought* (Oxford: Oxford University Press, 2006).

Matthews, J. T., 'Redefining Security', *Foreign Affairs* 68 (1989): 162–77.

Mattox, J. M., 'The Moral Limits of Military Deception', *Journal of Military Ethics* 1 (2002): 4–16.

May, L., *War Crimes and Just War* (Cambridge: Cambridge University Press, 2007).

—— *Aggression and Crimes Against Peace* (Cambridge: Cambridge University Press, 2008).

McClintock, C., 'The Evolution of Internal War in Peru: The Conjunction of Need, Creed, and Organizational Finance', in C. J. Arnson and I. W. Zartman (ed.), *Re-thinking the Economics of War* (Washington, DC: Woodrow Wilson Center Press, 2005).

McDermott, D., 'Fair-Play Obligations', *Political Studies—Journal of the Political Studies Association UK* 52 (2004): 216–33.

McDonald, M., 'Should Communities Have Rights? Reflections on Liberal Individualism', *Canadian Journal of Jurisprudence* 4 (1991): 217–37.

McIntyre, A., 'Doing Away with Double Effect', *Ethics* 111 (2001): 219–55.

McIntyre, A. and Weiss, T., 'Weak Governments in Search of Strength: Africa's Experience of Mercenaries and Private Military Companies', in S. Chesterman and C. Lehnardt (ed.), *From Mercenaries to Market: The Rise and Regulation of Private Military Companies* (Oxford: Oxford University Press, 2007).

McKeogh, C., *Innocent Civilians: The Morality of Killing in War* (Basingstoke: Palgrave, 2002).

McMahan, J., 'The Ethics of International Intervention', in A. Ellis (ed.), *Ethics and International Relations* (Manchester: Manchester University Press, 1986).

—— 'Killing, Letting Die, and Withdrawing Aid', *Ethics* 103 (1993): 250–79.

—— 'Innocence, Self-Defense and Killing in War', *Journal of Political Philosophy* 2 (1994): 193–221.

—— 'Self-Defense and the Problem of the Innocent Attacker', *Ethics* 104 (1994): 252–90.

—— 'Moral Intuitions', in H. LaFollette (ed.), *The Blackwell Guide to Ethical Theory* (Oxford: Blackwell Publishing, 2000).

—— 'The Ethics of Killing in War', *Ethics* 114 (2004): 693–733.

—— 'War as Self-Defense', *Ethics & International Affairs* 18 (2004): 75–80.

—— 'Just Cause for War', *Ethics & International Affairs* 19 (2005): 1–21.

—— 'The Morality of War and the Law of War', in D. Rodin and H. Shue (ed.), *Just and Unjust Warriors* (Oxford: Oxford University Press, 2008).

—— *Killing in War* (Oxford: Oxford University Press, 2009).

—— 'The Morality of Military Occupation', *Loyola International and Comparative Law Review* 31 (2009): 101–23.

—— 'The Just Distribution of Harm Between Combatants and Noncombatants', *Philosophy & Public Affairs* 38 (2010): 342–79.

McPherson, J., *Battle Cry of Freedom: The Civil War Era* (London: Penguin Books, 1990).

McPherson, L., 'Innocence and Responsibility in War', *Canadian Journal of Philosophy* 34 (2004): 485–506.

—— 'Is Terrorism Distinctively Wrong?', *Ethics* 117 (2007): 524–46.

Mehta, P. B., 'From State Sovereignty to Human Security (via Institutions?)', in T. Nardin and M. S. Williams (ed.), *Humanitarian Intervention: NOMOS XLVII* (New York: New York, 2006).

Meisels, T., *Territorial Rights* (Dordrecht: Springer, 2005).

—— 'Combatants: Lawful and Unlawful', *Law and Philosophy* 26 (2007): 31–65.

Melvern, L., *Conspiracy to Murder: the Rwandan Genocide* (London: Verso, 2006).

Miller, D., *On Nationality* (Oxford; New York: Clarendon Press, 1995).

—— 'Reasonable Partiality towards Compatriots', *Ethical Theory and Moral Practice* 8 (2005): 63–81.

—— *National Responsibility and Global Justice* (Oxford: Oxford University Press, 2007).

Miller, R. W., 'Respectable Oppressors, Hypocritical Liberators: Morality, Intervention, and Reality', in D. K. Chatterjee and D. E. Scheid (ed.), *Ethics and Foreign Intervention* (Cambridge: Cambridge University Press, 2003).

Miller, S., 'Osama Bin Laden, Terrorism and Collective Responsibility', in C. A. J. Coady and M. O'Keefe (ed.), *Terrorism and Justice: Moral Argument in a Threatened World* (Melbourne: Melbourne University Press, 2002).

—— 'Civilian Immunity, Forcing the Choice, and Collective Responsibility', in I. Primoratz (ed.), *Civilian Immunity in War* (Oxford: Oxford University Press, 2007).

Miller, S. C., 'Cosmopolitan Care', *Ethics and Social Welfare* 4 (2010): 145–57.

Moellendorf, D., *Cosmopolitan Justice* (Boulder, CO: Westview Press, 2002).

Moore, M. (ed.), *National Self-Determination and Secession* (Oxford: Oxford University Press, 1998).

Munkler, H., *The New Wars* (Cambridge: Polity, 2005).

Nabulsi, K., *Traditions of War: Occupation, Resistance, and the Law* (Oxford: Oxford University Press, 1999).

Nagel, T., 'War and Massacre', *Philosophy & Public Affairs* 1 (1972): 123–44.

—— 'The Problem of Global Justice', *Philosophy & Public Affairs* 33 (2005): 113–47.

Nardin, T., 'The Moral Basis of Humanitarian Intervention', *Ethics and International Affairs* 16 (2002): 57–70.

—— 'Introduction', in T. Nardin and M. S. Williams (ed.), *Humanitarian Intervention: NOMOS XLVII* (New York: New York University Press, 2006).

Narveson, J., 'Pacifism: A Philosophical Analysis', *Ethics* 75 (1965): 259–71.

Nielsen, K., 'Cosmopolitan Nationalism', *Monist* 82 (1999): 446–68.

Norcross, A., 'Comparing Harms: Headaches and Human Lives', *Philosophy & Public Affairs* 26 (1997): 135–67.

Norman, R. J., *Ethics, Killing, and War* (Cambridge: Cambridge University Press, 1995).

Nozick, R., *Anarchy, State, and Utopia* (New York: Basic Books, 1974).

Nussbaum, M. C., 'Patriotism and Cosmopolitanism', in J. Cohen (ed.), *For Love of Country: Debating the Limits of Patriotism: Martha C. Nussbaum with Respondents* (Boston: Beacon Press, 1996).

—— *Women and Human Development: The Capabilities Approach* (Cambridge: Cambridge University Press, 2000).

—— 'The Supreme Court 2006 Term. Foreword: Constitutions and Capabilities: "Perceptions" Against Lofty Formalism', *Harvard Law Review* 121 (2006): 5–97.

O'Brien, K. A., 'What Should and What Should Not be Regulated?', in S. Chesterman and C. Lehnardt (ed.), *From Mercenaries to Market: The Rise and Regulation of Private Military Companies* (Oxford: Oxford University Press, 2007).

O'Donovan, O., *The Just War Revisited* (Cambridge: Cambridge University Press, 2003).

O'Neill, O., 'Bounds of Justice', in O. O'Neill, *Bounds of Justice* (Cambridge: Cambridge University Press, 2000).

Okin, S. M., *Justice, Gender and the Family* (New York: Basic Books, 1989).

Orend, B., *The Morality of War* (Peterborough, ON: Broadview Press, 2006).

Otsuka, M., 'Killing the Innocent in Self-Defense', *Philosophy & Public Affairs* 23 (1994): 74–94.

—— 'Skepticism about Saving the Greater Number', *Philosophy & Public Affairs* 32 (2004): 413–26.

—— 'Saving Lives and the Claims of Individuals', *Philosophy & Public Affairs* 34 (2006): 109–35.

Øverland, G., 'Contractual Killing', *Ethics* 115 (2005): 692–720.

—— 'Killing Civilians', *European Journal of Philosophy* 13 (2005): 345–63.

Owen, W., *Dulce et Decorum Est*, ed. O. Knowles (London: Wordsworth, 2002).

Palmer-Fernandez, G., 'Cosmpolitan Revisions to Just War Theory', in M. Boylan (ed.), *The Morality and Global Justice Reader* (Boulder, CO: Westview Press., 2011).

Panagariya, A., 'Agricultural Liberalisation and the Least Developed Countries: Six Fallacies', in D. Greenaway (ed.), *The World Economy: Global Trade Policy* (Oxford: Blackwell, 2005).

Parfit, D., *Reasons and Persons* (Oxford: Clarendon, 1984).

—— 'Equality and Priority', *Ratio* 10 (1997): 202–21.

—— *On What Matters* (Oxford: Oxford University Press, 2011).

Parker, R. A. C., *The Second World War: A Short History* (Oxford: Oxford University Press, 1989).

Patrick, M., 'Humanitarian Intervention and the Distribution of Sovereignty in International Law', *Ethics & International Affairs* 22 (2008): 369–93.

Patterson, O., *Slavery and Social Death: A Comparative Study* (Cambridge, MA: Harvard University Press, 1982).

Pattison, J., 'Just War Theory and the Privatization of Military Force', *Ethics and International Affairs* 22 (2008): 143–62.

—— 'Whose Responsibility to Protect? The Duties of Humanitarian Intervention', *Journal of Military Ethics* 7 (2008): 262–84.

—— 'Deeper Objections to the Privatisation of Military Force', *Journal of Political Philosophy* 18 (2010): 425–47.

—— *Humanitarian Intervention and the Responsibility to Protect: Who Should Intervene?* (Oxford: Oxford University Press, 2010).

Paxton, R. O., *Vichy France: Old Guard and New Order, 1940–1944* (New York: Columbia University Press, 1972).

Percy, S., *Mercenaries: The History of a Norm in International Relations* (Oxford: Oxford University Press, 2007).

—— 'Morality and regulation', in S. Chesterman and C. Lehnardt (ed.), *From Mercenaries to Market: The Rise and Regulation of Private Military Companies* (Oxford: Oxford University Press, 2007).

Pettit, P., 'The Consequentialist Can Recognise Rights', *The Philosophical Quarterly* 38 (1988): 42–55.

Plato, *Republic*, ed. R. Waterfield (Oxford: Oxford University Press, 1993).

Pogge, T., *Realizing Rawls* (Ithaca, NY: Cornell University Press, 1989).

—— *World Poverty and Human Rights* (Cambridge: Polity Press, 2000).

Pogge, T. and Horton, K. (ed.), *Global Ethics: Seminal Essays: Global Responsibilities*, vol. II (St Paul, MN: Paragon House, 2008).

Pogge, T. and Moellendorf, D. (ed.), *Global Justice. Seminal Essays: Global Responsibilities*, vol. I (St Paul, MN: Paragon House, 2008).

Preston, P., *The Coming of the Spanish Civil War: Reform, Reaction and Revolution in the Second Republic*, 2nd edn. (London: Routledge, 1994).

Primoratz, I., 'The Morality of Terrorism', *Journal of Applied Philosophy* 14 (1997): 221–33.

—— (ed.), *Civilian Immunity in War* (Oxford: Oxford University Press, 2007).

Pufendorf, Samuel von, *On the Duty of Man and Citizen*, ed. J. Tully. (Cambridge: Cambridge University Press, 1991).

Quinn, W. S., 'Actions, Intentions, and Consequences: The Doctrine of Doing and Allowing', *The Philosophical Review* 98 (1989): 287–312.

—— 'Actions, Intentions, and Consequences: The Doctrine of Double Effect', *Philosophy & Public Affairs* 18 (1989): 334–51.

Quong, J., 'Killing in Self-Defence', *Ethics* 119 (2009): 507–37.

Radin, M. J., *Contested Commodities: The Trouble with Trade in Sex, Children, Body Parts and Other Things* (Cambridge, MA: Harvard University Press, 1996).

Rawls, J., *A Theory of Justice* (Cambridge, MA: Harvard: Harvard University Press, 1971).

—— *The Law of Peoples* (Cambridge, MA: Harvard University Press, 1999).

Raz, J. *The Authority of Law: Essays on Law and Morality* (Oxford: Clarendon Press, 1979).

—— 'Authority and Justification', *Philosophy & Public Affairs* 14 (1985): 3–29.

—— *The Morality of Freedom* (Oxford: Clarendon Press, 1986).

Reaume, D., 'Individuals, Groups, and Rights to Public Goods', *University of Toronto Law Journal* 38 (1988): 1–27.

Reynolds, D., *John Brown, Abolitionist* (New York: Vintage Books, 2005).

Richardson, L., *What Terrorists Want: Understanding the Terrorist Threat* (London: John Murray, 2006).

Ricks, T., 'Target Approval Delays Cost Air Force Key Hits', *Journal of Military Ethics* 1 (2002): 109–13.

Risse, M., 'How Does the Global Order Harm the Poor?', *Philosophy & Public Affairs* 33 (2005): 349–76.

Roberts, A., 'NATO's Humanitarian War over Kosovo', *Survival* 41 (1999): 102–23.

—— 'The Principle of Equal Application of the Laws of War', in D. Rodin and H. Shue (ed.), *Just and Unjust Warriors* (Oxford: Oxford University Press, 2008).

Robinson, F., 'After Liberalism in World Politics? Towards an International Political Theory of Care', *Ethics and Social Welfare* 4 (2010): 130–44.

Rocheleau, J., 'From Aggression to Just Occupation? The Temporal Application of *Jus Ad Bellum* Principles and the Case of Iraq', *Journal of Military Ethics* 9 (2010): 123–38.

Rodin, D., *War and Self-Defense* (Oxford: Clarendon Press, 2002).

—— 'The Ethics of Asymmetric War', in R. Sorabji and D. Rodin (ed.), *The Ethics of War: Sshared Problems in Different Traditions* (Aldershot: Ashgate, 2006).

—— 'The Moral Inequality of Soldiers: Why *jus in bello* Asymmetry is Half Right', in D. Rodin and H. Shue (ed.), *Just and Unjust Warriors* (Oxford: Oxford University Press, 2008).

—— 'Morality and Law in War', in H. Strachan and S. Scheipers (ed.), *The Changing Character of War* (Oxford: Oxford University Press, 2011).

Russell, F. H., *The Just War in the Middle Ages* (Cambridge and New York: Cambridge University Press, 1975).

Ryan, C., 'Self-Defense, Pacifism, and the Permissibility of Killing', *Ethics* 93 (1983): 508–24.

Sachs, J., *The End of Poverty* (London: Penguin, 2005).

Salter, J., 'Hugo Grotius: Property and Consent', *Political Theory* 29 (2001): 537–55.

Sambanis, N., 'What Is Civil War? Conceptual and Empirical Complexities of an Operational Definition', *The Journal of Conflict Resolution* 48 (2004): 814–58.

Sandel, M. 'What Money Can't Buy: The Moral Limits of Markets', In *Tanner Lectures on Human Values* (Salt Lake City: University of Utah Press, 1998).

Sanders, E. 'In Somalia, troops for peace end up at war', *Los Angeles Times*, 29 August 2009.

Sanders, J. T., 'Why the Numbers Should Sometimes Count', *Philosophy & Public Affairs* 17 (1988): 3–14.

Sangiovanni, A., 'Global Justice, Reciprocity and the State', *Philosophy & Public Affairs* 35 (2007): 3–39.

Satz, D., *Why Some Things Should not be For Sale: The Moral Limits of Markets* (Oxford: Oxford University Press, 2010).

Scahill, J., *Blackwater: The Rise of the World's Most Powerful Mercenary Army* (London: Profile Books Ltd, 2007).

Scanlon, T., 'Rights, Goals, and Fairness', *Erkenntnis* 11 (1977): 81–95.

—— *What We Owe to Each Other* (Cambridge, MA: Harvard University Press, 1998).

Scanlon, T. M., *Moral Dimensions: Permissibility, Meaning, Blame* (Cambridge, MA: Harvard University Press, 2008).

Scheffler, S., 'Conceptions of Cosmopolitanism', *Utilitas* 11 (1999): 255–76.

—— *Boundaries and Allegiances: Problems of Justice and Responsibility in Liberal Thought* (Oxford: Oxford University Press, 2002).

—— 'Doing and Allowing', *Ethics* 114 (2004): 215–39.

Schmitt, M. N., '"Target Approval Delays Cost Air Force Key Hits": Law, Policy, Ethics and the Warfighter's Dilemma', *Journal of Military Ethics* 1 (2002): 113–25.

—— 'Humanitarian Law and Direct Participation in Hostilities by Private Contractors or Civilian Employees', *Chicago Journal of International Law* 5 (2005): 511–46.

—— 'Precision Attack and International Humanitarian Law', *International Review of the Red Cross* 87 (2005): 445–66.

Searle, J., *Speech Acts: An Essay in the Philosophy of Language* (Cambridge: Cambridge University Press, 1969).

Selby, J., 'Oil and Water: The Contrasting Anatomies of Resource Conflicts', *Government and Opposition* 40 (2005): 200–24.

Sen, A. K., 'Rights and Agency', in S. Scheffler (ed.), *Consequentialism and its Critics* (Oxford: Oxford University Press, 1988).

—— *Development as Freedom* (New York: Oxford University Press, 1999).

—— 'Elements of a Theory of Human Rights', *Philosophy & Public Affairs* 32 (2004): 315–56.

Shaw, M., *War and Genocide* (Cambridge: Polity Press, 2003).

Shearer, D., *Private Armies and Military Intervention* (Oxford: Oxford University Press, 1998).

Shue, H., 'Torture', *Philosophy & Public Affairs* 7 (1978): 124–43.

—— 'Mediating Duties', *Ethics* 98 (1988): 687–704.

—— 'Bombing to rescue?: NATO's 1999 bombing of Serbia', in D. K. Chatterjee and D. E. Scheid (ed.), *Ethics and Foreign Intervention* (Cambridge: Cambridge University Press, 2003).

—— 'Limiting Sovereignty', in J. Welsh (ed.), *Humanitarian Intervention and International Relations* (Oxford: Oxford University Press, 2004).

—— 'Do We Need a "Morality of War"?', in D. Rodin and H. Shue (ed.), *Just and Unjust Warriors* (Oxford: Oxford University Press, 2008).

Simmonds, N. E., 'Rights at the Cutting Edge', in M. H. Kramer, N. E. Simmonds, and H. Steiner *A Debate Over Rights* (Oxford: Oxford University Press, 1998).

Simmons, A. J., 'The Principle of Fair Play', *Philosophy & Public Affairs* 8 (1979): 307–37.

Singer, P., 'Famine, Affluence, and Morality', *Philosophy & Public Affairs* 1 (1972): 229–43.

—— 'Sidgwick and Reflective Equilibrium', *The Monist* 58 (1974): 490–517.

Singer, P. W., *Corporate Warriors: The Rise of the Privatized Military Industry* (Ithaca, NY: Cornell University Press, 2003).

—— *Children at War* (New York: Pantheon Books, 2005).

SIPRI, *SIPRI Yearbook 2010* (Oxford: Oxford University Press, 2010).

Skerker, M., 'Just War Criteria and the New Face of War: Human Shields, Manufactured Martyrs, and Little Boys with Stones', *Journal of Military Ethics* 3 (2004): 27–39.

Slim, H., 'Dithering over Darfur? A Preliminary Review of the International Response', *International Affairs* 80 (2004): 811–28.

Smilansky, S., 'Terrorism, Justification, and Illusion', *Ethics* 114 (2004): 790–805.

Smith, M., 'Humanitarian Intervention: An Overview of the Ethical Issues', *Ethics and International Affairs* 12 (1998): 63–79.

Stacy, H., 'Humanitarian Intervention and Relational Sovereignty', in S. Lee (ed.), *Intervention, Terrorism, and Torture: Contemporary Challenges to Just War Theory* (Dordrecht: Springer, 2006).

Starr, J. R., 'Water Wars', *Foreign Policy* 82 (1991): 17–36.

Statman, D., 'Supreme Emergencies Revisited', *Ethics* 117 (2006): 58–79.

Steiner, H., 'Territorial Justice', in S. Caney, D. George and P. Jones (ed.), *National Rights, International Obligations* (Boulder, CO: Westview Press, 1996).

—— 'Working Rights', in M. H. Kramer, N. E. Simmonds and H. Steiner, *A Debate Over Rights* (Oxford: Oxford University Press, 1998).

Steinhoff, U., 'How can Terrorism be Justified?', in I. Primoratz (ed.), *Terrorism: The Philosophical Issues* (Basingstoke: Palgrave, 2004).

—— *On the Ethics of War and Terrorism* (Oxford: Oxford University Press, 2007).

Stiglitz, J., *Globalization and its Discontents* (New York: W. W. Norton and Company, 2006).

Stilz, A., 'Why do States have Territorial Rights?', *International Theory* 1 (2009): 185–213.

—— 'Nations, States, and Territory', *Ethics* 121 (2011): 572–601.

Strachan, H., *The First World War: To Arms*, vol. 1 (Oxford: Oxford University Press, 2001).

Strauss, S., 'Darfur and the Genocide Debate', *Foreign Affairs* 84 (2005): 123–33.

Suarez, F., '*De Bello*', in J. B. Scott (ed.), *Selections from Three Works of Francisco Suarez, S.J: De Triplici Virtute Theologica, Fide, Spe, et Charitate (1621)* (Oxford: Clarendon Press, 1944).

Tamir, Y., *Liberal Nationalism* (Princeton, NJ: Princeton University Press, 1992).

Tan, K.-C., *Justice Without Borders: Cosmopolitanism, Nationalism and Patriotism* (Cambridge: Cambridge University Press, 2004).

—— 'The Duty to Protect', in T. Nardin and M. Williams (ed.), *Humanitarian Intervention: NOMOS LVII* (New York: New York University Press, 2006).

Taurek, J., 'Should the Numbers Count?', *Philosophy & Public Affairs* 6 (1977): 293–316.

Taylor, F., *Dresden: Tuesday, February 1945* (London: Bloomsbury, 2004).

Teichman, J., *Pacifism and the Just War* (Oxford: Blackwell, 1986).

Temkin, L., *Inequality* (Oxford: Oxford University Press, 1993).

—— 'Egalitarianism Defended', *Ethics* 113 (2003): 764–82.

Tesón, F. R., *Humanitarian Intervention: An Inquiry into Law and Morality*, 2nd edn. (Irvington-on-Hudson, NY: Transnational, 1997).

—— *A Philosophy of International Law* (Boulder, CO: Westview Press, 1998).

—— 'The Liberal Case for Humanitarian Intervention', in J. L. Holzgrefe and R. O. Keohane (ed.), *Humanitarian Intervention: Ethical, Legal and Political Dilemmas* (Cambridge: Cambridge University Press, 2003).

—— 'Self-Defense in International Law and Rights of Persons', *Ethics & International Affairs* 18 (2004): 87–92.

Thomson, J. E., *Mercenaries, Pirates, and Sovereigns: State-building and Extraterritorial Violence in Early Modern Europe* (Princeton, NJ: Princeton University Press, 1994).

Thomson, J. J., 'Killing, Letting Die and the Trolley Problem', in J. J. Thomson, *Rights, Restitution, and Risk: Essays in Moral Theory* (Cambridge, MA: Harvard University Press, 1986).

—— 'Self-Defense', *Philosophy & Public Affairs* 20 (1991): 283–310.

—— 'Turning the Trolley', *Philosophy & Public Affairs* 36 (2008): 359–74.

Thornton, R., *Asymmetric Warfare: Threat and Response in the Twenty-First Century* (Cambridge: Polity, 2007).

Tolstoy, L. *War and Peace*, ed. H. Gifford (Oxford: Oxford University Press, 1991).

Ullman, R. H., 'Redefining Security', *International Security* 8 (1983): 129–53.

Unger, P., *Living High and Letting Die* (Oxford: Oxford University Press, 1996).

United Nations, *Human Rights in Palestine and Other Occupied Territories: Report of the United Nations Fact Finding Mission on the Gaza Conflict* (United Nations, 2009).

Vaha, M., 'Child Soldiers and Killing in Self-Defence: Challenging the "Moral View" on Killing in War', *Journal of Military Ethics* 10 (2011): 36–52.

Vallentyne, P., 'Justice in General: An Introduction', in P. Vallentyne (ed.), *Equality and Justice: Justice in General* (London: Routledge, 2003).

Vattel, E. d., *Le droit des gens, ou, Principes de la loi naturelle appliqués á la conduite et aux affaires des nations et des souverains* (Washington, DC: Carnegie Institute, 1916).

Vincent, R. J., *Nonintervention and International Order* (Princeton, NJ: Princeton University Press, 1974).

Vitoria, Francisco de, *On the Law of War*, in F. de Vitoria, *Political Writings* ed. A. Pagden and J. Lawrance. (Cambridge: Cambridge University Press, 1991).

Vlastos, G., 'Justice and Equality', in J. Waldron (ed.), *Theories of Rights* (Oxford: Oxford University Press, 1984).

Waldron, J., *The Right to Private Property* (Oxford: Oxford University Press, 1988).

—— 'Can Communal Goods be Human Rights?', in J. Waldron, *Liberal Rights* (Cambridge: Cambridge University Press, 1993).

—— 'What is Cosmopolitan?', *Journal of Political Philosophy* 8 (2000): 227–43.

Walzer, M., 'The Obligation to Die for the State', in M. Walzer, *Obligations: Essays on Disobedience, War, and Citizenship* (Cambridge, MA: Harvard University Press, 1970).

—— 'Political Action: The Problem of Dirty Hands', *Philosophy & Public Affairs* 2 (1973): 160–80.

—— 'The Politics of Rescue', in M. Walzer, *Arguing about War* (New Haven, CT: Yale University Press, 2004).

—— *Just and Unjust Wars: A Moral Argument with Historical Illustrations*, 4th edn. (New York: Basic Books, 2006).

—— 'Mercenary Impulse: Is there an Ethics that Justifies Blackwater?', *New Republic*, 12 March 2008, http://www.tnr.com/article/mercenary-impulse.

Wellman, C. H., 'Relational Facts in Liberal Political Theory: Is There Magic in the Pronoun 'My'?', *Ethics* 110 (2000): 537–62.

Welsh, J., 'Taking Consequences Seriously: Objections to Humanitarian Intervention', in J. Welsh (ed.), *Humanitarian Intervention and International Relations* (Oxford: Oxford University Press, 2004).

Wenar, L., 'Property Rights and the Resource Curse', *Philosophy & Public Affairs* 26 (2008): 2–32.

Wenger, M. and Denney, J., 'Lebanon's Fifteen-Year War 1975–1990', *Middle East Report* 162 (1990): 23–5.

Westhusing, T., '"Target Approval Delays Cost Air Force Key Hits": Targeting Terror: Killing Al Qaeda the Right Way', *Journal of Military Ethics* 1 (2002): 128–36.

Wheeler, N. J., 'Dying for "Enduring Freedom": Accepting Responsibility for Civilian Casualties in the War against Terrorism', *International Relations* 16 (2002): 205–25.

—— *Saving Strangers: Humanitarian Intervention in International Society* (Oxford: Oxford University Press, 2002).

Wiggins, D., 'Claims of Need', in D. Wiggins, *Needs, Values, Truth: Essays in the Philosophy of Value* (Oxford: Oxford University Press 1987).

Wolff, C., *Jus Gentium Methodo Scientifica Pertractatum* (Oxford: Clarendon Press, 1934).

Woods, N., *The Globalizers: The IMF, the World Bank, and Their Borrowers* (Ithaca: Cornell University Press, 2006).

Young, R., 'Political Terrorism as a Weapon of the Politically Powerless', in I. Primoratz (ed.), *Terrorism: The Philosophical Issues* (Basingstoke: Palgrave, 2004).

Ypi, L., 'Statist Cosmopolitanism', *Journal of Political Philosophy* 16 (2008): 48–71.

Zohar, N., 'Collective War and Individualistic Ethics: Against the Conscription of "Self-Defense"', *Political Theory* 21 (1993): 606–22.

—— 'Innocence and Complex Threats: Upholding the War Ethics and the Condemnation of Terrorism', *Ethics* 114 (2004): 734–51.

# Index

Lightning Source UK Ltd.
Milton Keynes UK
UKOW06f0749080515

251131UK00001B/3/P

9 780198 708575